The Great
Transformation
in Higher
Education

1960–1980

SUNY Series, Frontiers in Education

Philip G. Altbach, Editor

The Great Transformation in Higher Education

1960–1980

Clark Kerr

State University of New York Press

Published by
State University of New York Press, Albany

© 1991 State University of New York

For information, address State University of New York
Press, State University Plaza, Albany, N.Y. 12246

Production by M.R. Mulholland
Marketing by Bernadette LaManna

Library of Congress Cataloging in Publication Data

Kerr, Clark, 1911–
    The great transformation in higher education, 1960–1980 / Clark
Kerr.
        p.   cm. — (SUNY series, frontiers in education)
    Includes bibliographical references.
    ISBN 0–7914–0511–7 (alk. paper). — ISBN 0–7914–0512–5 (alk. paper
: pbk.)
    1. Education, Higher—United States—History—20th century.
2. Universities and colleges—United States—History—20th century.
I. Title. II. Series.
LA227.3.K45   1991
378.73—dc20   90–34456
                                                                    CIP

To the members of the Carnegie Commission and Carnegie Council on Higher Education, who gave so much good judgment and demonstrated so much goodwill in their many discussions of the great problems of higher education and their possible solutions at a time when so much of the future of higher education was still to be determined. . . .

Eric Ashby
Ralph M. Besse
William G. Bowen
Ernest L. Boyer
Joseph P. Cosand
E. Alden Dunham
Nolen M. Ellison
Nell P. Eurich
Daniel J. Evans
E. K. Fretwell Jr.
William Friday
Patricia Roberts Harris
David D. Henry
Theodore M. Hesburgh
Stanley J. Heywood
Carl Kaysen
Kenneth Keniston
Philip R. Lee
Margaret L. A. MacVicar
Katherine E. McBride

Frank Newman
Robert M. O'Neil
Rosemary Park
James A. Perkins
Clifton W. Phalen
Alan Pifer
Joseph B. Platt
Nathan M. Pusey
Lois D. Rice
David Riesman
David Z. Robinson
William M. Roth
William Scranton
Norton Simon
Stephen H. Spurr
Richard H. Sullivan
Kenneth Tollett
Pauline Tompkins
William Van Alstyne
Clifton R. Wharton, Jr.

They spoke wisely about higher education and not just for its narrow interests. They all became the best of friends.

Contents

Foreword

This volume of essays was undertaken on the initiative of Philip G. Altbach, who also contributed his always good advice.

Marian Gade assisted in the preparation of most of these essays, with her customary care and good sense, by collecting material for me, reviewing the manuscripts, and adding her helpful comments.

Maureen Kawaoka managed the manuscript, with good humor and precise attention to detail, from a scrawl inscrutable to everyone else, including me, to a finished product.

The individual essays are generally presented as originally published, since each is intended to reflect the time of writing. Occasionally there have been deletions, corrections, new data added, or notations of changed opinions, but mostly the essays stand unchanged, imbedded in time and place. While each essay was written for a specific occasion, I am surprised that they should add together as well as they do, that they duplicate each other so little, and that they provide as full coverage of the period as they have turned out to do. This was never intended at the time they were written.

Looking at these essays all together, I regret that they are written more from above the many battles than from within the individual battles, although I saw them from the inside as a participant as well as from the outside as an observer. I made more of an attempt at an analysis of what was going on than at a description of the infighting and the passions and how it all felt personally. I wish I might have been better able to say how it felt at the time along with telling what was going on and why. I wrote more from the perspective of a participating social scientist than that of an autobiographical novelist, a bent that reflects my background.

Prologue—Transformations

Three periods in the history of American higher education are of particular importance. The most recent of these is the focus of this series of essays.

1. The first such period came with the founding of Harvard and of William and Mary. Both schools took the classical curriculum from Oxford and Cambridge, but, much more significantly as it turned out, they adopted governance structures from Edinburgh and other Protestant Reformation institutions. This was to be expected at Harvard, which was Puritan, but not so clearly at William and Mary, which was Anglican; but the perceived indiscipline of students and faculty at Anglican Oxford argued for basic control by lay trustees as at Edinburgh and not by the professors. Thus arrived the introduction of boards of trustees and of strong presidencies into the American system from which so much else has flowed by way of the autonomy, diversity, flexibility, and competitiveness of American institutions of higher education. Also, Harvard and William and Mary both had religious connections, and this set the pattern for the origins of nearly all of the private colleges and universities in America; and the many Protestant sects, in turn, set the stage for so many varieties of colleges.

2. The second such period came after the Civil War (1870–1910);[1] and it was the first of the two great transformations. Science began to take over from religion and the classics, on the German model. This led, in turn, to greater specialization, the creation of departments, the introduction of graduate study for the Ph.D. degree, the rise of faculty influence in governance, and the advancement of academic freedom. Private institutions were among the leaders: MIT, Harvard, Johns Hopkins, Cornell, Chicago, and Stanford, among others.

Service, or "utility," was the particular theme of the land-grant universities. This meant mostly service to the productive elements of society—especially to agriculture and to industry. This led, in consequence, to placing more leaders of agriculture and of industry on boards of trustees, to more influence shifting to the states that promoted and financed the land-grant universities, and to more extension services to the external public. It also meant drawing on more elements of the population in recruiting students for the new occupations that lay beyond the old professions of theology, medicine, law, and teaching.

And students became less subject to the *in loco parentis* tradition of the older morality.

Growth was substantial: 50,000 students in 1870, 150,000 in 1890, and 350,000 in 1910; and the number of Ph.D. degrees conferred grew from 1 to 150 to 450.

The research university was the great result of this period.[2] The transition to the research university was led by some of the historic giants of American higher education: Eliot at Harvard, White at Cornell, Gilman at Hopkins, Angell at Michigan, Harper at Chicago, Jordan at Stanford, Wheeler at California, and Van Hise at Wisconsin.

This was also the time when most of the historically Black and the Catholic colleges and universities were founded—the first reflecting the end of slavery, the second the new immigrants.

3. The third historic period, and the second great transformation, was from 1960 to 1980, and once again higher education entered a new stage of history:

From 3.5 million students in 1960 to 12 million in 1980.

From a system nearly half private in terms of enrollment to one 80 percent public.

From a public system heavily comprised in 1960 of research universities and other institutions offering graduate instruction (50 percent of public enrollments) to one dominated in 1980 by comprehensive colleges and universities and by community colleges (75 percent of public enrollments).

The great growth of community colleges carried their enrollments from under 400,000 to over 4 million. As a result, particularly of the growth of community colleges, most states could be said by 1980 to provide universal access to higher education to all high school graduates who wished to attend—California had been the first to take this stand in 1960 under the Master Plan.

The great transition of teachers' colleges to comprehensive colleges and universities specializing in many professional fields, including particularly engineering and business administration, carried their enrollments from roughly 500,000 to almost 3 million.

From a professoriate of 235,000 to 685,000—and more of them part-time; and one-third of them unionized as against none in 1960.

From new doctoral degrees at a level of 10,000 in 1960 to 33,000 in 1980; and M.D. degrees from 7,000 to 15,000.

From federal expenditures on R&D within universities (not counting federal laboratories managed by universities) from $1,250 million to $3,000 million in 1980 dollars. Half of these expenditures were by twenty universities in 1963[3]; and by thirty in 1980,[4] demonstrating the increase in the number of universities with substantial national research responsibilities. Thirty-nine states and the District of Columbia in 1980 had one or more institutions designated as research universities in the Carnegie classification.[5]

Federal expenditures on student aid rose (in 1980 dollars) from $300 million to $10 billion.

From a curriculum dominated by letters and science departments to one dominated by the professional schools. In the short period from 1969 to 1976, undergraduate enrollments in the professions went from 38 percent to 58 percent.[6] This was the last and conclusive triumph of the Sophists over the Philosophers, of the proponents of the commercially useful over the defenders of the intellectually essential.

Some particular developments went beyond all prior experience:

The largest series of student revolts in American history

The greatest politicalization of the campus—both of faculty and of students

The most substantial shocks to governance mechanisms, with a decline in the comparative influence of boards of trustees and presidents

The greatest wave of attempted academic reform and the greatest wave of disappointments

The greatest public effort to achieve equality of opportunity to attend college with results that did not match the effort

The vast extension of mechanisms for the coordination of higher education by the states from twenty-four systems in 1960 to all but four in 1980 (Delaware, Michigan, Nebraska, Vermont); and, in general, the intensification of control.

Overall, the system in 1980 was bigger, more public, more a part of the totality of American life, more coordinated by the states than ever before; and there was no likelihood that it would, in any major respect, revert to the status quo ante of 1960. By 1980, 1960 was history long past; and 1980 had become the main starting point for the history yet to follow. In terms of student years on campus, two-thirds of the history of American higher education to 1980 had taken place from 1960 to 1980, as against one-third from 1636 to 1980. (See chart 1).

This was, in its totality, a particularly critical epoch in the life of American higher education.

Points of Observation

The participant, as I was during this period, has certain disadvantages as an observer. Participation may lead to too deep an immersion in detail with loss of overall perspective. It may also lead to too total a commitment

CHART 1:

Changing Dimensions of American Higher Education 1960–80

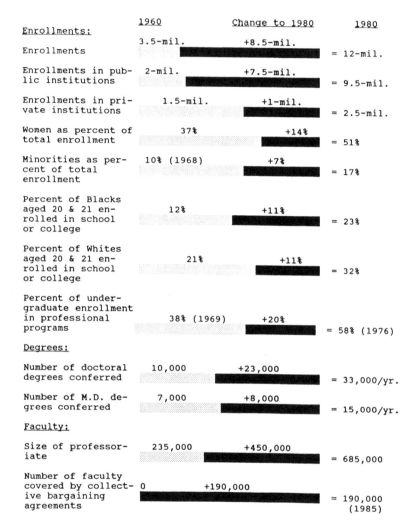

Enrollments:	1960	Change to 1980	1980
Enrollments	3.5-mil.	+8.5-mil.	= 12-mil.
Enrollments in public institutions	2-mil.	+7.5-mil.	= 9.5-mil.
Enrollments in private institutions	1.5-mil.	+1-mil.	= 2.5-mil.
Women as percent of total enrollment	37%	+14%	= 51%
Minorities as percent of total enrollment	10% (1968)	+7%	= 17%
Percent of Blacks aged 20 & 21 enrolled in school or college	12%	+11%	= 23%
Percent of Whites aged 20 & 21 enrolled in school or college	21%	+11%	= 32%
Percent of undergraduate enrollment in professional programs	38% (1969)	+20%	= 58% (1976)
Degrees:			
Number of doctoral degrees conferred	10,000	+23,000	= 33,000/yr.
Number of M.D. degrees conferred	7,000	+8,000	= 15,000/yr.
Faculty:			
Size of professoriate	235,000	+450,000	= 685,000
Number of faculty covered by collective bargaining agreements	0	+190,000	= 190,000 (1985)

to positions taken in the past. It is difficult to be in the battle and yet to stand above it at the same time.

Participation, however, has certain advantages. The individual is given a chance to know the many pressures and the many considerations that enter into decision making, the role of personalities as against more objective factors, the weights actually given to different factors as against the assumptions and guesses of outsiders, the knowledge available at the time of

	1960	Change to 1980	1980
Institutions:			
Number of institutions	2,000	+1,200	= 3,200
Number of public institutions	700	+800	= 1,500
Number of private institutions	1,300	+400	= 1,700
Enrollment in public institutions as percent of total	60%	+20%	= 80%
Percent of public enrollment in community colleges & comprehensive colleges & universities	50%	+20%	= 70%
Enrollment in community colleges	400,000	+3,600,000	= 4-mil.
Enrollment in public comprehensive colleges & universities	600,000	+1,800,000	= 2.4-mil.
Federal & state support:			
Federal R&D to universities (1980 $)	$1,300-mil.	+$3,000-mil.	= $4,300-mil.
Federal student aid (1980 $)	$300-mil.	+$9.7-bil.	= $10-bil.
State expenditures on operations of higher education institutions (1980 $)	$4-bil.	+$17-bil.	= $21-bil.

decision making, the alternatives weighed, the total oral record as well as the selective written documents, and much else.

And nonparticipant, outside observers also have their prejudices and their commitments that must be taken into account. I have never read what I have considered a fully objective account of events in which I have directly participated, either by an outside observer or by a participant. I have, consequently, developed a certain skepticism about all histories. History is an art and not an exact science, and an art of passion as well as of analysis. One should write, as one should read, with realization of the limitations of all histories.

My vantage points to witness the great transformation of 1960 to 1980 were several.

1. I was chancellor at Berkeley from 1952 to 1958. This was the time of preparation for the "tidal wave" of students. Almost endless consultations

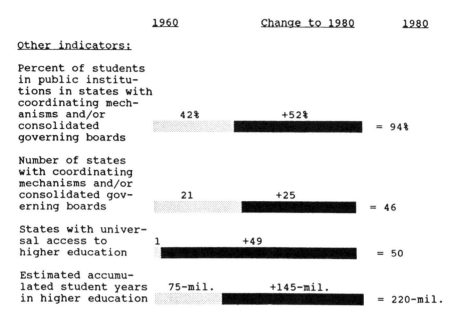

Other indicators:

Percent of students
in public institu-
tions in states with
coordinating mech-
anisms and/or   42%   +52%
consolidated   = 94%
governing boards

Number of states
with coordinating
mechanisms and/or
consolidated gov-   21   +25
erning boards   = 46

States with univer-
sal access to   1   +49
higher education   = 50

Estimated accumu-
lated student years   75-mil.   +145-mil.
in higher education   = 220-mil.

took place on the maximum size we desired for the Berkeley campus. We agreed on 27,500 and convinced the Regents to accept this figure: the UCLA campus later decided on a size of 27,500 plus a medical school. Many considerations entered into selecting this figure. The most generally applicable one was the judgment of the largest size at which a department could function well with all senior members knowing each other and particularly knowing and taking an interest in the progress of their junior colleagues. If anything, we set the figure too high, and several departments found that they had passed the size of full effectiveness when they grew to seventy or eighty members. The 27,500 figure at Berkeley and at UCLA, however wise it was, forced the Regents to create new campuses. These years were ones of intense competition in recruiting faculty members and in securing funds; for Berkeley, they were the most intense in its history as it took the actions that led it to be rated as the "best balanced distinguished university in the country."[7]

2. As president of the University of California from 1958 to 1967, it was my responsibility to guide the development of three new campuses at San Diego, Irvine, and Santa Cruz, each of which was to have its own distinctive personality, and transformations at Davis, Santa Barbara, and Riverside. This again led to almost endless discussions of how improvements could be made—if they could be made—on the standard models of Berkeley and UCLA; or of how variations could be introduced to give each

campus its separate characteristics. The new campuses, and other developments, necessitated the largest governance reorganization of the university in all of its history, in the direction of massive decentralization.

I also initiated and guided the development of the California Master Plan of 1960, which gave me a chance to come to know in detail the capacities, ambitions, and prospects of the community colleges, state colleges, and, to a lesser extent, private institutions in the state. The Master Plan not only guaranteed universal access to college for all high school graduates for the first time anywhere, but it also set up a system of clear differentiation of functions among the segments of higher education.

Then came the student revolts that engulfed Berkeley sooner and more intensely than most campuses in the United States, and the subsequent adverse public reaction that engulfed me in conflict with the new governor, who had been elected in substantial part on the basis of the adverse reactions.

3. Then I spent thirteen years (1967–80) as chairman of the Carnegie Commission on Higher Education (later the Carnegie Council), which undertook the largest and most important survey of higher education in American history. Meetings were held with local leaders of colleges and universities in every region of the United States. Thirty-seven reports with recommendations, and some 130 sponsored research reports, were issued. The major concerns were:[8]

Equality of opportunity
Provision of higher skills and new knowledge
Quality of academic programs and possible reforms
Adequacy of governance
Resources available to higher education
Purposes and performances of higher education
Demographic prospects

Eric Ashby, Vice-Chancellor of Cambridge University, called this "the most thorough analysis of a nation's higher education which has ever been made."[9]

Digression—An Internecine Battle in Higher Education

The Carnegie Commission, along with the Rivlin Commission, became a party to the most intense internal warfare in the history of higher education in the United States.[10] The federal government in the late 1960s and early 1970s was prepared to give substantial funding to support higher education in order to accommodate the millions of new students, advance equality of opportunity, and build new "human capital," which was one of the great themes at that time. The American Council on Education and *all* the other leadership associations agreed on and pledged themselves irrevocably to support a program of lump-sum grants to institutions as such. We disagreed and were even on occasion verbally accused of "treason." We disagreed for these reasons:

We did not believe that the federal government was prepared to take over *institutional* support of colleges and universities in addition to project support as in research contracts and aid to individual students.

If it did, we feared that the states would start to withdraw their commitments, and we believed that the states were a better long-run source of support than was the federal government, which had to remain flexible financially in order to meet urgent emergency demands for defense, or for counter-cyclical actions, or for tax relief. As it turned out, support to higher education institutions as such would have been very vulnerable during the Reagan years as compared to the grants and loans that aided millions of students and their parents—"entitlements" to individuals were more politically secure than subsidies to institutions.

Also, if the federal government did give institutional support, we thought it would have greater difficulty selecting institutions to support, as compared with selecting individual students, in part because of the separation of church and state in a situation where many colleges still had church connections.

We also thought that the federal government would have to impose more conditions on the autonomy of institutions than if aid went through individual students.

We also believed that higher education in the long run was better off in the hands of fifty competitive states than in the hands of a single federal government, and that the states could better reflect the many regional variations across the nation.

Additionally, we thought it was better, and more in keeping with federal obligations, to aid low- and lower-middle–income students to attend college, thus increasing equality of opportunity, which was an historic national promise. This was our overwhelming consideration.

We also favored using the student market, rather than bureaucratic rules, to distribute funds.

We also considered that it was better that any great political issues affecting higher education be handled at the state and local levels rather than at the national level as was happening in Europe at the time of the student troubles.

In any event, we won decisively. The new Pell Grants and the older loan programs provided by the Higher Education Amendments of 1972 were greatly increased—Pell Grants alone, by the late 1980s, went to three million students in an amount of $4 billion per year; and equality of opportunity was advanced modestly. Had we not had our alternative available, nothing would have happened and an historic opportunity might have been missed. I was surprised along the way by two things about higher education: (1) how committed it became to a program that I did not believe was, and, more importantly, turned out not to be, politically viable; and (2) how willing it was to make a Faustian bargain of incurring long-run dangers of national control as the price for receiving short-term, lump-sum checks. Fortunately this was a single episode in an otherwise good record of approaches to the federal government by organized higher education.

4. Subsequently, I spent eight years (1981 through 1988) studying three projects[11] in the area of governance, under the auspices of the Association of Governing Boards of Universities and Colleges. The preparation of these reports included the most extensive national field investigation ever undertaken of the operation of presidencies and boards of trustees. These investigations included more intimate contact with the inner workings of all types of colleges and universities than any other similar projects were ever privileged to have.

5. Additionally, I have had the opportunity to participate in many conferences and programs on higher education around the world—particularly under the auspices of the International Council for Educational Development, chaired by James A. Perkins—that provided a comparative view of the American system.

Convictions

My basic intellectual convictions about the role of education in society are quite simple and quite standard for an American:

> That "the wheel of education, once set in motion, moves at an ever faster pace." (Plato)
>
> That "useful knowledge" can make great contributions to the welfare of society. I agree with Franklin that "it would be well if they [students] could be taught everything that is useful, and everything that is ornamental: but art is long, and their time is short. It is therefore proposed that they learn those things that are likely to be most useful and most ornamental, regard being had to the several professions for which they are intended." (Benjamin Franklin)
>
> That universal-access education is essential to the workings of a democracy. "I think by far the most important bill in our whole code

is that for the diffusion of knowledge among the people. No other sure foundation can be devised for the preservation of freedom, and happiness.'' (Thomas Jefferson)

That the quality of education is one major determinant of the quality of a society.

These convictions have been intensified by my personal history. My mother, with only a grade school education, worked as a milliner making fancy hats in store windows on customer orders and was not willing to marry until she had saved enough money to send her children to college; as a consequence of her devoted efforts, my three sisters attended Oberlin and I went to Swarthmore. My father, of Scottish ancestry, was both a teacher and a farmer in rural Pennsylvania (as was his father before him). The highest priority of all, in our family, was placed on education, and on hard work.

More specifically, I saw how intellectual activities seemed to progress best in a face-to-face, caring community, as in a one-room schoolhouse at the end of ''Spook Lane'' near Stony Creek in Berks County, Pennsylvania, where our teacher, Miss Elba, loved all her students, and as at Swarthmore College. Living on a farm in the Oley Valley where neighbors helped neighbors, I learned the general value in human relations of the sense of community obligations. As a consequence, I have always been concerned with the welfare of smaller communities, such as departments and ''cluster colleges,'' within the larger academic world.

My interest in a broad liberal education was first kindled by my father, who once taught in the Reading Classical School, of which he was co-founder, and whose small library at home was composed of the most famous of the Greek, Roman, and English classics. Later at Swarthmore, in the Frank Aydelotte years, a liberal education was a great intellectual challenge, just as it was useful thereafter.

Additionally, as a convinced Quaker and longtime practitioner of mediation and arbitration in industrial disputes, I developed an intense opposition to both the immorality and the ineffectiveness of the use of force, as a first resort, in the solution of disputes; and this later led me into confrontations with advocates of force both on the left and on the right.

These are some of the ways in which my autobiography has influenced my beliefs and my actions in higher education. Thus, as with so many others, so much of my choice of educational policies has been influenced by personal experiences.

In approaching the great transformation of 1960 to 1980, it is appropriate to observe with Pindar that: The test of a person ''lies in action.'' So also of institutions. And there was plenty of action in those two decades testing American institutions of higher education. How well did they meet this test?

Notes

1. For an excellent history of this period, see Laurence R. Veysey, *The Emergence of the American University* (Chicago: University of Chicago Press, 1965). At the time, William James was very perceptive regarding the long-run consequences of the changes then taking place. (See "The Ph.D. Octopus," in *Memories and Studies* [New York: Longmans Green, 1911], 329–47). He saw that the Ph.D. was coming to dominate American higher education and that the degree held was the test of adequacy rather than "brilliance."

2. The original members of the Association of American Universities, founded in 1900: University of California at Berkeley, The Catholic University of America, University of Chicago, Clark University, Columbia University, Cornell University, Harvard University, Johns Hopkins University, University of Michigan, University of Pennsylvania, Princeton University, Stanford University, University of Wisconsin, and Yale University. By 1910, the following had been added: University of Virginia, University of Illinois, University of Minnesota, University of Missouri, Indiana University, University of Iowa, University of Kansas, and University of Nebraska.

3. Listed in order of amount of funds received: Massachusetts Institute of Technology, University of Michigan, Columbia University, University of California at Berkeley, Harvard University, University of Illinois, University of Chicago, Stanford University, University of California at Los Angeles, University of Minnesota at Minneapolis–St. Paul, University of Wisconsin at Madison, Cornell University, Johns Hopkins University, New York University, University of Washington, Yale University, University of Pennsylvania, Ohio State University, University of Rochester, University of Texas.

4. Listed in order of amount of funds received: Johns Hopkins, MIT, Stanford, University of Washington, University of California at San Diego, UCLA, Harvard, Columbia, University of Wisconsin at Madison, Cornell, University of Minnesota, University of Michigan, University of Pennsylvania, Yale University, University of California at San Francisco, Washington University, University of Chicago, University of Illinois at Champaign-Urbana, University of California at Berkeley, Penn State, University of Southern California, University of Colorado, Duke University of California at Davis, University of North Carolina at Chapel Hill, University of Rochester, Yeshiva University, University of Texas at Austin, NYU, Ohio State.

5. Carnegie Council on Policy Studies in Higher Education, *A Classification of Institutions of Higher Education* (Berkeley, CA: Carnegie Council on Policy Studies in Higher Education, 1976).

6. Carnegie Foundation for the Advancement of Teaching, *Missions of the College Curriculum* (San Francisco: Jossey-Bass, 1977), 103.

7. Allan M. Cartter, *An Assessment of Quality in Graduate Education* (Washington, DC: American Council on Education, 1966), 107.

8. For summaries of the work of the Commission and Council, see Carnegie Commission on Higher Education, *A Digest and Index of Reports and Recommendations, December 1968–June 1972* (Berkeley, CA: Carnegie Commission on Higher Education, 1972); and Carnegie Council on Policy Studies in Higher Education, *The Carnegie Council on Policy Studies in Higher Education: A Summary of Reports and Recommendations* (San Francisco: Jossey-Bass, 1980). See also Lewis B. Mayhew, *The Carnegie Commission on Higher Education* (San Francisco: Jossey-Bass, 1973); and Jack Embling, *A Fresh Look at Higher Education: European Implications of the Carnegie Commission Reports,* Amsterdam: Elsevier, 1974).

9. Eric Ashby, "The Great Reappraisal," in *Universities Facing the Future: An International Perspective,* eds. W. R. Niblett and R. F. Butts (San Francisco: Jossey-Bass, 1972), 29–44.

10. See Carnegie Commission on Higher Education, *Quality and Equality: New Levels of Federal Responsibility for Higher Education* (New York: McGraw-Hill, 1968). Also see Alice Rivlin, *Toward a Long-Range Plan for Federal Financial Support for Higher Education,* a report to the President (Washington, DC: U.S. Department of Health, Education, and Welfare, Office of the Assistant Secretary for Planning and Evaluation, January 1969).

11. See the following: Commission on Strengthening Presidential Leadership (Clark Kerr, chairman and director), *Presidents Make a Difference: Strengthening Leadership in Colleges and Universities* (Washington, DC: Association of Governing Boards of Universities and Colleges, 1984); Clark Kerr and Marian L. Gade, *The Many Lives of Academic Presidents: Time, Place & Character* (Washington, DC: Association of Governing Boards of Universities and Colleges, 1986); and Clark Kerr and Marian L. Gade, *The Guardians: Boards of Trustees of American Colleges and Universities,* (Washington, DC: Association of Governing Boards of Universities and Colleges, 1989).

PART I

The American System in Perspective

Introduction—The American System in Perspective

The American system is a unique one. To understand the great transformation of 1960 to 1980, it is first necessary to understand the system within which it occurred and that was changed so significantly by it.

1. The American Strategy among Several Alternatives. The American system of education is only one among several actual alternative systems. The American alternative was not chosen consciously all at once—quite the contrary. It developed over the centuries out of the special history of the nation itself. In particular, it was never intended to be as elitist as were some other national systems, for example, the English, although early enrollments were very limited. Inherently, given its Puritan philosophical origins, it was always subject to potentially great expansion, which transpired first toward a mass basis after the Civil War and then later—and as the first to do so anywhere in the world—toward universal access after World War II. The manifest destiny of the American system was from the beginning to serve all of the people all of the time.

Five possible overall strategies for education are these:

Elite-oriented
Production-oriented
Universal-access
Horizontal
Atomistic

The American system is a combination of the second, third, and last of these orientations.

2. Heritage. The American system of education is marked not only by a special combination of strategies: it is also noteworthy for the comparative emphasis it has placed on education among other activities within t'¹ society. Historically this emphasis has only been matched or surpasse⸍ Scotland, which was the original model, and by contemporary Japan, ' is the current chief competitor. The American system has been calle⸍ with changing emphasis over the centuries, to

advance individual aspirations,
perpetuate religious convictions,

extend effective political participation,
assist economic growth,
aid absorption of new immigrants, and
enhance national power externally and regional advantage internally.

3. Structure. The American system of higher education has a very special structure. It has both an influential private sector as well as a strong public sector. Within the public sector, the control of institutions is comparatively highly decentralized. Sources of funds are both private and public in both public and private institutions. Of special note, significant public funds are distributed as though they were private. Structures of higher education around the world are of the following types:

Independent private
Dependent private (as in some church-led institutions)
Independent public
Semi-independent public (state/guild type)
Semi-independent public (state/trustee/guild type)
Dependent public

The American mixture consists of institutions in the first, third, and fifth of these types, with the third (independent public) constituting a particularly significant category within the United States; this mixture stands as a possible model for developments elsewhere—showing how it is possible to be both public and private at one and the same time! This innovation, along with the land-grant university and the community college, stands as a particular contribution of American higher education.

4. Functions. An ancient conflict, going back to the Greeks in their classical age, is whether higher education should be concerned with what is important to philosophers (as to Socrates, Plato, and Aristotle) or with what is useful to the people in their everyday lives (the view of the Sophists, who thought you could never know the absolute truth but you could learn how to make a good argument about it); or with both in some balance. This conflict continues to this day and may well continue into eternity.

Higher education in the United States has many functions and they keep on growing—and these involve not just the research of Flexner or the continuation of the great philosophical dialogue of Hutchins. Higher education in practice is a strung-along enterprise without a single preferred function to concentrate its efforts. Its functions respond to time and to place. It is the idealists (such as Flexner and Hutchins) who look for the one and only true faith, while the pragmatists look at whatever works best. The former are exclusionist and perfectionist, the latter inclusionist and adaptive. My views, quite obviously, are more of the pragmatic persuasion: the overall goal of education is to serve the people as they wish to be served or can be persuaded to be served, and this leads to several, sometimes conflicting, functions—but they should be kept in some reasonable balance.

Several "pure" models are

The Research University (Flexner)
The Classical College (Hutchins)
The Community of Scholars (Goodman)

The Dissenting Professor
The Dissenting Academy
The Partisan Camp

The actual reality, however, is what I call "the pluralistic university in the pluralistic society."

"The Pluralistic University in the Pluralistic Society" looks at the long-term contest over functions. At the most fundamental level, this contest is over whether to perpetuate the past, advance some vision of the future, serve the present, or develop some combination of these. In serving the present, in turn, the battles are over how much attention should be given to the production, consumption, and citizenship functions of higher education. It is suggested here that American higher education has done best with its production functions, least well with its consumption functions, and middling with its citizenship functions.[1]

5. Remembering Flexner. This is my commentary on the Flexner model of the research university. The greatest of the historic critics of the American university have been Abraham Flexner; Thorstein Veblen, who thought that the Captains of Industry controlled the Captains of Erudition; Upton Sinclair, who thought Big Business not only controlled but exploited the Big University;[2] and Robert Maynard Hutchins, who thought that salvation clearly lay through the Great Books.

6. Disagreeing with Hutchins. Hutchins was the great proponent of the Classical College, and of the Great Books as the center of the classical college. The Great Books method, however, appears to me to be one alternative approach to a liberal education, within the several purposes of higher education, and not the one and only way.

7. Performance. Another way of looking at higher education is to examine goals and effectiveness in reaching chosen goals. This is to enter a swamp. There are ideal goals and actual goals. There is good evidence, bad evidence, and no evidence of effectiveness; but mostly bad or non existent evidence. However, the American system may be said to be marked by a particularly wide and flexible series of goals that are highly responsiv to the wishes of the great mass of citizens, and these wishes grow incrementally. It also may be said that, on a comparative basis (contrary to what we have at other levels of education), it performs well in areas that can be measured.

Notes

1. The Carnegie Commission (see *The Purposes and Performance of Higher Education in the United States* [New York: McGraw-Hill, 1973]) set out five purposes for higher education: the development of the individual student (the consumption function); the advancement of human capability (the production function); the enlargement of educational justice, the advancement of learning and wisdom, and the critical evaluation of society (the citizenship functions). This report also gave first place in performance to the production function.

2. Thorstein Veblen, *The Higher Learning in America* (Stanford, CA: Academic Reprints, 1954 [originally published 1918]); and Upton Sinclair, *The Goose Step: A Study of American Education* (New York: AMS Press, 1970 [first published, 1923]).

CHAPTER 1

The American Strategy among Several Alternatives—
Five Strategies for Education, and Their Major Variants*

This essay was part of a series of five lectures I gave at the University of Nairobi. Kenya was then considering moving from a system of higher education modeled on England to a more American type; and I was arguing, indirectly, for the American type. My lectures were identified as Gandhi Memorial Lectures because the Indian community in Kenya, then under increasing attack, supported them as a goodwill gesture.

Education takes many forms in many places. It is not one, but many things. One errs in talking about *the* contribution of education to national development without specifying what kind of education, for whom, at what stage of development, and where. Some kinds of education for certain kinds of people under one set of circumstances may be very helpful; and the same kind for different people under other circumstances may be equally harmful. Western models do not work equally well in Africa or Asia. Education is a multiform, not a uniform, phenomenon.

Model I. Elite-oriented Education

One strategy for education is to consider it as serving a small elite only. This elite may be defined by birth—an aristocracy, or by demonstrated talent—a meritocracy, or by some combination of both. The difference between definition by birth and by talent, however, is a substantial one. The persons chosen will be quite different because talent does not uniformly follow family origin. The method of selection is quite easy when based on birth and quite difficult when based on talent. The latter basis requires much better primary and secondary schools that are widely distributed and better methods of examination. The tone of the educational process varies also, from a leisurely one when based on birth to a highly competitive one when based on talent.

Yet there are substantial similarities in education serving elites defined by birth or by talent. In each case, small numbers are involved. The curriculum tends to be of the classical type: all students receive much the same background in terms of the central content of the curriculum and the style of approach in residential living and codes of personal conduct. Once a student is on the ladder, the effort of the system is expended on his or her support as an individual and on the student's preservation within the elite group. Graduates enter into a distinct class status raised far above that of nongraduates. The quality of academic degrees is held, wherever possible, to a single "Gold Standard." A degree has a certain value for all holders regardless of what field they study or their personal performance. Graduates have an assured status.

The British system of higher education until the middle of the nineteenth century was elitist, and largely hereditary elitist. Entry into Oxford and Cambridge was limited by rule to males who were members of the Anglican church and in fact mostly to sons of the gentry and the upper middle classes. During the next century, reliance gradually was placed more on talent and less on heredity. Good preparatory schools based on talent were developed, and effective sorting examinations were devised. Harvard, in the United States, followed a somewhat similar historical course. The Scottish universities were always more open to talent. Sub-Sahara Africa with its missionary schools and French lycées followed the meritocratic elite system then in effect in Britain and France. China had such a system to prepare its mandarins for two thousand years.

Higher education in Latin America, by and large, has not yet given up selection on the basis of family position in favor of selection based on talent. One reason for this is that the good secondary schools are almost universally private and costly, although higher education is generally tuition free. Thus only the children of the wealthier families can qualify for the university through prior attendance at the better secondary schools. And, once they arrive at the universities, they are often but not always heavily subsidized from the public purse. A largely unconnected mass elementary system of low quality exists for the children of peasants and workers. There is almost no way for talent to rise through the formal system of education. It is more likely to emerge through the military forces. Much of the Moslem world parallels the pattern found in Latin America. Ancient Rome also had an elitist system for children of the upper class based on tutors and private schools and a large-scale elementary system for the masses.

There are, then, at least three major elitist approaches: (1) The hereditary elitist, which may be visualized as a ladder that leads from entry almost automatically to exit. (2) The meritocratic elitist, which has a broader base: able young persons are sought more widely than in the wealthy classes alone and are subject, in the early stages of education, to intense competition through which some are eliminated. (3) The hereditary elitist, with a separate, largely unconnected, low-level egalitarian system at the primary level, looking like a disconnected figure L (see fig. 1)

FIGURE 1

a, Hereditary elitist; *b*, meritocratic elitist; *c*, hereditary elitist with a separate
mass elementary system

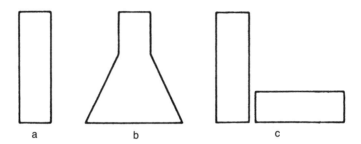

Model II. Production-oriented Education

The University of London, which was founded in 1836 with a different orientation than that of Oxford and Cambridge, was much more open to bright young people drawn from the total population and not only trained them to be scholars and gentry, but also prepared them for a much broader variety of professions. A great system of training for the health professions was developed there long before Oxford and Cambridge took any broad interest in such training. The redbrick universities in England followed London's lead.

The most dramatic step toward the occupational orientation of higher education took place in the United States with the founding of the land-grant universities at the time of President Lincoln. These institutions aimed to serve the children of farmers and workers. They turned their backs on the classical curriculum of the day and, instead, sought to fill the needs of developing industry and agriculture for managers and technical experts. They were oriented not at all toward class status but clearly toward productive effort.

Russia, after 1917, moved in the same general direction, but with more ideological content, more centralized control, and even more emphasis on technocratic aspects. The purpose in Russia, as in the United States, was to aid the economic growth of an advancing society and, simultaneously, to open up new opportunities for more of the youthful population.

Japan, since World War II, has enormously expanded and diversified its national system of higher education. Adopting a production-oriented approach to education, Japan has put less emphasis on university-based research than either the United States or Russia. Applied research in Japan has been left principally to large private industry, and basic research, until recently, has been comparatively neglected.

The tendency in all production-oriented systems is to concentrate at first on high-level manpower and then, more gradually, on paraprofessional manpower. This development reflects three factors. First, full recognition of how many paraprofessionals are needed to make good use of the highly skilled professional is usually not forthcoming. Second, for educating paraprofessionals, to the extent that they are used, reliance is initially placed on secondary schools and on on-the-job training. Later, provision of some formal training at the postsecondary level as well is usually found desirable. Third, paraprofessional training has lower status and is avoided by students if they have the alternative of professional training. As industrial growth proceeds, however, this impediment is less effective, and paraprofessional training becomes more common. Policy conclusions based on these three considerations have contributed to the rise of community colleges with two-year programs in the United States. They are now, in enrollment, the largest single element of American higher education. In Canada, community colleges and comparable institutions more than doubled in size in the 1960s. The British government recently has particularly aided the polytechnics, and Australia has done the same for the institutions of technical and further education.

A modified occupation-oriented approach is the civil-servant approach: education, particularly secondary and higher education, is designed to turn out civil servants rather than the whole range of professionals and paraprofessionals required by an industrializing or industrialized nation. This narrower concentration has marked France, India, and much of Africa until very recent times. Napoleon in France and the British colonial authorities in India both concentrated on the need of the state for well-trained civil servants. In both countries today teachers are included in the class of civil-servants.

Another variation of the production- or occupation-oriented model entails preservation of elements of the older classical system reformed to include a meritocratic base and the addition of a new technocratic system. The land-grant universities were founded while the older liberal-arts colleges continued to thrive in the United States; the redbricks were added on to Oxford and Cambridge; the technical universities to the Humboldt-type universities in Germany; and now, in Latin America, new technical universities are being started while older universities, such as San Marcos, remain largely unchanged. Over a period of time, classical institutions, in competition for funds and students, begin to look more like the newer, technocratic institutions. There is a movement of the classical institution toward the production-oriented institution, and the civil-servant institution begins to train for a wider range of careers—thus also merging toward the dominant modern type.

The pyramidal model may change shape, as in the United States, when more jobs require more training and more persons can afford more education. The sides will slope less steeply as more people stay in school for a longer period of time, and the apex will be rounded off as many more positions require training at quite advanced levels. The shape becomes that of a haystack.

There are, then, at least five major production-oriented approaches: (1) The pure pyramid, which is closely tied to manpower planning, with a universal base of literacy, topped by successively smaller components of training for clerks and technicians, advanced technicians, scientists, scholars, and advanced professionals. Within higher education in Russia, only 10 percent of the students are in universities; 90 percent are in technical colleges. The United States demonstrates a more varied approach because dynamics of the labor market, rather than manpower planning, fit education to jobs, and because the system responds to student demand for education beyond the needs of industrial production. (2) The truncated pyramid, or partially truncated pyramid, as in Japan, where great emphasis is placed on primary and secondary education and less (until the postwar period) on higher education. (As a corollary, the universities are weak in basic research.) This pyramid has a reduced apex. (3) The half pyramid, found historically in France and India, with emphasis on training for the public civil service rather than for private industry and commerce. (4) The pyramid rising alongside an older elite system, as in England where until recently the redbricks drew heavily on the public grammar schools while Oxbridge continued to draw substantially on private schools like Eton and Harrow. (5) The advanced-stage pyramid with a more rounded top, when more and more occupations require more and more training (see fig. 2).

One may note that the pyramidal approach applies within higher education, as well as to the totality of education, and results within higher education in an emphasis on differentiation of functions—some elements have higher academic value and some, lower. Thus, the binary system in England; the universities versus the technical institutes in Russia; the tripartite system of community colleges, state colleges, and universities in California; the institutions of technical and further education, the colleges of advanced education, and the universities in Australia; and so forth. There is no Gold Standard. There is instead a diversity of programs, standards, and status. In all pyramidal systems the emphasis is on identifying and

FIGURE 2

a, Pure pyramid; *b*, truncated pyramid with reduced emphasis upon higher education, including research; *c*, half pyramid, directed toward civil-service occupations; *d*, pyramid arising alongside an older elitist system; *e*, advanced-stage pyramid

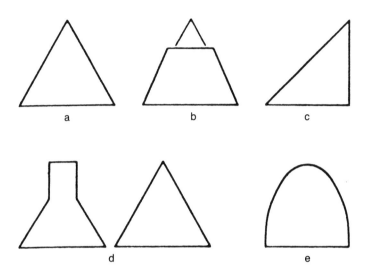

eliminating the less able individual and on preserving within the system only the most able. Less able students drop off as the slopes rise higher.

Model III. Universal-Access Education

A third approach is universal schooling and open enrollment in higher education, which is open to all persons eighteen years of age and over. California (1960) and New York City (1970) are examples in the United States, and within the foreseeable future, 95 percent of all Americans will be within commuting distance of an open-access college. The first community college in the United States was founded in 1902, and the University of Chicago opened its adult extension division in 1892. Community colleges and adult extension are the two great devices tried in the United States to date to achieve universal open access.

As other examples, Britain has now established (1970) the Open University; Japan has begun (1971) the "University of the Air"; Sweden is establishing regional centers attached to its universities; Spain is planning an "open university"; the University of Nairobi has a "Mature-Age Entry Scheme."

The open-access approach to higher education in industrialized nations follows four developments: first, the prior creation of universal primary and secondary education; second, the continuing need by employed persons for technical retraining in the midst of dynamic technological changes; third, the widely held view that education should be a continuing part of the lives of all people who wish it for whatever purpose; and fourth, the new electronic technology which makes an open-access approach possible.

Open access to higher education relates to a basic question: Does education exist for the sake of an elite in a class society, for the sake of productive efficiency in an industrial society, or for all people throughout their lives in a populist-oriented society? Given the financial resources and necessary levels of prior education, the concept of open access to higher education demands that education be available to all who wish it. The courses taught will cover many more subject areas than either elitist or production-oriented higher education. Many courses, for example, will be oriented toward consumption activities. An elitist curriculum is more directed toward development of political leadership; a production-oriented curriculum, toward the needs of the labor market; and the open-access curriculum, toward the interests of daily life. Academic standards will be lower, on the average, in an open-access system and may even disappear in some areas in favor of mere attendance. Remedial work for adults will be a major component. Relevance is not defined as what a highly educated person should know, nor as what an expert must know, but, rather, as what any person may want to know for whatever reason.

Open access may extend to college-age youth only, or to persons of all ages.

The open-access approach may not only develop in wealthy industrial, fully modernized, societies but also in largely rural societies with a low level of per capita wealth. Gandhi, for example, wanted to make "basic education" available to all the people living in a village to assist them in all aspects of their lives. Tanzania has advocated "education for self-reliance" for its entire population. Modern China has instituted literacy training and basic education throughout its vast country. A century ago, Denmark began its rural folk schools. "Store front" schools, in a few American ghettos, follow the same general pattern. An industrializing nation may adopt a form of open access at some level, or levels, of education based on an egalitarian ideological drive, or as a way of letting everybody in—for political reasons—on some of the improvements in society, or as a way of keeping people in rural areas so that they will not swamp the modern sector.

Open access may be developed as a pure system, standing by itself, as Gandhi essentially wanted since he did not favor industrialization. Or it may be added onto a production-oriented system serving modern industry and government.

There are, thus, at least two major forms of open access: (1) The pure type with equal educational opportunity for all citizens. (2) The alternative type where an open-access system of education stands as an alternative to the meritocratic system (see fig. 3).

FIGURE 3

***a*, Pure open access; *b*, open access as an alternative**

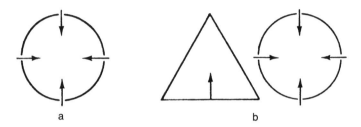

a   b

Of course, comparatively heavy emphasis in the second type may be placed on the pyramid (as in the United States), or heavy emphasis may be placed on the circle (as in Tanzania).

In any event, open access can arise under quite diverse circumstances: as a chosen instrument in a progressive, egalitarian, largely rural society; as an adjunct to the modernizing sector of society—perhaps as part of a rural development program; or as a supplement to the meritocratic educational system of a highly industrialized society with populist tendencies. As open-access approach may be combined in various ways, and for various reasons, with a pyramidal system. Open access, however, is essentially incompatible with an elitist—particularly a hereditary elitist—approach. Egalitarianism and hereditary elitism make strange bedfellows in education, as in society as a whole.

Model IV. Horizontal Education

Recently, the suggestion has been made that education, which has historically been vertical in the effect on social stratifications, be laid on its side horizontally. The "knowledge commune" has been posited as a central aspect of "horizontal collectivism."[1] In a society fitting such a model there would be no highly trained experts; people would rotate from job to job as they saw fit. There would be equality among teachers and students in the knowledge commune—no "chair" professors, no assistants, no subservient students. No one would be allowed to rise above a certain fixed level. Society, as well as the education system, would have a flat profile when projected graphically. Education would be an instrument of leveling conformity.

This model may be visualized as a horizontal line or, perhaps better, as a wide room with a low ceiling (see fig. 4a).

This is a vision that is beautiful to some but one that I do not believe realistic. Some experts, meritocratically selected and trained, are needed to make an atom bomb, even in Maoist China. The little Red Book does not suffice in this case, nor in the provision of surgical care or the building of bridges and dams. No modernized or modernizing system can get along without technical experts and the necessarily pyramidal educational structure to train them. Modernization is not a necessity, but a pyramidal structure of education is essential if modernization is undertaken.

Horizontal equalization of all citizens in all aspects of their lives engenders enormous pressures for conformity, and these pressures require a supreme charismatic personality or a strong bureaucratic hierarchy—or both—to give inspiration and to assure control of the masses. The greatest personality cult in the world today is that surrounding Mao Tse-tung, who during his lifetime had the backing of an all-pervasive military establishment. Furthermore, different people have different tastes, interests, and abilities, and it would be both unwise and impossible to confine them all on a horizontal level forever. The leveling of humanity to one universal standard is inconsistent with both human nature and the realities of the modern world.

Nevertheless, the horizontal approach has been tried recently in a modified form in China during the cultural revolution. A political and military elite remained, however, above the mass of the people, as well as a small technological elite with an educational background. The experience of China may be termed a modified horizontal approach with two small elite classes rising above the horizontal mass—one raised through on-the-job training and selection (political and military leaders) and the other through formal education (technical experts) (see fig. 4b). This approach, in fact, looks something like that found in Latin America, but it is quite different because the Chinese elite groups were chosen on the basis of ideology and merit, not heredity, and through on-the-job selection and training as well as education. The mass of the population was held to low levels of education, not as a result of poverty but as the consequence of an ideology emphasizing the interchangeability of persons in the essential roles of soldier-peasant-worker. Enforced homogenization, politically determined, was the force at work in China rather than socially and economically determined neglect.

The horizontal approach is quite different from open access. The open-access approach allows an individual to obtain whatever education he or she wants, at any time and at any level. The horizontal approach not only sets a ceiling on individual aspirations but also prescribes a set curriculum for everyone regardless of individual interests. The curriculum is heavily oriented toward literacy, ideology, vocational skills, and "coping" skills in health, nutrition, etc.

FIGURE 4

a, Horizontal-egalitarian; *b*, modified horizontal approach with elite groups

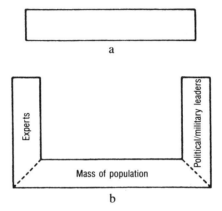

Model V. Atomistic Education

This may be viewed as the oldest, or the newest, or the most constant form of education: oldest because education began informally in the family and on the job, newest because of recent proposals for the "deschooling of society,"[2] and most constant because education always takes place informally as well as formally—in the home, on the job, in the library, beside the radio, in front of the TV screen. The emphasis in atomistic education is on the individual being educated as a by-product of some other activity or on his own, but not through a system of formal education. Atomistic education might be represented by a series of random dots (see fig. 5). Such a system can coexist with any of the other systems we have discussed, but it is most consistent with the open-access approach. The atomistic system if dominant will supplant all other systems; its central theme is ultimately incompatible with the organized character of the other models.[3]

FIGURE 5

Atomistic education

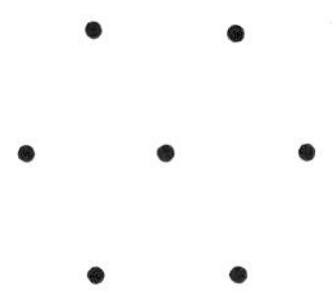

Current interest in atomistic education comes from philosophical anarchist sources. Proponents argue that most, or at least many, people in the world are not now receiving formal education and that universal formal education is too expensive to attempt to realize; that formal education unwisely elevates some people above others and does more harm than good by smothering interest in learning and alienating youth from manual labor; and that schools serve to perpetuate the status quo against the real interests of the people by teaching them to be passive consumers of whatever the society offers. Apprenticeship training and informal learning centers, which people can enter and leave when they wish, are favored instead of formal schools. The argument calls for the abolition of all compulsory attendance in education and of all degrees and certificates.[4] The content of individual learning programs would be highly idiosyncratic.

Conclusion

The five pure models of educational systems I have presented vary from a vertical line to a pyramid, a circle, a horizontal line, and a series of dots.

I have set forth these several strategic approaches to education first to reinforce the point that education is many different things and must be looked at in its specific forms rather than as a single form, and second to emphasize the range of strategic choices that societies have chosen and may choose among.

The elitist approach responds to social class in a stratified society. All persons who step on the lowest rung of the ladder are expected to climb to the top, and most do so. Dropout rates are low. Emphasis is on the selection and training of political leaders.

The occupational approach to structuring education responds to dramatic insistence on national economic growth, to skill needs in a production-

and service-oriented society. Students drop out when they face increasingly difficult competition or when they choose to withdraw. Emphasis is on the selection and training of experts for industry, commerce, and the professions, on the skills related to the production of goods and services.

The open-access approach responds to populist pressures, to the interests of all the people all of the time. The circle is open to them at any time and contains any subject they may want to study. Sir Eric Ashby has written about this, in the American context, as "any person, any study."[5] Nobody drops out by definition. Some persons may choose to stop out, however, precisely as they may choose to stop in. The emphasis is on everybody and free choice.

The horizontal approach is grounded in an egalitarian ideology that emphasizes the homogenization of the masses who have no free choice.

The atomistic approach turns its back on all formal schooling as not only unproductive but even counterproductive.

The elite approach fits best a nation under either dynastic or colonial leadership; and the occupational model fits an industrializing society with middle-class or nationalistic, socialistic, or communistic leadership.[6] The open-access approach best fits an egalitarian rural society, or serves as an adjunct to the modernizing sector of a developing nation, or stands as an alternative and supplement to the meritocratic structure in a modernized society. The horizontal approach is found, in modified form, in an ideologically managed political and military dictatorship. The atomistic approach is connected with anarchistic thought and the socioeconomic conditions of primitive society.

Notes

* First presented as the Gandhi Memorial Lectures, University of Nairobi, 1972, and adapted from a chapter in Clark Kerr, *Education and National Development: Reflections from an American Perspective during a Period of Global Reassessment* (Nairobi: East African Publishing House, 1979). Reprinted from *Comparative Education Review* 23, no. 2 (June 1979): 171–82. Used by permission of The University of Chicago Press.

1. Johan Galtung, "Social Structure, Education Structure and Life Long Education," mimeographed (Paris: OECD, November 1970).

2. Ivan Illich, *Deschooling Society* (New York: Harper & Row, 1971). Also see Paul Goodman, *Compulsory Miseducation* (New York: Horizon, 1964), and his essay in *Summerhill: For and Against* (New York: Hart, 1970), 205–22.

3. While atomistic education is not a viable total approach to education in industrialized and industrializing societies, proponents of atomistic education have

added impetus to some developments which have been taking place for other reasons, such as (1) more efforts to find talent throughout all elements of the population, (2) more attention to lifelong learning opportunities, (3) more active participation by learners in the educational process, (4) more acceptance of individualized learning programs, and (5) more use of noneducational institutions for educational purposes.

4. See Everett Reimer, *School Is Dead: Alternatives in Education* (Garden City, NY: Doubleday, 1971).

5. Eric Ashby, *Any Person, Any Study: An Essay on Higher Education in the United States* (New York: McGraw-Hill, 1971).

6. For a discussion of the various elite groups that lead the industrialization process and their several strategies, see Clark Kerr, John T. Dunlop, Frederick H. Harbison, and Charles A. Myers, *Industrialism and Industrial Man: The Problems of Labor and Management in Economic Growth* (Cambridge, MA: Harvard University Press, 1960).

CHAPTER 2

Heritage—

Education in the United States: Past Assignments and Accomplishments*

A conference on the "World Crisis in Education" had contributions from authors from several nations, each seeking to describe the essential nature of the educational systems of their nations. This is what I said, in part, about the United States.

Few nations in history have relied so fully and for so long on education for solutions to so many problems as has the United States. And yet today, after more than three centuries of devotion to education, the American people face their most serious educational crisis. This crisis is not universal in its impact, for much is done effectively and even superbly. It is, rather, a crisis comprised of inadequacies—some minor and some major—in specific aspects of educational performance. The failures of today are related, in part, to unique features of the American scene; but, in part also, they are indicative of difficulties to be faced by any highly developed industrial society.

Formal education in the United States now absorbs a little over 6 percent of the gross national product. Over the past decade, resources put into education have risen proportionately by more than one-half. The increase by over one-half in a single decade is the most substantial of any similarly short period in American history. It reflects both the high priority placed on educational effort and the great rise after World War II in the number of persons of school age.

The daily lives of more than one-quarter of the American people are involved in formal education. School and college enrollments total 55,000,000 [59,500,000 in 1987], out of a population of 200,000,000 [243,000,000 in 1987]. Teachers number 2,500,000. Beyond formal education lies an enormous amount of organized training in industry, government, the military, the churches; and related to education is the creation of new knowledge and the general dissemination of information. Fritz Machlup has estimated that the production and distribution of knowledge—in all of its many forms—accounts for 25 percent of the national income, and that this form of activity is growing at twice the rate of the economy as a whole.[1]

This brief review will be concerned with the historic relations of formal education to American development.

Historical Review

Historically six major purposes have been served by education.

1. Individual Aspirations. Immigrants to the United States came largely from countries that, at the time of the immigration, confined educational opportunities to members of the aristocracy and the upper middle class. One of the reasons for immigration was to secure opportunities for personal advancement, and this included access to education. Education was an important aspect of the "pursuit of happiness." Schools were started as soon as the original colonies were settled. As the population moved westward, new schools were begun as each new community was founded.

This populist, egalitarian approach rejected the older elitist view of education from the very founding of the new nation. Universal access to education was first assured at the primary level and then at the secondary level. Now in the middle of the twentieth century it is in the process of being assured at the early levels of higher education. Tuition-free junior colleges are open to all high school graduates in California, the state with the most fully developed community college movement; and junior colleges are now the most rapidly expanding segment of education in the United States. In 1900 there were eight; today there are over eight hundred [1987: almost one thousand]. They carry open access, as a matter of right, through fourteen years of formal education. At the national level nearly one-half of all high school graduates enter an institution of postsecondary instruction.

This irresistible and massive wave of individual aspirations has been the most elemental force affecting education in America. Education to ever higher levels has taken on aspects of a social right. It is also a highly valued consumers' good in a high-consumption society. Nor is this historical process yet at an end. It is not clear what may be the ultimate level of general aspirations for available years of education, and how these years may be spread throughout the average lifetime. This ever-rising tide of educational aspiration and attainment is one of the great triumphs of the human spirit.

2. Religious Convictions. Religious institutions, in order to perpetuate their religions and to express the ideals of their religions, have given great leadership to educational development. Many of the early primary and secondary schools were founded by Protestant religious groups. Until the Civil War most of the colleges, including the first, Harvard, were started by one or another of the Protestant denominations. Since the Civil War the Catholics have been the more active in establishing their own parochial schools

352412

and colleges. Ten percent of all elementary and secondary students are in Catholic schools today. And 10 percent of the colleges, with a little less than 10 percent of all enrollments, are Catholic.

The impact of religion on education, while historically most significant, is now fading. Many institutions, once religious in their leadership and with a religious emphasis in their curricula, have now become fully secular, particularly the originally Protestant ones; even Catholic colleges are beginning to move toward lay boards and even some lay administrative leadership.

Few new institutions are being started by religiously oriented groups. The initiative has passed to the public sector, and increasingly public funds are being sought and also being supplied for support of institutions still essentially religious in their orientation. This creates constitutional and political problems in a nation dedicated to separating church and state, but the two systems of education—religious and secular—are going through an historic process of closer accommodation.

3. Political Participation. The founding fathers of the American democracy were convinced that an educated electorate was a prerequisite for political health. To Jefferson, the ownership of land and a degree of education for all the people were the bases on which a democracy could be built, and this theme of education for democratic participation has continued throughout the history of the United States. The educational expectation of citizens has moved from literacy to a primary education and now to a secondary education. As society becomes more complex, the standard expectation may rise yet higher. School-leaving age has generally been raised to sixteen, and in some states to eighteen, largely on the grounds of the educational requirements for citizenship participation.

4. Economic Growth. Benjamin Franklin was the first prominent American to emphasize the practical contributions of education to agriculture, commerce, and industry. He opposed the classical education of the day in favor of useful knowledge. A century later that view gave rise to the land-grant university movement, which placed higher education at the service of the total economy and all elements of the population. Technical high schools and vocational specializations in the community colleges carry on this theme.

Economic growth is a complex phenomenon, and its requirements vary from one stage of development and one situation to another. The postwar economic miracle in Western Europe has been based primarily on large-scale injections of new labor and new capital, using technology already developed. It is not certain that the educational quality of labor, on the average, rose substantially in Western Europe during this period, and in some cases it may have dropped. The United States during this same period has had less access to vast new inputs of labor into industrial pursuits and capital investment on a percentage basis. It has had to rely more heavily on other sources of growth. A recent study by Denison shows education was a major source of growth. For the period from 1955 to 1962, Denison claims, more than one-fifth of the increase in national income per person employed is explained by higher educational levels. "Advances in knowledge," related particularly to higher education, added about another one-fourth.[2] Facing the future, the United States must rely increasingly on greater skill and better technology as sources of economic growth, and both are based on education.

Job content is rising rapidly in the American and the Canadian economies. From 1940–44 to 1960–61, jobs in the top three (out of five) content levels rose from 45 to 59 percent of the employed labor force in the United States and from 40 to 57 percent in Canada.[3] Job families classified as "research and design," "health," "clerical," and "inspection" each rose in size three times or more than the average. There is, of course, no precise way to relate rising job content to higher educational requirements.

Whatever the exact measure, education has increasingly been shown to be a basic and important element in carrying nations to higher levels of economic output, as Benjamin Franklin intuitively sensed two centuries ago.

5. *Absorption of Immigrants.* The United States received waves of immigrants, from changing locations and in changing volume from about 1840 up to World War I [and now again in the 1980s]. The problem of absorbing these new people into the American system of life as it had been developed by the earlier English and German settlers became an insistent issue beginning with the vast migration of the Irish in the 1840s. The assimilation problem continued as the source of later immigrants moved to Eastern and Southern Europe [and now from Latin America and Asia]. The schools were relied upon to provide literacy training for the first generation and full or nearly full Americanization for the second generation. This burden of amalgamation of different language and cultural stocks historically has been carried out with great success.

6. *National Power and Regional Advantage.* Beginning with World War II, there has been an increasing correlation between the quality of the educational system and both national power and regional development, particularly through science and technology based on science. The United States has moved into a clear first place in numbers of leading scientists. From 1901 to 1918, 5 percent of the Nobel Prize awards went to Americans; from 1946 to date, the percentage is 40.

Within the nation certain regions, particularly the Boston metropolitan area and the State of California, have used the quality of their educational systems, and especially of their front-rank universities, to attract modern, scientifically related industry. The competition is now being intensified, above all by the Middle West and Texas.

Thus education has served many purposes and has been the basis for many accomplishments in the United States. It has reflected the uncommon aspirations of the common person, the religious convictions of a more religious people, the historic effort of making America safe for democracy, the combination of greater skill and dexterity in the people with greater technological effectiveness in the capital, the absorption of many people from many backgrounds into a single culture, and the requirements of national and regional influence in a scientific age. Over three centuries the emphasis has shifted. Religious and democratic concerns have been less in the forefront, and greater attention has been given to serving economic growth and national and regional power: the spiritual and the political have been joined by the material and the national. Two concerns have maintained a more steady course: the rising aspirations of individuals for the benefits that education can bring, and the need for a mechanism to introduce unassimilated groups into fuller partnership in American society—this latter concern is at the moment most intense.

Notes

* Paper presented at the International Conference on the World Crisis in Education, Williamsburg, Virginia, 1967. Originally titled "Education in the United States: Past Accomplishments and Present Problems," in *Essays on World Education: The Crisis of Supply and Demand*, ed. George Z. F. Bereday (New York: Oxford University Press, 1969), 297–303. Copyright 1969 by Oxford University Press. Reprinted by permission.

1. Fritz Machlup, *The Production and Distribution of Knowledge in the United States* (Princeton, NJ: Princeton University Press, 1962), 362, 374.

2. Edward F. Denison, assisted by Jean-Pierre Poullier, *Why Growth Rates Differ: Postwar Experience in Nine Western Countries* (Brookings Institution, 1967), 299.

3. J. G. Scoville, "Job Content of the Canadian Economy 1941–1961," *Special Labour Force Studies, No. 3* (Dominion Bureau of Statistics, April 1967): 11.

CHAPTER 3

Structure—

The American Mixture of Higher Education in Perspective: Four Dimensions*

This paper was given at a conference on "privatization" of higher education organized by the International Council for Educational Development. I seek to describe how there is a halfway house between "public" and "private" systems of higher education, and how that half-way house was built in America.

The understanding of systems of higher education is impeded not only by their inherent complexities but also by the tendency to oversimplify their descriptions. In the American system, for example, it is misleading to separate higher education solely into "public" and "private" segments, by ownership, which misses a great deal of reality. There is, more generally, a regrettable tendency to overemphasize the importance of (1) ownership as against (2) actual control, and, also, to look only at (3) the sources of financing as against (4) the mechanism of financing.

In the current concern for "privatization" of higher education in several countries of the world,[1] it is assumed that the best way to "privatize" is by having "private" institutions, when a more universally effective way may well be to privatize "public" institutions.

These points are made below, mostly by reference to the American system, by looking at four major dimensions of higher education and their variations.

The American mixture is now of interest elsewhere, at least in the U.K. as recently stated by the Secretary of State for Education and Science: "The diversity and flexibility so evident across the Atlantic represents the future toward which we in Britain—and, I hope, throughout Europe—will want to move."[2] The American mixture is also of current concern in the United States, as the private sector has declined from 50 percent of enrollments in 1950 to 20 percent now, lest this decline reduce, in particular, "diversity and flexibility."

So what is the American mixture, particularly of controls as well as ownership and of methods of distributing funds as well as sources of funds?

Four Dimensions. Dimension one is ownership—public or private; yet the University of California ("public") is much more like Stanford ("private") than like the University of Moscow (also "public").

Dimension two is control—whether essentially external or internal and, in each case, by whom and for what purposes. The basic difference between the Universities of Moscow and California is that control is heavily external in the former and internal in the latter.

Dimension three is financing—private or public funds in terms of origin.

Dimension four is mechanisms for public financing—public funds treated as public versus public funds treated as private; in other words, who controls the specific distribution of the funds. There is, of course, also the possibility and sometimes actuality of private funds being treated as public.

In the American context, "private funds" include gifts and grants, income from endowments, tuitions and fees, income from auxiliary enterprises, and sales of services. "Public funds treated as public" are appropriations for specifically designated purposes, in the extreme in the form of line-item budgets. "Public funds treated as private" include costs of public loans and grants to students, public research grants and contracts awarded to faculty members, and lump-sum state appropriations to institutions.

Concentration alone on any one of these four dimensions, particularly the first and the third, not only gives too simplistic a view of higher education but can result in a false one as well. Some institutions that are "public" in terms of ownership but controlled by lay boards and/or faculty guilds, are more private, in the sense of independent, than are some "private" institutions that are controlled, at least occasionally, by churches. And some "private" institutions appear more "public," when looking only at their funding sources, than some "public". Total expenditures by "private" Cal Tech, for example, with heavy financing by federal research funds, are 80 percent from public funds, which is higher than by some "public" campuses with comparatively high tuitions and private gifts—for example the Berkeley campus of the University of California (75 percent from public funds).

It is not so much who owns as who controls—a point made long ago by Berle and Means in their classic study of the "modern corporation";[3] and not so much who funds as how they distribute their funds.

A minimum series of categories to reflect worldwide reality, while acknowledging many intermediate situations, is the following:

I. *Independent private*—independent in ownership, control, and basic financing. This is the model of Harvard. A subcategory here is institutions, including Harvard, with heavy federal funding as against liberal arts colleges, like Swarthmore, without much federal financing. Federal funding brings many bureaucratic and annoying controls over expenditures of funds. Private funds are also, sometimes, for narrowly specified purposes but no uniform policy of control is involved.

II. *Dependent private*—independent in ownership and in financing but dependent in control (as some church-owned institutions). This is the model of the early University of Paris.

III. *Independent public*—dependent in ownership but independent in control and in substantial part in financing. This is the model of Michigan, with a strong lay board of trustees, a strong presidency, a strong faculty with shared authority to govern, and public sources of financing heavily through lump-sum appropriations by the state and through support of individual students and individual faculty researchers by the federal government.

IV. *Semi-independent public (state/guild type)*—dependent in ownership, mixed in control, and heavily dependent in financing. The mixed control is by the state in external and some internal affairs, for example, in the curriculum, and by the faculty guilds that elect their own deans and control academic personnel matters. This is the Napoleonic model as in France, and the practice in Italy, Spain, and most Latin American nations.

V. *Semi-independent public (state/trustee/guild type)*—mixed control by the state, academic guilds and, additionally, lay boards of trustees (and presidents); but with heavily state-controlled financing. A strong form of mixed control, including by lay boards, is found in many state colleges in the United States and in a weaker form in Great Britain, particularly in the polytechnics.

VI. *Dependent public*—dependent in ownership, control, and financing. This is the Communist model of University of Moscow.

Most nations have institutions mostly or entirely of a single category, as the Napoleonic in France, or the Communist in the U.S.S.R., and the semi-independent public (state/trustee/guild type) in Great Britain. Some have mixed systems, as in Japan, with semi-independent public institutions of the state/guild type (a few of them very good and very powerful) and many independent private; as also in Korea, Indonesia, Mexico, Puerto Rico, Colombia, and the Philippines.

A schematic outline of these categories is shown in table 1.

Dimensions of the American System—Controls. A unique feature of higher education in the United States is that it has institutions spread across four categories—I, II, III, and V, but with category I (independent private) historically setting the tone for the other three. It is this model that most

TABLE 1

Categories of Institutions of Higher Education

Categories	Ownership		Control				Financing		
	Private	Public	State	Church¹	Guild	Trustees and Presidents	Private	Public Funds Treated as Private	Public
Independent Private (I)	*				*̲	*̲	*̲	*	
Dependent Private (II)	*			*̲	*̲	*̲	*̲	*	
Independent Public (III)		*			*̲	*̲	*	*̲	*
Semi-independent State/Guild Type (IV)		*	*̲		*̲			*	*
Semi-independent State/Trustee/Guild Type (V)		*	*		*	*			*
Dependent Public (VI)		*	*̲						*

Notation: Underlining shows strong emphasis on this aspect.

1. Degree of church control varies enormously from fully dependent to semi-independent to largely independent. This category could well be divided into three, much as there are also variations within each of the other general categories.

sets the spirit for institutions in the other three categories. Most institutions seek to be as "independent private" as they can be. (Most, and increasingly so, institutions still with church affiliations in the United States are essentially "independent private," but some remain semi-dependent upon church authority. In general, lay boards and faculty-shared governance have replaced or greatly reduced church control, over the course of history.)

This worship at the shrine of the independent private institution has led to a very diverse, competitive, and flexible system of institutions in the United States with great capacity to adjust to changing situations. Special aspects of the system as a whole are a comparatively strong chief executive, substantial reliance on several sources of funds including tuitions and gifts, and, of course, comparative freedom from government controls via the independence of boards and trustees.

Other unique features of the American system are (1) the degree of access to the system, which is roughly double that in other advanced industrial nations taken together—roughly 40 percent versus 20 percent of the college-going age group; (2) the historic emphasis on service to the productive segments of American society including agriculture and industry; and (3) the distribution of very high-level academic institutions in both the private and state-owned sectors.

Private institutions have had and still exert strong influence on the following aspects of independent and semi-independent public institutions:

- independent boards of trustees (although largely or wholly selected by public authorities in state-owned institutions)
- influential chief executives
- institutional control over individual student admissions
- institutional control over curriculum
- institutional control over specific budget expenditures (although much less so in the semi-independent public institutions
- institutional control over academic personnel policies
- institutional control over legal affairs, investments, grounds, and buildings
- institutional control over research
- recognition of academic freedom

Also, the private institutions set the goals for all institutions in their provision for the care of individual students and in setting yardsticks for the reasonableness of state formulas for expenditures per student.

Taken together, these emphases result in the absence of strong "ministries of education" at the federal and state levels.

The state-owned institutions, however, have much less control than the private over

• the establishment and location of new institutions,
• the general mission of each institution,
• the selection of trustees,
• the general level of expenditures,
• the general level and composition of admission requirements, and
• the auditing of expenditures;

and they are far more subject to inter-institutional coordination.

Dimensions of the American System—Methods of Financing. Table 2 shows the generalized financing, which is quite mixed, of educational activities of institutions of higher education in the United States, but the situation is even more complex than this table indicates:

1. Auxiliary enterprises (housing, bookstores, food services, hospitals) are largely but not solely financed by private funds. They account for the following percentages of *total* expenditures (not educational alone):
   Public institutions—19 percent
   Private institutions—21 percent
2. Tuitions and fees are counted as private, although some money for these purposes comes from federal and state grants to students. Loans, of course, are subject to repayment but there is a net cost to public funds. (Also, children in college are likely to be shown as tax deductions by parents, but the amounts involved are not included in our calculations.)
3. Gifts and endowments benefit from tax preferences, and perhaps as much as 30 percent might be counted as a cost to public sources. Tax preferences are known technically as "tax expenditures."
4. Some appropriations by states are of a lump-sum nature, as to the universities of Michigan and California, and should, if known in their totality, be added to "public funds treated as private."
5. Property taxes are not assessed on any college or university, and this constitutes a hidden public subsidy.

A rough estimate of allowances for the impact of the inclusion of the first three of these considerations upon the ultimate sources of funds is given in table 3.

Private and privatized support for public institutions takes different forms, depending on the category. Public research universities not only receive federal funding for research on the same basis as do private universities, but they also receive other donations in a similar pattern with substantial support from alumni, foundations, and corporations.

TABLE 2

Sources of Revenues for Institutions of Higher Education in the United States, 1984–85, for *Educational Activities*, in Percentages

	Publicly Owned Institutions	Privately Owned Institutions
Private money:		
Tuition and fees	18	52
Gifts and income from endowments	5	20
Subtotal	23	72
Public money treated as private (cost of student loans and grants, and research grants and contracts to faculty members):		
Federal[1]	10.5	20
State and local	2.5	2
Subtotal	13	22
Public money via direct appropriations:		
Federal	3	1
State[2]	55	1
Local[3]	4	0
Subtotal	62	2
"Other"	2	4
Totals	100	100

Sources: Various reports, U.S. Department of Education.

1. Federal grants and contracts for research are largely to faculties in research universities.
2. Eight states have some form of appropriations for private institutions (other than via assistance to students). These states are Connecticut, Florida, Illinois, Maryland, Michigan, New Jersey, New York, and Pennsylvania.
3. Local appropriations are almost entirely for community colleges.

The comprehensive colleges and universities in the public sector, many of them former teachers' colleges, are less privatized than the research and doctorate-granting universities. Few have developed strong alumni organizations; they conduct less research and thus are not recipients of large amounts of federal funding; and they are not prime candidates for individual or corporate philanthropy since they are viewed as essentially supported by public monies.

Community colleges reflect their public control and orientation to an even greater extent. Much of their private support is "in-kind," in the form

TABLE 3

More Ultimate Sources of Revenues of and Subsidies to Institutions of Higher Education—Rough Approximations in Percentages

	All Public Institutions	Pure Form of Independent Public Institutions	Private Institutions
Private money[1]	35	36	**64**
Public money treated as private[2]	16	**62**[3]	34
Subtotal	51	98	98
Public money treated as public[4]	**49**	2	2
Total	100	100	100

Note: The bold number indicates the major source of funds, for each category.

1. Sales of services by auxiliary enterprises are counted here as private funds, although not all of them are private in their ultimate sources.
2. In addition to the items in table 2, 20 percent of tuition and fees (estimated as paid from public grants) and 30 percent of gifts and endowments (foregone taxes) are counted here as public money treated as private.
3. Lump-sum state appropriations counted as public money treated as though it were private, in addition to items in table 2.
4. Public appropriations except lump-sum.

of donations of supplies and equipment from local businesses. Alumni support is minimal as graduates tend to identify with their baccalaureate college or university, if any. However, 700 out of 950 community colleges have established "foundations" engaged in securing private funds, with total assets of $200 million, mostly for purposes closely tied to each local community and its needs.

What Consequences Does It Have to Be "Private" or "Public"? The great historic models are Harvard for the private institutions and Michigan for the state-owned. Michigan was actually founded as a private institution in 1817 and became public in 1835. It was given (1850) the following constitutional protection, a protection that was later extended to, among others, the University of California:

> The Board of Regents shall have the general supervision of the university, and the direction and control of all expenditures

Michigan has fought hard politically and in the courts to preserve its autonomy—and very successfully.

The degree of privatization decreases when moving from the level of Michigan to other state-supported research universities, to the state-supported comprehensive colleges and universities, and to the public community colleges, some of which come perilously close to inclusion in the dependent public category, as in California where legislative provisions have taken six hundred pages to detail, including 2,800 separate statutes. Most community colleges, however, and also most public comprehensive colleges and universities, are more like the British polytechnics (which operate under a stronger form of public control than do institutions in the "autonomous" sector of universities) than they are like the Michigan model. A few community colleges and a few state-supported comprehensive colleges and universities have, however, achieved an independent public status.

At the research university level, the differences between institutions that follow the Michigan model and those that follow the Harvard model are as follows:

For faculty members—essentially no differences.

For students—some differences, including more formal admission requirements and much lower tuition in the Michigan type than the Harvard.

For presidents—many differences; including more time spent in the state capitol and less at the clubs of business leaders and at alumni gatherings; more bedevilment by special-interest groups in the body politic; much less influence over the selection of trustees, who tend to have more an attitude of surveillance and less one of support; more subjection of their personal conduct to public scrutiny—including by the press; less intense attention to the recruitment and retention of individual students, who pay less tuition—and also to their parents; less in the way of personal salary and fringe benefits; shorter terms of office on the average; more time spent with the governor of the state and less with the chairman of the board of trustees; less sense of freedom to speak out on public issues; more likelihood of having to deal with unions of faculty members; more attention directed to agriculture and industry and less than their private counterparts to the historic professions of law and medicine and theology; more time spent on relations with coordinating mechanisms and less experience of the feeling of heading up a freestanding institution; and less time spent raising private gifts.

For boards of trustees—several differences; including mostly publicly appointed (or elected) trustees rather than self-selected ones and usually, thus, originally less familiarity with and devotion to the institution; more trustee concentration on the role of supervisors than on the role of supporters of the institution; board operations more subject to the operation of Sunshine (open meeting) laws and policies, including open-session discussion of many internal affairs; and less freedom of boards to try experiments and otherwise control their own affairs.

The differences increase, particularly for presidents, in the categories of comprehensive universities and colleges and of community colleges, and in the same general directions. Among other things, the attention to the welfare of the individual student declines very considerably, and state control over detailed decisions increases very considerably. The differences for presidents between a private liberal arts college and a four-year public college, for example, are much greater than those for presidents between private and state-supported research universities.

Recent developments (since about 1960) affecting the differences between public and private institutions include the rise in the public, but not in the private sector, of coordinating mechanisms in many states with centralized budgetary control, and of massive systems under a single governing board with 100,000 or more enrolled students (there are fifteen such systems).

Overall, presidents and boards notice the differences between private and public institutions far more than do faculty and students.

The current distribution of institutions and enrollments among the above categories is shown in figure 1. For historical perspective, 1940 enrollments are shown in figure 2.

The American System in Historical Perspective. The American system has always been a mixed one, although ownership (whether private or public), control (whether private or public), financing (whether private or public), and the mixtures in between have been very unstable over time.

The original nine colonial institutions, starting with Harvard in 1636, were, with one exception, part private and part public in their initiatives (see table 4).

Private-sector institutions after the colonial period originated mostly in initiatives by religious organizations. These religious organizations were very diverse, from Southern Baptists to Quakers, and the institutions they created were also very diverse and very competitive. This private sector was early protected from public absorption by the Supreme Court in the Dartmouth College Case (1819), which validated the private contract that established Dartmouth.

The first strictly state-initiated universities were Georgia (1785) and North Carolina (1795). They were state-initiated and -owned, but with independent boards of trustees from the very start. The colonial colleges were their models. They followed an early accepted tradition of comparatively limited direct public control, and started the tradition of the independent public institution. This sector has been greatly strengthened in recent times by federal policy in two areas:

The granting of research funds on merit to individual scholars by a series of public "foundations" (World War II)

The granting of aid to higher education via students and not directly to institutions (particularly the "GI" Bill at the end of World War II and the Higher Education Act of 1972).

FIGURE 1

Higher Education in the United States by General Category, 1987

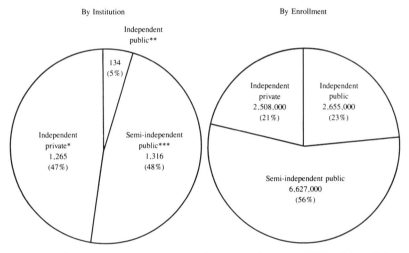

Source: *A Classification of Institutions of Higher Education,* 1987 edition (Princeton, NJ: The Carnegie Foundation for the Advancement of Teaching, 1987). Omitted from this figure are 642 "specialized" and 32 public "liberal arts" institutions that the *Classification* includes.

*Included here are all church-affiliated institutions, some of which are in fact "semi-independent" and a few of which are "dependent" on their churches.
**Included here are research universities and doctorate-granting universities, although some of them, particularly in the latter group, might more appropriately be listed as "semi-independent."
***Included here are comprehensive colleges and universities, and community colleges, although some of them might better be described as "independent" and a few as "dependent."

FIGURE 2

Higher Education in the United States by General Category, 1940

By Enrollment

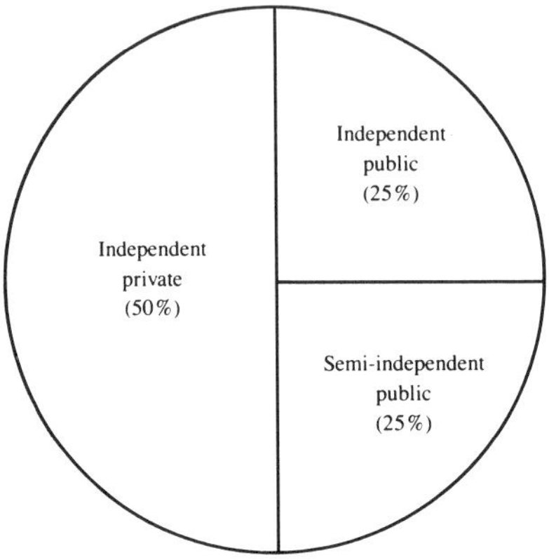

Source: Calculated from *World Almanac 1941;* and *Biennial Survey of Education in the United States,* U.S. Office of Education, *Bulletin,* 1940.

A countervailing tendency at the state level has been the great increase in comparative importance in terms of enrollments, particularly in the 1960s, of the more clearly public sectors (see fig. 2). This came about with the great expansion of state teachers' colleges into comprehensive colleges and universities, and the fast growth of the community college system. These segments are generally under more public control than the publicly supported institutions that originated earlier with a more independent tradition, but, nevertheless, they operate under lay boards usually with substantial independence.

The public comprehensive colleges and universities were mostly originally state teachers' colleges which added many additional programs. Teachers' colleges historically were typically governed by the state board of education that also supervised the schools. The state board of education, with the colleges as with the schools followed a pattern of homogenization of mission (training teachers) and of strict control over expenditures, line-item by line-item. Most public comprehensive colleges and universities have moved substantially away from the state school board model and now have their own boards of trustees, but it has been a slow development and the old patterns of control have left their legacy.

About half of all community colleges were built on the high school model, often actually originating in the high school system, with elected

TABLE 4

The Nine Colonial Colleges

Institution	Year of Opening	Colony	Founding Organizations	Current Status
Harvard College	1638	Massachusetts Bay	Colony; Congregational	Private
College of William and Mary	1694	Virginia	Colony; Anglican	Public
Yale College	1702	Connecticut	Colony; Congregational-Presbyterian	Private
College of New Jersey (Princeton)	1747	New Jersey	Colony; Presbyterian	Private
King's College (Columbia)	1754	New York	Colony; Anglican	Private
The College, Academy, & Charitable School of Philadelphia (University of Pennsylvania)	1755	Pennsylvania	City; Colony; Anglican; Presbyterian; Society of Friends	Private
College in the Colony of Rhode Island (Brown University)	1765	Rhode Island	Colony; Baptist	Private
Queens College (Rutgers, The State University)	1771	New Jersey	Dutch Reformed	Public
Dartmouth College	1769	New Hampshire	Colony; Congregational	Private

Based on Jurgen Herbst, *From Crisis to Crisis: American College Government 1636–1819* (Cambridge, MA: Harvard University Press, 1982), Appendix A.

boards of trustees and a tradition of strict administrative control. The other half were modeled more after the less selective private liberal arts colleges with appointed trustees (mostly local residents) and with less emphasis on control of administrative detail.

These two huge public sectors (comprehensive colleges and universities, and community colleges) have a heavily "public" historical background.

Public control has been additionally enhanced in recent times, affecting particularly the community colleges but also the public comprehensive colleges and universities, as a result of

the large sums of money and of numbers of students involved inviting public attention, the greater public interest in admissions' policies,

the enhanced labor market concerns of productive elements of society, and

the improved capacity of governments to supervise funding and operations.

The mixed system that has resulted—part private, part private-public, part public—has the following overall sources:

The American emphasis on private as well as on public initiatives.

The Protestant Reformation with its concentration on lay control versus state or guild control (guilds of priests or of faculty members). The primary governance model was Calvinist and particularly via Scotland. This has resulted in the existence of strong lay boards and of influential presidents that the public and state authorities can hold accountable.

The strongly supported separation of church and state, with institutions of higher education often originating in the church and inheriting the autonomy of the churches.

The existence of now fifty states with primary authority for education located in the states and not in the federal government.

The constitutional protection of private contracts in the Dartmouth College case.

The rise of the concept of "shared governance" with faculty, beginning particularly with the founding of the American Association of University Professors in 1915.

Tax laws that support private giving (including gifts in kind); and tax exemptions for both public and private colleges and universities.

A long tradition of private contributions to private and even selected public endeavors (particularly higher education). De Tocqueville early noted the tendency of Americans "to sacrifice a portion of their time and property to the welfare of the State." Of the twenty universities with the largest endowments, three are public, although each of them is a system of campuses—Texas, Texas A&M, and California.[4] Of the top twenty campuses in terms of current receipts of private gifts and bequests, six are public—Minnesota, Illinois, California–Los Angeles, Michigan, California-Berkeley, and Ohio State.[5]

Public policy decisions at the federal level (1) to make higher education the primary instrument for basic research, with support through public agencies acting much like private foundations; and (2) to give aid through students and not directly to institutions.

The success of the system that leads to its perpetuation. It works better with substantial independence. Among other things, the sense of independence raises what Harvey Leibenstein[6] has called the "x-efficiency factor"—the morale of the enterprise.

The role of alumni in the more selective institutions (both public and private) in supporting the independence of their colleges and universities, financially and politically.

The American distrust of public agencies and public control.

The restraints accepted by public authorities in the exercise of their inherent powers.[7] Institutions of higher education have no God-given right to independence. In part, society has acceded it to them; and, in part, they have earned it by good conduct.

The heavy role of the student market in influencing the size of institutions and their internal compositions among fields, and in bringing financial support through tuitions and through enrollment-driven state financial formulas. This role is conceded both by the institutions themselves and by state authorities.

Consequences. This mixed system has had some important positive consequences:

Unusual autonomy for many nominally public institutions, particularly the research universities.

Great diversity among institutions; and a consequent ability to reflect the intricate geographic and human mosaic of American society.

Intense competition among institutions that occupy the same general categories.

Flexibility, institution by institution, in undertaking adaptations to new and changing circumstances. Now one and now another type of institution responds to social needs: the research universities after Sputnik in the 1950s, the community colleges with the emphasis on equality of opportunity in the 1960s, the comprehensive colleges and universities with the greater need of the economy for middle-level skills in the 1970s and 1980s.

The existence of private institutions as role models for the public institutions in the areas of academic freedom, institutional autonomy, and the ability to be diverse and to innovate; and for state authorities in judging the appropriateness of levels of financing.

The protection of academic freedom and the extension and endurance of academic tenure as a result of the competition among institutions for the best, or at least better, faculty members. Violations of academic freedom or removal of tenure provisions would be a great competitive handicap.

Significant attention to the welfare of individual students who pay tuition and who become alumni with a tradition of subsequent financial support.

A concern for service to surrounding communities.

Quick adaptation to labor market demands.

The system has some dangers inherent within it:

It is, in some parts, overresponsive to temporary labor market requirements.

Some institutions are unduly influenced by alumni, or by their supporting churches, or by demands from related industries (as once strongly from agricultural interests), or by changing fads in public or student opinion.

The academic core is sometimes not adequately insulated from pressures and becomes eroded.

The University–Industry Axis. The close contacts with industry through direct financial support and through indirect influences within the political processes are consequential:

Drawing activity toward favored areas, as, for example, business administration and engineering, and in earlier times agriculture, and away from the liberal arts; and, more generally, away from what Martin Trow[8] has called the "autonomous functions."

Within research, drawing activity in a more applied direction.

Generally, aiding larger more than smaller establishments.

Creating, overall, a disproportion of support within higher education in favor of (a) technologically oriented research universities and (b) labor-market-responsive four-year colleges and community colleges versus other types of institutions.

Diverting thought, time, and energy from teaching and research to more entrepreneurial activities by some faculty members; thus also creating a two-class professoriate of higher-income entrepreneurial-academics as against less-well-remunerated academic-academics.

Capturing, by individual companies, of first access to new discoveries; and giving special favors to cooperative faculty members in return.

Tempting faculty members to use academic facilities for private gain.

More generally, promoting opportunistic as against academic mentalities in the professoriate; and encouraging the emergence of a netherworld of intellectual activity.

Undertaking efforts to directly influence the "ideology" of academic institutions—only very occasionally successful.

Indirectly increasing the proportion of students and faculty in the more politically "safe" areas of the campus, such as engineering and business administration, and reducing the counterculture areas, such as sociology.

Drawing academic institutions, as the result of one or the other of the above impacts, into public controversies; as, for example, over the greater support to agribusiness than to the family farm.

These impacts, some of them potentially and actually negative, are, on balance, more than offset by these positive advantages:

Adding additional funds to higher education directly from industry and indirectly by support of public funding.

Encouraging substantial contributions by higher education to economic growth generally, and to specific industries and areas.

Aiding greater contact by academics with the realities of the productive activities of society.

Engendering greater public support for higher education as beneficial to economic and social advance, including job creation.

And some of the potentially negative impacts can be mitigated by internal policies of universities and colleges, such as consciously seeking to pursue a reasonable academic balance among fields, requiring faculty members to record their outside endeavors that may result in conflicts of interest, controlling the amount of time faculty members can spend on nonacademic activities and their use of academic facilities for private gain, protecting academic freedom, insisting that research results be made available on an open basis, and insisting on the integrity of academic endeavors.

Dangers that some social critics predicted would result from an industry–university alliance have not come to pass: by Thorstein Veblen that the "Captains of Industry" would dominate the "Captains of Erudition"; by Abraham Flexner that there would be a degradation of academic life in general and specifically of the academic spirit; and by Marxists that the transformational contributions of higher education would be subjugated to the reproductive functions.

There have been individual abuses rather than any general subversion of the academic ethic. MIT and Cal Tech have not sold their souls to the devil. What Faustian bargains are made are more by institutions of lesser stature and particularly by certain segments of and faculty members within them—also of lesser stature.

Industry has never exerted the influence and control over related aspects of academic life that was exerted in past times by the ancient professions of theology, medicine, and law in their respective areas of concern.

The role of industry needs to be put in perspective. It is a source, through grants and contracts and gifts, of less than 3 percent of all income of institutions of higher education; but this 3 percent is quite unevenly distributed, creating potentially significant leverage in some areas in some institutions. Industry support is divided almost equally between private and public institutions.

Conclusion. The American system has been noted, among other national systems, for the creation of the land-grant university and the community college movement as instruments of service to their communities.

It is, perhaps, even more unique and even more of a potential model in its demonstration of how a significant independent public segment, and an even larger semi-independent public segment, can be created and sustained. The U.K., in the Golden Age of the University Grants Committee, is the other historical model.

The overall shift of emphasis, over time since the founding of Harvard in 1636, has been from private to independent public to semi-independent public approaches in terms of enrollments. There are currently no clear shifts for the future that can be predicted with any certainty. It can be said, however, given the history of American higher education, that potentially high public policy priorities in prospect are (1) to preserve in strength the private sector,[9] and (2) to preserve and increase the private aspects of the public sectors. These private aspects include independent boards of lay trustees and influential presidencies, shared governance by faculty, access to private funds, and public funds distributed lump-sum or via students or faculty members.[10] Concerns over these two priorities, it may safely be said, will continue far into the future.

In the meantime, wherever the goal is "greater institutional differentiation and diversification in a market-led and multi-funded setting" with a correspondingly "greater institutional autonomy and flexibility" (Baker 1989), as now advanced in the U.K., the American mixture demonstrates the importance of forms of control as well as of ownership, and of means of distribution of funds as well as of sources of funding.

Notes

* First prepared for a conference chaired by James A. Perkins, of the International Council for Educational Development, at Wingspread Conference Center, Racine, Wisconsin, June 18, 1987. Reprinted from *Higher Education*, 19, no. 1, (January 1990). Reprinted by permission of Kluwer Academic Publishers.

1. R. L. Geiger, *Privatization of Higher Education: International Trends & Issues* (Princeton, NJ: International Council for Educational Development, 1988), conference report, International Council for Educational Development, Racine, Wisconsin, June 15–18, 1987; and Research Institute for Higher Education, *Public and Private Sectors in Asian Higher Education Systems* (Hiroshima: Research Institute for Higher Education, Hiroshima University, 1987).

2. K. Baker, "Higher Education: The Next 25 Years," *Speeches in Education* (London: Department of Education and Science, 1989), speech given at a conference at Lancaster University on January 5, 1989.

3. A. A. Berle and G. C. Means, *The Modern Corporation and Private Property* (New York: Macmillan, 1932).

4. *Chronicle of Higher Education* 34, no. 38 (1 June 1988): A35.

5. Brakeley, John Price Jones, Inc., *Higher Education and American Philanthropy, A Report for 1985–86* (Stamford, CT: Brakeley, John Price Jones, 1987).

6. Harvey Leibenstein, *Inflation, Income Distribution, and X-Efficiency Theory* (London: Croom Helm, 1980).

7. For a discussion of the importance of restraint and of the sources and the means of the policy of restraint, see Martin Trow, "Defining the Issues in University–Government Relations: An International Perspective," *Studies in Higher Education* 8, no. 2 (1987): 115–28.

8. Martin Trow, "Reflections on the Transition from Mass to Universal Higher Education," *Daedalus* 99, no. 1 (1970): 1–42.

9. For a discussion of the problems of maintaining a strong private sector, see Education Commission of the States, *The Preservation of Excellence in American Higher Education, Report of the Task Force on State Policy and Independent Higher Education* (Denver: Education Commission of the States, 1990).

10. For a discussion of the problems of maintaining strong presidencies and strong lay boards, see National Commission on Strengthening Presidential Leadership (Clark Kerr, chair), *Presidents Make a Difference: Strengthening Leadership in Colleges and Universities* (Washington, DC: Association of Governing Boards of Universities & Colleges, 1984); C. Kerr and M. L. Gade, *The Many Lives of Academic Presidents: Time, Place & Character* (Washington, DC: Association of Governing Boards of Universities & Colleges, 1986); and C. Kerr and M. L. Gade, *The Guardians: Boards of Trustees of American Colleges and Universities* (Washington, DC: Association of Governing Boards of Universities & Colleges, 1989).

Functions—

The Pluralistic University in the Pluralistic Society*

The occasion for this essay was the Great Ideas Today *series of the* Encyclopaedia Brittanica, *which in 1969 concentrated on* The University Today. *Robert M. Hutchins, the great sponsor of the* Encyclopaedia, *later in life chaired the Center for the Study of Democratic Institutions, to which he invited me as a regular participant. I was a member of his committee of consultants throughout the period of his leadership, and I admired him greatly as a personality. At a Center meeting, he once said that my ideas on pluralism placed me down in the Agora doing the "bumps and grinds" while he preferred to live up on the top of the Acropolis thinking philosophical thoughts. His thoughts, he believed, were a continuation of the great dialogue that began in Greece at the time of Socrates, Plato, and Aristotle. Hutchins's vision, from my point of view, is fine, but there is more to education than that alone.*

The battle over functions has been and will continue to be fought at many times and in many places. The monists glory in their rectitude and their rhetoric; and the pluralists struggle in the mud of reality.

The functions of the university have always been more or less complex and never as simple as some have supposed. The historical tendency has been for university functions to become more complex, and to leave simplicity ever farther behind. Yet there are still those who cry for the simple life, the homogeneous institution.

The university, through its expanding functions, is also ever more central to the life of society; more involved in more of the affairs of more individuals and institutions. Yet there are still those who say the university should stand outside society, or should stand within but serve only one social force—and that social force the one they favor.

The functions of the university have often been controversial and not fully accepted by everyone. Currently the controversy is more intense than in earlier periods. Yet there are those who think that controversy should be foreign to the university.

Complexity, centrality to society, and controversy mark the American university of today. Is this inevitable? Is it to some extent undesirable? And, to the extent it is deemed undesirable, what should be done?

The American university is now one hundred years of age. The first true university was Johns Hopkins in 1876; Harvard transformed itself from a college into a university during the immediately subsequent period. There were other new beginnings, such as at Chicago and Stanford, and many additional transformations by the time of World War I.

Two points should be made clear in advance of discussing the problems of the American university today.

One point is that the problems of the university assume different but related forms in Rome, Berlin, Paris, London, Tokyo, Calcutta, Madrid, Warsaw, Prague, Moscow, Peking, Buenos Aires; they are found wherever great universities with their concentrations of intellectuals come into contact with the surrounding industrial society, and, of almost equal importance, with their own myriad selves.

The other point is that this is not the first time in history that the functions of the university have been under intense discussion. In England, for example, there were violent discussions when Henry VIII separated Oxford and Cambridge from the Church, when Cromwell separated them from the Crown, when Parliament in the middle of the last century separated them from the Anglican aristocracy; in Germany, at the time of the Thirty Years' War, with the battle over the Reformation that also tore the universities apart, and again when Humboldt started the University of Berlin at the beginning of the nineteenth century; in France, when Napoleon took moribund institutions and sought to turn them into servants of the new state; in the United States, when the newly created modern university began taking over from the classical college a century ago, and later when Lowell and then Hutchins attempted a counterrevolution.

The university in the toils of intense controversy is not limited to this one place—the United States—and this one time—the second half of the twentieth century. The university in many places and at many times has been torn by internal and external conflict; the ivory tower of fond but forgetful memory has often been a bloody battlefield. And the university has always survived, though often changed. It, and the church, are the two most persistent institutions society has known. This has been true in the past. It is true now. It will be true in the future.

Returning to a Golden Age

There are those who would like the university to return to a Golden Age of purity and harmony. They see in the past their hopes for the future.

But which golden age? At least three golden ages now seem attractive to one or another of those concerned with a better vision for higher education. Each of these golden ages is quite distinctive; each is essentially incompatible with the others; each has its merits.

1. The "Golden Age of Research" hearkens back to the Johns Hopkins of 1876, and the Humboldt of Berlin in 1809. The emphasis is upon pure research, upon the autonomous scholar, upon "isolation and freedom" and the "pure idea of learning," to quote Humboldt.[1] "It is a further characteristic of higher institutions of learning that they treat all knowledge as a not yet wholly solved problem and are therefore never done with investigation and research." Discovery of truth is the great challenge, the highest aspiration of the academic.

Abraham Flexner,[2] in particular, but many before and since, lamented the fall from grace that came with desertion of the single-minded pursuit of the Holy Grail of Truth. The path down from Humboldt's "summit" led to applied research, to service (the "service station"), to the new professions like business administration, to football stadia, to correspondence courses. This was the "false path" that was followed by all American universities, even Harvard and John Hopkins. Rockefeller University alone would have been seen as staying at the "summit."

Many in the modern university support this emphasis on pure research, on truth, on new knowledge. They and their precursors have made enormous contributions to knowledge and, through knowledge, to society, and, in the course of doing so, to the growth and prestige of the university. We know more about physiology, and the health of the people has been improved; about agriculture, and there is more food and fiber; about sources of energy, and there are more material goods; and much else. The pursuit of truth has carried society and the university a very long way forward.

But this golden age had its seamy side. It led to the dominance of the full professor in the German university and of the science "star" in the American. It led to ultraspecializaton in the curriculum and rigidity in course sequences, as against the broader point of view sought by many students. It led to heavy dependence on the state as the source of research funds in the older Germany and the newer United States alike. It led to a single-minded pursuit of truth in narrow field after narrow field with little or no concern for the broader consequences of the application of piecemeal truth. It led to heavy emphasis on the areas of science where new discoveries could most easily be made, to the neglect of other areas, especially the humanities.

Nor was the purity of the approach easy to defend. How pure is "pure" research? The tendency was always for some scholars to move down the seamless web from the very pure to the wholly applied, with no clear place to draw the line and call a halt. Moreover, it turned out that contact with actual problems to be solved enhanced even the purest of research. World War II was an enormous stimulus to pure research in science, just as the Great Depression was to pure theory in economics. Also, knowledge and service tend to merge. The people with knowledge often have a passion to make it available, and those who can use it want access to it. The transition from knowledge to service, from the laboratory to the ''service station,'' drew inspiration from both the producers and consumers of the new knowledge. The path to this version of sin was downhill all the way; the fall from the ''summit'' was both inevitable and irreversible. Yet individual summits of pure research have dominant positions in all the great universities.

2. The ''Golden Age of the Classics'' is a vision that looks back to Cardinal Newman's[3] ''idea of a university,'' to John Stuart Mill's[4] ''accumulated treasure of the thoughts of mankind,'' to Thomas Aquinas, to the Lyceum of Aristotle and the Academy of Plato. The best historical model would perhaps be Oxford as seen by Newman a little over a century ago, before it was changed by Parliament and the scientists. The search was for wisdom as found in the classics, in the ''Great Books''; and as refined and applied through dialogue and ''free speculation.'' The ''intellectual'' and the ''moral'' were intertwined, as Mill noted in his *Inaugural Address* at St. Andrews in 1867; ''knowledge'' and ''conscience'' supported each other. The university should make students ''more effective combatants in the great fight which never ceases to rage between Good and Evil.'' The emphasis was not on the new truth but the old wisdom, on the ''liberal knowledge'' that Newman thought prepared a man ''to fill any post with credit, and to master any subject with facility.'' The university was for the generalist, not the scientific specialist; it was ''a place of teaching universal knowledge''; it was a beautiful ivory tower.

Hutchins and Barzun have led the current laments of those who regret the fading of this great ideal; and Hutchins sought with great courage and some modest effect to resurrect it at Chicago. To Hutchins[5] the university has become a ''nationalized industry'' as a result of the ''rise of the nation-state and the beginning of the Industrial Revolution.'' Hutchins saw as evil influences both the ''service'' that Flexner hated, and the ''research'' that Flexner loved, for research leads to specialization and a degradation of the teaching function. The purpose of a university is to have people ''think together so that everybody may think better than he would alone,'' and not to have each go off in his own direction in pursuit of new knowledge or added skills. ''Many large American universities appear to be devoted to three unrelated activities: vocational certification, child care, and scientific research.'' This is a long way from the ''ancient ideal'' of the ''autonomous intellectual community'' where ''unity and clarity of purpose are fundamental.''

To Barzun,[6] "the fabric of the former single-minded, easily defined American university" has been torn apart. Where Hutchins looks all the way back to Aristotle in Athens, Barzun looks back only to Nicholas Murray Butler's rule at Columbia; for the decay Barzun sees has taken place since Butler's retirement at the end of World War II. The university has become "bankrupt in mind and purse" now that it is no longer a "sheltered spot for study only," now that it has entered "the marketplace." The Manhattan Project, the GI Bill of Rights, the legacy of faculty participation in the New Deal and of academic advice to a world power are markers on the road to ruin; and the university has come to cater to "proletarian culture"—even Chicago and Columbia. Only St. John's College, Annapolis, which draws much of its inspiration from Hutchins, remains true to the classics. Barzun is critical of "service," such for example, as helping to meet the needs of urban life. Yet all institutions have rendered service to some segment of society. The service that Barzun favors is service best fitted to the interests of an aristocracy and of the "liberal professions" that draw their members from an aristocracy and cater to it.

This ideal of a perpetual discourse about general ideas today holds the allegiance of many students and a few teachers. It gets resurrected on a grand scale, not as a continuing pursuit but as an *ad hoc* inspiration, when great issues such as civil rights and the war in Vietnam rend the nation. And the university does remain as one of the few places in modern society where fundamental discussions of basic issues can and do take place. In a world of specialists, the university is one of the last hunting grounds for the generalist; and society can be as much aided by better general views as by better specialized research.

Oxford and Cambridge before 1850 and Yale College in 1828 (at the time of the famous faculty report defending the classical curriculum) did not appear so golden to their own contemporaries, except to the guilds that ran them. The classical approach looked more to the past than to the present or the future, and thus had a conservative cast. As a result, the campus seemed isolated from the contemporary reality. General discussions lacked the sharpness that comes from attention to actual and specific cases, and often became ideological and sectarian in their nature—it was no accident that many of the teachers were trained in theology. The whole approach either led to or was at least compatible with an *in loco parentis* approach to the students, an insistent concern with a rigid curriculum and the development of "character." Moreover, the approach had greater appeal to the children of an hereditary aristocracy and of a comfortable upper-middle class than to those of workers and farmers; it made a greater contribution to the would-be gentlemen than to the ex-artisans. It was sometimes hostile to science—one of the great and growing streams of human thought. And the contest of Good against Evil came to be fought at least as much by the middle class and the working class, without benefit of a classical education, as by the members of the aristocracy, who were supposed to be the "more effective combatants" by virtue of their education.

The Classical College did not and indeed could not survive as *the* model of the university, nor could it be restored. The spread of democracy meant that opportunity had to be made available to new elements of the population to whom a classical education did not prove so attractive. Industrialization demanded new skills beyond those of a merchant class or a colonial service or the historic professions; it demanded engineers and architects and administrative specialists. No longer could the professions of real value be limited to those that had served the upper classes: the doctors, the lawyers, and the ministers. New professions arose and the university came to train for them also. The welfare state brought new demands for teachers, public administrators, and public health personnel. And science could not be ignored. The new culture might be called "proletarian." It was also more democractic, more technological, more oriented toward the general welfare, more scientific. And any university that limited itself to the classics for the aristocracy would have condemned itself to oblivion in the new age—but none chose to do so.

Yet elements of the old Classical College grace any system of higher education, and merit preservation as well as encouragement. In fact, the new leisure class of affluent students is bringing a resurrection, a renewed attention, to "knowledge" and to "conscience."

3. The "Golden Age of the Scholarly Community" looks back to the Middle Ages when small bands of scholars met in face-to-face discussions in a legendary "community of scholars"—with more emphasis on "community" and less on "scholars." One modern version is that of Paul Goodman,[7] who favors educational communities of a couple of hundred students (150 is suggested as ideal) meeting in free discussion with a few senior persons drawn from practical pursuits in the surrounding society. The historical model cannot be that of the early Bologna, for the students ruled the rebellious professors there; nor of the early Paris, which was under the domination of the church. It may be the early Oxford and Cambridge, before they became highly organized and subject to traditions; or perhaps the religious discussion groups around the monks that congregated at Glendalough in Ireland. In any event, the model, past or proposed, assumes small communities of scholars voluntarily formed, in which everyone participates as equals, but with some having more experience than others. One such community, although rather large in size from this ideal point of view, is the new student-run Rochdale College on the edge of the University of Toronto; another, the early Kresge College of the University of California at Santa Cruz.

The tutorial and the seminar and the "bull session" may be taken as modern counterparts of the ancient communities of scholars; and each has made and does make a substantial contribution to personal and intellectual development.

The "scholarly community" would seem to fit best those aspects of education which benefit from the oral tradition, the personal example, and the experimental doing of things, like an apprenticeship. It relies less on books and not at all on laboratories—the library is at the center of the Classical College, and the laboratory of the Research University; the small discussion group takes their places in the Scholarly Community. Tests and degrees and formal curricula are not an inherent part of it; in fact, they are rather anathema to it. This approach is better at effecting sensitivity and understanding than at imparting high skills and deep knowledge, or discovering new and complicated relationships.

In a world that also calls for high skills and deep knowledge and new discoveries, the "community of scholars" can at best be an aspect of or an appendage to higher education. It could be the totality of higher learning only when knowledge was more limited and consisted more of beliefs and observations than of intricate theory and complicated facts—only when the world was a simpler place.

And yet this personalized kind of education about the general nature of the world and the individual's place within it holds great and valid attraction for many students in the fragmented and mechanized world of today.

The "golden age" of the Community of Scholars goes back to the days before the printing press, when the oral tradition was supreme; that of the Classical College to an era before the laboratory, when the classical texts were the greatest source of knowledge; and that of the Research University, to an epoch before egalitarianism and the welfare state became such central features of society and when science was viewed as the great and even the only key to progress. Each "golden age" relates to its own layer of history; each has its great contributions; each has left an important legacy within the higher education of today. Yet no one of these models was as "golden" when it existed as hindsight makes it appear; and none could serve as the sole model for the university of modern times. The earliest of these golden ages fitted the religious orders of a more religious era; the next, the aristocracy of a less democratic society; and the last, the scientific elite in a period of rapid industrialization. Why were these earlier models abandoned, and why can they not be recreated readily? Basically the reason is that each one, in turn, became increasingly incompatible with the changed conditions of its society.

Flying the Flag of Dissent

Others view the functions of the university from the perspective not of past models but rather of future possibilities. They emphasize the function of evaluation, criticism, dissent as a central purpose of the university. This function of dissent was a possible activity of each of the "golden age" universities, but it was not a main function. Social change might be a consequence of scientific research; it might be accepted and accommodated effectively by leaders trained in the classical tradition; it might flow from the little communities of scholars. But social change was not the avowed *raison d'être* of any of them as they actually existed.

Those who see dissent as a central function of the university may be divided into three general groups, with many variations and refinements within each grouping.

1. First, there are those who emphasize the "dissenting professor" and his or her protection—the professor who individually and of his or her own free will decides to criticize some aspect of society or society in its totality. The rules governing academic freedom and tenure grow out of the concept of the "dissenting professor." Some believe that the professor, out of his or her knowledge, has an obligation to provide a free and independent criticism of the surrounding society in his area of specialty. Others view the professor as having a more generalized obligation, as an educated man or woman and a free agent, to comment upon the affairs of society outside as well as inside his or her specialty. They argue that few other persons are so well stationed and so well equipped to perform this essential service to society. Many of the policies of the American Association of University Professors are aimed at guarantees of his right to dissent. The *Lehrfreiheit* of the German universities was to protect this function. Acceptance of this role, as *a* role of the professor, is almost universal among the best of the American universities.

2. A more recent development is the call for the "dissenting academy," to use the phrase of Roszak.[8] Here the responsibility of providing dissent is collective, rather than individual: the "central business of the academy is the public examination of man's life with respect to its moral quality"; universities should "cease functioning as the handmaidens of whatever political, military, paramilitary, or economic elite happens to be financing their operations." Galbraith[9] sees this responsibility (or possibility) as extending beyond the universities to the wider circle of the "educational and scientific estate," which, with its increasing numbers and new positions of power, can become a major force for social change. "The responsibility of intellectuals," says Chomsky,[10] is "the creation and analysis of ideology," not just the creation of experts to run society.

The supporters of the "dissenting academy" see the academy, as a collectivity, helping to change society. They seek to have faculties and professional associations as a whole, such as the sociologists, take positions on public issues. Some even seek to have "the University" as a corporate body take positions on the great issues of the day, for "a university that will not speak for man . . . has ceased to be a human enterprise."[11] They do not support violence in these efforts of the academy, on the grounds that violence has no moral validity in an intellectual community and, in any event, is ineffective against the armed power of the state. The reliance is on persuasion and also, perhaps, on passive disobedience. To perform this dissenting function effectively, the academy requires corporate autonomy and freedom from external obligations for its individual members. The campus becomes, in the words of Tussman,[12] "the most crucial of battlefields" where "the essential vitality of society is tested."

3. Beyond the "dissenting academy" lies what may be called the concept of the "partisan camp," the university which serves as a base for guerrilla activity against the surrounding society. This was the successful strategy of Mao in China and of Castro in Cuba, and the unsuccessful effort in 1968 of the student rebels in France and of some faculty members and students of Berkeley in the late 1960s to "reconstitute" the university into a mechanism intent on reconstituting society. The universities were also one base for violent activity as Hitler conquered Germany. It is argued that the trustees and administrators of the traditional university must be viewed as "occupying powers" and that "terror reigns,"[13] and that the occupying powers should be thrown out and the terror ended. A university, to become "partisan," must have autonomy from control by the police, and internal authority must rest largely in the hands of the students.

Individual dissent is now well accepted within the modern university; the basic battles have been won. It is protected by the rules of the campus and the efforts of the administration. Its costs in public support are generally accepted. It is part of the reality of the pluralistic university as it now exists.

The "dissenting academy" is not accepted. The proponents seek rules or informal actions that discourage or prohibit service and research involving actual or implied commitments to the established order (particularly the "military-industrial complex"), that reward individuals for their contributions to dissenting activities or punish them for "improper" service to the established order, and also, perhaps, that favor the appointment to the faculty of persons with a record of dissent or potentialities for dissent. They may also seek actions by the collective faculty or the collective profession or both attacking policies of the estabished order, and appropriate policy statements from the university as a corporate body. For these tasks it is essential to have faculty control of university governance, or at least substantial influence over it, perhaps with student allies. Efforts at such results lead to great internal strains within a faculty, or, if successful, to the development of a faculty or segments of a faculty with a single point of view; to major battles over governing authority with trustees and public bodies; and to public distrust of an institution that is inclined to constant and unified dissent rather than to more or less balanced comments. Some German universities during the Reformation were captured by the Protestants, and others remained under the Catholics, as German society divided. The "dissenting academy" was a divided academy; and this may be the natural tendency at all times and in all places.

The "partisan camp" either helps destroy society or is destroyed by society.

These three dissenting views reflect the essential natures of the liberal, the radical, and the revolutionary university. Dissent for the first is an important product; for the second, the main product; and for the last, the sole product.

Dissent, in any of these three forms, has never (with a few temporary exceptions) been the sole or even the central function of actual universities; it has never been the basic organizing principle in the long run. Yet dissent is one function of an academic institution, and a particularly important one if handled effectively, especially now that so many other sources of independent comment, such as the church, the trade union, the independent newspaper editor, have become muted. Even the "partisan university" may have its occasional and temporary place in acting against a clearly oppressive regime (as Harvard and Columbia did before and during the American Revolution, and as Charles University in Prague did in a restrained fashion in the face of the Russian invasion in 1968). The appropriateness of the nature of dissent is related to time and to place.

Criticisms of the modern university made from the side of dissent sound like many of those from the several versions of the "golden age." Proponents of each view quote one another in condemnation of the actual university. None, for example, like the "service station" aspect of the modern university; all speak for "free speculation"; and all prefer a simplification of present functions. They vary greatly among themselves, however, in what they would put in place of the university today—the Research University with its laboratories, the traditional College with its classics, the small community of participating scholars and practitioners, the academy dissenting as a collectivity, or the partisan camp. The critics seem united against the modern university, but they stand divided as architects of the new institution that is to take its place. They are comrades in arms as they attack the status quo, but enemies when it comes to putting something new in place.

Serving the Special Interests

Criticism comes also from sources other than from the philosophical positions we have been discussing. It flows from a sense that the university is not providing adequate service for some point of view or some group.

These special interests either accept the modern university in general but criticize it specifically, or they are unconcerned with the totality and concentrate only on their own claim for service. The philosophical positions set forth above are more eternal and global in their approach; these special interest positions, more current and particular.

The special interest criticisms spring from many groups:

From the conservatives, including many parents, who feel that the university is not properly socializing the students in the manners and beliefs of the surrounding community, that the campus is not politically quiet and culturally orthodox, that the campus neglects its duties *in loco parentis.*

From the organized alumni, often conservatives and often parents, who believe that the old campus traditions are not being maintained.

From the employers of the graduates, the consumers of the research, the users of the services, who complain that the work of the university is not practical enough, not useful enough, that industry or agriculture or the trade unions or the elementary and secondary schools or the government are not getting the immediately effective services they want; from all those who say that the graduates should have better vocational skills, research more geared to their immediate needs, services more responsive to their requests.

From students in general, who say that teaching is neglected, that the curriculum is too rigid and too irrelevant, that the routine "grind" goes on endlessly, that even their own parents can no longer perform the *parentis* role; from black students, in particular, who say the academic life of the white culture is repugnant to them and must be changed.

From neglected areas of the campus such as the humanities, the lesser professions, and the creative arts, which claim more of a place in the sun.

From historically neglected areas in society, such as religious institutions and the newer professions (like real estate), or newly neglected areas, such as the American Legion with its interest in ROTC, which claim their share of attention.

The first four groups want "better" service; the latter two, more service or even some service.

These views about functions demonstrate the variety of expectations that have come to converge on the modern university: that it conserve the past; that it give useful service to the currently powerful forces in society; that it not neglect any group that feels a claim upon its attention. These concerns indicate the myraid groups that feel related to the university, and the extent to which the university is many different things to many different people. A full view of the university requires an appreciation of the claims of these special interests on its functions, an understanding of how potentially useful it has become to how many people.

The Intricate Web of Functions

It is customary to say that the university has three functions: teaching, research, and service. Actually, as the above discussion has indicated, the pattern of functions is more complicated, and any effort to understand the problem must include a comprehension of the complexities. Neither the actual criticisms of functions nor the possible solutions can be evaluated with the simplified threefold system of categorization.

Higher education may be said to perform a series of services related to production, to consumption, and to citizenship.

1. The functions related to production are all those that potentially add to the output of goods and services in society:

The talent hunt.—The selection, guidance, rating, and placement of students for productive occupations. Higher education acts as a great sorting machine. It rejects as well as selects and grades.

The training in vocational, technical, preprofessional, and professional skills.—This is carried on at three levels: terminal vocational work often included in the junior college program leading to a certificate or an Associate in Arts degree, introductory technical training leading to the Bachelor's and Master's degree, and advanced professional training leading to the Doctor's degree. Related to this is postgraduate retraining.

Research.

Service.—Through formal and informal advice and consultation.

All of these functions are best carried out by specialists and through highly organized programs that proceed in sequence, step by step. They draw support from industry, government, the professions, and the academic world itself. The test of performance is technical competence. The line of authority is from the expert to the novice.

2. The consumption functions are those that relate to current consumption of goods and services by the students or by others in the campus community, or to "durable" consumption through changed tastes, sensitivities, skills, and opportunities that lead to a fuller life for the individual:

General education.—This gives students a better understanding of their cultural heritages and perhaps of other cultures as well, and assists them to understand more deeply themselves and their relationships with others. The classics, with their emphasis on personal character, were once the single chosen instrument for general education. Now there are several approaches available. General education for cultural and recreational purposes is increasingly demanded and is available also at the older adult level.

Provision of community life on campus.—Once this life was highly moral and religious; later it came to be predominantly collegiate—athletics, journalistic activities, fraternities, sororities, and so forth. Currently the emphasis is more on external political activity, on service projects to aid others, on experimental cultures of dress and conduct, on artistic affairs; and increasingly there is the tendency to consider people other than strictly defined members of the campus as part of the "community"—the walls fall down. In the early American colleges, community life was determined by the college itself. Beginning with the movement for student control of extra-curricular activities a century ago, the nature of the community life has been more responsive to the changing interests of the students, to the wishes of the peer group.

Custodial.—Students, somehow, must be housed and fed, given medical care and personal counseling, and preferably kept out of trouble during the period between the time they leave the homes of their parents and start their own families.

Holding operation.—Many students, particularly at the lower division, but also at the M.A. level, are uncertain about what they want to do—get a job, get married, get more education, choose a new field of emphasis. The college provides a place for them to be and an excuse for being while they survey their opportunities and make up their minds. The high dropout rate at these levels can also be viewed as a high "drop-in" rate to other activities. The college, by providing a holding pattern for many students, extends their practical range of choices and the time to make these choices, and thus may improve the quality of the choices.

These several functions are best assisted by persons oriented not so much toward subject matter as toward students as individual human beings and through programs that are flexible and diversified in response to the changing and varied interests of the students. These functions consider the student—not industry, government, the professions, or the academic world—as their main source of orientation. The test of performance is less in technical competence and more in student acceptance. The line of authority is more from the consumer (the student) and less from the teacher and the administrator. Influence over the student relies more on guidance than on control of a technical program. This is the realm for the generalist, not the specialist.

3. The citizenship functions of higher education are those that relate to the performance of students, alumni, and faculty members in relation to their civic responsibilities:

Socialization.—This involves giving the student a basic understanding of the nature of and the rules governing political, economic, and community life. Some would add: indoctrination.

Evaluation.—This calls for critical analysis of the purposes and conduct of established society, and for opportunities to voice objections and make proposals. Some would add: direct social action.

Remedial.—Students drawn from many types of homes, many different communities, many diverse school systems come to the campus with quite different qualities of preparation. Once there, the concept of equality of opportunity requires that provision be made so that deficiencies can be made up and subsequent competition put on a more equal footing.

Returning for a moment to our earlier discussion, the Research University approach ties in most closely to the talent hunt, high-level training, and research; the Classical College, to general education; the Community of Scholars, to community life; and the several approaches to dissent, to the function of evaluation.

Higher education over the past few years has seen an enormous shift in the concern attached to these several functions. During and after World War II, with the emphasis upon military and material strength, and going back a century to the rapid industrialization of the United States, the emphasis was upon the functions tied to production. Prolonged prosperity and personal affluence are shifting the emphasis toward the functions tied to consumption, and internal and external political controversies of great intensity, toward functions tied to citizenship. Jobs are more taken for granted, and public policy is less accepted. Higher education is now caught in the turmoil of these historical shifts. The shift is from domination by production considerations toward consumer sovereignty and citizenship participation. Russia, by contrast, still conducts higher education under the domination of production considerations and "socialization" of its own sort. In England, the trends are more mixed, partly because the functions related to production were never so heavily emphasized. Other shifts are taking place around the globe in the comparative emphasis upon one function or another. As the emphasis from function to function shifts, the institution is, of course, changed—also the roles and the lives of individuals within it, and they are not passive about these shifts.

The Functioning of the Functions

Toynbee has noted that "there seems to be a worldwide consensus that the traditional system of higher education does not meet, any longer, the educational needs of a more and more rapidly changing society."[14] I should now like to examine how the present functions of higher education relate to a changing society, how adequately they are being performed when viewed one at a time, and how they may best be related to each other in different types of institutions.

1. Higher education is a part of society, not apart from it. It is a partially autonomous subsystem of society. It draws on the material resources of society, and may add to them in the long run as much as or more than it draws out. It reflects the political arrangements of the surrounding society and seldom has much more freedom than is generally provided other institutions and their members, and it almost never has much less freedom. It draws on the accumulated cultural resources of its society and, beyond that, of the world, but it can never be far in front of the cultural resources of the world. Thus higher education benefits from rich material resources, a favorable political climate, and cultural growth, and, generally, the more it adds to each, the more in turn it will benefit from each.

Society is changing, and the functions of higher education are changing. The university, like all other human institutions, has always survived by changing, and change always starts from where you are.

The changes now needed in the functions of American higher education related to production, reflecting changes in society, would seem to be these:

A search for talent from more elements of society, particularly from low-income groups and disadvantaged minorities

The extension of training into advanced adult levels and newly arising professions and occupations

The development of research into the general consequences of specific research, now that research is increasingly viewed as a potential enemy of humanity rather than only as a constant friend

Service to urban life such as the land-grant university has previously provided to rural life

In the functions related to consumption, the changes encouraged by changes in society include these:

A great new emphasis on general education, perhaps reoriented around social problems and field service, reflecting the interests of the new generation of affluent students facing a life of greater opportunity beyond work and thus more like the aristocratic clientele of the older Classical College, a new general education that may also include place for more such subjects as the creative arts and religious philosophy

Much greater stress on the intensity and diversity of community life, reflecting the new vitality and sense of freedom of students, the attraction to them of the view that life is drama, their craving for a variety of personal experiences, their emphasis on peer-group culture

The rejection of custodial functions by the campus, reflecting the greater maturity of students and the more permissive environments from which they have come—the campus can no longer be a "company town"

More realization of the importance of the holding-pattern function of some campuses, as access to higher education becomes more nearly universal and is made available to many who may not be fully committed to it

The first of these directions of change in the functions related to consumption will please Hutchins; the second, Goodman; the third, nearly all students; the fourth, the half of the students who do not go straight through.

The major changes in the functions related to citizenship may well be these:

A tendency to count more on the high school for the socialization function

An inevitable increase, at least temporarily, in remedial work

A new attention to the function of evaluation, both because society is undergoing such great change and because elements on campus are taking such great interest in the direction of these changes

2. Higher education has fulfilled its individual functions with varying degrees of success.

Generally, the production functions have been well performed. Skilled personnel has been supplied at a high level of skill for an expanding economy, and research has moved well in advance of technology to assist ever higher levels of productivity. However, there are inadequacies aside from lack of full adaptation to the changing nature of the external society as noted already. The talent hunt, according to the best available evidence, has often eliminated some of the most creative, experimentally minded students. Secret research is anathema to the open nature of a campus in that it places students and professors in untenable categories of the "cleared" and the "not cleared"; yet it has been accepted on many campuses.

The consumption functions have been poorly performed. The undergraduate curriculum for the student wanting a liberal education, rather than a vocational preparation, is often a disaster area. It has come under the dictatorship of the graduate program, as Riesman[15] has noted, with its emphasis upon specialization and its downgrading of undergraduate instruction. It serves the research interests of the faculty more than the educational concerns of the students. The guild has been dominant over the interests of the consumers. William Rainey Harper, when founding the University of Chicago, was one of the few who realized how the graduate emphasis of the university might overwhelm the undergraduate concerns of the college, and how they might be incompatible. The development of attractive and inspiring communities for undergraduates has been sadly neglected, with little realization of what a major aspect of their lives is determined by the quality of the communities in which they live. Too little attention has been paid to the possibilities of placing auxiliary enterprises, like residence halls and cafeteria, in the hands of private entrepreneurs or student cooperatives so that consumer tastes and preferences can be reflected more readily than through institutional policies and rules. Additionally, the holding function calls for an affirmative attitude toward the experimental dropout, and not one of condemnation and retribution.

The citizenship functions are always more delicate in a society in turmoil than in a society more content with itself. Generally the function of socialization has been handled with balanced description and comment, not with the rigid indoctrination of communist nations. The remedial function has been neglected; it has too often been assumed that all students enter on an equal footing; and too little has been done in working with high schools to improve their performances. The function of evaluation, as noted earlier, is subject to great internal and external debate. To be effective it must be carried out with a reasonable sense of balance so that no important point of view dominates unfairly or is excluded—this approach is in keeping with the morality of academic life that all voices should be heard, and with the need to preserve the credibility of the academic community before the surrounding society; with an emphasis on constructive proposals rather than destructive criticisms alone, for the sake of drawing society toward better solutions; and with reliance on persuasion, since resort to violence is antithetical to devotion to reason and can readily lead to reactions that endanger the essential freedoms of the academic community and even of society.

In a volatile political climate tending toward polarization, the academic community should be one of the strongholds of reflection and reason and the arts of persuasion. Generally this has been the approach of the "liberal university" now under such aggressive attack from the more extreme supporters of the "dissenting academy" and all of the supporters of the "partisan camp." The academic community needs to give the most careful consideration to the performance of its evaluative function so that it abides by its own highest principles and helps to meet the needs of the society for better solutions to urgent problems.

Overall, the individual functions more poorly performed are general education and the creation of exciting communities; and the function most in need of clarification is the function of evaluation.

3. Higher education must live with itself as well as with society. Not all functions are equally well performed when combined with others, since some are inherently contradictory. Not all institutions of higher education need be alike; some can specialize in one set of functions and others in another. How best may the several functions be combined?

The two-year community college and the four-year urban college can best serve in the areas of technical training (including related adult education); performance of the holding function (including providing options for advancing into general education and preprofessional work); and remedial work.

The liberal arts college, either as an independent institution, or as a largely independent entity with its own budget and its own curriculum but attached as a "cluster college" to a university, can best perform the functions of general education and the provision of an effective community life, and can help provide general evaluation of society. To perform these functions well, these colleges should glory in their diversity and their flexibility. The university best supplies advanced technical and professional training (along with the specialized technical school, the state college, and the independent professional school—each in its area of competence and at the appropriate level), research, and service; and its particular contribution to evaluation is in the more technical and specialized areas. General education is less well performed in the monolithic university because of its inherent nature; it is carried on better in a different environment from that of the university, where it has been a notable failure.

It might be said that the community colleges and the urban colleges best serve certain of the citizenship functions; the liberal arts colleges, certain of the consumer functions; and the universities, certain of the production functions. Since the production functions are now particularly well performed, it is the other functions that require the intensified attention that over the past century has been paid to the production functions almost alone.

Each campus must live with itself. Perkins[16] has suggested the goal of "internal coherence": Each activity on the campus should "strengthen the others." The more modest goal suggested above is that the activities be able to coexist effectively with each other, each drawing strength from, and hopefully also adding strength to, the common campus environment; and, thus, that essentially incompatible functions be eliminated—ones that are weakened by others or weaken others. Beyond the compatibility of functions lie the questions of whether they are worthwhile in and of themselves, whether they are suitable to the campus or are more suitably performed elsewhere, and whether they are of a level of quality that matches the general quality that matches the general quality of the overall endeavor. The campus does not have a residual function that requires it to fulfill all the otherwise unmet needs of society. It must pick and choose. Internal consistency is one important principle of choice.

It deserves a passing note that functions affect other aspects of the university. One is scale. The liberal arts college performs best when small, when it is a community; the junior college when it is moderate in size, when locally oriented; and the university when it is large enough to warrant adequate library and other research facilities, when nationally and internationally oriented. Another aspect is governance. The liberal arts college needs to be particularly responsive to its students, the junior college to its community, and the university to its faculty. A third aspect is financing. The production and citizenship functions have more of a claim on public funds, and the consumption functions on private money.

In summary, five competing views about the proper nature of higher education in the United States now confront the reality of the existing system: the Research University serving the specialized pursuit of knowledge, the Classical College serving the generalist, the Community of Scholars serving the changing and diverse interests of students, the Dissenting Academy serving the reform of society, and the Partisan Camp serving revolutionary change in society. The reality is a pluralistic system in a pluralistic society serving many functions including constant evaluation of society. The single-purpose campus is as unlikely as the single-purpose wife or husband; the nature of both is to serve more than one function. Nor can there easily be a single model for the multipurpose campus, since some functions combine better than others and there are a number of functions in totality to be performed by higher education.

It is relatively easy to attack the current reality from the perspective of a Golden Past that is no longer totally relevant or from that of a Utopian Future that may never be totally realized. It is more difficult to assist higher education as it actually exists, to change as society changes, to improve its individual functions, to preserve its own integrity. This is the greater challenge.

Notes

* From *The Great Ideas Today 1969* (Chicago: Encyclopaedia Brittanica, 1969), 6–29. Reprinted by permission of the publisher.

1. Wilhelm von Humboldt, *Humanist Without Portfolio: An Anthology of the Writings of Wilhelm von Humboldt*, trans. and intro. by Marianne Cowan (Detroit: Wayne State University Press, 1963).

2. Abraham Flexner, *Universities: American, English, German* (New York: Oxford University Press, 1930).

3. John Henry Cardinal Newman, *The Idea of a University Defined and Illustrated* (London, 1873). Originally *Discourses on the Scope and Nature of University Education, Addressed to the Catholics of Dublin* (Dublin, 1852).

4. John Stuart Mill, "Inaugural Address," delivered to St. Andrews University, February 1, 1867, *Dissertations and Discussions: Political, Philosophical, and Historical,* vol. 4 (Boston, 1867).

5. Robert M. Hutchins, *The Learning Society* (New York: Frederick A. Praeger, Inc., 1968; originally "Education: The Learning Society," in *Britannica Perspectives*, ed. Harry S. Ashmore [Chicago: Encyclopaedia Britannica, Inc., 1968], vol. 2).

6. Jacques M. Barzun, *The American University: How It Runs, Where It Is Going* (New York: Harper & Row, 1968).

7. Paul Goodman, *The Community of Scholars* (New York: Random House, 1962).

8. Theodore Roszak, ed., *The Dissenting Academy* (New York: Random House, 1968).

9. John Kenneth Galbraith, *The New Industrial State* (Boston: Houghton Mifflin, 1967).

10. Noam Chomsky, "The Responsibility of Intellectuals," in Roszak, *The Dissenting Academy.*

11. Richard Lichtman, "The University: Mask for Privilege?" *The Center Magazine,* January 1968.

12. Joseph Tussman, "The Collegiate Rite of Passage," *Experiment and Innovation*, July 1968.

13. John R. Seeley, "The Fateful Trumpet, II" (unpublished manuscript, April 1966).

14. Arnold J. Toynbee, "Higher Education in a Time of Accelerating Change," Academy for Educational Development, paper no. 3, 1968.

15. Christopher Jencks and David Riesman, *The Academic Revolution* (New York: Doubleday, 1968).

16. James A. Perkins, *The University in Transition* (Princeton, NJ: Princeton University Press, 1966).

CHAPTER 5

Vignette—
Remembering Flexner*

Abraham Flexner was a great critic and reformer of American higher education. As a critic, he hated what he saw. I was asked to write an introduction to a new issuance of a famous book of his. But I mostly liked what I saw. Flexner wanted the pure research university and only the pure research university. I wanted that but more than that alone.

For more than a half-century, Abraham Flexner devoted his prodigious talents and energies to the cause of education in America. As participant and contributor, as chronicler and critic, and as innovator, he helped shape the course of American education—and particularly medical education—during a great period of modernization and growth. He was a student at the influential German universities during the early 1900s, and a frequent visitor and perceptive observer of Oxford and Cambridge and the other great European centers of learning throughout his active life. In 1928 he was invited to give the Rhodes Lectures at Oxford. Those lectures—a distillation of his observations, criticisms, and ideals of "the modern university"—formed the basis for this volume, which, since its publication in 1930, has become a classic in the literature of higher education.

Flexner's first encounter with American higher education was singularly propitious, and its influence was to last a lifetime. Through the financial sacrifice of an older brother, Flexner, then seventeen, was sent to Johns Hopkins University in 1884. The university was less than ten years old, but, under the dynamic presidency of Daniel Colt Gilman, it was well launched on the course of advanced study, research, and high academic standards that earned its position as the first fully modern university in America. An aura of intellectual excellence, excitement, and challenge pervaded the institution. "My attitude toward the university, toward President Gilman, toward the members of the faculty . . . was one of reverence," Flexner later wrote. And, again, "Those who know something of my work long after Gilman's day . . . will recognize Gilman's influence in all I have done or tried to do."[1]

Flexner had just enough funds to spend two years at Johns Hopkins. With the characteristic energy and determination that marked his whole career, he made do. Electing the rigorous classics course, he taught himself sufficient Greek in six weeks to catch up with the regular classics students. He was excused from physics classes after passing an oral examination, and from English composition after he showed faculty members the communications which he had already had printed in *The Nation*. For the rest, he simply doubled up on classes. When the first year-end examinations came, he found that several test times conflicted. He took his problem to Gilman, and the astonished president, after investigation, authorized rescheduling of the conflicting examinations. In the two years at his disposal, Flexner earned his degree.

Returning to Louisville and a teaching position in the local high school, he immediately put to the test his commitment to academic excellence. He was nineteen, and teaching Greek to many of his fellow students of three years earlier. At the end of the first year, he failed an entire class of eleven students. This unprecedented action became a local *cause célèbre,* reached the newspapers, and culminated in a school board hearing at which Flexner was sustained.

But Flexner was anxious to have a freer hand with curriculum and class organization. At the age of twenty-three he left the high school to form his own school, preparing boys for entry into Eastern universities. Nine years after "Mr. Flexner's School" opened its doors, Flexner received a letter from President Eliot of Harvard, whom he had never met. Eliot stated that boys from Flexner's school were entering Harvard younger and graduating more quickly than students from any other school. "What are you doing?" he asked. Flexner outlined his approach and, at Eliot's suggestion, wrote an article about it for *The Educational Record,* the first of his many writings in the educational field. He closed the school in 1905 to do graduate study at Harvard and in Germany, but his interest in secondary school matters continued. When, subsequently, both he and President Eliot were members of the Rockefeller-endowed General Education Board, Eliot revived the topic of "Mr. Flexner's School" and the Board asked Flexner to write about the school and his ideas in the secondary field. The resulting pamphlet, "A Modern School," published in 1916, led to the endowment of the experimental Lincoln School of Columbia Teachers' College, which pioneered in secondary education for three decades.

After a year at Harvard, Flexner spent two years in Europe, studying in the great German universities whose programs of advanced study and research had guided Gilman in the design of Johns Hopkins. From the perspective of his foreign studies Flexner wrote his first book, *The American College: A Criticism*. The book created little public stir, but led to his being asked by The Carnegie Foundation for the Advancement of Teaching to undertake a study of medical education in America. When Flexner pointed out that he had never set foot in a medical school before, foundation officials replied that what they wanted was not a practitioner but an observant educator.

They got precisely that. In the next eighteen months Flexner set foot in every one of the 155 medical schools then existing in the United States and Canada. He found medical education in a sorry state, with rare exceptions such as Johns Hopkins Medical School. Students were often admitted with less than two years of high school education. Laboratories were nonexistent or pitifully underequipped. Hospitals were not generally under the control of the medical schools, and there was almost complete separation of the scientific and the clinical instruction. Flexner minced no words when he wrote *Medical Education in the United States and Canada* in 1910. His scathing report aroused broad concern and inspired a revolution in the teaching of medicine in America. He recommended that 120 of the then existing medical schools be closed as inadequate, and he identified them by name. As a matter of fact, nearly all of them did disappear, in substantial part because of his report. It had the cutting edge of a surgical knife.

From 1913 to 1928 Flexner worked for the General Education Board, which had been established by Rockefeller in 1902 as the first strictly educational foundation to operate on a nationwide basis in the United States. As a member of the Board and its secretary, Flexner was at first involved in projects for assisting Negro educational institutions and for helping Southern states to develop statewide systems of secondary education. But his interest returned repeatedly to medical education, and he was instrumental in encouraging Rockefeller to provide a total of fifty million dollars for the modernization of American medical schools, and in helping to allocate the huge sum. Flexner was particularly instrumental in the establishment or renovation of the medical schools at Washington University in St. Louis, Rochester, Cornell, Vanderbilt, and Iowa—schools that remain among the greatest to this day. He could write with truth that "the revolution this accomplished brought American medicine from the bottom of the pile to the very top."[2]

In 1928 Flexner retired from the General Education Board, only to plunge into his preparation for the Rhodes Lectures and the writing of the present volume. As an immediate consequence of its publication, he was approached by two people who wished his advice about the educational use to which "a considerable sum of money" might be put. The sum was, in fact, five million dollars; the donors, a prominent New Jersey merchant, Louis Bamberger, and his sister, Mrs. Felix Fuld. The use proposed by Flexner was the establishment in the United States of a center for advanced scholarship and science resembling the Rockefeller Institute in the field of medicine; and, undoubtedly also, All Souls College where he had stayed during his Rhodes Lectures, and the Kaiser Wilhelm Gesellschaft (now the Max Planck Institute), which he so greatly admired. The donors accepted

Flexner's proposal on the condition that he should head the new center, and thus was created the Institute for Advanced Study at Princeton. At the age of 64, Flexner entered yet another career in education, this time as director of the Institute, a post he held until his retirement in 1939. Under his directorship the Institute took form and assembled distinguished scholars, including Albert Einstein, from throughout the world, some of them refugees from the once-great German institutions Flexner had so profoundly admired. The Institute continues today to play a distinguished part in the intellectual life of the United States.

Nearly all of Flexner's contributions to education—whether writings, proposals, negotiations, or administrative actions—were addressed to immediate problems, and they had an immediate impact. He thought of himself not as a philosopher but as "something of a practical idealist" with "enthusiasm for the feasible."[3] Of all his contributions, this present volume has had the least direct impact on the course of American education. Yet it seems destined to stand as a milestone in the philosophical discussions of the university and its place in society. Why?

The American historian Daniel J. Boorstin has pointed out that certain writings may acquire an "afterlife" which makes them significant far beyond the times in which they were created, and sometimes for far different reasons than the author envisioned.[4] Thus it was with Flexner's *Universities*. Flexner thought he was describing the ideal modern university—an institution whose outlines he had glimpsed at Johns Hopkins and Berlin and whose realization throughout America, England, and Germany awaited only certain reforms which he enumerated. Instead, as the passage of history has revealed, he was writing a valedictory to a university form which was already passing—already evolving to a new stage. In so doing, he preserved for us, in perhaps its purest and most completely reasoned form, the "idea of a modern university" at a crucial stage of its development, just as Cardinal Newman, seventy-five years before, had so eloquently preserved the "idea of a University" at an earlier, equally important, and equally passing stage. By the time Flexner wrote in 1930, Johns Hopkins, he sadly noted, had become a "local institution" due to "dilution" by too many students and "adulteration" by the addition of too many low level functions,[5] and the German universities were on the brink of their greatest catastrophe.

The expression of such ideal types, however, is immensely valuable both to the understanding and the evaluation of our contemporary institutions. They contain the roots of the past, "the soil out of which we grow," to use Flexner's own words, "accumulated treasures of truth and beauty, and knowledge, experience, social, political, and other, which only a wastrel would ignore."[6] They stand as a yardstick against which to measure the accomplishments of the present. They provide reference points for trends from past to present, and so help us to speculate about the future course of our institutions. Thus the student of present-day universities may read Newman and Flexner with greater benefit than he will receive from most of the more contemporary analyses.

The university of Cardinal Newman focused upon one essential function—the conservation of knowledge and ideas and their transmission to an elite body of largely undergraduate students. Newman believed that research should be performed outside the university. "If its object were scientific and philosophical discovery," he wrote, "I do not see why a University should have any students."[7]

The "modern university" of Flexner, taken from the German model, united for the first time the functions of advanced teaching and research—particularly research in science. The university became, as Flexner pointed out, "an institution consciously devoted to the pursuit of knowledge, the solution of problems, the critical appreciation of achievement and the training of men at a really high level."[8] Thus the university broadened its mission—but there were strict limits. Flexner rejected—or urged rejecting—much undergraduate teaching which he thought was really on the secondary level and ought to be done elsewhere. He believed that most professional training, except for the traditional university training in medicine and law, ought also to be done elsewhere. Similarly with most adult education, consulting, "business" research, and a host of other activities that we now regard as the service function of today's university.

Flexner did not disapprove of these activities *per se*. He simply thought they had no place in a university, as Newman before him had thought research had no place in a university. Flexner's fear was that these activities would dilute the university's commitments to advanced teaching and research. He warned: "A university . . . may thus readily find itself complicating its task and dissipating energy and funds by doing a host of inconsequential things."[9]

Time has proved Flexner's fear largely groundless. The service function and undergraduate instruction have been interwoven with the advanced teaching and research functions in many of America's great institutions of learning. The university is performing a far broader mission in today's society, and certainly few would argue that graduate teaching and research have been thereby weakened or endangered. Rather, graduate teaching and research have weakened undergraduate instruction, and have become dominant over service activities; they are not the subservient elements.

Flexner saw the university as "an organism, characterized by highness and definiteness of aim, unity of spirit and purpose."[10] Had the university retained an organic structure, its efforts might well have been diluted and dissipated by the addition of numerous professional schools, the multiplication of undergraduate students, the performance of a broad array of service activities. But the contemporary university is not an integrated organism. It is a pluralistic organization with many component parts, each of them capable of "highness and definiteness of aim, unity of spirit and purpose," each of them (in the best of all university worlds) possessing the energy and the funds to accomplish its specific task.

Today's university, then, is not Flexner's. But it owes a debt to that earlier university, and retains its finest elements: the high regard for academic excellence, the firm alliance of advanced teaching and research, the partnership of graduate student and professor, the commitment to intellectual discovery. For his eloquent espousal of that university model, scholars everywhere are in Abraham Flexner's debt. His strictures against an overemphasis on intercollegiate athletics (paying the coach more than the president), against "absurd topics for the Ph.D.," against the "shameless humbuggery" in some curricula,[11] against "wild, uncontrolled, uncritical expansion"[12] echo down the decades in the hallways and faculty clubs and committee rooms of academe.

Flexner's strictures echo down the decades, but Flexner, in the essential viewpoint he expressed in *Universities,* was wrong.

1. "Neither Columbia, nor Harvard, nor Johns Hopkins, nor Chicago, nor Wisconsin is really a university, for none of these possesses unity of purpose or homogeneity of constitution."[13] Without either unity or homogeneity, the greatest of American universities, including several on this list, have taken their places among the outstanding universities of the world—surpassed by none, equaled by few.

2. "Fifty years ago, the degree of Ph.D. had a meaning in the United States; today it has practically no significance. The same is true of research."[14] Yet, only 5 percent of the Nobel Prizes were held by Americans before World War I; and 40 percent after World War II.

3. "The American professoriate is a proletariat."[15] Today it is quite obviously part of the affluent society, and not the least part.

4. Many American universities, "more especially in the South and West—though the East is not free—are hotbeds of reaction in politics, industry and religion, ambitious in pretension, meager in performance, doubtful contributors, when they are not actual obstacles, to the culture of the nation."[16] Hotbeds they indeed may be today, but not of reaction; and the cultural awakening in America finds much of its impetus on the campus.

The really Golden Age was not behind the American university in 1930, but ahead. And the path was not one laid by Flexner. The Harvard Graduate School of Business, "pretentious and dangerous,"[17] did not become the "Boston School of Business," separated from Harvard as suggested by Flexner. Teachers' College at Columbia did not disappear from the face of the earth. Nor did the College at Columbia or at Chicago. The "most incomprehensible"[18] Institute of Human Relations at Yale survived. There was no "ruthless abolition of trivial courses, trivial chairs, trivial publications, and ridiculous research."[19] "The make-believe professions" and "majors, minors, units, credits"[20] were not driven out of the temple. The universities that "thoughtlessly and excessively catered to fleeting, transient and immediate demands"[21] kept on doing so, and prospered— even in advanced teaching and research. Universities became, even more, "administrative aggregations"[22] instead of "organisms"; and they also be- came more productive in scholarship. There came to be more institutes, not less. The universities did all the wrong things—undergraduate instruction, professional schools (other than law and medicine), service activities, voca- tional courses, extension work. They did all the wrong things—and they entered their most Golden Age.

Flexner thought *Universities* had laid out the one correct road to Mecca: "It made a great stir among academic folk and in the newspapers, for once more I had told the truth."[23] "How much effect the Rhodes Lec- tures have had, I have no way of knowing, but time will work in their favor."[24] But the road to Mecca went the other way; and time worked in a contrary fashion. Why?

1. Flexner was too enamored with the Hopkins of 1884 to 1886. He saw too little in the Harvard of 1930, which was really leading the way.

2. Flexner was too respectful of the German university. In 1930 he could write that "the political upheavals which occur in American universities are beyond imagining in Germany"; the "most serious" problem was "lack of money."[25] In 1930, German universities were class institutions in a class society; centers of reaction in a nation well on its way into facism. They were dominated by the few full professors and excessively dependent on the will of public officials. There was less of merit in the German university of 1930 and more in the University of London than Flexner thought.

3. Flexner saw too much in criticism as a driving force. It had worked with the medical schools, which in 1910 were too often schools for butchers. It worked less well in 1930 for the universities as a whole, which were both much better and moving more favorably than the medical schools of 1910. Shock treatment was less justified and less effective.

4. Flexner did not realize how many functions can be combined within a single university—even apparently inconsistent functions. Particularly, he did not see how service functions might draw support and money to a university, so that it could perform better also in

advanced teaching and research. American universities did not "break beneath the incongruous load placed upon them."[26] He saw too much in unity and cohesion, and too little in pluralism and diversity.

5. Flexner drew a clearer line of distinction between law and medicine, with their "intellectual and altruisitic purposes" and their "code of honour,"[27] on the one hand, and the "make-believe professions" of business and religion and library science, on the other, than the facts would warrant. Law and medicine were more distinguished by traditional acceptance than by the special virtues that Flexner thought they alone upheld.

6. Flexner did not understand that quality and quantity could be combined. Hopkins did not lose out because it came to have too many students. Berkeley came to be rated both as the highest-quality graduate center in the United States (by the American Council on Education in 1966) and also as the most productive undergraduate source of doctoral degrees (by the National Academy of Sciences in 1967).

7. Flexner saw too much in Gilman, and too little in all the forces that drive an institution ahead. The university president can be a key figure, particularly in a new institution, a fast-growing institution, a period of fundamental change in higher education; but there may be other key figures too—among trustees and faculty members and government leaders. In particular, Flexner underrated "faculty government" as "confusion worse confounded."[28] And yet he greatly admired Oxford and Cambridge which gloried in the most faculty-oriented government of all. He also saw the German universities which "were more highly developed, more nearly autonomous, far more highly respected and exerted a wider influence"[29] than any other—and they had no presidents; instead they had Ministries of Education. And he worked with Eastman and Brookings—the successful business men—in bringing modern medical schools to Rochester and Washington University. There were few Gilmans in American universities, but there were other constructive forces at work.

8. Flexner saw too little in America, too little in overall social forces. America was moving forward to world leadership, and so were its universities. Germany was facing upheaval, and so were its universities. England was coming to share leadership with others, and so were its universities. The university system cannot be separated from the performance of the society that supports it; it is not a thing apart. The German and English universities of today look more to American universities than the other way around.

9. Flexner correctly saw the university as "an expression of the age,"[30] but he did not understand the age in America—the populist drive for more education as against the elitist traditions of the older

aristocracy, the desire of a technological society for knowledge made more available through service, the rise of new professions to stand alongside the old.

Thus Flexner saw too much in decaying institutions and too little in the new buds of growth, too much abroad and too little at home, too much in criticism and too little in the existing reality, too much in research and too little in service, too much in purity and too little in the creative tensions of divergent forces, too much in the old professions and too little in the new, too much in small size and too little in the possibilities inherent in growth, too much in presidential leadership and too little in the other animating forces, too much within the institution and too little in the environment that sustains it, too much in the forces of the past and too little in the urgings of the present. The "truth" he sought too often lay on the other side of the argument.

Flexner was also right. He was right in developing a clear-cut model of the university against which other models and reality could both be tested. He was right in being among the first to recognize the importance of the university in society and to study it carefully. He was right in wishing to reform the university, in trying to make it better, for then as now it can be made better. He was right, in particular, in his desire to eliminate the "rubbish." He was right in fighting for a better university, as he had so effectively fought for better medical education. He was right in fighting for it on the actual battle line: "Utopia, in so far as humanly possible, can be realized only by 'trench warfare'."[31]

Notes

* Originally appeared as the introduction to *Universities: American, English, German*, by Abraham Flexner. Copyright 1930 by Oxford University Press, Inc.; renewed 1958 by Abraham Flexner. Introduction copyright 1968 by Clark Kerr. Reprinted by permission of the publisher.

1. Abraham Flexner, *I Remember* (New York: Simon and Schuster, 1940), 52, 59.

2. Flexner, *I Remember*, 308.

3. Flexner, *I Remember*, 399.

4. Daniel J. Boorstin, ed., *An American Primer* (Chicago and London: The University of Chicago Press, 1966), xvii.

5. Flexner, *Universities* (1930 edition), 191.

6. Flexner, *Universities* (1930 edition), 4.

7. John Henry Cardinal Newman, *The Idea of a University* (New York: Longmans Green, 1947), xxvii.

8. Flexner, *Universities* (1930 edition), 42.

9. Flexner, *Universities* (1930 edition), 25.

10. Flexner, *Universities* (1930 edition), 178–79.

11. Flexner, *I Remember*, 355.

12. Flexner, *Universities* (1930 edition), 222.

13. Flexner, *Universities* (1930 edition), 179.

14. Flexner, *Universities* (1930 edition), 124.

15. Flexner, *Universities* (1930 edition), 179.

16. Flexner, *Universities* (1930 edition), 45.

17. Flexner, *Universities* (1930 edition), 162.

18. Flexner, *Universities* (1930 edition), 112.

19. Flexner, *Universities* (1930 edition), 204.

20. Flexner, *Universities* (1930 edition), 215.

21. Flexner, *Universities* (1930 edition), 44

22. Flexner, *Universities* (1930 edition), 178.

23. Flexner, *I Remember*, 355.

24. Flexner, *I Remember*, 356.

25. Flexner, *Universities* (1930 edition), 348, 360.

26. Flexner, *Universities* (1930 edition), 222.

27. Flexner, *Universities* (1930 edition), 30.

28. Flexner, *I Remember*, 335.

29. Flexner, *Universities* (1930 edition), 345.

30. Flexner, *Universities* (1930 edition), 3.

31. Flexner, *I Remember*, p. 399.

CHAPTER 6

Vignette—
Disagreeing with Hutchins*

This was my reply to the most publicized criticism of the Carnegie series. The great critic was Donald McDonald, editor of the Center Magazine *at Robert M. Hutchins' Center for the Study of Democratic Institutions, who wrote of the "Six Million Dollar Misunderstanding." (He took his title from that of a novel,* The Great Misunderstanding, *on how a grandmother gave her college-student grandson one hundred dollars for books and he spent it on a weekend of illicit pleasure instead!) The six million dollars was what the series of over one hundred studies and reports cost. The "misunderstanding" that he saw was that we did not endorse the study of Great Books as the one and only solution to all the problems in higher education.*

Donald McDonald undertook a review of certain limited aspects of the work of the Carnegie Commission on Higher Education. He concentrated on curricular content, particularly general education, and on teaching. He ignored, however, many other aspects of the endeavors of the Commission. We were concerned, in particular, with the historic transition of higher education from mass attendance to universal access, with its many attendant problems such as those of structure, financing, equality of treatment. We started to study eight issues—the functions of higher education, the structure of higher education, the governance of higher education, innovation and change, the demand for higher education, the expenditures for higher education, available resources, and effective use of resources—and then added others along the way. This was *our understanding* of the most pressing current issues confronting higher education in the United States and these issues involve elements amenable to early action.

I note Mr. McDonald's selective approach only because anyone seeking a rounded view of the Commission will wish to consult its publications more generally than does Mr. McDonald or read a more comprehensive review such as that by Eric Ashby ("The Great Reappraisal" in *Universities Facing the Future*, Jossey-Bass, 1972, W. Roy Niblett and R. Freeman Butts, editors). Ashby states that the publications of the Commission constitute "the most thorough analysis of a nation's higher education which has ever been made" and "the most massive and courageous effort to plan the future for American youth that any group of men have ever attempted." This evaluation by Ashby is rather contrary to the impression that Mr. McDonald leaves in seeking to set Lord Ashby versus the rest of the Commission. However, because the article spent so little time on the bulk of the Commission's work and concerned itself with only one important issue, I will restrict my comments to that issue of curriculum content.

I agree with most of what Mr. McDonald sets forth in his review, since most of it consists of quotations from the publications of the Commission! I also agree that he writes as a proponent of what he calls the "classical liberal education viewpoint." This viewpoint is a respectable one, and I hope it is never lost as *a* viewpoint. I personally believe that there is much to be said for this approach to higher education, as *one* among several. But the proponents of what he has called the "classical" model of higher education have become what has been called the "Great Stuck Whistle"! They keep advancing the classical approach as the one and only model, which it has not been for a very long time and is unlikely ever to be again. The classical model largely neglects the sciences, the social sciences, the professions, which are also important ways of knowing. Nor is it a model which was all that effective in its own day. It was largely rejected after over two centuries of criticism by many students and increasing numbers of faculty members, and by many outside the academic halls, including the Royal Commissions that reviewed it in Great Britain. Indeed, as historical criticism shows us, the classical model was never as golden, when it reigned supreme, as it now appears to those who glance back at it so longingly from such a distance.

The Carnegie Commission has favored more diversity than this one approach allows, more options for students and faculty members to choose among diverse approaches, more competition among ways of knowing. And it is the Commission, not any one person, which, after intense discussion, established the policies for each report.

The Commission *was* deeply concerned with general education, which is the central concern of Mr. McDonald, and it was critical of performance in this area of higher education in particular—calling it a "disaster area" is at least an implied form of criticism even in an age when the language of criticism has become so exaggerated and even though Mr. McDonald thinks we were much too soft on criticism. We also make a suggestion for a remedy which some institutions, including Stanford, have found helpful, a suggestion which we consider to be a most hopeful one. It involves the development of a series of options for broad learning experiences as set forth in our report, *Reform on Campus.*

The Commission was also deeply concerned in the same report with the quality of teaching and has made many suggestions for its improvement.

The Commission did recognize, however, that the issues of curricular content and teaching methods are most complex, have been discussed by many people for centuries, and are not subject to simple and easy solutions. The "relationship between teaching and learning on the one hand and human growth in understanding and wisdom on the other" has been under discussion for at least 2,500 years, without any definitive conclusions. We did not consider, consequently, that we could add as a group as much in these areas as in certain others in the time available to us. Dubin and Taveggia in the *Teaching-Learning Paradox* (University of Oregon, 1968), for example, summarize the results of many studies and conclude that the total wisdom gained from them is "in a word—nothing." We are not so pessimistic, but we are realistic in acknowledging the complexities—there are many ways of teaching many things to many people and no one model, including the classical, is appropriate to all subjects and all students.

The Commission sought to advance higher education on several fronts, not to try to direct it down one long-neglected and overgrown lane, as Mr. McDonald would have had us do. The full truth, we believe, is still subject to further discovery. The Commission, as Mr. McDonald rightly notes, was more pluralistic, less absolutist, in its approach. We were generally more favorable to the Golden Mean of Aristotle than to more monistic approaches; to the cause of checks and balances than to the dogmatisim of the "true believer."

Mr. McDonald has, however, raised the flag high once again for the classical model with its Great Books. I hope he keeps on doing so. There should be Saint John's-type colleges and there should be Centers like that on Eucalyptus Hill in Santa Barbara. I have been a longtime supporter of the Center for the Study of Democratic Institutions from the very early days when it was less well-established and much more controversial than it has now become. But I think higher education would lose if Saint John's were the only type of college; and the intellectual life of America would be poorer if the Center on the hill were the only model for intellectual discourse. Long live the classical model—as *one* model among many.

Notes

* Originally titled, "Follow-Up/The Carnegie Report," *The Center Magazine* (Center for the Study of Democratic Institutions), vol. 6, no. 6, November/December 1973, 46–47. (Response to Donald McDonald, "A Six Million Dollar Misunderstanding," *The Center Magazine,* vol. 6, no. 5, September/October 1973, 32–52.) Reprinted by permission.

CHAPTER 7

Performance—

Goals for and Effectiveness of Systems of Higher Education*

This was another paper for the International Council for Educational Development chaired by James A. Perkins. It looked at the American system, on a comparative basis, in terms of what it tried to do and how well it did it. I was skeptical, however, about all formal goals and of most statistics on performance, as I still am.

I. Goals: Varied and Changing

It is deeply embarrassing to ask a woman about her age; a man about his wealth; a teenager about his or her pimples; an old person about his or her sex life; and a university about its goals.

Systems of higher education vary enormously in their attention to explicit goals. Yet there is a certain method to this apparent madness. Statements of goals are means, and, as means, they are of more use in some situations than in others.

We shall be dealing here with goals for systems as wholes or for major parts of a system. These goals are sometimes officially stated and sometimes only unofficially recognized. We note that there are other goals than just those for systems—for example, those of individual participants within the system, or those of external persons relating to the system, or those of particular institutions within the system—and that all of these various goals may be more or less consistent or inconsistent with or even contradictory to the more official or semiofficial goals for the system itself.

Which Systems Have Goals?

It appears from a review of the reports of the twelve ICED studies[1] and, from other literature, that countries are more likely to have an official or semiofficial set of goals for higher education when

the country has a planned economy, and higher education is part of the plan (Poland);

the country operates on the basis of a consensus (a "rolling consensus") among its political parties and its principal economic partners (Sweden);

the country is newly developing its system of higher education and wants a plan for its development (Iran); or

the country is undertaking a major reorientation of its higher education system (Japan in 1947; the U.K. at the time of the Robbins report in 1963; France in 1968).

There are less likely to be statements of goals when the country operates in a pluralistic fashion, and particularly when the system of higher education is well established and not undergoing any planned overall change. Federal systems of government (Australia, Canada, Germany, U.S.) are the least likely to have a set of national goals; so also, systems with a substantial private sector (Japan, U.S.). Likewise, loosely organized societies (Mexico, Thailand), regardless of any other characteristic, are less likely to have specified and continuing national goals than more highly organized ones.

Goals May Be a Necessity. A statement of goals can serve affirmative purposes to guide the development of a planned economy, draw together a consensus for action in a society with great self-discipline, set priorities for the development of a new system, and indicate general aims for a higher education system which is being pointed in new directions. In each of these situations, a statement of goals can be useful, but difficult to develop.

When Stated Goals Are Not Necessary, They Can Be a Menace. The effort to set forth goals can be highly divisive, as different individuals and groups seek to advance their points of view and to gain an advantage. The effort can also be unproductive, either because it results in listing meaningless generalities, or, if specific enough, tends to confirm and entrench the status quo. Moreover, there is a better way to reaffirm goals and to change them—and that is through the budget process or by specific, item-by-item policy actions. The budget process allows for almost infinitely small increments or decrements of support, thus avoiding all-or-none confrontations: money is not a principle and so it can be compromised without anyone losing face by abandoning principle; and commitments are short term, not forever. This is the standard incrementalist approach of a slowly but constantly changing pluralistic society, in contrast to the more comprehensive approach of a more centralized or rapidly changing society.

There is also a matter of taste, and taste is not so easily subjected to debate or analysis. Those who are more idealistically, ideologically, moralistically, or intellectually oriented seem to prefer having goals out in front to be set and followed. Those who are more practically, pragmatically, realistically, or affectively oriented seem to prefer goals that are more implicit than stated, more flexible than rigid, more multiple than singular. There is a great difference between those who start from a clear central principle and then move to its application in reality—"mind over matter"—and those who start with action and only dimly infer from their actions what their principles really are. Some are adept at both ways, as is sometimes said of the French—good principles *and* flexible practical actions, which may or may not relate to each other, but each of the two approaches, on different occasions, can be skillfully utilized. The communist countries of today and the Catholic and Protestant worlds of the past fall more in the first category as to taste; the Anglo-American tradition falls more in the second.

Goals are also a matter of tactics. Conservatives are likely to insist upon goals to support the status quo, radicals in order to attack the status quo, reformers in order to change the status quo (as in the Canadian province of Alberta). Moderates and liberals and those generally in positions of active political leadership are more likely to be wary at least of specific goals as causing unnecessary controversy and reducing freedom of action. The former (conservatives, radicals, reformers) are likely to look upon goals as a way of mobilizing and directing efforts; the latter (moderates, liberals, administrators) as a source of divisiveness and rigidity. Those closer to the two ends of the political spectrum, or out of power, are more likely to think in terms of goals than those closer to the middle or in power.

Thus, whether as a result of historical factors, intellectual taste, or choice of tactics, countries and elements within them are quite divided in the extent to which they set forth explicitly and comprehensively their goals for higher education. For example, Poland, with its planned economy, has an official policy for higher education. Sweden first began developing a set of goals for higher education in the 1950s; these were made more explicit in the "U68" policy statement as the country sought a consensus for change. Nigeria developed a new plan for the development of higher education including a set of goals, particularly through the Ashby report of 1960.

Napoleon had as the goal of his reforms the training of civil and military leaders; Humboldt advocated the advancement of "learning" as the great goal for the reform of the German university system. Cornell, the first great land-grant university in the United States, had as its goal the creation of a place "where any person can find instruction in any subject"—each of these goals pointed to new directions.

Canada, with a decentralized federal system, has never had an official statement of the goals for higher education. The United Kingdom, with its pragmatic approach to governance, never had a list of goals, even a semi-official one, until the Robbins report. The United States and Japan, with large private sectors, have never had a statement of goals for these sectors.

Newman and Hutchins and Mao have been more interested in setting forth eternal goals for higher education than Ashby or Conant or Churchill.

What Goals do Systems Have?

We now turn to the goals of systems, whether explicit or implicit—which, in the latter case, involves assigning goals to systems when they have never acknowledged them.[2] We begin with three observations. First, most, perhaps all, systems experience an accretion of goals over time. The initial goal for most systems was to prepare students for the professions: at Bologna—lawyers, accountants, managers for commercial firms; at Paris, Oxford, and Cambridge—priests and teachers; at Harvard—"ministers and leaders of state and society"; at Tokyo—high-level civil servants. But, in each instance, other goals were added.

Second, there are major constellations of goals which seem to form a pattern: for the LDCs—the development of skilled manpower; for the communist nations—provision of skilled manpower, assurance of egalitarian access, and advancement of "political and civic education"; for the more developed noncommunist nations with a narrow range of goals—skilled manpower, transmission of culture, and opportunity for individual development (France before 1968 is an example); for the more developed noncommunist nations with a wide range of goals—egalitarian access and research, and perhaps also public service may be added (United States since the land-grant movement is an illustration).

Finally, goals, while carrying the same designation, are often defined differently from nation to nation and from time to time within nations.

Trained Manpower

Manpower is a new word in the language. It does not even show up in the *Oxford English Dictionary*. It seems to have been first used in connection with military service during World War I. Yet the idea of using universities or academies to develop trained personnel goes back in the classical tradition to the Sophists (teachers, architects, etc.), in the European tradition at least to Salerno (medicine), in the Chinese tradition to Confucius (civil servants), and in the Islamic tradition to translators, astronomers, and mathematicians. The individual universities of Europe were founded on two models—one was the guild, the other the church—both interested in training for the professions of the day.

The general progression of training in the West since the Middle Ages has been as follows: for the classic professions (law, medicine, clergy, teaching); for the state and the military (civil servants and officers); for the economy (the many new professions); and for an advanced economy where certain basic learning skills are needed by all workers (basic skills to be provided within postsecondary education when not obtained at earlier levels of education), and where special technological and managerial training is needed by many persons.

Classical professional training mainly served the old aristocracy; the preparation of civil servants and military officers supported the newly arising nation states. Later, new professions were added to meet the technical demands growing out of the industrial revolution.[3] Now there is a need to absorb all persons to the maximum extent into "productive labor" and since "unskilled labor" jobs have largely disappeared, this may require teaching remedial skills even at the post-secondary level. Thus the expansion of the definition of this assignment to higher education has reflected less its own internal evolution and more the transformation of the surrounding society.

The planned economies place more stress on matching training with the needs for specific manpower skills; and the less planned economies emphasize more general training for several possible employments. The LDCs generally first emphasized the classic professions (particularly law), then civil servants, and only later the technological professions.

No system of higher education has ever been without this goal of providing trained manpower in fact if not in theory. It must be considered the most basic and universal of all. It is also the goal which has evolved most uniformly among nations in relation to their stages of economic development and their related techniques and technologies.

Transmission of a Common Culture

Here again, all systems seek to transmit a cultural emphasis, but this emphasis varies greatly according to content and intensity. Some of the elements of culture to be transmitted may be identified as follows:

A Religious Culture. The Pope once established new universities primarily to combat heresy. Many American private colleges were formed for the purpose of perpetuating one or another religion, and many so continue. The University of Sydney was established to advance "religion and morality"— in a nation, however, more noted for attendance at sporting events than at church. This emphasis on religion has been declining in importance in modern times.

A Democratic Culture. Thomas Jefferson believed that students should be taught the "principles of government" on which the "United States were genuinely based." Many state universities to this day require instruction in American government and institutions. The U68 in Sweden proclaims a goal of teaching for "democracy."

A Socialist Culture. Marxists believe that the creation of "socialist man" is one of their greatest purposes; and that universities must be concerned with "political and civic education."

An Attachment to the Historical Culture. This is a strong emphasis in France, which has a most highly developed culture, but also in Japan, and to a lesser extent in Thailand.

A Moral and Ethical Culture. The Robbins report in the United Kingdom put an emphasis upon "the common standards of citizenship," and higher education in Japan in 1947 had as one purpose the development of "intellectual and moral character."

Nationalism. This was, before World War II, a very strong emphasis in Japan and Germany.

Internationalism. This is a new official purpose in Sweden and of some concern, at least, in Canada.

A Culture of Change. In Sweden, there is a clear concern to prepare students to assist in and adjust to social change.

A Scientific and Intellectual Culture. The Robbins report referred to the need to "promote the general powers of the mind." Also a great concern of Cardinal Newman, this is an implicit goal in many nations, particularly within the academic community itself in nations such as Poland and Germany and more generally within the Anglo-American and Protestant traditions.

Several of these, especially the first four, place an emphasis upon the classic texts of the cultural tradition. At least two of these approaches— religious/culture and nationalism—are often an embarrassment to the academic profession when pushed to an extreme; the other approaches vary in their compatibility with the inclinations of the members of the academic profession. All but the last may be incompatible if pushed too intensively and too rigidly.

National culture is clearly an area where the policy of the society may not be in accordance with the goals of faculty members and students. Many of the battles, great and small, between societies and their institutions of higher education have been over the "transmission of a common culture." The approach taken also divides nations and reflects their differing internal characters and historical traditions.

The goal of training manpower parallels in its variations the more or less common flow of historical stages of development. The transmission of the common culture, by contrast, reflects the different points of origin and the different routes taken by different societies. Manpower development is a uniting theme, cultural transmission a divisive one, in the world of higher education.

Individual Development

The development of the individual student is a byproduct of any system of higher education, regardless of the goals. Even a system that concentrates on manpower training adds to the individual development of students. Some systems, however, have individual development as a theme in its own right. They are more likely to be in capitalist than in socialist countries. Marxist theory emphasizes that the individual fulfills himself only as he serves the community. The goal of individual development also seems to be a theme more of systems which were started early in history than of those begun in later times when technical training came to be more important and "leadership" preparation less important. Individual development is also emphasized more in those countries which had "upper classes" which institutions of higher education primarily served. The theme is more the "whole person" than the "whole society."

Individual development, in British tradition, has had a series of themes[4]—training in taste and manners, in character and leadership, in critical intelligence, in universal knowledge and universal truth, in humanism, and in moral philosophy, among others. The American, Canadian, and Australian traditions have to varying degrees and in varying places followed the British.

The methods used to encourage individual development range from heavy emphasis on residential living, as in the colleges of Oxford and Cambridge, to a heavy component of "general education" in the curriculum, to strong emphasis on counseling and guidance, to a rich cultural, ethical, and athletic environment, to active and comprehensive student organizations, such as the "nations" in Swedish universities. This has been a stronger theme in Anglo-American-type nations and Sweden than in France, where students traditionally have been put much more on their own, or in Mexico or Iran; and it varies from one institution to another—more attention at Chulalongkorn in Thailand, for example, than at a poly-technic in England.

Overall, this approach has an element of class origins in it and is of generally decreasing importance, in any event, in an age of mass enrollments in technical programs. The Battle of Waterloo may have been "won on the playing fields of Eton" but modern wars and peace-time economic contests are not; they are more likely to be won in the classrooms of the polytechnics.

Research and Scholarship

Some scholarly activities have been a part of institutions of higher education at almost all times and places. Such scholarship as there was at the time was concentrated in the Cathedral schools that preceded the founding of the medieval universities. But research, particularly scientific research, became a major theme only with the rise of the Humboldt-type university in Germany and its predecessors over the prior century; although Uppsala was a great center for science (Linnaeus and Celsius) before Humboldt, and there was Newton at Cambridge. However, it was the German-type university that became the model for much of the world.

Basic research is more likely to be a preoccupation of universities in highly developed and wealthy economies in the LDCs. Within the developed economies, however, there are variations. Some countries follow the German model; others the French, where research is concentrated in the Academy and its instrumentalities rather than in the universities. France has become the model for the socialist world, via Russia and Peter the Great, although there is now some tendency to place more research in the university setting. Japan is a special case. Research there is largely imported or undertaken within industrial or governmental laboratories.

Applied research within the universities has been particularly developed within American universities, starting first with the application of science to agriculture.

Public Service

Most activities of institutions of higher education are "services," even public services. The concept of public service, however, got its start with the land-grant movement in the United States. Public service takes four major forms:

Criticism and advice by members of the academic community on technical problems and social issues in the external community

Provision of cultural and athletic events, open to the general public

Offering of noncredit courses to the general public

Preservation of cultural heritages for their own sake, and for public consumption (a museum function), in addition to or aside from scholarly study

Higher education has frequently performed the first of these services regardless of whether the external community desired it or not. Abelard, one of the progenitors of the University of Paris, was charged with heresy for his critical views. Still, this type of public service is the most widespread of all, but muted on the social-issue side in socialist and authoritarian nations. Programs of public events and noncredit courses are particularly typical of the United States and Canada. Such diverse nations as Poland and Thailand stress attention to cultural heritages.

Egalitarian Access

Access, traditionally, has been for a small elite group of students defined by class origin, wealth of their parents, professions of their fathers, as well as (or sometimes instead of) their talents. In more modern times, the emphasis has been more and more upon academic merit regardless of the student's socioeconomic class. The land-grant movement helped to pioneer this emphasis. Still more recently there has come to be a concern for compensatory advantages in access, particularly within socialist and social-democratic nations—giving certain preferences to children of workers and peasants (Poland) or of low-income or minority families, or to persons of more advanced age and with work experience (Sweden). More attention is also being paid to access in neglected geographical areas (as in Thailand in areas outside of Bangkok).

Concluding Note

Systems of higher education may be differentiated in many ways, including by the goals they follow, either explicitly or implicitly; by how they define these goals; and by what weight they give to them.

The goals they choose or that are thrust upon them reflect the stages of economic development, as in the different types of trained manpower they produce; the central social orientation of each nation and its specific history, as in the different cultural emphases it seeks to transmit, the comparative attention to social and to individual needs, the kinds of public services provided, and the attention it gives to egalitarian access; and the status of the nation among nations, as in its contributions to basic research.

Looking at goals, it appears that systems of higher education might be grouped as follows: less developed economically; communist; capitalist and social democratic—with narrow assignment of goals; and capitalist and social democratic—with broad assignment of goals. The similarities of goals within each type are greater than between types. Individual systems can roughly be assigned within these categories, with some in transition from one category to another. These categories help to make the point that systems of higher education cannot be understood without reference to the nature of the larger society of which they are a part. Higher education more follows than leads society.

Comparative Effectiveness: Unknown and Mostly Unknowable

> Higher education has many effects, but whether and particularly to what extent it is independently effective in producing decisive and desired results— that is another question and no one fully knows the answers.

Any current consideration of the comparative effectiveness of systems of higher education is bound to end in failure, but it may be an instructive failure.[5] The reasons for the inevitable failure are mainly these: First, there is no consensus on desired outcomes in many nations—highly planned economies are an exception; and effectiveness must be related to goals. Second, there are many unintended side effects of higher education even where there is a consensus, and some of these side effects are at least partially hidden from sight and long-delayed in their expression. Some of these side effects also run counter to desired results. What happens along the way is often more important that the purpose of the journey. Third, even if there were a consensus on desired outcomes and the side effects were all readily visible, the data to evaluate them are often nonexistent and, when existent, inadequate. Comparisons among nations and over time in a single nation are extremely difficult even in any single area of evaluation, and impossible over a modest range of areas. Also, most effects have more than one cause; and most causes have more than one effect. And so, it is very difficult to assign causes to effects, and thus to analyze the origins of effectiveness.

Moreover, systems have quite different roles to play within their nations, and both the systems and the nations may be at quite different levels of historical development. It can even be argued "that one can understand the structure and the functioning of higher education systems only in the context of the society that creates this system of higher education, its economic and political structure as well as its cultural and value systems."[6] Those who strongly adhere to this argument believe that effectiveness consequently must be examined only within nations, and not across nations.

Finally, academics, who study all other institutions of mankind critically and analytically, have been less inclined to study their own. There is only one substantial effort at an overall evaluation of higher education—Howard Bowen's *Investment in Learning: The Individual and Social Value of American Higher Education*[7]—and it applies to only one nation.

Consequently, higher education is more often described than evaluated. We know more about its history, structure, governance, human composition, instructional content than we know about its consequences. Higher education may seek the truth but largely ignores even the measurable consequences of that search.

Gross Results

All this having been said, there are some broad tests of effectiveness-albeit crude and elemental—that do apply across nations and across time. Effective systems of higher education do the following:

Endure. Most systems of higher education, once established, have survived, especially those created in modern times. Ancient systems in China, Greece, Rome, and the Islamic world ceased to exist only in the course of cataclysmic changes in the societies that supported them. Universities are among the oldest continuing institutions in Europe and the Americas.

Grow. In modern times, the number of institutions within each system has increased substantially, and the institutions have become more diverse (table 1).

Attract More Resources. The percentage of the GNP spent on higher education is almost universally higher than it was a century ago, half a century ago, even a decade ago.

Attract more students. Student numbers have risen faster than the population as a whole in almost every nation over recent decades (table 2).

Satisfy their students. What studies there have been on this test—United States, United Kingdom, France, Australia, Sweden, Japan, Germany—all indicate a high level of satisfaction by students with their experience in higher education (table 3).

Draw public support. To the extent that public opinion data are available (as in the United States), they show higher education to rank among the very top institutions enjoying public confidence (table 4).

Increase their functions. The functions of institutions of higher education have not only changed in internal definition over time but have been augmented by accretion of new functions with little offsetting diminution.

TABLE 1

Growth of Higher Education Systems since 1950

Country	Number of Higher Education Institutions	
	1950	1975
Australia	175	279
Canada	181	256
France	N.A.	110[2]
Germany (West)	136	235
Iran	9	70
Japan	555	999
Mexico	12[1]	208
Poland	64	89
Sweden	16	132
Thailand	8	135
United Kingdom	207	300
United States	1,851	3,026

Sources: For this and the succeeding tables, see original tables in *12 Systems of Higher Education,* except tables 3, 4, 8, and 9.

1. Data available for universities only.
2. Does not include *grandes écoles;* total approximately 282, with *grandes écoles.*

TABLE 2

Students Enrolled in Higher Education as Percentage of Total Population

Country	1965	1975
Australia	1.2	5.8 (1976)
Canada	1.9	3.5[1] (1976)
France	1.1	1.9
Germany (West)	0.7	1.4
Iran	0.2 (1967)	0.5 (1976)
Japan	1.1	1.9 (1976)
Mexico	0.3	0.9
Poland	0.8[2]	1.4
Sweden	0.9	1.3[2]
Thailand	N.A.	0.6
United Kingdom	0.6	1.0
United States	3.0	5.2

1. Does not include part-time students in nonuniversity institutions.
2. University-type enrollments only.

TABLE 3

Student Satisfaction with Education

Country	"Satisfied" and "More or Less Satisfied"[1] %	"Dissatisfied" and "More of Less Dissatisfied" %	No Answer[2] %
Australia	82	17	2
France	62	35	4
Germany (West)	76	18	6
Japan	63	33	4
Sweden	80	16	4
United Kingdom	55	7	38
United States	84	16	1

Source: Youth Research Institutions, survey on "Consciousness of Youth in the World," sponsored by the Prime Minister's Office, Tokyo, Japan, 1977.

1. The question asked was "Are you satisfied with your school life or not?" Respondents were eighteen to twenty-four years old.
2. Totals may not add up to 100 because of rounding.

The overall, long-term record is impressive; matched by that of few other human institutions.

Analytical evaluation of higher education is in a primitive state of development. But higher education itself is not. The evaluation of it, informal and impressionistic as it may have been, by many societies and by numerous individuals can only have been favorable; otherwise, it would not have endured and so expanded its functions. And this is the evaluation that really counts—not the analytical evaluation of the cost–benefit experts with their inadequate data and narrow visions. Moreover, the very fact that the institutions have endured and grown—without economic, political, and military power—attests to their effectiveness.

The expansion of functions is of particular importance to any evaluation of effectiveness both because it implies increasing usefulness and also because it makes evaluation more complex—a single-function institution is easier to test than a multiple-function one.

TABLE 4

Public Confidence in Higher Education, United States

"As far as people in charge of running higher education are concerned, would you say you have a great deal of confidence, only some confidence, or hardly any confidence at all in them?"

Year	Great Deal of Confidence %
1966	61
1975	36
1976	31
1977	41

Source: Louis Harris and Associates, New York.

"Do you have 'a lot of,' 'some,' or 'not much' confidence in universities and colleges?"

Year	A Lot of Confidence %	Some Confidence %	Not Much Confidence %
1973	25	62	11[1]
1975	28	43	24
1976	27	47	18
1977	32	48	13

Source: San Francisco *Chronicle*, May 12, 1977, 12.

1. "No opinion" accounts for the difference between the sum of each row of figures and 100%.

Expansion of Functions

Institutions change in part as the range of their functions increases or diminishes. Institutions that have diminished in function over recent centuries have been organized religion, the family, and even the business enterprise (as compared with the earlier guild, which generally had more functions to perform than the modern public or private economic enterprise). Institutions that have increased their functions have been, above all, the nation-state but also higher education. For higher education, there are not only more functions but, of at least equal significance, older functions have taken on new and expanded definitions.

Training of skills has moved from the small-scale preparation of persons for the ancient professions, to education of members of social elites, to preparation of high-level civil servants, to training for the fantastic array of modern professions and occupations, to remedial instruction in basic skills for the upwardly mobile. This training once applied to a fraction of 1 percent of the youthful population; now it comprises 20 percent and more in several economically advanced nations.

Conversion of the class structure has changed in emphasis from a combination of perpetuating an hereditary elite while adding gradually to it, to development of a new class—the meritocracy, to reduction of class lines both by helping to create almost infinite gradations of occupations and by serving to narrow income and status differentials in the long run. The last of these contributions is a much more complicated assignment than the first.

Advancement of learning has expanded from preservation and interpretation of the classics, to reformulation of doctrines and ideas, to basic research, to applied research in an ever-expanding variety of fields.

Aiding the individual development of students, which once meant instruction aimed at their moral, intellectual, and social growth, has increasingly included developing the students' physical skills and artistic creativity; and, of course, it now serves more students. In nations with a Marxist orientation, individual self-fulfillment is considered to occur only in service to society, and this adds another dimension to the personal development of students.

Providing public service, where it has been undertaken, has come to include advice on an ever broader range of technical and social issues, and concern for the interests of a wider range of noncampus constituencies.

Contributing to social justice in the form of providing wider access for women, for members of lower-income groups, and for minorities is a rapidly expanding responsibility of higher education in a substantial number of nations. This function entails a responsibility for finding and advancing talent whatever its social points of origin, and sometimes includes a responsibility for providing compensatory equality of opportunity.

Undertaking a residential responsibility for unattached youth is an actual function in a few nations and is just developing in others. The need to provide a location for activity for unemployed or otherwise unattached youth is a function more recognized in practice than in official rhetoric. In several countries, student enrollments tend to increase when jobs are less available and to decrease when the labor market is able to absorb larger numbers of inexperienced youth. This counter-cyclical functions of higher education occurs partly by design and partly because of market forces.

Adding to quality of life takes many forms and higher education makes a contribution in at least two ways: by providing "durable consumer goods" to be enjoyed by students throughout their lifetimes in the form of skills, interests, and life orientations; and by providing current consumer services that result in satisfaction with aspects of life related to the educational environment.

Encouraging social change is a result of higher education and thus a function in fact if not an officially acknowledged goal in many circumstances. Social change comes about as a result of several of the functions already noted: by raising the general level of skills and knowledge; by creating technicians and experts to help operate society at higher and higher levels of complexity; by helping to transfer top leadership to trained professionals and away from the earlier hereditary or politically identified elites; by reordering the class structure of society; by adding new knowledge and disseminating it; by advancing social justice; and by adding to the quality of life of individuals, which, in turn, results in new consumer demands for goods and services. Some systems directly use higher education to obtain social changes. In Poland and in other communist countries, there is a direct effort to develop a new type of "socialized individual." In Sweden, students are prepared to participate in and to accept change, and also to become and to view themselves as citizens of the world. Among the side effects of higher education, when permitted, are introduction of new forms of cultural behavior and participation in political efforts directed at a fundamental reordering of the social structure whatever it may be.

If being of more use to more people in more complicated ways is one aspect of effectiveness, then higher education has been becoming more effective in more nations around the world in recent decades. In terms of the breadth and depth of functions performed, systems of higher education may be classified as performing the following functions:

Elementary functions, particularly skill training, in developing countries such as Iran, Mexico, and Thailand

Centrally planned functions, as in Poland, with particular attention to skill training, development of "socialist man," and pursuit of social justice in attendance patterns (In Sweden, "consensus" is substituted for a plan but is much less confining)

Functions limited by official choice, as in France and Japan, where research is mostly carried on outside the universities

Functions partially limited by internal choice, as in Germany and the United Kingdom, where the parameters of the systems are defined in part by attachment to historic academic orientations that act as constraints

Functions increasingly responsive, at least in some segments of the system, to consumer demand, as in the United States, Canada, and Australia

The most effective systems may be those which have the most constructive impacts on the greatest proportion of the population and on the life of the nation; these are the systems to which societies, formally and informally, have given the greatest responsibilities. This is the ultimate overall test of effectiveness.

Specific Tests of Effectiveness

Some goals of individual systems are not subject, by their very nature, to comparative evaluation. For example, it is not possible to compare "individual development" with "socialist development" of students in any meaningful way; or, except by observation, to compare the capacity to transmit desired cultural patterns, since these patterns vary so substantially. Furthermore, we cannot realistically compare effectiveness in attaining social change, since some systems want one kind of change and others another and some none at all; or the impact on the quality of life, since "quality" is subject to so many different interpretations; or the adequacy of public services, since the services desired vary so greatly; or the discharge of any residual responsibility for youth, since in some nations this is assigned to other agencies or is not assigned at all; or the diversity within systems, which depends so greatly on their size and on the span of their functions as well as on the choice of unitary, binary, or pluralistic approaches. This eliminates vast areas of great importance where evaluation may be possible within a single nation or among two or more highly comparable nations but not on a broadly comparative basis.

Some other possible tests must also be rejected. One test, within some systems, is the dropout rate—with a low dropout rate considered better than a high one, but this test can easily be manipulated by lowering standards. Also, elite systems will always win this test and open-access systems always lose it. Another test of effectiveness might be to measure the system's net contribution to the GNP, but it is technically not possible, despite valiant attempts, to apply this test either by estimating "residuals," of which training in higher education is only one of several; or contributions to "advancement of knowledge," of which higher education within a nation is only one source; or by calculating "social returns" to higher education, which are based on quite different wage and salary structures some of which, at least in part, do not reflect productivity. Other suggested tests have been the degree of integration of higher education with primary and secondary education and the degree of consistency with the economy and polity—with the assumption that the greater the integration and consistency, the better; but some systems are designed to work with less precise integration and less complete consistency and prefer it that way. A most attractive evaluative mechanism would be tests of student competence, as pioneered so successfully at lower levels of education by Torsten Husén,[8] but postsecondary education has so many diverse patterns of study that competence tests are much more difficult to devise and administer than at lower levels where subject matter is much more uniform. Still, such tests may become a basis for evaluation to some extent in the future.

Nevertheless, there are some specific tests of effectiveness that might be applied to the extent that data are available:

Percent of GNP drawn into support of its functions by higher education in competition with other segments of society (table 5)

Total enrollments, full-time and part-time, as a percentage of the age cohort, as an indication of choices in the expenditure of time and of opportunities available (table 6)

Distribution of enrollments by sex (table 7), by socioeconomic status (table 8), by ethnic and racial origin, by geographical location, by age, as a test of equality of access

TABLE 5

Percentage of GNP Spent on Higher Education

Country	% GNP Spent on Higher Education	Year
Australia	2.2	1975
Canada	2.2	1976
France	0.8	1975
Germany (West)	1.3	1975
Iran	N.A.	N.A.
Japan	1.0	1973
Mexico	1.0	1976
Poland	1.2	1977
Sweden	0.7	1975
Thailand	0.6	1975
United Kingdom	1.5	1971
United States	3.0	1975

TABLE 6

Total Higher Education Enrollment as Percentage of College-Age Cohort

Country	% Enrolled
Australia (17–22)	19 (1976)
Canada (18–24)	32 (1976)
France (18–23)	20 (1975)
Germany (West) (18–24)	14 (1975)
Iran (20–24)	2 (1976)
Japan (18–24)	17 (1976)
Mexico (20–24)	14 (1975)
Poland (20–24)	14 (1975)
Sweden (19–22)	25 (1974)
Thailand (19–22)	4 (1975)
United Kingdom (18–22)	14 (1974)
United States (18–24)	40 (1975)

Table 7

Equality of Access by Sex

	% Male	% Female	Year
Australia	51	49	1975
Canada	53	47	1976
France	52	48	1976
Germany (West)	64	36	1975
Iran	63	37	1975
Japan	70	30	1973
Mexico	78	22	1971
Poland	51	49	1975
Sweden	55	45	1975
Thailand	58	42	1975
United Kingdom	61	39	1974
United States	55	45	1975

Percentage of the most qualified young persons academically (say the top 10 percent or 20 percent) drawn into the system of higher education, as an indication of the success of the talent hunt

Voluntarily expressed satisfaction by students

Voluntarily expressed confidence by the public at large

Surpluses and deficits in the provision of trained manpower

Contribution to the narrowing of income and status differentials as between graduates of institutions of higher education and all employed persons[9]

The national origins of decisive new ideas in the sciences and social sciences (table 9)

This list constitutes more an agenda for research than a statement of what is known.

There are dangers, however, in all such attempts. Many important areas of evaluation are not subject to quantification. When some areas are quantified and others are not, there is a tendency to emphasize the first and neglect the second, and this leads to imbalance in evaluation and possibly in actions. Knowing half of the truth can lead to ill-founded policies and actions. Also, setting up quantifiable tests can lead to efforts to satisfy these quantities, one way or another, including in some cases by reduction of quality. These all can lead to a new kind of "numerology" and "numerology easily leads to suboptimization."[10]

TABLE 8

Equality of Access by Socioeconomic Status (in percentages)

Country	Year	Socio-occupational Category[1]				
		A	B	C	D	E
England and Wales	1961	61.0	13.0	—	—	26.0
	1970	46.0	27.0	—	—	27.0
France	1960	55.2	34.4	5.8	—	4.6
	1968	47.0	30.7	6.3	—	11.9
Germany (West)	1961	34.2	29.0	3.6	14.7	5.4
	1970	26.2	35.7	4.2	14.3	12.6
Sweden	1950	55.0	39.0	—	—	6.0
	1960	48.0	39.0	—	—	13.0
	1968	40.0	37.4	—	—	22.6

Source: Jean-Pierre Pellegrin, "Quantitative Trends in Post-Secondary Education, 1960–1970." *Towards Mass Higher Education: Issues and Dilemmas* (Paris: Organization for Economic Co-operation and Development, 1974), table 12.

1. Classification: A = upper stratum
                    B = middle stratum
                    C = independent agriculture
                    D = other independent
                    E = lower stratum

TABLE 9

Research Accomplishments in the Natural and Social Sciences

Nobel Prizes in Natural Sciences 1930–1975	Origins of Social Science Breakthroughs	Country
102	53	United States
43	17	Great Britain
23	10	Germany
7	5	Russia
7	2	France
6	2	Switzerland
5	1	Sweden
3		Denmark
2	4	Austria
2	1	Italy
2		Argentina
2		Australia
2		Belgium
2		Japan
2		The Netherlands
1	1	Czechoslovakia
1	1	India
1		Canada
1		Finland
1		Hungary
1		Ireland
1		Norway
1		Portugal
	1	Chile
	1	China
	1	South Africa

120	100	40	20	0	20	60	80	100

Source: For origins of social science breakthroughs: K. V. Deutsch, J. Platt, and D. Senghass, "Conditions Favoring Major Advances in Social Science," *Science,* 1971, 450–59.

Concluding Impressions

A review of the country studies prepared for ICED and other related materials leads to the following impressions. First, the generally best performed function is provision of trained manpower. There seems to be some tendency to overproduce lawyers in early stages of development and to underproduce "hard" scientists and technicians; but, overall, manpower needs of industrializing and industrialized societies are met. One reason for this is the flexibility of humans in the use of their talents. An exception to the general rule of adequacy in supplying trained manpower occurs in some very rapidly developing economies, such as Iran.

The function most subject to widespread attention at the present time is advancement of social justice. In many nations, intensified efforts are being made to draw in once neglected groups of students.

A function claiming constantly more attention in a number of nations is quality of life. This leads away from the historic attention to the production aspects of higher education and toward the consumption aspects.

Another function claiming more attention is contribution to social change, whether in the form of "affirmative action" as in the United States, or inculcation of global perspectives as in Sweden.

The research function in higher education on a worldwide basis is largely concentrated in a few countries—particularly the United States, the United Kingdom, Germany, France, Sweden, Russia, and Switzerland. Some nations cannot afford their own basic or even applied research on any substantial scale (the LDCs); others largely borrow basic research from abroad (Japan). Some concentrate basic research in an academy or in other agencies (France and Poland).

In almost all nations, postsecondary education is becoming an increasingly major route for youth to enter adult life. The functions of higher education will continue to expand secularly since greater knowledge and higher skills (along with new social structures) are the main ways in which human evolution now takes place.

Qualitative impressions of broad contributions of systems of higher education are more useful than quanitative tests of specific results. Evaluative efforts of whatever sort, however, will always end up as an "instructive failure"; but along the way they do instruct in the different natures of national systems, in the importance of the different stages of national development, in the inherent complexity of evaluating multipurpose institutions, in the paucity of our specific knowledge, and in the inadequacy of our tools of analysis—a valuable lesson in humility.

The most needed new set of functions includes the development of a global perspective for students, the creation of mechanisms on national and international levels for studying global problems—almost every great national problem today has a global aspect—and the encouragement of intellectual frameworks which can encompass an analysis of world systems and deal with the future in terms of broad interrelationships, as against the current fragmentation of knowledge into what Bertrand Russell once called "fiercer specialisms." This will require a great leap forward. The world needs, as never before, an international community of scholars working on world problems. The ultimate test of the effectiveness of higher education may well come to be its effectiveness at the world, not the national, level, for as Torsten Husén notes: "The academic ethos implies universalism."[11] Finally, efforts to evaluate effectiveness might possibly signal a period of at least temporary stasis: "A culture is in its final flower before it begins to analyze itself."[12]

Notes

* Reprinted from *12 Systems of Higher Education: 6 Decisive Issues* (with John Millett, Burton Clark, Brian MacArthur, and Howard Bowen) (New York: International Council for Educational Development, 1978), 1–10, 157–77. Reprinted by permission.

1. *Systems of Higher Education,* New York: International Council for Educational Development, 1978. Canada (Edward Sheffield, Duncan D. Campbell, Jeffrey Holmes, B. B. Kymlicka, and James H. Whitelaw); France (Alain Bienayme); Federal Republic of Germany (Hansgert Peisert and Gerhild Franheim); Iran (Abdol Hossein Samii, M. Reza Vaghefi, and Deriush Norwrasteh); Japan (Katsuya Narita); Mexico (Alfonso Rangel Guerra); Poland (Jan Szczepánski); Sweden (Rune Premfors and Bertil Östergren); Thailand (Sippanondha Ketudat, Wichit Srisa-an, et al.); United Kingdom (Tony Becher, Jack Embling, and Maurice Kogan); United States (Alan Pifer, John Shea, David Henry, and Lyman Glenny).

2. The list that follows does not include some items, occasionally listed as system goals, which seem to relate more to process or to means than to end goals: "autonomy," "recurrent education," "student participation in governance," and "multidisciplinarity."

3. Enrollment in "higher schools" and the mining-manufacturing index developed in almost identical fashion in Japan from 1875 to 1960. See: OECD, *Recurrent Education—Japan* (Paris, 1976), figure 3.

4. See Sheldon Rothblatt, *Tradition and Change in English Liberal Education* (London: Faber and Faber, 1976). For recent American definition, see Carnegie Commission on Higher Education, *The Purposes and Performance of Higher Education in the United States* (New York: McGraw-Hill, 1973).

5. Melvin M. Tumin writes of his attempt, with Marvin Bressler, "to create a model for the measurement of the effectiveness of educational systems" and of how it ended in "failure, albeit an instructive one." ("Evaluation of the Effectiveness of Education," *Interchange* 1, no. 3 (1970).

6. Jan Szczepański, *Higher Education in Eastern Europe,* International Council for Educational Development, Occasional Paper Number 12, 1974, 5.

7. Howard Bowen, *Investment in Learning* (San Francisco: Jossey-Bass, 1977).

8. See the nine-volume report of the IEA Six Subject Survey, conducted from 1966 to 1976 by the International Association for the Evaluation of Educational Achievement and published by Almquist and Wiksell International (Stockholm) and by John Wiley and Sons (New York) as *International Studies in Evaluation* (individual authors and titles vary).

9. See, for example, the study of the Netherlands by Jan Tinbergen, "Education, Inequality and Life Chances: A Report on the Netherlands," *OECD, Education, Inequality and Life Chances,* vol. 2 (Paris, 1975), 404–26.

10. Kenneth F. Boulding, "In Praise of Inefficiency," *Association of Governing Boards Reports* 20, no. 1 (January–February, 1978): 44–48.

11. Torsten Husén, "The Community: Its Nature and Responsibilities," in *Higher Education in the World Community,* ed. Stephen K. Bailey (Washington, DC: American Council on Education, 1977), 198.

12. Alfred North Whitehead, *Dialogues of Alfred North Whitehead,* as recorded by Lucien Price (Boston: Little, Brown, 1954), 16.

PART II

The Unfolding of the Great
Transformation: 1960–1980

Introduction—The Unfolding of the Great Transformation: 1960–1980

Like Proteus, the great transformation in the period from 1960 through 1980 took on several forms as circumstances changed, and its appearance to the observer altered as it was seen in advance, in midstream, and in retrospect. At first it looked like a great challenge—even the greatest challenge ever; later like a bad dream that would never end about a Hydra-headed monster; and finally like a complicated mosaic of diverse aspects of the larger human drama as played out within higher education at that time and place. Actually there were three periods. The first (1960–65) was dominated by the advancing "tidal wave" of students—getting ready for growth and adjusting to it; the second (1965–75) by the student revolts and the public reactions to them, and also by the series of recessions brought on by the OPEC crisis; and the third (1975–80) by shaky restabilization in a sadder and wiser and more doubtful mood. The first was a Golden Age; the second, a descent into a time of troubles for much of higher education; the third, a grey day of reality following survival, of innocence gone forever.

Like a major earthquake that exposes the layers below the surface, so higher education was forced to display its substructures and to recognize that it had them. It became more conscious of how it was composed internally and of how it related to the surrounding society that constitutes its environment and that nurtures it. It demonstrated both some strong features and some hidden weaknesses; and some of what it learned about itself it did not like. And it would never be the same again, not only because it was so fundamentally changed but also because its perceptions of itself were so altered, leading to less self-confidence in and more uncertainty about itself and about relations with society.

8. *Ex Ante*. In advance, there was a combination of sense of great challenge and of some fear. The challenge was to accommodate the "tidal wave" of students, the research surge after Sputnik, the new opportunities arising in the intellectual world, and the added need for skills—and all at once. This meant that each institution had to rethink its own size and mission; and that new campuses had to be built and their missions chosen, their sites selected, and their programs developed. The fear was that not enough time was available, not enough money would be forthcoming, and quality would deteriorate—"bigger is worse." Growth was the dominating concern.

9. In Transitu. Growth there was, but there was much more than growth. Growth was handled well; in fact, very well. The "much more" was not. The "much more" was made up, mostly, of two surprises. The first was the rise of political activism on campus to the highest levels in national history and of negative counterreactions also at the highest levels; and the second was the establishment of the cartel by oil-producing nations that sent economic shocks around the world. Not only were these developments not anticipated, but they were inherently hard to handle. Additionally, higher education, it turned out, had grown faster than the labor market and we had, for a time, the phenomenon of the "overeducated American" with reduced economic returns to higher education.[1] The public turned against the campus, and the campus, in part, turned against itself. Government stepped more in to "coordinate." Instead of growth, the theme, all of a sudden, was political and economic survival.

10. Ex Post. Looking back, it was all a lot more complicated than it seemed to be either when the dominant theme was growth or when it was survival, or than when at first it was mostly hope or when later it was mostly fear. Higher education did grow and it did survive, and it did learn quite a lot about itself. It learned how flexible the system was and what an asset this turned out to be; and it learned that it could grow and maintain quality at the same time. It learned how important to it were developments completely outside its control, such as demographics and worldwide economic fluctuations—it was not the keeper of its own fate as it had fantasized it was, but a plaything of larger forces. It also learned that it was not easily subject to internally originated academic reform—it was so conservative about its own affairs; and that attempts to use it for external political transformations could be counterproductive—it was too marginal to society to be effective and too antagonistic to society in its tactics to be persuasive. Additionally, it found out that many aspects of its governance could be and were amended but that the overall structure had surprising endurance.

11. Faculty. An observation about the faculty, at least as represented by those members who wrote their views, that emerges from the experience of these years is how the dominant intellectual mood, from euphoria to depression, may swing farther up and farther down than the objective circumstances in the longer run seem to warrant—a mild manic-depressive case.

12. Students. An observation about the activist students is that they had excessive expectations about the impacts they could have and were going to have on American society—the expectations that they and they alone could generate a revolution in a nonrevolutionary period in a nonrevolutionary democracy. While they hoped for too much, reactionary elements in society almost equally feared too much—thus demonstrating a lack of faith in the secure future of their society. Both the hopes and fears seemed to me, then and now, to be without adequate foundation in the realities of the national situation; but they nevertheless were strong forces to be confronted.

13. Society. The labor movement was once perceived, particularly in the first half of the twentieth century, as the great political challenge to the American system and the workers as the rising new class of power. The workers turned out, however, not to be a revolutionary force—in fact quite the contrary in some ways; but still with substantial evolutionary impacts. Then in the 1960s, the student movement came along and was perceived by some as the new mechanism for revolutionary change, but once again the American system proved its stability and its ability to absorb, adapt to, and contain the student movement as it had the labor movement. American society did not, by and large, overreact—a few bad episodes to the contrary. It did instead, by and large, act in constructive ways—the war in Vietnam was ended, social justice was improved, young persons were given the vote at age eighteen. The major lesson of this event in history was how resilient the American system, in response to this new challenge, proved to be, as it had before in its history.

14. A Possible Residue. We may not have heard the last of the student–faculty political revolts of the 1960s. Significant proportions of the faculty then expressed basic doubts about the American system, and basic sympathy for a revolt against it—at a level of one-fifth to one-third. And many of the veterans of the student revolt later became faculty members themselves in the 1970s. Has the campus become *the* center of the "adversary culture," and is it on an historic "collision course" with American society? A new period of massive political unrest, if it should develop, will give an answer to this question.

Notes

1. Richard B. Freeman, *The Overeducated American* (New York: Academic Press, 1976).

CHAPTER 8

Ex Ante—

The Frantic Race to Remain Contemporary*

Daedalus *had a volume (1964) on* The Contemporary University: USA *and asked me to say how I saw it as a university president. The editor said that I showed a "relaxed acceptance" of the status quo. Actually, I then felt personally about as "frantic" as the title to my essay said higher education was.*

"The true American University," David Starr Jordan once observed, "lies in the future." It still does; for American universities have not yet developed their full identity, their unique theory of purpose and function. They still look to older and to foreign models, although less and less; and the day is coming when these models will no longer serve at all.

The American university is currently undergoing its second great transformation. The first occurred during roughly the last quarter of the nineteenth century, when the land-grant movement and German intellectualism were together bringing extraordinary change. The current transformation will cover roughly the quarter century after World War II. The university is being called upon to educate previously unimagined numbers of students; to respond to the expanding claims of government and industry and other segments of society as never before; to adapt to and channel new intellectual currents. By the end of this period, there will be a truly American university, an institution unique in world history, an institution not looking to other models but itself serving as a model for universities in other parts of the globe. This is not said in boast. It is simply that the imperatives that are molding the American university are also at work around the world.

Each nation, as it has become influential, has tended to develop the leading intellectual institutions of its world—Greece, the Italian cities, France, Spain, England, Germany, and now the United States. The great universities have developed in the great periods of the great political entities of history. Today, more than ever, education is inextricably involved in the quality of a nation. And the university, in particular, has become in America, and in other nations as well, a prime instrument of national purpose. This is new. This is the essence of the transformation now engulfing our universities.

American universities are currently facing four great areas of related adjustments: (1) growth, (2) shifting academic emphases, (3) involvement in the life of society, and (4) response to the new federal involvement. The direction of adjustment in each of these areas is reasonably clear; the detailed arrangements and the timing are not. There are several other areas where adjustments will be necessary but where the direction of adjustment is as yet by no means clear; and four such areas will also be noted below.

Growth

The number of university and college students in the United States will almost double during the 1960s. This addition of three million will duplicate in one decade the growth of the three centuries since Harvard was founded. The proportion of graduate students will rise considerably, and there are already 25,000 post-doctoral students.

Existing university campuses are being enlarged and many new one founded. The University of California, for example, now has seven campuses and a total enrollment of 65,000 students. Four of those campuses will triple or more in size in the next decade. One campus admitting undergraduates for the first time this fall, and two entirely new campuses admitting students for the first time in 1965, are being planned to accommodate ultimate enrollments of 27,500 each.

But university expansion alone cannot begin to meet the demand for some kind of education beyond the high school level. In the years before World War II, post–high school study was the exception; it is rapidly becoming the norm. In California today four out of every five high school graduates seek further education; soon it will be even more. This great shift in the pattern of American education will call for many more four-year colleges, both public and private. And a particularly large number of junior colleges will be formed as the community college movement becomes nationwide. Problems of differentiation of function will arise among public sectors of higher education—junior colleges, four-year colleges, and universities—as they compete for state support. The State of California has already met that problem through legislative adoption of a Master Plan for Higher Education, and other states are working along similar lines. However the total demand for higher education may be parceled out among the public and private institutions of varying types, one fact is clear: this will be the most unprecedented period of campus development in American history, or indeed in the history of the entire world.

To accommodate the great increase in enrollments, many academic calendars are being rearranged, particularly in state-supported institutions, to permit more nearly year-round use of physical facilities. Students will be able to accelerate their work if they wish, and general students will come and go with less reference to their "class"; more of them will drop in and drop out as suits their particular schedules and needs.

There will be some further mechanization of instruction (television, language laboratories, programmed learning) to improve quality and to save faculty time for other endeavors; including more individual work with students. The sciences will almost eagerly embrace these aids to learning. The foreign language departments will be rather reluctant, because these devices can threaten their structure of faculty employment and the recruitment and utilization of graduate students.

Because of the competition for faculty members, salaries will continue to rise; fringe benefits of all sorts will be devised to tie professors to a particular campus. In addition to competition among universities, there is also intensified competition with industry and government. This competition has obvious advantages in raising faculty income, but it has its negative aspects. As the market becomes more active, internal equity will be injured, for some disciplines are much more in demand in the market than others. Teaching loads will be competitively reduced, sometimes to zero, although more teachers are needed and students are complaining about lack of attention. The identification of the professor with his university will be generally loosened—he will become more a member of a free-floating profession. The rules regarding how much time a professor can spend away from his university assignments, and those affecting the sources of his income within the university, will continue to be in great flux.

This current phenomenon of rising salaries and benefits, however, may be of relatively short duration, lasting, perhaps, for the remainder of this decade. Faculty salaries have been catching up with incomes in other professions after a historical lag. By 1970, also, the personnel deficit of today may be turning into the surplus of tomorrow as all the new Ph.D.'s roll into the market. A new plateau of compensation may be reached in the 1970s.

In addition to the great expansion of individual institutions of higher learning, there will be an increasing tendency for university centers to cooperate and even coalesce for added strength, particularly in their graduate research programs. Allan Nevins has put it this way: "Observers of higher education can now foresee the inexorable emergence of an entirely new landscape. It will no longer show us a nation dotted by high academic peaks with lesser hills between; it will be a landscape dominated by mountain ranges." The highest peaks of the future will rise from the highest plateaus.

One such plateau runs from Boston to Washington. At the universities and laboratories situated along this range are found 46 percent of the American Nobel Prize winners in the sciences and 40 percent of the members of the National Academy of Sciences. A second range with its peaks runs along the California coast. C. P. Snow has written: "And now the scientific achievement of the United States is moving at a rate we all ought to marvel at. Think of the astonishing constellation of talent, particularly in the physical sciences, all down the California coast, from Berkeley and Stanford to Pasadena and Los Angeles. There is nothing like that concentration of talent anywhere in the world. It sometimes surprises Europeans to realize how much of the pure science of the entire West is being carried out in the United States. Curiously enough, it often surprises Americans too. At a guess, the figure is something like 80 percent, and might easily be higher."

The California mountain range has 36 percent of the Nobel laureates in science and 20 percent of the members of the National Academy of Sciences. The Big Ten and Chicago constitute a third range of academic peaks, with 10 percent of the Nobel laureates and 14 percent of the members of the National Academy of Sciences. These three groupings of universities —the East Coast, California, and the Big Ten and Chicago—currently produce over three-quarters of the doctorates conferred in the United States. Another range may be in the process of development in the Texas–Louisiana area.

This concentration of talent partly follows history—the location of the older private and public universities. Partly it follows industrial strengths and population centers. But it also has its own logic. No one university can cover all specialties, or cover them well enough so that there is a sufficient cluster of close intellectual colleagues. The scholar dislikes intellectual isolation, and good scholars tend to swarm together. These swarms are extraordinarily productive environments. No library can be complete, nor any graduate curriculum. Some laboratories, to be well used, must be used by more than one university. Thus the Big Ten and Chicago, through their Committee on Institutional Cooperation, are merging their library resources, creating a "common market" for graduate students, diversifying their research laboratories on a common-use basis, and parceling out foreign language specializations. Something similar is happening in the University of California system, and between Berkeley and Stanford. Harvard and MIT, Princeton and Pennsylvania, among others, run joint research enterprises. These clustering universities in turn have clustering around them scientifically oriented industrial and governmental enterprises. To match the drawing power of the great metropolis, there now arrives the Ideopolis. The isolated mountain can no longer dominate the landscape; the constellation is greater than the single star and adds to the brightness of the sky.

The rate of growth being forced upon American universities and colleges by the surging enrollment wave will present difficult problems. As President Johnson said in his 1964 Commencement address at the University of Michigan: ". . . more classrooms and more teachers are not enough. We must seek an educational system which grows in excellence as it grows in size." A period of rapid growth is necessarily a period of both flexibility and ingenuity. Institutions can readily adopt on new campuses ideas and programs that would require costly reorganization on older campuses. The University of California, for example, is building its new Santa Cruz campus as a series of small residential colleges, each with its own subject field orientation. The University's new Irvine campus will explore ways of involving organized research units in the formal process of instruction. The new San Diego campus of the university will subdivide its ultimate enrollment of 27,500 students into a series of smaller colleges, with groups of four such colleges constituting largely self-contained subcampuses of varying academic emphases. The University of the Pacific, in Stockton, California, has established a new residential college in which the entire curriculum is conducted in Spanish. Thus the enrollment explosion may bring unusual opportunities for colleges and universities, along with the heavy burden of numbers.

The current surge in higher education is not, of course, unique to the United States. In Canada the proportion of eighteen- to twenty-one-year olds in higher education is expected to double in the decade from 1962 to 1972. In France the total enrollment in higher education is expected to soar from around 200,000 now to 500,000 by 1970. In Britain, the much-discussed Robbins Committee Report recommends doubling the number of universities by 1980. These figures reflect the rapidly growing pressures resulting from a vast increase in secondary enrollments throughout much of the world. The decade of the 1950s has seen a world increase of 81 percent in secondary enrollments and an increase of 71 percent in college enrollments.

The data both from this country and abroad clearly indicate that we are witnessing everywhere the demise of two long-held notions: that higher education ought to be restricted to a small elite minority, and that only a small percentage of a country's population is capable of benefiting from some kind of higher education. Growth is having quite uneven impacts on American universities. Some, and they are almost always private, are building walls around themselves as aristocratic enclaves protected from the swirling currents of the population explosion. Others, and they are mostly public, are engulfed with more than their share of accommodation to the new hordes, that do not wish to be barbarous, advancing through their gates. The aristocratic enclave offers refuge to the faculty member who wishes protection from the new invasion, and many do; but it will become a more and more isolated element within the society of the future. The university with the open door will suffer the pangs of adjustment, but it will become in the process a more central element in a dynamic society. The one will be a pleasant place to be but increasingly out of tune with the surrounding society. The other will be a less pleasant place to live but will provide a more challenging and exciting environment, and will be more a part of the evolving life around it. Each will have its place, but the places they occupy will grow farther and farther apart.

Shifting Academic Emphases

A second major factor in the changing scene for American higher education is that knowledge is exploding along with population. There is also an explosion in the need for certain skills. The university is responding to all these explosions.

The vastly increased needs for engineers, scientists, and physicians will draw great resources to these areas of the university. Also, some new professions are being born. Others are becoming more formally professional, for example, business administration and social work. The university becomes the chief port of entry for these professions. In fact a profession gains its identity by making the university the port of entry. This creates new roles for education; but it is also part of the process of freezing the structure of the occupational pyramid and assuring that the well-behaved do advance, even if the geniuses do not. The university is used as an egg-candling device; and it is, perhaps, a better one than any other that can be devised, but the process takes some of the adventure out of occupational survival, and does for some professions what the closed shop has done for some unions. The life of the universities for a thousand years has been tied into the recognized professions in the surrounding society, and the universities will continue to respond as new professions arise.

The fastest-growing intellectual field today is biology. Here there is a veritable revolution where the doctrine of evolution once reigned supreme. To the classifying efforts of the past are being added the new analytical methods of the present, often drawn from chemistry and physics. There are levels of complexity to be explored in all living structures. The ''code of life'' can now be read; soon it will be understood, and soon after that, used. It is an intellectual discovery of unique and staggering proportions. The secrets of the atom, much as they have changed and are changing human activity on this planet, may hold no greater significance than the secrets still hidden in the genetic code. If the first half of the twentieth century may be said to have belonged to the physical sciences, the second half may well belong to the biological. Resources within the universities will be poured into the new biology and into the resulting new medicine and agriculture, well supported though medicine and agriculture already are. Medical education and research may be, in particular, on the threshold of revolutionary change.

Another field ready to bloom is that of the creative arts, hitherto the ugly duckling or Cinderella of the academic world. America is bursting with creativity in painting, music, literature, the theater, with a vigor equaled in few other parts of the world today. Italy, France, Spain, Germany, Russia, England, the Low Countries have had great periods of cultural flowering. America is having one now. In the arts the universities have been more hospitable to the historian and the critic than to the creator; the latter has found his havens elsewhere. Yet it is the creativity of science that has given the sciences their prestige in the university. Perhaps creativity will do the same again for the humanities, though there may be less new to create than has recently been true in science, and though the tests of value are far less precise. A very important role remains for the historian of past ages of creativity and for the critic of the current productions. But the universities need to find ways also to accommodate pure creative effort if they are to have places on stage as well as in the wings and in the audience in the great drama of cultural growth now playing on the American stage.

These possibilities for expansion—in the training of engineers, scientists, physicians, and the newer professionals, in biology, and in the creative arts, among various others—raise the problem of balance. As James Bryant Conant has noted, the Western world has had for a thousand years a continuing problem of "keeping a balance between the advancement of knowledge, professional education, general education, and the demands of student life."

But the balance is always changing; this is the unbalancing reality. The balance is not equal treatment, the provision of equal time in some mechanical and eternal way between teaching and research, or between the humanities and science. The dynamics of balance did not give equal treatment to the available scientist in Padua in 1300 when Giotto was painting his chapel, or to the available artist in Padua in 1600 when Galileo was lecturing from his crude platform. Balance cannot be determined on the scales by blind justice, field versus field and activity versus activity.

The essence of balance is to match support with the intellectual creativity of subject fields; with the need for skills of the highest level; with the kinds of expert service that society currently most requires. None of these measures is constant. Balance requires, therefore, a shifting set of judgments which relates facilities and attention to the possibilities inherent in each field, each skill, each activity at that moment of time in that environment, yet preserves for all fields their essential integrity. To know balance is to know the potential creativity, the potential productivity, the potential contribution of each competing activity in an unfolding pattern of time and an evolving landscape of environment. To know balance is to know more than anyone can ever know in advance. But decisions must nevertheless be made, and time will tell how well. The only certainly wrong decision is that the balance of today must be preserved for tomorrow. Where will the world's work and the university's work best be done? The answer to that question is the true definition of balance.

Involvement in the Life of Society

The third great change affecting the contemporary university is its thoroughgoing involvement in the nation's daily life. At the heart of this involvement is the growth of the "knowledge industry," which is coming to permeate government and business and to draw into it more and more people raised to higher and higher levels of skill. The production, distribution, and consumption of "knowledge" in all its forms is said to account for 29 percent of the gross national product, according to Fritz Machlup's calculations; and "knowledge production" is growing at about twice the rate of the rest of the economy. Knowledge has certainly never in history been so central to the conduct of an entire society. What the railroads did for the second half of the last century and the automobile for the first half of this century may be done for the second half of this century by the knowledge industry: that is, to serve as the focal point for national growth. And the university is at the center of the knowledge process.

So the campus and society are undergoing a somewhat reluctant and cautious merger, already well advanced in some fields. MIT is at least as closely related to industry and government as Iowa State ever was to agriculture. Indeed, universities have become "bait" to be dangled in front of industry, with drawing power greater than low taxes or cheap labor. Route 128 around Boston and the great developing industrial complexes in the San Francisco Bay area and southern California reflect the universities in these areas. The Gilpatric report for the Department of Defense explained that 41 percent of defense contracts for research in the fiscal year 1961 were concentrated in California, 12 percent in New York, and 6 percent in Massachusetts, for a total of nearly 60 percent, in part because these were also "centers of learning." Sterling Forest outside New York City seeks to attract industry by location next to a new university campus. In California, new industrial laboratories were located next to two new university campuses before the first building was built on either of these campuses. Sometimes industry will reach into a university laboratory to extract the newest ideas almost before they are born. Instead of waiting outside the gates, agents are working the corridors. They also work the placement offices. And the university, in turn, reaches into industry, as through the Stanford Research Institute.

The university and segments of industry are becoming more alike. As the university becomes tied into the world of work, the professor—at least in the natural and some of the social sciences—takes on the characteristics of an entrepreneur. Industry, with its scientists and technicians, learns an uncomfortable bit about academic freedom and the handling of intellectual personnel. The two worlds are merging physically and psychologically.

The rapid production of new knowledge has given new significance to university extension slogans about "lifelong learning." Television makes it possible for extension to reach into literally every home; the boundaries of the university are stretched to embrace all of society. The student becomes alumnus and the alumnus continues as student; the graduate enters the outside world and the public enters the classroom and the laboratory. Knowledge has the terrifying potential of becoming popular, opening a Pandora's box.

Extension divisions are proving to be increasingly effective administrative devices for linking campus and community in the further pursuit of knowledge. Freer of traditions and rules than regular university academic departments, extension units can respond quickly and in a variety of patterns to meet society's needs for current information and training. Professional schools and colleges, in particular, are making widespread use of extension programs for "refresher" and "continuing education" courses for the active practitioners in their fields. University of California Extension, for example, now enrolls in its courses one of every three lawyers and one of every six physicians in the state. Its total enrollment now numbers some 200,000 students, and it sponsors a remarkably wide range of academic activities including workshops, resident seminars and conferences, theater groups, symposia attracting participants of world renown, and even, recently, a notable scientific expedition to the Galapagos Islands. During the summer of 1964, in response to the growing concern with problems of school integration, University Extension was able to present several short-term workshops and courses on this urgent subject. The new role for knowledge is bringing a new and potentially quite exciting role for extension divisions in American higher education.

The campus becomes a center for cultural life; it has a ready-made audience in its students and faculty, and it has the physical facilities. Persons attracted by the performing and visual arts and the lectures come to live around the campus—also assorted crackpots. As the downtown areas in some cities decay, the campus takes its place as the cultural center of the community. A new dimension has been added to the land-grant idea of service.

The New Deal took professors to Washington from many campuses, the New Frontier from more than just one. In Wisconsin before World War I, the campus and the state house in Madison were exceptionally close. Today the campus is being drawn to the city hall and the state capitol as never before. The politicians need new ideas to meet the new problems; the agencies need expert advice on how to handle the old. The professor can supply both. Keynes concluded his *General Theory* as follows: ". . . the ideas of economists and political philosophers, both when they are right and when they are wrong, are more powerful than is commonly understood. Indeed the world is ruled by little else. Practical men, who believe themselves to be quite exempt from any intellectual influences, are usually the slaves of some defunct economist. Madmen in authority, who hear voices in the air, are distilling their frenzy from some academic scribbler of a few years back. I am sure that the power of vested interests is vastly exaggerated compared with the gradual encroachment of ideas." As, for example, the ideas of Keynes.

The university must range itself on the side of intelligent solutions to sometimes unintelligent questions. These questions more and more arise from abroad as well as at home; and the quality of the answers has been made all the more crucial in a world swept by Communist and nationalist revolutions.

There are those who fear the further involvement of the university in the life of society. They fear that the university will lose its objectivity and its freedom. But society is more desirous of objectivity and more tolerant of freedom than it used to be. The university can be further ahead of the times and further behind the times, further to the left of the public and further to the right of the public—and still keep its equilibrium—than was ever the case before, although problems in this regard are not yet entirely unknown. There are those who fear that the university will be drawn too far from basic to applied research and from applied research to application itself. But the lines dividing these never have been entirely clear, and much new knowledge has been generated at the borders of basic and applied research, and even of applied knowledge and its application. Whitehead once wrote of the creative margin when the "adventure of thought" met "the adventure of action."

Involvement with the Federal Government

Growth and shifting emphases and involvement in society all take money; and which universities get it in the largest quantities will help determine which of them excel a decade or two hence. Will federal support be spent according to merit or according to political power? Will private donors continue to do as well as they recently have done for those universities that have done well already? Will the states find new sources of revenue or will their expenditures be held under a lid of no new taxes? The answers to these questions will help predict the standings on the next rating scale of universities.

Of key importance to American universities is the role of the federal government, particularly through federal support of scientific research. This support, which received its great impetus during and after World War II, had already changed the face of the leading American universities almost as much as did the land-grant program a century earlier. Federal support had today become a major factor in the total performance of many universities, and the sums involved are substantial. Higher education in 1960 received about $1.5 billion from the federal government—a hundredfold increase in twenty years. About one-third of this $1.5 billion was for university-affiliated research centers; about one-third for project research within universities; and about one-third for other things, such as residence hall loans, scholarships, and teaching programs. This last third was expended at colleges as well as universities, but the first two-thirds almost exclusively at universities, and at relatively few of them.

The $1 billion for research, though only 10 percent of total federal support for research and development, accounted for 75 percent of all university expenditures on research and 15 percent of total university budgets. Clearly the shape and nature of university research are profoundly affected by federal monies. The effects of this extensive federal aid and the new problems that have arisen as a consequence are many and varied, but the more important of them might be grouped under the two general headings of "federal influence" and "balance."

1. Federal control as a substantive issue is, as Sidney Hook has said, a "red herring." With a few exceptions—the generally necessary exception of secrecy in certain types of work, and the unnecessary exception of the disclaimer affidavit once required by the National Defense Education Act—there had been no control in any deleterious sense. The real problem is not one of federal control but of federal influence. A federal agency offers a project. A university need not accept—but, as a practical matter, it usually does. Out of this reality have followed many of the consequences of federal aid for the universities; and they have been substantial. That they are subtle, slowly cumulative, and gentlemanly makes them all the more potent.

A university's control over its own destiny has thus been substantially reduced. University funds from tuition and fees, gifts and endowments, and state sources go through the usual budget-making procedures, and their assignment is subject to review in accordance with internal policy. Federal research funds, however, are usually negotiated by the individual scholar with the particular agency, and so bypass the usual review process. Thus 20 to 50 to 80 percent of a university's expenditures may be handled outside the normal channels. These funds in turn commit some of the university's own funds; they influence the assignment of space; they determine the distribution of time between teaching and research; to a large extent they establish the areas in which the university grows the fastest. Almost imperceptibly, a university is changed.

The authority of the department chairman, the dean, the president is thereby reduced; so also is the role of faculty government. This may have its advantages. The university's internal process of distributing funds would be generally less selective and less flexible than the federal research project approach. Within a university, the tendency is to give each faculty member about the same opportunity and once having given it to keep giving it thereafter; but the project method allows more attention to exceptional merit and has the advantage that all projects may end some time. Additionally, federal agencies are more responsive to particular national needs than the universities would be, given the same amount of money to spend according to their own priority system.

There are, however, clearly detrimental effects. Some faculty members come to use the pressure of their agency contacts against their university. They may try to force the establishment of a new administrative unit or the assignment of land for their own special building, in defiance of general university policy or priorities. These pressures, of course, should be withstood; they speak well neither of the professor nor of the agency. Also, some faculty members tend to shift their identification and loyalty from their university to the agency in Washington. The agency becomes the new alma mater. There are especially acute problems when the agency insists on the tie-in sale (if we do this for you, then you must do that for us) or when it requires frequent and detailed progress reports. Then the university really is less than a free agent. It all becomes a kind of "putting-out" system with the agency taking the place of the merchant-capitalist of old.

2. The question of "balance" in federal aid arises in relation both to support of specific fields within an institution and to distribution of support among institutions of higher learning. Among the totality of university functions, federal support has been heavily concentrated on research and on graduate and postdoctoral training in fields of national interest. Expenditures have been largely restricted to the physical and biomedical sciences, and to engineering, with only about 3 percent for the social sciences and hardly any support for the humanities.

All this is said to have destroyed the "balance" among fields, and it is generally concluded that something should be done about it. The balance among fields, however, has never been a static thing. If it were, philosophy, theology, and the classics would still be the dominant areas of study, as they have not been for a long time. Assuming that the balance of 1942, say, was appropriate for 1942, this does not mean it would have been appropriate for 1962. It is not enough to say that the old "balance" has been destroyed. The real question is what should be the proper balance today. It is clear that the flowering of the Renaissance should have affected the "balance" in the sixteenth century. It would seem likely that the splitting of the atom and the deciphering of the genetic code should in their turn affect the balance of the twentieth century. We should expect the most money and the brightest students and the greatest prestige to follow the most exciting new ideas. By and large they have done so, and this is one way of defining the nature of balance.

The real question, it seems to me, is not one of balance in any historical or monetary sense, but rather what is most appropriate to each field in each period. "All fields are equal, only some are more equal than others." There should be no effort to do the same things in the same amounts for each field. Each should receive support in accordance with its current potentialities, and potentialities vary. There are no timeless priorities.

Federal research expenditures have also been heavily focused on relatively few institutions. If both project research and large research centers are included, six universities received 57 percent of the funds in a recent fiscal year, and twenty universities received 79 percent. If project research alone is considered, the figures are 28 and 54 percent. As a percentage of total university expenditures for all purposes among the leading twenty recipients, federal funds have amounted to 20 to 50 percent when project research alone is counted, and from 20 to over 80 percent when the research centers are added. These twenty universities are only about one-tenth of all universities in the United States. They constitute the primary "federal grant" universities.

The project approach almost automatically led to concentration of federal research effort in a relatively few universities. The universities best equipped to undertake the research were also those with the faculty and facilities to provide for the training of Ph.D.'s. It is no coincidence that the six universities with a little more than 25 percent of project funds graduated about 25 percent of the Ph.D.'s; and a similar situation prevails for the top twenty universities. If "only the best will do," this concentration of effort is inevitable. A different result would have been quite surprising.

The concentration of effort has undoubtedly strengthened the facilities and improved the quality of faculties of universities already in the front rank. It has probably widened the gap between those of the first and those of the second and third ranks. It may, in fact, have actually injured universities of the second and third ranks and some colleges by turning their potential faculty members into research personnel in the front-rank universities. The good are better; the poor may well be worse. And it has greatly accentuated the differences between colleges and universities.

The general policy of federal agencies in allocating research grants to universities for the last two decades has been one of "seeking excellence wherever it is." The period has been one of what I have called "intuitive imbalance." We are now clearly entering a new phase of federal support policy, one that might be called "bureaucratic balance."

The new balance calls for developing a larger number of outstanding centers of graduate instruction and research. The Seaborg report of 1960 suggested expansion from the present fifteen or twenty centers to thirty or forty over a fifteen-year period. The National Education Improvement Act of 1963 envisaged expansion from twenty to seventy. Teaching is being emphasized along with research. Summer refresher courses for teachers of science, improvement of science textbooks, and language laboratories are programs already established. The National Science Foundation has a large effort under way to improve and renovate equipment for undergraduate teaching in the physical sciences. Undergraduates, as well as graduate students, are being assisted by loans and scholarships. The social sciences are receiving increasing sums of money. More funds are being granted to colleges as well as to universities, and to universities of all ranks.

A particularly significant step in the direction of broadening institutional support is the new science development program announced in the spring of 1964 by the National Science Foundation. This program is specifically designed to raise the overall quality of science programs in good institutions to the level of the excellent. Distinguished institutions are excluded: "Institutions already recognized as being outstanding in science should continue to depend on existing programs for assistance."

Undergraduate as well as graduate institutions will be eligible, and the grants (up to $5 million per institution) may be used in any way the institution chooses to strengthen single departments or related departments, to create new departments, or to improve the entire science program. *Science* magazine, commenting on the NSF plan, said, "It is probably safe to say that the success or failure of this program is going to have a far-reaching influence on the evolution of higher education in the United States."

The approach to a university "as an institution" has interesting implications. If additional universities are to be selected to become centers of strength in research and graduate instruction, then it will be necessary for the federal government to be concerned with the "general health of the institution." This will be a notable departure from historical practice, except in agriculture. If we are to move toward federal orientation to the "total function of the university," then the University Grants Committee in Great Britain is the outstanding precedent, and one that has received some support in the United States. However, there are only about thirty universities in Great Britain, and it is clear what is and what is not a university. Additionally, the University Grants Committee has come to exercise more influence over the establishment of new programs, the cost and size and even the appearance of new buildings, the equalization of faculty salaries among institutions, and the determination of admission policies than would currently be acceptable if it came from the federal government in this country.

Some hard choices must be faced. The decentralized project approach of the last two decades has much to recommend it. It is selective on merit, flexible in accordance with quality of performance, and responsive to national goals. The universities and their scholars retain substantial freedom. But such dominant reliance on the project approach is no longer likely. It is said that support to institutions as such will "give a university the necessary autonomy'' and will permit dispersion of effort and better balance in several directions. It is difficult, however, to assess the merit of a total institution as complex as a modern university. One alternative is to rely on a formula, as in the case of agriculture in the land grant institutions. Another is to be guided by political influence; and this is increasingly happening. Inter-university competition is being taken from the quasi-academic arena of the agency committee to the legislative halls.

The partnership of the federal government with higher education and particularly with the federal grant universities over the last two decades has been enormously productive in enlarging the pool of scientific ideas and skills. Now we are entering a new phase of widening and deepening relationships. This new phase can carry the American commitment to education to new heights of endeavor. It can also preserve the traditional freedom of higher education from excessive control. It can enlarge the horizons of equality of opportunity. It can maintain and even increase the margin for excellence. The challenge is to make certain it does all these things.

However this turns out, the scene of American higher education will continue to be marked by great variety, and this is one of its great strengths. The large and the small, the private and the public, the general and the specialized all add their share to overall excellence. The total system is extraordinarily flexible, decentralized, competitive—and productive. The new can be tried, the old tested with considerable skill and alacrity. Pluralism in higher education matches the pluralistic American society. The general test of higher education is not how much is done poorly, and some is; rather it is how much is done superbly, and a great deal is, to the nation's great benefit.

Changes Still to Come

But there are some problems still to be fully faced; and they are problems of consequence.

1. One is the improvement of undergraduate instruction in the university. The much-advertised conflict between teaching and research puts the problem the wrong way. The teaching of graduate students is so closely tied to research that if research is improved, graduate instruction is almost bound to be improved also. And the almost universal experience seems to be that federal research support has improved graduate instruction. At the undergraduate level, however, a "subtle discounting of the teaching process" has been aided and abetted.

The reasons for the general deterioration of undergraduate teaching are several. Teaching loads and student contact hours have been reduced. Faculty members are more frequently on leave or temporarily away from the campus; some are never more than temporarily on campus. More of the instruction falls to teachers who are not members of the regular faculty. The best graduate students prefer fellowships and research assistantships to teaching assistantships. Postdoctoral fellows who might fill the gap usually do not teach. Average class size has been increasing.

There seems to be a "point of no return" after which research, consulting, and graduate instruction become so absorbing that faculty efforts can no longer be concentrated on undergraduate instruction as they once were. This process has been going on for a long time; federal research funds have intensified it. As a consequence, undergraduate education in the large university is more likely to be acceptable than outstanding; educational policy from the undergraduate point of view is largely neglected.

Improvement of undergraduate instruction will require the solution of many subproblems: how to give adequate recognition to the teaching skill as well as to the research performance of the faculty; how to create a curriculum that serves the needs of the student as well as the research interests of the teacher; how to prepare the generalist as well as the specialist in an age of specialization looking for better generalizations; how to treat the individual student as a unique human being in the mass student body; how to make the university seem smaller even as it grows larger; how to establish a range of contact between faculty and students broader than the one-way route across the lectern or through the television screen; how to raise educational policy again to the forefront of faculty concerns.

2. Another major task is to create a more unified intellectual world. We need to make contact between the two, the three, the many cultures; to open channels of intelligent conversation across the disciplines and divisions; to close the gap between C. P. Snow's "Luddites" and scientists; to answer fragmentation with general theories and sensitivities. Even philosophy, which once was the hub of the intellectual universe, is now itself fragmented into such diverse specialities as mathematics and semantics. However, the physical sciences are drawing together as new discoveries create more basic general theories; the biological sciences may be pulled together in the process now going on; the social sciences might be unified around the study of organizations and the relations of individuals to and within them. Biochemistry and social psychology may come to be central focalizing fields. As knowledge is drawn together, if in fact it is, a faculty may again become a community of masters; but "a sense of the unity . . . of all knowledge" is still a very long way off.

3. A third problem is to relate administration more directly to individual faculty and students in the massive institution. We need to decentralize below the campus level to the operating agencies; to make the collective faculty a more vital, dynamic, progressive force as it now is only at the departmental level; to bridge the growing chasm between the department

that does the teaching and the institute that does the research, with the faculty member torn between; to make the old departments and divisions more compatible with the new divisions of knowledge; to make it possible for an institution to see itself in totality rather than just piecemeal and in the sweep of history rather than just at a moment of time; to bring an understanding of both internal and external realities to all those intimately related to the process, so that there may be greater understanding; to see to it that administration serves and stimulates rather than rules the institution, that it is expendable when necessary and flexible all the time; to assure that the university can do better what it does best; to solve the whole range of governmental problems within the university.

4. Additionally, there is the urgent issue of how to preserve a margin for excellence in a populist society, when more and more of the money is being spent on behalf of all of the people. The great university is of necessity elitist—the elite of merit—but it operates in an environment dedicated to an egalitarian philosophy. How may the contribution of the elite be made clear to the egalitarians, and how may an aristocracy of intellect justify itself to a democracy of all men? It was equality of opportunity, not equality *per se*, that animated the founding fathers and the progress of the American system; but the forces of populist equality have never been silent, the battle between Jeffersonianism and Jacksonianism never finally settled.

George Beadle, president of the University of Chicago, once implied that the very large American university (but not his own) might be like the dinosaur which "became extinct because he grew larger and larger and then sacrificed the evolutionary flexibility he needed to meet changing conditions"; its body became too large for its brain. David Riesman has said that the leading American universities are "directionless . . . as far as major innovations are concerned"; they have run out of foreign models to imitate; they have lost their "ferment." The fact is that they are not directionless; they have been moving in clear directions and with considerable speed. These directions, however, have not been set as much by the university's visions of its destiny as by the external environment, including the federal government, the foundations, and surrounding and sometimes engulfing industry.

But the really new problems of today and tomorrow may lend themselves less to solutions by external authority; they may be inherently problems for internal resolution. And these solutions, if they are to come, are more likely to emerge on the campuses of those old, private universities which have prided themselves on control of their own destiny, and on the totally new campuses of the state universities in America (and the new public universities in Britain). The university for the twenty-first century is more likely to emerge from these environments than from any others. Out of the pride of the old and the vacuum of the new may come the means to make undergraduate life more exciting, intellectual discourse more meaningful, administration more human. And perhaps there will arise a more dynamic demonstration of how excellence makes democracy more vital and its survival more assured. Then the contemporary American university may indeed rise to "the heights of the times." Then it may demonstrate that it has a mind as well as a body.

Notes

* *Daedalus* 93, no. 4 (Fall 1964): 1051–70. Reprinted by permission.

CHAPTER 9

In Transitu—
What We Might Learn from the Climacteric*

Daedalus *had another volume on higher education about ten years later (1975) than the one in which the prior essay had appeared; now with a title of* Toward an Uncertain Future. *The age of survival was coming to an end but was still fresh in all of our minds. I wrote about what we might have learned from the ten years since the prior* Daedalus *volume. The editor now noted that the past ten years had "had momentous consequences for American colleges and universities," and chose my essay to introduce the volume.*

Higher education in the United States has been passing through one of the great turning points in its history, a climacteric period when unfamiliar forces affected its development and its future was pointed in new directions.

After accepting but complaining in the 1950s about the "apathetic generation," higher education in the United States in the later years of the 1960s was swarmed over by the political activists, as had earlier happened in Latin America and Japan. After more than three centuries as a strong component of what Ruth Benedict once called the special American "magic" of education, higher education has seen confidence in its institutions and its leadership drop almost by one-half over the past six years according to the public opinion polls. After largesse from the horn of plenty had been poured on it after World War II, it recently entered the "new depression." After the labor market had for so long eagerly sought its graduates, it began around 1968 to declare them in oversupply. After a century of steady growth, doubling enrollments every ten or fifteen years, higher education now faces much slower growth and then at least a decade of enrollment decline in the 1980s. And science, the great genie and source of inspiration to our universities for a century, has now come to be seen by many, as by Hannah Arendt, as having reached the "point of negative returns."

Seldom has so great an American institution passed so quickly from its Golden Age to its Age of Survival.

There follow some reflections on higher education as it is passing through its greatest "time of troubles." What has this period of trauma revealed about higher education, about its several constituencies, about its environment? With what weaknesses and what strengths does it face its future? These reflections are in the form of generalizations, and there are, of course, many important exceptions in individual situations. Several of these reflections apply more particularly to research-oriented institutions than to others.

The Widening Gap with the Public

The public at large has clearly lost some confidence in higher education. This process of decay antedates the student unrest of the 1960s, which, however, both exacerbated it and brought it to general attention. The decline of agriculture in national and state affairs cut one most favorable base of support; heavy income and inheritance taxes another. Many institutions moved away from their regional or denominational focus, becoming instead national or even international institutions and losing contact in the process with some historic friends. Science was already, even before the 1960s, becoming suspect by some. I first noticed this new attitude toward science in public contacts at the time that the biological code of inheritance was being unraveled—a frightening prospect to many. The cost of higher education, as another negative factor, rose from 1 to 2.5 percent of the GNP in the 1960s; and other priorities began attracting public attention. Additionally, many citizens resented what they considered misuse of the campuses at their expense as taxpayers; many of them had not themselves had the advantage of a college education and this added to their resistance. Operating resources grew at a slower rate. Public bond issues for higher education failed to pass.

Higher education needs to develop, in fully legitimate ways, better contacts with the public. It cannot prosper in isolation. More concern for the health care of all individuals is one way to encourage favorable reactions; wider availability of off-campus instruction and cultural programs is another.

More attention needs to be paid to reactions as well as to actions. The political activism of the late 1960s, for example, seemed to disregard the possible reactions. The left inflamed the more powerful right to the detriment of higher education. The center did not seem to be sufficiently alert to this possibility, or this inevitability. In particular, freedom of speech on campus must be fully protected, not only from attacks from without but also from within. This is fundamental. It is, and it appears, most hypocritical to defend freedom in principle and then not to protect it in practice against its internal enemies, as has happened on occasion in recent times.

Generally, higher education needs to be less introspectively concerned with itself alone and more alert to its environment.

A House Partially Divided

Higher education lacks unity. This is a virtue, for it is a result of the great diversity of endeavors and it allows for many pluralistic initiatives. But it also has its costs. Higher education is now being folded, for state planning purposes, into "postsecondary education," and the several elements have so little in common that it is a forced and likely unhappy combination.

Within higher education, the interests of the expanding community colleges are not identical with those of the contracting comprehensive colleges. And private and public higher education, which lived in general harmony in times of expansion, are now potentially in greater conflict over tuition policies and state subsidies. When private institutions could hold their absolute numbers of students, they were less concerned with public competition than they are now when retention of these numbers is threatened. An agreement under which the private institutions support low public tuition in return for the public institutions support of state subsidies for the private segment may be possible; but it is not yet clear whether such an agreement, if arrived at within higher education, will gain legislative support. If it does not, then there will be an intensified conflict between the segments.

Higher education is only loosely held together. The coming struggle for survival may demonstrate how loosely.

The Vulnerability of Higher Education

Three centuries of almost constant growth in size—growth faster than that of the nation as a whole—and in importance led to an assumption of an assured place in the future. This feeling of certainty has been shaken, and not only by the apparent fickleness of public support and by the divisions within higher education.

Higher education, now that the percentage of the age group going to college has reached a plateau, is highly dependent for its enrollments on general demographic trends, and these have again proved their inconstant nature.

The possibility of public control has always existed, but the reality has never been exercised as it is today. At the same time that increasing attention was riveted on academic freedom for individuals, autonomy for the institution was being steadily eroded. The academy appears almost defenseless before the Leviathan.

Higher education has no monopoly on the services it supplies. More and more research is being carried on by industry and by government bureaus and by independent agencies like Rand and Brookings. They stand as an alternative. More teaching is taking place on the job, and in nonprofit and proprietary technical schools. The plant and the office and other elements of "postsecondary education" stand as alternatives. More service is provided by consulting firms and by professional associations. They also stand as alternatives. It is, all of a sudden, a more competitive world.

The mass media now place selected, and usually the more odd or extreme, aspects of college activities in every home. The college was once more safely dependent on more rounded knowledge held by fewer people.

The campus is open to the public, and thus open to the intrusions of off-campus activities and of "street people," to crime and to drug traffic.

Higher education has its soft underbelly. Accustomed to the advancement of criticism against others, it discovers itself also open to criticism. Take a case in point: The current national administration has been the subject of intense critical comment by many within higher education, for, among other things, not having done enough for women and minorities. This attack by the academics was from the high ground of principle. But the national administration pressed forward with strong programs of "affirmative action"; and higher education found itself not only on the defensive but situated on the low ground of its own abysmally inadequate record of consideration for women and minorities. The "unprogressive" administration thus demonstrated it was more progressive than the "progressive" academy; and the academy was set against itself internally. The forces of higher education found themselves in some disarray. Or take another case in point: Higher education spoke of its concern for equality of opportunity for all youth and particularly the very poor. But then it turned out that its concern, when it approached the federal Congress, was as much or more for institutional support for itself and subsidies for its existing middle-class students. It seemed to be placing its interests above its principles; and it lost some congressional friends.

Dependent on demography, dependent on the judgment of public authority, dependent upon the comparative performance of its competitors, dependent on the mercies of the mass media, open to the surrounding community, vulnerable to attacks against its own inadequacies, higher education today, as contrasted with a decade ago, is becoming more conscious that it is a subsystem within the total society and that it does not lead a life entirely of its own design.

Even Harvard: "For a long time, many, perhaps even most members of the Harvard community thought that 'it couldn't happen here.' They were wrong" (Committee of Fifteen, *Interim Report on the Causes of the Recent Crisis,* June 9, 1968). Even Harvard is vulnerable.

The Volatility of the Academic Community En Masse

Students usually come and go as individuals, pursuing their careers and their pleasures. Once in a while they coalesce into a "movement," only to have it later disappear almost without trace. This cyclical history was repeated again in the 1960s. This time, however, the cycle was unique in first the height of its peak in May 1970, and second the suddenness of its decline in the summer of 1970. But there seems to have been at work not only a cycle of short-term student political activity but also an underlying long-term trend toward amplification of intensity from one cycle to the next— from the 1930s to the 1960s, for example. When may the next wave come, for there surely will be one; and what special forms will it take, for it will be different; and will it also be further amplified?

Recently, such student activism as there is seems to be taking the form of guerrilla attacks by small groups bereft of mass support, not only in the United States but also in Britain and elsewhere. Hobsbawn has written of the "frenzied ultra-left gestures" indulged in by "a small activist minority." Is this the end of the last wave or the start of the next or something in between? In any event, the sense of permanent immunity from student political activism that marked so much of American higher education after World War II until the middle 1960s should be identified in the future, if it again manifests itself, only as self-delusion.

Faculty members in the late 1960s also became politically active beyond prior experience, usually in support of student-initiated causes. They lined up generally to the left of the electorate at large, but were more widely divided among themselves than any other major grouping of citizens. So cautious and conservative in the actions taken in committee meetings, they often displayed quite opposite characteristics in mass meetings. The chemistry of the situations was almost wildly different.

The academic world seems to be divided into two contrasting parts. First, there is the part of activity—the overwhelming part—that takes place in the classroom, the laboratory, the committee meeting, the study hall. In these environments, the emphasis is upon technical specialization, observance of the facts, careful analysis, individually arrived-at conclusions. And then there is the other part, so visible to the public when it is operative, that takes place in the highly charged atmosphere of mass meetings. There it is generalized issues, myths and rumors, slogans, and group actions that so often hold sway. The two parts seem to be so unrelated to each other— the one highly cognitive, the other highly affective. It can be confusing, and not only to the outside observer, that these two aspects of behavior of the same group of people can be so different not just in degree but even in kind. It appears like a split personality.

The academic mind, so dedicated to the eternal verities, is not immune to the current emotions; is not always superior to the nonacademic mind in its rationality.

The Fragility of Sentiments

Colleges and universities are (or were) systems of sentiments as well as administrative structures. They have often liked to view themselves over the centuries as "communities of scholars" bound together by an element of affection.

Much of this veil of tender fraternal attachment was torn away in recent years, particularly in the elite institutions which also were most likely to pride themselves on their sense of community. Volatility begot fragility. Faculties broke into left, right, and center. The bulk of the trustees moved to the right, the bulk of the faculty to the left—the former seeking to be "sound" and the latter to uphold doctrinal purity. Faculty members and students who were friends on the picket lines discovered they were more likely than not to be antagonists across the tables where changes in academic authority were being discussed. Administrators were rejected, like football coaches whose teams had lost too many games too recently. Alumni were alienated.

Cleavages between interests and along political lines had always existed, but they were largely ignored or even hidden. They were now revealed, and once revealed were hard to forget and to cover over again. The united community of old was, it turned out, made up in fact of strangers and even enemies, as well as of friends. Illusions were destroyed. Cautious suspicion often replaced the prior confidence almost automatically given.

With the bonds of sentiment so frayed, how could institutions show such strength, as I shall suggest later on that they have? The answer is: mutual survival. Faculty and students and administrators all need one another when the situation is looked at coldly. Each role is essential to the others. A more businesslike attachment of necessity came to replace, so very often, the earlier reality (or pretense) of affection.

An element of sentiment also earlier united the academic world and the external public. The campus was surrounded with an aura of dignity and even awe. This was shattered. The campus now looked to many on the outside like just another business, or trade union, or government bureau, and not too well run at that.

With the internal sense of community and the external vision of academic dignity both shaken and even destroyed, what remained? A more businesslike set of internal and external relationships calculated increasingly on the basis of costs and benefits, transaction by transaction. Higher education was located ever less on the Acropolis and ever more in the Agora.

The campus was found to consist of many constituencies, not just one gathered around revered Alma Mater; and the public of many interest groups, some not sure that higher education was worth what it cost economically and politically. Something of value was lost.

The Importance of Choosing the Right Time

With all these swirling events and developments, timing has become much more important than in more placid eras. What is just right at one time may be just wrong at another.

1. It was much easier to build a research university starting in 1957 just before Sputnik and the expanding demand for Ph.D.'s than in 1967, when federal R&D appropriations were turning down and the future market for Ph.D.'s was becoming less assured. Many made it starting in 1957; few, if any, in 1967.

2. It was far easier for a "comprehensive college" to "emerge" from teachers' college status when teachers were still in great demand than after the bottom fell out of that market.

3. The president with a long established prior record had a better chance of surviving 1968–70 than one who had just recently assumed office. The president who entered office in the fall of 1970 was an instant hero as student unrest on his campus disappeared as soon as he took office—*post hoc ergo propter hoc.*

4. The Miller bill to support the teaching of science came along too late in the 1960s to capitalize on the science wave. The Green bill to give institutional support so that more students could be absorbed came along too shortly before the time in the 1970s when colleges could absorb more students than there were around.

5. Higher education is getting more tenured-in just as student interests are becoming more volatile. Either development would be easier to handle by itself.

6. The Ph.D. candidate in 1960 could not miss; one in 1980 will be lucky to make a hit. Higher education expanded its capacity to train Ph.D.'s too greatly in the 1960s and now runs the danger of contracting it too severely in the centers of highest quality. Two maladjustments may well have been accomplished within the course of two decades.

7. A reform that might succeed in one year might fail the next. Generally, the academic and governmental reforms of the late 1960s have left little residue in the early 1970s. The "great reforms," beyond the normal

changes that would have taken place anyway, have had a lasting effect on the totality of higher education probably in the range of plus or minus one percent.

The conditions of the present are not so likely to continue into the future as once seemed to be the case. Consequently, both more advance consideration and more flexibility are in order. Risk and uncertainty mark the situation. It is more of a time for gamblers or astrologers or Pareto's "foxes." A homogenized view of time—that any one time is as good as any other—no longer holds.

The Strength of the Individual Institutions

Few colleges, and no universities, have been lost as higher education rounded all the recent sharp turns in circumstances at such high speeds, and these few colleges have represented an almost infinitesimal percentage of total enrollments. Many institutions had financial deficits in 1968–70; almost none by 1972–74. The reversal was remarkable, considering what was required. Many institutions that were increasing expenditures per student at a rate of the cost of living plus 5 percent per year in the 1960s went to plus 1 percent or even minus 1 percent in the early 1970s. New dispute–settlement mechanisms were introduced. Faculty and students and administrators united, or at least drew together, against external opposition. As a consequence, institutions generally became more stable internally, not less. Campus after campus made major rearrangements in its curricula and its faculty resources to reflect the new conditions of the job market and the new interests of students.

Great survival capacity and underlying institutional stability have been demonstrated in the face of the greatest series of more or less simultaneous shocks to higher education in American history.

Institutions of higher education and their component parts seem to behave more responsibly and more rationally under external attacks than their record in handling internal conflicts might imply. Under the circumstances of internecine strife, they may seem to be falling rapidly apart, as in the late 1960s; under the conditions of reduced support or even attack from outside, they seem to be solidly structured, as in the early 1970s. This, of course, does not distinguish them from many other types of institutions, but it does help explain the appearances of disintegration in the late sixties and the reality of consolidation in the early seventies.

A High Capacity for Progressive Renewal?

Higher education in the United States has a remarkable historical record of constructive adaptation to changing circumstances. In response to science and industry, the classical college became the modern university. The community college movement was an innovative reaction to the transition from mass-access higher education to universal access. The G.I. rush was accommodated most successfully. The answer to Sputnik was a triumphant one. The "tidal wave" of students was accepted without loss of quality.

Now new challenges are being faced—from a strong base of past accomplishments, and of intellectual and administrative resources. In retrospect, from the vantage point of the year 2000, the challenges may once again have been met and it may come to appear that, just as the early 1960s were marked by greater euphoria than subsequent circumstances warranted, the early 1970s were marked by too great a despondency. The moods of higher education seem to swing farther up and farther down than reality fully warrants. And it may turn out to be easier to accept pleasant surprises in the 1970s and beyond, than it was the unpleasant surprises of the latter half of the 1960s.

We are not yet, however, at the year 2000. And higher education must now summon its many strengths to demonstrate once again, as it has so often in the past, that it is capable of self-renewal. It needs to become less backward-looking and defensive in its posture, and more forward-looking and constructive; to do less running in the face of unfriendly forces and to challenge them aggressively instead; to stop groping for solutions and to decide on new thrusts; to spend less time regrouping for the sake of survival and to pay more attention to renewed progress.

Notes

* *Daedalus* 104, no. 1 (Winter 1975): 1–7. Reprinted by permission.

CHAPTER 10

Ex Post—
The Climacteric in Review*

The University of Washington, where I had once been a young faculty member, asked me to return to give the Walker-Ames Lecture and to look back on what had happened, 1960 to 1980, as I then saw it. If I had been in a "plus" mood in 1964 and a "minus" mood in 1975, I was by now (1980) looking at the "pluses" and the "minuses." I still see the same pluses and the same minuses now ten years later.

Higher education in the United States has just completed a very distinctive period in its history of three and one-half centuries. The past twenty years have been both its Golden Age but also its Age of Survival. Enrollments (headcount) quadrupled from three million to twelve million. If history were to be measured in terms of enrollment years of students, then more than half of the life of higher education in this nation has been experienced in the past two decades. If history were to be measured in terms of research effort, the same observation would hold. Growth in enrollments and in research activity were part of the story but so also were the student revolts and the series of recessions following the OPEC price shocks. What have we learned from these experiences, both good and bad? I should like to reply to this question from the viewpoint of a participant-observer over the period and going back into earlier years as well.

1. The Great Flexibility of the System. The system has responded to the great emphasis on research after Sputnik, to the transition for potential students from mass-access to universal-access education, to the demands of new vocations and occupations, to the interests of new types of students— in each case, rapidly and effectively. It did this while each type of institution and often each individual institution remained much as it was, remained remarkably unchanged, kept its functions, and maintained its ethos. Research universities did not change in kind—only in degree, as with community, comprehensive, and liberal arts colleges. The size and the number of institutions of each type grew, or occasionally contracted, but the central characters of individual institutions continued constant. The Harvard of 1980 was still the Harvard of 1960; Fresno City College was still Fresno City College; Slippery Rock State College was still Slippery

Rock State College; Oberlin was still Oberlin. Yet three revolutions had taken place: the research revolution, the access revolution, and the occupational revolution.

The system was more flexible than its individual constituent parts. When the national research effort exploded by 80 times from 1940 to the middle 1960s,[1] the research universities responded; when universal access was provided as a matter of public policy—first in California in 1960 in the Master Plan—the community colleges responded; when new occupations required college preparation, the comprehensive colleges (many originally teachers' colleges) added more specialties in engineering, business administration, nursing, and almost countless other fields—they remained occupationally oriented but became more comprehensive. When more adults and more part-time students participated, the community colleges and the comprehensive colleges were ready to receive them. At a more specific level, when Protestant fundamentalism underwent a renaissance, as it has recently, the Protestant fundamentalist colleges, like Oral Roberts University and Bob Jones University, were there to accommodate it.

Diversity is the secret to this flexibility. In the United States, a whole series of types of institutions has been created over the centuries by private initiatives and by actions of federal, state, and local governments. No one planned it this way. But contrast the American situation with that in some European and non-European nations where there is only one accepted model—the research university. New models have been attempted but they have either failed to gain acceptance or they have become more and more like the old university model (as have the colleges of advanced technology—the CATS, in England).[2] Or, the old universities have tried to absorb the new functions and the new students, as in Italy, and have ended up in internal chaos and their nations with a mismatch between the degrees given and the actual needs of the labor market. The historic American policy of "any person, any study"[3] (and it might be added "any place" and "any auspices") has served the nation well. It is clearly better in the modern world to have several models to utilize as needed than only one. Japan, Australia, and Canada most closely, among industrialized nations, approximate the American model.

2. The Remarkable Ability of the System to Preserve Quality. High school test scores, as is well known, have gone down steadily and significantly for two decades. Many reasons are given for this[4]—the competition of TV and of street life for student attention, the lessened emphasis in the curriculum on basic skills, the reduction in parental care and discipline, the alleged decline of the work ethic generally, new elements in the changing student population taking the tests (including members of minority groups), the loosening of discipline in the schools, social turbulence in the 1960s and

1970s, and less motivation to learn. There are many reasons, and they apply almost across the board—from the ghettos of New York City to Westchester County.

Test scores out of college have also gone down but to a lesser degree. This means that the colleges have at least maintained their "value added," that colleges have added at least as much value as before but on a lower base.[5] How can this be? College students also watch TV, have access to street life, are subject to less parental and institutional discipline, may reflect the alleged decline in the national work ethic, are more composed of persons from lower-income families and minority backgrounds, and experienced the turbulence of the 1960s and 1970s. Yet all of these influences which have affected the decline at the high school level do not seem to have had the same impact on value added at the college level. The colleges seem to have been immune to these great social forces. Why?

I have some opinions which are nothing more than that; no proof. Accreditation, which is the approved institutional effort to assure quality, is not the cause; it affects few institutions and these only marginally. The introduction of more remedial work in basic skills almost certainly has helped some students. I would credit three other sources, however, for the good record under the circumstances. First, there is something to be said for the concept of "academic standards" and for the devotion of many faculty members to their maintenance. Second, students in college have been provided with better libraries, better laboratory equipment, and better facilities generally. Real expenditures per student on instruction rose about 20 percent from the average of the 1960s to 1980 (most of the rise taking place in the 1960s) and perhaps by as much as 50 percent from the start of the 1960s to 1980.[6] Much of this increase was accounted for by higher real salaries for faculty members. But many colleges were clearly more adequate places for study in 1980 than in 1960. Third, and I think most important, the colleges are in a much more competitive environment than the high schools. Colleges compete with each other in a way that high schools do not. The latter have their local monopolies in terms of student attendance but the colleges do not. There is not only competition at the college level among institutions, but also within colleges and universities between departments and in some places among faculty members for students, research grants, and prestige. College students also compete with each other in order to get into graduate school or to obtain preferred jobs in a way that high school students do not generally compete with each other to get into college or to get jobs. The high school diploma is enough to get into some colleges under a policy of universal access, and the diploma itself (not the grades associated with it) is the important document in obtaining most jobs directly out of high school. Neither the college market nor the job market is as selective and as sophisticated out of high school as out of college. The whip of competition has been on the backs of the colleges and their students as it has not been on the high schools and most of their students.

It should be noted, however, in all fairness, that the colleges have an easier assignment than the high schools. Attendance is voluntary, not compulsory. As a consequence, colleges draw the more academically talented, socially disciplined, and highly motivated young persons. Their students are also older and more responsible for their own conduct. Additionally, high schools often encompass more social conflict, by their very location and their use to advance integration, than do colleges. Also, it may be that college teaching has greater rewards than high school teaching and draws abler people into it; and that college administrators have more freedom and prestige, which may also draw abler people into these positions.

3. The Now-Dominant Influence of Changing Demographics. Higher education historically has been devoted to high thought and to training for advanced skills but now dances to the tune of base demographics as never before. It responds not just to the instructions of the mind but also to the forces that determine the net fertility rate. What made the Golden Age so golden was mostly demographic growth. The role of demography was earlier evident in time of war, as in the decline in student numbers during World War II and in the rise during the GI rush afterward; but was not so insistently evident in times of peace. The number of students in higher education rose from 10 in 1638 (all at Harvard) to about 50,000 in 1870; or at less than 250 per year on the average. From 1870 to 1960 there was generally steady growth at a compound rate of 5 percent a year. Then came the explosion with almost a million more students in a single year (1975).[7] This explosion was the result of the "baby boom" after World War II, the shift from mass to universal access to higher education, and the great labor market demand for teachers and technicians of all sorts with a resultant high rate of return on the investment in a college education (it peaked in the late 1960s).

Now we face a twenty-five percent decline over the next twenty years in the size of the traditional college-going age cohort. After that, the trends are open to almost unbounded speculation. It is highly unlikely, however, that there will ever again be over three centuries the slow and then moderate but always quite steady growth as from 1636 to 1960—aside from times of war. Pressing demographic considerations are likely here to stay as unwelcome guests for the possible future—no more smoothly rising curves. At least for the final forty years of this century, demographic shifts will have played a dominant role.

The demographic explosion of the Golden Age had many consequences. An additional eleven hundred (net) campuses were established. They were mainly community colleges (over six hundred), and community college enrollment, a minor component in 1940, came to account for one-third of the total. The size of the average campus of all types taken together doubled. The comprehensive colleges grew especially rapidly, as they became more comprehensive in their offerings.

The size of the national professoriate almost tripled. Promotions were easier. Real incomes rose faster than for the national employed labor force as a whole. Mobility of faculty members among institutions increased in a seller's market. Capacity to produce Ph.D.'s more than tripled. The number of administrators also almost tripled, and they also got their promotions more readily.[8] It was a time of euphoria in the academic world. All this began to be reversed in the later 1970s. But while fast growth lasted, the staffs in higher education never had it so good. Now they think they have never felt so bad since the growth has stopped.

Academic programs were greatly affected. It was easier to open up new academic fields such as the environmental sciences; to introduce new occupational specialties such as computer programming; to undertake academic experiments such as cluster colleges; and to balance faculty–student ratios as new faculty were added in areas where these ratios were low; and thus it was easier to get rough internal equity and to offset accumulated discrepancies.

Impacts on the labor market were substantial. Gradually the supply of graduates caught up with the enhanced demand. The comparative monetary value of a college degree for a time fell in relation to a high school degree. The rate of return on the investment in a college education went down by about one-third before rising again. A huge deluge of college graduates into the labor market was created. Within this deluge of graduates there was intense competition, reduced chances for promotion, increased occupational frustrations, and, incidentally, a heightened demand for additional higher education. The generation that was crowded in the elementary schools, in the secondary schools, and in tertiary education was now crowded in the labor market. Some day it will crowd the ranks of retirees and then the cemeteries. Current undergraduates seeing the toughened competition in the labor market have turned to more vocational courses. The proportion of students with professional school majors rose by over 50 percent between 1969 and 1975; and majors in the social sciences and humanities declined proportionately by 50 percent.[9]

In terms of financing, public sources of funds became more important and public control more intensified. Total funds spent on higher education rose from about 1 percent of GNP in 1960 to over 2 percent in 1980, with great expansion efforts made by colleges and universities in the process of doubling their comparative share of the nation's output of goods and services. Also, and of great importance, state support of higher education was generally based on average costs per student. As student numbers rose on each campus, marginal costs were less than average costs. Marginal costs in the short-run in a period of expansion are about 70 to 80 percent of average costs as existing overhead is spread over more students. The colleges were better off. They made a "profit" on each student added. This was the main source for improvements in real increases in salaries for faculty members and in facilities for students. Federal student aid funds, also, led to enrichment of programs in some colleges.

Growth was not neutral in its impacts. The structure of the total system changed rapidly, reflecting the new demands placed upon it; it became more compatible with the needs of the surrounding society. Faculty members and administrators were, for a time, much better off. Academic program adjustments were facilitated. The labor market became more competitive for persons with high-level skills. Students shifted their academic programs in response. Colleges got more public money and more public control. Campuses became larger and more impersonal in nature. Growth generally enriched the academic community, but there were costs along the way— particularly in the loss of a sense of community on many campuses and in the intensification of public control and supervision.

The student enrollment cycle sets into motion other cycles that are more exaggerated than the student cycle and not in consonance with it. The actual student cycle rose for twenty years (1960–80) and now stabilizes or declines for twenty years (1980–2000). But the faculty cycle set into motion runs about forty years in length from new hires to retirements. The building cycle runs about twenty-five years before major repairs and perhaps fifty years before replacement. The top year for student enrollments was 1975. The faculty then hired will retire in 2015; the buildings then dedicated may need renovation or replacement in 2025. Demographic fluctuations in student numbers set into motion other fluctuations that complicate planning, financing, and administering higher education.

In the 1950s, as the "tidal wave" of students came closer, it was common in academic circles, particularly in Great Britain but also the United States and Canada, to say that "bigger means worse." As it actually turned out, "bigger" generally meant "better"! Growth has been the American way of life, not only on Main Street but also along College Drive and University Avenue; not only for Babbitt but also for Mr. Chips. Now growth has ended.

4. The Failure of Intended Internally Originated Academic Structural Changes.[10] The two great periods of academic change in American higher education were after the Civil War, with the land-grant movement, and the modernizing efforts of Eliot at Harvard, White at Cornell, Gilman at Johns Hopkins, and others, and in the 1960s. In between there were minor change efforts mostly aimed at a return to "general education," as under Lowell at Harvard. The 1870s and the 1960s had at least two things in common—a spurt of growth in enrollments that made additions of new faculty and new programs much easier, and new surges forward in national efforts in which higher education could participate.

The national efforts in the 1870s were to industrialize rapidly and to settle the whole continental United States, which meant new agricultural crops in new areas. Higher education became a source of science and technology, of engineers and farm agents, going far beyond the earlier classical education for the historic professions of teaching, medicine, the law, and the ministry. The national efforts in the 1960s were to advance science and technology after Sputnik and to provide more equality of opportunity for members of lower-income groups and for minorities and for women. Higher education intensified its emphasis on science and technology, and, within the system as a whole, moved from mass access to universal access in higher education and opened up several professional fields to minorities and women. These national efforts in the 1870s and 1960s were generally successful, least so in the area of provision of greater equality of opportunity in the 1960s; and higher education at both times played a constructive role.

The internal academic changes that accompanied these forward movements were generally fruitful after the Civil War but generally not in the 1960s. I note this latter fact with sadness.[11] I had high hopes for academically inspired changes and participated actively in their promotion, particularly, as president of the University of California, in the creation of the Santa Cruz campus, about which Gerald Grant and David Riesman once wrote that "no university . . . has achieved a more vibrant pluralism in the forms of intellectual, social, and aesthetic experiences for undergraduates";[12] and as chairman of the Carnegie Commission and later the Carnegie Council on Higher Education, which made so many proposals for academic changes, especially in a report entitled *Less Time, More Options.*[13] I also watched the failure of the Tussman and Strawberry College experiments at Berkeley and, as a member of the governing board, watched the only partially effective efforts to maintain and restore the honors program at Swarthmore—the great innovation of Frank Aydelotte in the 1920s. I know of no inventory of intentional academic changes of the 1960s that shows their survival rate,[14] but I would guess that in the vicinity of 90 percent were discontinued or so attenuated as to disappoint their authors.

Why? The essential conservatism of faculty members about their own affairs is certainly one reason. This is abetted by the tendency to rely on consensus in making decisions and on the opinions of the older members of any academic group. Also, there are no rewards to the faculty members who seek academic innovation, only the burden of long, drawn out, and often disappointing consultation. Most academic reforms are in fact initiated by students, who are notoriously inconstant in their efforts, partly because of their rapid turnover and their responsiveness to current fads; and by administrators who are usually, except in new endeavors, such as a new campus, restrained by convention and by faculty committees from participating actively in academic affairs. Also, adaptations over past decades and centuries may well have found the best way of doing things, the tried and true. More fundamentally, there often may be no best way, only different ways.[15] Half a dozen different ways may be equally effective or ineffective, so there is no strong argument for change. The big research university is particularly impervious to structural changes.

But I think there are three more reasons why the attempted changes of the 1960s largely failed. Many changes at that time in American history attracted faculty members and students who, by their nature—often disaffected and disenchanted as they were with academic life—would not let anything work well, particularly somebody else's attempted reform. Reforms were killed by the customers of reform; reforms were stung to death by the hornets they attracted. The reforms of the 1870s, by contrast, attracted the upwardly mobile children of farmers and immigrants, not the sliders down the meritocratic pyramid of success that had been built up by the 1960s.

Another reason is that the changes of the 1960s moved mostly in directions that most faculty members by and large opposed. They often called for more time, often much more time, spent with students, and a broader coverage of subject matters in "integrated" programs. The changes of the 1870s moved in ways many faculty members (but by no means all) liked— toward specialized courses, specialized and self-governing departments, graduate work, student electives, research.[16] The new faculty members and particularly the new scientists were avid supporters even though the older classicists kicked and screamed all the way. The changes of the 1870s had a central theme—enhancement of expertise, science, and scholarship. The attempted changes of the 1960s were oriented not so much toward the advancement of knowledge but more toward improved environments for students, usually in ways that cost faculty members in time and attention and emotion. Faculty members at Santa Cruz often complained of how time was taken from their research and how their emotions were drained by contact with students. The changes of the 1870s liberated faculty members; the changes advanced in the 1960s tied them down to their offices and to their undergraduate students. The changes of the 1870s liberated faculty members from *in loco parentis* and those of the 1960s enslaved them again. It was the students of the 1960s who wanted *in loco parentis* in terms of personal attention but hated it in terms of impersonal rules enforced by the dean of students—the form it came to take after the 1870s.

The one most successful academic change advocated by the Carnegie Commission, which coined the phrase and argued its merits, was the "stopout." "Stop-outs" were troublesome to registrars and housing supervisors but not to faculty.

The academic changes of the 1960s originated in student bull-sessions and in the minds and hearts of administrators who listened to students; they died in the faculty clubs. An exception was the reform at MIT which brought undergraduate students into participation with faculty members on research projects. This reform originated with faculty members and paralleled faculty interests.

An additional reason for the differences between the 1870s and the 1960s was that the national thrusts of the 1870s required fundamental academic changes, specifically the creation of the modern university with its emphasis on research and occupational training. The national thrusts of the 1960s, however, could be accommodated within the existing structures; they did not require such great changes. Additionally, presidents, who are the great change agents, had much more power in the 1870s than in the 1960s, and faculties much less.

Some changes of the 1960s were based not on academic but on political concerns, and were forced into practice by student pressure, such as black studies and women's studies. White, male faculty members generally never liked them; in fact, barely tolerated them. Born in the passion of the student activists, they have mostly withered or at least wilted in the cold embrace of faculty committees.

I introduced this section with the phrase "intended internally originated academic structural change" and have suggested that the attempted reform movement was a flame that burned brightly for a while and then flickered out, its extinction mourned by only a few. I count myself among those few. But there were academic changes on a major scale that originated in the marketplace external to educational policy considerations; and these "popular reforms" succeeded where the "telic" reforms failed.[17] These changes consisted of the fundamental shift from liberal to vocational studies, and, within vocational studies, from one field to another—with engineering, for example, going up and down like a yo-yo. Business administration and the paramedical specialties were the great gainers. The composition of overall instructional effort must have changed by at least one-third over two decades. This was a revolution of major proportions in what faculty members taught, what students studied, what librarians bought, which departments faded or grew in importance, what kinds of classrooms and laboratories were built and where they were located on campus. In American higher education, changes influenced by the market are accepted in a way that reforms originating in concerns for educational policy are not. An appropriate emblem for the American college might be the traditional open book, but an open book lying on a sales counter.[18]

The Golden Age, because of growth, was a comparatively favorable period for academic idealism; some basic improvements could then have been made; but the opportunities were largely missed.

5. Limits to the Use of the College and University as a Direct Instrument of Social Reform. Colleges and universities throughout American history have been looked upon as instruments of social reform. Harvard was founded in part to "advance *learning* and perpetuate it to Posterity; dreading to leave an illiterate Ministry to the Churches, when our present Ministers shall lie in the Dust."[19] In the 1960s and 1970s there were two major efforts to use the university deliberately to change society.

One such effort was by the federal government to increase equality of opportunity. This was done, in part, by offering grants to college students based upon their comparative ability to pay and, in part, by forcing colleges and universities to change their policies to admit more minorities and women, particularly into professional schools, and to employ more minorities and women as faculty members. Many more minorities and women have attended institutions of higher education but mostly from the higher income groups. Progress in increasing attendance from low-income groups has been meager. (See table 1.) It has been easier to change policies and practices and preferences that make distinctions on the basis on sex and race than those that distinguish based on income group. Attendance can be made more possible, but the choice to attend remains voluntary; and developed academic ability and interest is not equally distributed across income groups.[20]

In terms of participation of minorities and women at the faculty level, again progress has been slow. The, as yet, small sizes of the pools of trained persons is one reason; so also the late start of the federal government after the massive new hiring of the 1960s was past. Another reason is the difficulty governmental agencies have in challenging the autonomy of universities and their meritocratic standards; and prejudice on campus too may play a role. The hope that many of us had that higher education by 1976 would draw equal proportions within ability groups regardless of family income has been disappointed.[21] This remains a still remote but still achievable goal. And, in my judgment, more of the progress that has been made has been because of the new temper of the times and the aroused consciences of the academic community and less because of direct federal intervention.

All those federal billions of dollars in student aid did more to raise college attendance than to change its composition in terms of source of students by the level of their family income. It may have had a good political effect, however, by indicating public concern for and commitment to equality of opportunity; and by creating a situation where lack of attendance was more a matter of choice than of necessity. It also brought more money into higher education. It also subsidized middle-income hedonism by reducing financial burdens on middle-income parents.

The second effort was by students with some faculty support. It sought to use the campus as a staging ground to "reconstitute" society through

TABLE 1

Changing Enrollment Patterns, 1960–79

	1960	1979
Women		
Percentage of undergraduate enrollment	38.0[a]	51.3[b]
Percentage of graduate enrollment	29.0[a]	47.0[b]
Percentage of faculty and other professional staff	22.0[c]	24.8 (1978)[d]
Minorities		
Percentage of undergraduate enrollment	6.6[e]*	13.0 (1978)[f]
Percentage of graduate and professional enrollment	6.1[e]*	5.8 (Black only; 1978)[f]
Percentage of faculty (1960 and 1977)	N.A.	8.8[g]
Black	3+[h]	4.4[g]
Asian	N.A.	2.6[g]
Hispanic	N.A.	1.5[g]
Native American	N.A.	0.2[g]
Percentage of total population (1960 and 1977)		
Black	10.5[i]	11.6[i]
Asian	0.6[i]	1.4 (1980)[j]
Hispanic	N.A.	5.3[k]
Native American	0.3[i]	0.6 (1980)[j]
Low-income students		
Percentage of students from families in bottom one-fifth of national income distribution	8.7[l]	14.0[m]

* Includes Black, Asian, and Native American

Sources:

a. National Center for Education Statistics, *Projections of Education Statistics to 1975–76* (Washington, DC: U.S. Government Printing Office, 1966), tables 11 and 12.

b. National Center for Education Statistics, *Opening Fall Enrollment 1979* (Washington, DC, unpublished data, 1980).

c. Calculated from National Center for Education Statistics, *Digest of Educational Statistics, 1968* (Washington, DC: U.S. Government Printing Office, 1968), table 100.

d. Digest of Education Statistics, 1979, 101. Women constituted 25.9 percent of full-time instructional faculty in 1979–80. (National Center for Education Statistics, "Women Faculty Still Lag in Salary and Tenure for the 1979–80 Academic Year," Early Release, NCES 80-342.)

e. United States Census of Population, 1960, Subject Reports, *School Enrollment,* Final Report PC(2)-5A.

f. Institute for the Study of Educational Policy, *Equal Educational Opportunity,* Fourth Status Report, Preliminary Draft, September 1980.

g. "Higher Education Staff Information—EEO-6," Report of the U.S. Equal Employment Opportunity Commission, 1977.

h. Institute for the Study of Educational Policy, *Affirmative Action for Blacks in Higher Education: A Report* (Washington, DC: Howard University, 1978), 25.

i. *Statistical Abstract of the United States, 1979* (Washington, DC: U.S. Government Printing Office, 1979).

j. *Statistical Abstract of the United States, 1986* (Washington, DC: U.S. Government Printing Office, 1986), table 32.

k. U.S. Bureau of the Census, *Current Population Reports,* series P-20, no. 329, "Persons of Spanish Origin in the United States, March 1977" (Washington, DC: U.S. Government Printing Office, September 1978), table B.

l. U.S. Bureau of the Census, *Current Population Reports,* series P-20, no. 183, "Characteristics of Students and Their Colleges, October 1966" (Washington, DC: U.S. Government Printing Office, 1969), table 2; and *Current Population Reports,* series P-60, no. 105, "Money Income in 1975 of Families and Persons in the United States" (Washington, DC: U.S. Government Printing Office, 1977), table 13.

m. U.S. Bureau of the Census, *Current Population Reports,* series P-20, no. 346, "Population Characteristics: School Enrollment—Social and Economic Characteristics of Students: October 1978" (Washington, DC: U.S. Government Printing Office, October 1979), table 25; and *Current Population Reports,* series P-20, no. 120, table 5.

political discussion, demonstration, and protest. The major targets were racial injustice and the Vietnam war, but also environmental pollution and nuclear power, among others. In no case did the students initiate these issues; they did, however, draw each issue more insistently to national attention. In my judgment, the student use of the colleges and universities was largely ineffective. The blacks quickly rejected the proffered leadership of their movement by the middle-class whites on campus, thus beginning a new form of separatism. The federal government, and particularly President Nixon, adroitly used student protest as one way of temporarily increasing acceptance of continuation of the Vietnam war through encouraging the backlash of public opinion against the students. And, in any event, students abruptly abandoned their efforts in the summer and fall of 1970. The student effort was divisive on campus and off; and costly in morale internally and in support externally. I believe that the student effort was not bound inherently to be so ineffective. It was ineffective because of excessive and alienating rhetoric and the occasional use of force. A more reasoned, persuasive approach might have worked. Rage, however understandable, had its costs. The student lobbies of the 1970s have, by way of comparison, been effective.

Higher education, however, does reform, or at least change, society indirectly in many ways. New knowledge is one of the great moving forces in our society. The more education that people have, the more liberal their attitudes are on issues such as race, sex practices, and abortion; the more likely they are to be well informed about public issues and to vote in elections; the more likely they are to take better care of their health, to act prudently as investors, to purchase effectively as consumers; and the more likely they are to accept and to adapt to change.[22] Styles of life are affected. The counterculture did not originate on campus, but it was avidly embraced there and distributed from there in the writings of faculty members and the actions of students and graduates. The "new breed," as Dan Yankelovich identifies it, is essentially defined by acceptance of the counterculture and now constitutes, it is said, about half of the American population as against the largely noncollege "old breed."[23]

The direct political use of the university as an instrument of social reform has had a recent record, depending on source, purpose, and methods, that has ranged from partially effective to counterproductive. The academic activities of institutions of higher education is society, on the other hand, have had many fundamental long-term consequences. The presence of the university carrying out its normal functions changes society fundamentally; but the attempted manipulation of the university, for the sake of specific political reforms, changes the university for the worse more than it changes society for the better.

6. *Shifts at the Level of Governance.* One of the great themes of the student (and left-wing faculty) revolts of the late 1960s and early 1970s was to "reconstitute" the university internally and particularly in the direction of "participatory democracy." This intended, in particular, more of a role for activist students and for junior faculty members in governance. "All power to the people" meant not to society in general and to its elected representatives in particular, but to the then-dissident groups. What actually happened within the several layers of governance during the crisis period from 1960 to 1980?

Student interest in formal governance rose and fell very quickly; it did not endure. Some boards of trustees added students to their memberships but with little net impact; so also with faculty committees. The big radical student impact has been, instead, at the informal level, particularly in the direction of Marcuse's "repressive tolerance"[24]—that there should be no tolerance for people with whom you disagree. This had meant, in practice, more faculty caution in classroom discussions and fewer right-wing speakers invited on campus where intensely committed groups may cause trouble. Conservative boards of trustees once limited, by rule, access to speakers on the far left (for example, Communists); now small groups of students and their faculty supporters limit, in practice, access to speakers on the far right. Limitations on free speech have shifted from sources on the right to the left. Another informal student impact has been on the declining acceptance of administrative but also of faculty authority.

Faculty interest in governance, by contrast, had remained quite constant, with one major exception. By and large, faculties have not sought membership on boards of trustees. They have insisted instead on extension of "shared governance," particularly in academic affairs, which has meant consultation in many areas of full control in a few. This has been the historic AAUP approach. The major exception has been the introduction of collective bargaining, which now covers about 32 percent of the professoriate in about 31 percent of the institutions, mostly community and state colleges. Collective bargaining has essentially meant more academic participation in decision making in the less elite academic institutions via unions but along the lines already practiced by academic senates in the more elite institutions. The biggest impact of all has been where union representatives are elected to boards of trustees and very occasionally come to constitute a majority of board members, as in a few community colleges.

Faculties, by and large, have proven themselves less willing to defend themselves against attacks from the internal left than from the external right, and more accepting of attacks on presidents than on themselves.

Presidents, in the 1960s and 1970s, were shown to be vulnerable to the assaults of protest groups—to be "emperors who had no clothes." Many other forces have also reduced their former authority.

Boards of trustees were much less affected than presidents by internal campus events, but the rise of coordination at the state level has diluted their authority in many public institutions.

The federal government demonstrated over this period that its interests in higher education are instrumental and rise and fall and change—now in research, then in greater economic equality in student access, and then again in affirmative action at the faculty and staff levels. State support, by contrast, has been much more constant and committed across the board. Legislatures also, by and large and even surprisingly and remarkably, held steady during the period of student protests, passing few antagonistic laws and maintaining fiscal support even as public opinion became largely critical. State legislatures proved to be the most constant sources of support and the greatest centers of stability with much rhetoric but little adverse action. Governors varied greatly—some protecting higher education, some attacking. Overall, governors, in the area of public higher education, have become the one most dominant force, but with differing and changing agendas. They have become the new persons of power in public higher education.

More campuses now fall within systems of coordination. In the public arena, 70 percent of all students are on campuses within systems.

The record shows that the greater forces for stability in governance, in the midst of a crisis period, were legislatures, boards of trustees and presidents; and the greater forces for instability were students, left-oriented faculty, and public opinion; with governors and faculties in their entirety having mixed records. The record also shows that, in terms of power, students first gained some power and then used it little at the formal level, but gained substantially at the informal level; that faculties made evolutionary gains in shared governance; that presidents lost; that boards in many public institutions lost to coordinating mechanisms; and that coordinating mechanisms and governors gained over the period.

What has been the result of all the battles won and lost, in addition to shifts in the loci of power and influence? More formal rules, certainly, but there were always a good many and all of society is moving that way. More internal and external reports and consultations, but, again, this is a universal trend. A lessened sense of campus community and institutional autonomy but, here again, many institutions are becoming more consolidated. A more conservative, cumbersome, time-consuming system of governance. It is ironical that "participatory democracy," meaning that all the "people" should be consulted, which was supposed to result in more radical decisions, in more speedy and more responsive actions, has meant, instead, more veto groups, less action, more commitment to the status quo—the status quo is the only solution that cannot be vetoed. Instead of releasing the pent-up energy of the masses, it has confirmed the power of special interest groups to stop changes they do not like.

The most serious consequences of the governance changes for the continued dynamics of American higher education are, I believe, the following:

The loss of tolerance toward the presentation of controversial issues in the classrooms and on campus platforms; and more timidity in the face of group pressure

Weakened administrative leadership

Less autonomy on campus in many public institutions

Overall it was discovered, or at least rediscovered, that formal arrangements in governance, such as students on boards of trustees and on faculty committees, or mechanisms for supra-campus coordination, or collective bargaining by faculty, are only a part of the dynamics of governance.

The second leg of the three-legged stool of governance is attitudes, such as the degree of tolerance for the opinions of others and the comparative respect for authority. The spirit that animates conduct, the mentalities that inform approaches to problems, can turn the same system of formal governance from a low level of Paradise to an advanced level of the Inferno.

The third leg is the informal system of decision making at the individual level. Most decisions are really made outside the formal system of governance; they are made in more informal, less bureaucratic ways. The more visible superstructure of governance is less important than the less visible infrastructure in terms of number (and often also in importance) of decisions made. Most decisions about teaching, curriculum, research topics and methods, and amount and form of public service are made by individual faculty members. Most decisions made about majors selected, courses taken, time spent on study are made by individual students. Looking only at what is happening to the formal superstructure of governance is looking only at a part of the whole; important, but not all that decisive. What are faculty members deciding individually? How are students voting with their feet?

In looking at the three layers of governance, I have noted these changes:

1. *Formal structures:* comparatively modest changes with modest impacts
2. *Mental attitudes:* major changes with major impacts
3. *Informal structures of decision making:* little change in methods, but some impacts in decisions made due to changing attitudes

It is in the second of these areas that higher education underwent a transformation.

Other countries had other experiences. China, Germany, France, Sweden, Denmark, and The Netherlands, among others, undertook fundamental changes in the formal structures of academic governance on a nationwide basis, mostly with negative consequences for academic life. The United States (also the U.K., Canada, and Australia) muddled through. The United States, in particular, made mostly case-by-case adjustments. This was possible only because of the power and influences of independent boards of trustees; it was also advantageous.

7. The Importance of Surprises—Past and Future. So much of the history of the past twenty years have been written by surprises and by the responses to them. A long series of surprises began with Sputnik in 1957 and continued with the sudden onset of state coordinating mechanisms in the early 1960s, the student revolts of the middle and late 1960s, the OPEC crises in the 1970s, the glut of Ph.D.'s and the decline in attendance rates by majority males after the end of the Vietnam war, the continuing decline in the fertility rate that became clear about 1965 and that cut that rate in half, the heavy shift of students to vocational courses, and the sudden interest of some schools' faculty members in collective bargaining, among others. In retrospect, most of these should not have been surprises; we can now see that there were prior warnings. For example, the surplus of Ph.D.'s was predicted as early as 1965,[25] and the decline in majority-male attendance was implied by the 1969 findings of a Carnegie survey that about 15 percent of males at the time of the Vietnam war were "reluctant attenders" and were in college against their wishes.[26]

For twenty years there was a continuous effort, particularly by top administrators, to adjust to each new surprise, each new crisis. This is not to suggest that there were not surprises in earlier times, such as the Great Depression and World War II, but only that the rate of arrival of new surprises seems to have increased. And it is likely to keep on increasing; there may be more shocks in the future. The United States is now more than ever susceptible to developments elsewhere around the world, to the impact of new technologies, to new styles of life, to new mentalities—as in the "new breed," and all these have repercussions on higher education.

One of the obligations of top leadership is to help anticipate new developments and to adjust quickly and well to them. The apparent fact of a rising crescendo of surprises makes the role of leadership more rather than less important just at a time when it is more circumscribed than at any time at least in the past century. The more uncertainties there are in society and the more uncertainties there are for higher education, the more need there is for effective leadership in higher education. As the once-central participant in selecting chancellors for the nine campuses of the University of California, I stressed at first interpersonal and public relations talents, ability to handle administrative matters, good citizenship within the university and the broader world of higher education, and long-term academic leadership on campus; but I came to add the ability to adjust to new developments, to handle the sudden crisis, to be more of a line officer and less of a staff type. This ability will become even more important in the future.

Notes

* Walker-Ames Lecture, University of Washington, Seattle, Washington, October 29, 1980.

1. In constant 1972 dollars, federal funds for research and development were approximately $229 million in 1940, before the World War II research effort began. They rose to $4,643 million in 1953; $12,681 million in 1960; $18,183 million (the highest in history) in 1966; but fell to $16,215 million (estimated) in 1980. *Sources:* 1940 calculated from data in *Historical Statistics of the United States* (U.S. Government Printing Office, 1976), 613. Other figures from National Science Foundation, *National Patterns of Science and Technology Resources 1980*, (Washington, DC: U.S. Government Printing Office [NSF80-308], 1980), 29.

2. Ladislav Cerych, "Retreat from Ambitious Goals?" *European Journal of Education* 15, no. 1 (1980): 5. For an analysis of "drift" toward the older university model in England, France, Norway, and Yugoslavia, see Guy Neave, "Academic Drift: Some views from Europe," *Studies in Higher Education* 4, no. 2 (October 1979): 143–59.

3. Eric Ashby, *Any Person, Any Study* (New York: McGraw-Hill, 1971). Ezra Cornell said, "I would found an institution where any person can find instruction in any study." (Walter P. Rogers, *Andrew D. White and the Modern University* [Ithaca, NY: Cornell University Press, 1942] 47.)

4. *On Further Examination*, Report of the Advisory Panel on the Scholastic Aptitude Test Score Decline, Willard Wirtz, Chairman. (New York: College Entrance Examination Record, 1977).

5. Scores of college graduates on examinations for entrance to graduate schools, the Graduate Record Examination and the Graduate Management Admissions Test, have dropped about 5 percent in recent years, while Medical College Admissions Test scores have risen slightly. (Data from Educational Testing Service, Princeton, NJ, and from M. Golladay, *The Condition of Education, 1977*, vol. 3, pt. 1 [Washington, DC: National Center for Education Statistics, 1977].)

6. Margaret S. Gordon and Charlotte Alhadeff, "Supplement I: Instructional Costs and Productivity, 1930–1977," Carnegie Council on Policy Studies in Higher Education, *Three Thousand Futures* (San Francisco: Jossey-Bass, 1980), 319.

7. The greatest increase in the 1960s came in 1965, when 641,000 more students enrolled than in 1964.

8. Full-time faculty increased from 170,000 in 1960 to 445,000 in 1978; all faculty numbers increased from 296,000 to 809,000 in the same period. (U.S. National Center for Education Statistics, *Projections of Educational Statistics to 1976–77* [Washington, DC: U.S. Government Printing Office, 1967], table 28; U.S.N.C.E.S., *The Condition of Education, 1980* [Washington, DC: U.S. Government Printing Office, 1980] table 3.10.)

Earned doctoral degrees conferred increased from 9,829 in 1959–60 to 32,131 in 1978. (U.S. National Center for Education Statistics, *Digest of Education Statistics, 1977–78* [Washington, DC: U.S. Government Printing Office, 1978], Table 120; U.S.N.C.E.S., *The Condition of Education, 1980*, table 3.14).

Executive administrators numbered 34,362 in 1959–60 and 101,263 in 1976. (Information from National Center for Education Statistics.)

9. *Missions of the College Curriculum, A Commentary of The Carnegie Foundation for the Advancement of Teaching* (San Francisco: Jossey-Bass, 1977), 103.

10. I am choosing my words carefully here. I say "intended" in the sense of planned by the institution in advance as compared with adjustments made in response to political or market pressures. I say "internally originated" to contrast with changes externally imposed or influenced. I say "academic" to indicate affecting instruction. I say "structural" to mean doing things in a different way and to exclude content change in courses which goes on all the time. I say "change" as a more neutral word than *reform*, which carries the implication that it is better in some way than what it replaces.

11. I was much interested in a number of changes which were then attempted. Particularly I was concerned about giving more attention to undergraduate students

in research universities, creating more of a sense of an academic community, reducing the fractionalization of the intellectual world, adding more options for the more diversified students to choose among. Also, I felt that experimentation gave a sense of life and dynamism to the academic endeavor; that is drew forth energy and enthusiasm—as in the Hawthorne experiments in industry; that it served as a check and balance against the old way of doing things; that it released some faculty and students from their sense of frustration and impotence. I was opposed, however, to changes which reduced academic quality (such as academic credit for experi ence), which repudiated the value of cognitive learning (such as emphases on affective "touchy-feely" experiences), and that led to excessive early specialized vocationalism.

12. Gerald Grant and David Riesman, *The Perpetual Dream: Reform and Experiment in the American College* (Chicago: University of Chicago Press, 1978), 296.

13. Carnegie Commission on Higher Education, *Less Time, More Options* (New York: McGraw-Hill, 1970).

14 Ann Heiss, *An Inventory of Academic Innovation and Reform* (Berkeley, CA: Carnegie Commission on Higher Education, 1973), discussed innovations adopted in the late 1960s and early 1970s, but at a time too close to their inception to estimate their survival rates. For a description and evaluation of thirteen major curriculum reforms, over half of which are still in existence, see Arthur Levine, *Handbook on Undergraduate Curriculum* (San Francisco: Jossey-Bass, 1978), ch. 13. Levine chose to consider the more permanent of the attempted changes. See also Levine, *Why Innovation Fails* (Albany: State University of New York Press, 1980).

15. A review of forty years of research on methods of teaching concluded that "no particular method of teaching is measurably to be preferred over another when evaluated by student examination performances." (Robert Dubin and Thomas C. Taveggia, *The Teaching–Learning Paradox: A Comparative Analysis of College Teaching Methods* [Eugene, OR: Center for Advanced Study of Educational Administration, 1968], 31.)
However, offering a variety of instructional options may be useful because "student learning processes vary across individuals. Students can exploit their comparative learning advantage if numerous pedagogies are offered, enabling each student to choose the teaching technique that he thinks suits his learning process best." (John J. Siegfried and George H. Sweeney, "Bias in Economics Education Research from Random and Voluntary Selection into Experimental and Control Groups," *Papers and Proceedings, American Economic Review* 70, no. 2 [May 1980]: 30.)
Attempts to determine characteristics of institutions that have significant impacts upon students have generally concluded that the characteristics of incoming freshmen have much more to do with the "output" of institutions than do any other factors. One study of "productivity" of undergraduate institutions (in terms of proportions of students who eventually earned a doctoral degree) found that a few institutions were much more productive than were others with whom they were matched in terms of intelligence, sex, and major field of study of students. Among

the "overproductive" institutions were three campuses of the City University New York and three campuses in the state of Utah. Even in these cases, however, it was "difficult to determine whether the overproductivity of these groups can be attributed to the effects of the institutions themselves. Certain ethnic or religious characteristics of the students entering these institutions may be important factors in the colleges' productivity . . . in addition to the factors of sex, college majors, and intelligence level." (Alexander W. Astin, " 'Productivity' of Undergraduate Institutions," *Science*, [13 April 1962], 129–35.)

16. For a detailed discussion of the elements of academic change in the late nineteenth century, see Laurence R. Veysey, *The Emergence of the American University* (Chicago: University of Chicago Press, 1965).

17. See the discussion in Gerald Grant and David Riesman, *The Perpetual Dream: Reform and Experiment in the American College* (Chicago: University of Chicago Press, 1978).

18. Abraham Flexner once wrote that American universities "have thoughtlessly and excessively catered to fleeting, transient, and immediate demands" (*Universities: American, English and German* [New York: Oxford University Press, 1930, 1968], 44.) This was his central complaint. I, however, take the present situation as a fact, and with strong arguments for it, as compared with any other system of decision making.

19. "New England's First Fruits, 1643," in Richard Hofstadter and Wilson Smith, eds., *American Higher Education: A Documentary History,* Vol. 1 (Chicago: University of Chicago Press, 1961), 6.

20. For a discussion of the effects of ability and socioeconomic status on enrollment rates in four advanced nations, see Roger L. Geiger, "The Limits of Higher Education: A Comparative Analysis of Factors Affecting Enrollment Levels in Belgium, France, Japan and the United States," Yale Higher Education Research Group Working Paper, YHERG-41, New Haven, February 1980.

21. "By 1976, the two-hundredth anniversary of the Declaration of Independence, the Commission proposes: That all economic barriers to educational opportunity be eliminated, thus closing the present probability differentials for college access and completion, and graduate school access and completion, among groups of equal academic ability but unequal family income level." The Carnegie Commission on Higher Education, *A Chance to Learn* (New York: McGraw-Hill, 1970), 27.
As much as 15 percent of the high-quality talent that might be expected to go on to college does not now do so, based on the shortfall of students in the top quartile in ability from low- and moderate-income families as compared with the attendance rate of similar-ability students from more affluent families. (National Opinion Research Center, Chicago, private communication, September 1980, based on college attendance plans of sample of high school graduates, June 1980.)
See also the discussion by Alice Rivlin, "Reflections on Twenty Years of Higher Education Policy," in *Educational Access and Achievement in America* (New York: The College Entrance Examination Board, 1987).

22. Howard R. Bowen, *Investment in Learning* (San Francisco: Jossey-Bass, 1977); F. Thomas Juster, et al., *Education, Income, and Human Behavior* (New York: McGraw-Hill, 1975); Stephen B. Withey, *A Degree and What Else?* (New York: McGraw-Hill, 1971). For a summary of some outcomes of higher education, see Charlotte Alhadeff and Margaret S. Gordon, "Supplement E: Higher Education and Human Performance," in Carnegie Council on Policy Studies in Higher Education, *Three Thousand Futures* (San Francisco: Jossey-Bass, 1980).

23. Daniel Yankelovich, "Work, Values and the New Breed," in *Work in America: The Decade Ahead*, eds. Clark Kerr and Jerome Rosow (New York: Van Nostrand, 1979), 10.

24. See Herbert Marcuse, "Repressive Tolerance," in Robert Paul Wolff, Barrington Moore, Jr., and Herbert Marcuse, *A Critique of Pure Tolerance* (Boston: Beacon Press, 1965), 81–117.

25. Allan M. Cartter, "A New Look at the Supply of College Teachers," *Educational Record* 46, no. 3 (Summer 1965): 267–77; and "The Supply and Demand of College Teachers," *Journal of Human Resources* 1, no. 1 (Summer 1966): 22–38.

26. *Less Time, More Options, A Special Report and Recommendations by the Carnegie Commission on Higher Education* (New York: McGraw-Hill, 1971), 7.

CHAPTER 11

Vignette—
Faculty: The Moods of Academia*

The American Council of Education invited me to give a major address before the assembled college and university presidents at its annual meeting in 1973. I charged the faculties, and by implication the presidents also, with having lost an historic perspective; and with having lost faith. I had the sense that they did not believe me—that what was happening was all just too awful to look at in the rosy glow of a brighter, longer-range future.

Higher education in recent decades has gone through a series of cycles of development, each lasting about five to seven years. Each cycle has had one or two dominant themes. During World War II the theme was one of "standby" for the duration. Then came the GI rush with efforts to accommodate vast numbers of returning soldiers and to respond to their attitudes and aspirations. This was followed by a "return to normalcy," and by the "apathetic generation" of students. Then came the period of advance planning and of great growth to meet the "tidal wave" of students and adjust to the accent on science after Sputnik—the theme was "full speed ahead." This was followed by an abrupt change into a period of political and financial depression—it came like a bolt of thunder out of an almost cloudless sky. Now we are in a cycle of recovery and austerity, a time for looking inward and more at the immediate concerns of the present. What may the next turn of history bring? Most probably, it now seems, a period of change and transition. Such a period offers both opportunities and dangers, and thus requires careful consideration and wise judgments; it is a time to look outward as well as inward, at the future as well as the present. I should like to discuss how we may wish to approach this time of transformations, in what kind of a mood.

We probably all have on our shelves, read or unread, books with titles or subtitles like these staring out at us:[†]

Academia in Anarchy (1970)
Academics in Retreat (1971)
Academy in Turmoil (1970)

American Universities in Crisis (1968)
Anarchy in the Groves of Academe (1970)

So much for some of those starting with A. Among the Bs, including one reprint:

Back to the Middle Ages (1969)
Bankruptcy of Academic Policy (1972)
Blow It Up (1971)
Blind Man on a Freeway (1971)

And among the Cs:

Chaos in Our Colleges (1963)
Confrontation and Counterattack (1971)

And among the Ds:

Death of the American University (1973)
Destruction of a College President (1972)
Degradation of the Academic Dogma (1971)
Down and Out in Academia (1972)

And among the Es and Fs:

Embattled University (1970)
Exploding University (1971)
Fall of the American University (1972)

And so on down the alphabet. They leave in the mind associated ideas like Academic–Anarchy; College–Chaos; Dogma–Degradation.

People in the past also were critical but they did not seem to strive so hard to display their criticism on their jacket covers, as though negativism would sell books in competition with sex. Veblen had his grave doubts but he called his book *The Higher Learning in America;* and Hutchins chose the same title for his attack; and Flexner used the neutral *Universities: American, English, German* for his aspersive comments.

One supposition might be that these titles were put on the books by their publishers in order to get wide distribution for them. Academic books, however, are mostly read, if at all, by academic people, and it gives one cause for thought as to why smart publishers think that smart academic people are more likely to read books if they have negative titles. Why?

But it is not just the promises held out by the titles—behind the scary titles lie some scary contents. Look inside:

> Indignation in some, passivity in others conspired to establish as a universal truth that the American university was an engine of oppression, rotten to the core, a stinking anachronism [from a former academic provost].[1]

> we sense acutely the tragedy that is occurring before our very eyes. . . . as if Nemesis had once again struck . . . [two university professors].[2]

> Most of us . . . are beyond the point of mere rebelliousness and mere paralyzed dismay. The academy is already a shambles: we need devote no further energy to bringing it down [a former college professor].[3]

> Today's colleges are not worth the price. In fact, they are probably doing more harm than good . . . [a college professor].[4]

> there has arisen a despair that transcends simple description [a college professor].[5]

This is what some of our "best" and our "brightest" in higher education—defined as those who get books published—think about us. But not only they, so also some of those in power and close to power, some of those who have sold in Peoria and seem to have known what sells in Peoria. Some seem to have believed that higher education badly needed to be saved, was itself solely responsible for the fact that it needed to be saved, and that nobody outside could or would come to its rescue:

> And it is time for the responsible university and college administrators, faculty and student leaders to stand up and be counted, because we must remember, only they can save higher education in America. It cannot be saved by government. . . . Listen to this: If the war ended tomorrow, if the environment were cleaned up tomorrow morning, and if all the other problems for which government has responsibility were solved tomorrow afternoon—the moral and spiritual crisis in the universities would still exist [Speech, Kansas State University, September 16, 1970].[6]

Another high official, in an attack on the Scranton Commission report, said:

> responsibility . . . does not belong on the steps of the White House . . . [but] on the steps of the university administration building and at the door of the faculty lounge [Statement, September 29, 1970][7].

And the wife of a then highly influential Cabinet member locked herself in her bathroom, called up a reporter, and had this to say:

> The academic society is responsible for all of our troubles in this country. . . . The whole academic society is to blame. . . . the professors in every institution of learning. . . . They are totally responsible for the sins of our children [September 20, 1970].[8]

Some of us say it about ourselves. Some of our elected leaders and those close to them say it about us. Is it true?

Yes, in part:

- Responsibility for the recent turmoil in the academy did lie at the doors of college presidents and faculty members, but at many other doors as well. Higher education is responsible for some of the unrest of youth, but so are many other elements of society. We should neither ourselves insist upon nor should we accept all of the blame.
- We did have the greatest series of episodes of campus unrest in American history; but not "anarchy"; and that period is now in the past—at least for the time being. Ending the draft and the war in Vietnam actually did help. The campuses, as institutions, have shown remarkable long-run organizational endurance; and their "moral and spiritual crisis" no longer seems to be so great, or at least so visible.
- We have entered a "new depression" financially—but not "bankruptcy" —at least not in many places; a "fragile stability" has been restored; and, throughout most of the history of higher education in the United States, it has been subject to genteel and sometimes to not so genteel poverty; "down" yes but not "out."
- We have fallen in the esteem of the American public, fallen badly for a time; but not "degradation" in the sense of public disgrace; and other institutions have lost favor as much or more, and the level of esteem for higher education may now be rising. A recent California Poll report, in a state where higher education has known its recent disappointments, starts out this way: "The California public today has a very high opinion of the value of a college education." Only 25 percent of those surveyed disagreed with the statement that "colleges and universities are being blamed for a lot of things these days that aren't really their responsibility." And 80 percent disagreed with the statement that "The way colleges and universities are being run nowadays, a person is better off not going to one." These opinions, in what has been a bellwether state, are all the more surprising since the public learns about the campus largely from the news. And bad news—and there has been a lot of it—makes news more than does good news.
- We have our current problems, even crises—how to adjust to collective bargaining, how to handle tenure, how to absorb into our faculties more

women and more members of minority groups, and many others; but we do not have "chaos"; and all these problems, given time and good judgment, are potentially subject to reasonable solutions.

- We do now experience a decline in the rising rate of student enrollments and the prospect of a decline in absolute numbers during the 1980s; and this will mean modest overall curtailment for a few years in the numbers to be taught, affecting some institutions much more than others, but not "retreat" for the system of higher education as a whole—not for its research, not for its service activities, not for its essential contributions to society in their totality.

- We are now faced with a less favorable job market for our graduates; but this does not mean "death" for our efforts at the higher education of youth. It does, however, mean many adjustments by many people.

Now I fully realize that I have used several of these terms in a different sense and context than employed by the authors themselves in their books; but I have been responding to the general tone of these many treatments of higher education, to their themes of derogation and even denigration rather than to their specific arguments.

Another set of words could have been employed in the titles of recent books on the state of higher education, and I think more accurately—words such as "The Campus Muddles Through" or "Modest Successes in Academia." Higher education has been and is going through a time of troubles, but it is more likely that it will survive and surmount the challenges it now faces than that it will decline and fall—those with visions of the Apocalypse to the contrary. There are some favorable signs as well as unfavorable:

- Students are generally satisfied or even very satisfied with their colleges and with the education they receive.
- Alumni also show general satisfaction with their college experiences.
- Faculty members nearly universally like their profession and their institutions, and would choose each again if they had the chance.
- State legislators, even at the height of student disturbances, showed considerable understanding of the problems of higher education and a desire to continue their support.
- The states have kept on appropriating funds for higher education in an almost unbroken rise in the burden placed on per capita personal income. It is remarkable what aid most states have given.
- Private contributions are at an all-time high.
- The federal government has, for the first time in history, committed itself to remove financial barriers to access to college, although the appropriations as yet are woefully inadequate.

- High school graduates who are blacks, for the first time in history, are entering college at the same rate as whites.
- Deficits in health manpower are being overcome quite rapidly with the full cooperation of higher education.
- The truly historic transition from the more selective arrangements of the past into a system of higher education where access is guaranteed for all high school graduates into some institution of advanced education, as is now the case in several major political jurisdictions, has been taking place with remarkably few difficulties considering the magnitude of the change.
- Enrollment rates are disappointing to many, but most of this is due to demographic changes that cannot and should not be reversed; and some quite temporary forces have also been at work, such as (1) the decline of military inductions, which has added more to the civilian labor force than to college enrollments and thus has reduced the percentage of civilians in the age group who are in college, (2) lifting of the recession which has drawn more young persons into gainful employment, and (3) the significant rise in the "stop-out" rate (now apparently about 10 percent) with a temporary impact on enrollments. These short-run factors should not be cause for alarm. And the colleges can offset some of the longer-range demographic impacts by more consideration for community college transfers and for part-time enrollees and for adults. Also, the reduction of enrollment pressures will make it easier for the federal and state governments to finance equality of opportunity than would otherwise be the case.

I cite these facts not to argue that all is well, for it is not, but to note that there are grounds for hope as well as for despair, and that there are accomplishments as well as failures. I find myself much more in sympathy with the following evaluation by Alan Pifer than with that by the doomsayers: "In view of the formidable burden the nation has placed on its higher educational system, the astounding fact is how well it has succeeded, not how badly it has failed."[9]

Why then have so many within the groves of academe been so subject to the "doomsday syndrome"? Roger Heyns, last year in speaking to the American Council, ascribed it to "the masochistic need that is perhaps our [meaning the academics] most prominent common personality trait." Perhaps so; but perhaps we are just given to moods. Not so long ago we were euphoric—science would have the world and the campus was the "home of science"; growth would go on forever; there was an almost endless need for more Ph.D.'s; faculty salaries would keep on transporting us into a standard of living to which we would like to become accustomed; the university was the center of the postindustrial society—not the farm, not the factory, not the government bureau; and so on. There were few—hardly any—

"Chicken Littles" then, when we needed some words of caution, and the sky subsequently did, for a time, seem to be falling down.

This swing in moods does raise some questions about the quality of our collective judgments, particularly since we are supposed to be, as academics, in a better position to view the long run more analytically and to see basic forces at work more objectively than almost any one else. It may turn out, however, that we are just as likely to project short-run circumstances into long-run laws of development as are nonacademics, perhaps even more so. To project the present unchanged into the future ignores the lessons of history; to do so in a crescendo fashion, like Ravel's "Bolero," does so to an even greater extent. As an example, we once overdid student apathy; then we overdid the students on the march to revolution; and now we may be overdoing the apathy theme again.

Some elementary truths we all know: (1) There are always adjustments that are made to any major development. (2) Nearly always there are countervailing forces at work. (3) Also, positive trends have their negative aspects, and negative trends have their positive aspects. (4) And there are surprises. Rothblatt, in writing about the University of Cambridge a century ago, noted:

> In a plural society, . . . it is entirely possible that the university and society will be in subtle and complex states of disagreement as well as agreement with one another, that the direction of university change may not be completely obvious, that surprises will occur. It is entirely possible that disagreement and agreement together constitute the peculiar quality of the modern university. . . . A university which is being asked to reform, but is still allowed a high degree of internal freedom, may restructure itself to acquire an identity which few expected.[10]

So also today.

The mood of the times on campus, and not just of the authors whose titles I have listed above but of many others as well, may have recently carried us too far along a one-track concentration on despondency. A. P. Herbert, during World War II, wrote a take-off on a strategic services training center under the title "Number Nine." One section was concerned with psychological testing. The participants were asked to show how their minds worked by starting in with a word given to them and then filling words into three subsequent blank spaces, to show how they associated ideas. One young lady had the same fourth word, for example:

Shell   Fish   Oyster   Bed
Class   First   Sleeper   Bed

For many in higher education today the sequence might start with "collective bargaining" and end up with "despair"; or with "tenure" and end up with "despair"; or with "budgets"; or with any one of a number of other key words and end up with "despair."

Should we just note this moodiness, if moodiness it is, as a possibly interesting but minor social phenomenon and then forget it? Or should it be a matter of concern? I believe it should be a matter for concern. First, because it has external impacts that can be harmful. If we do not believe in ourselves, how much should others believe in us, when we provide so many of our own self-chosen gravediggers and they are in such unseemly haste? Second, because it has internal impacts. The current mood of so many administrators is one of survivalism—to survive one more year, to keep, as Roger Heyns described it last year, a "low profile." The current mood of so many faculty members is to doubt the future, to hang onto past gains as best they can. There has been, as the Carnegie Commission states in its final report, "too much excessive, almost paralyzing, criticism."[11]

It takes social energy to carry out functions effectively, to undertake reforms, to prepare the way for a better future. An attitude of "back to the Middle Ages" or even, as I heard one academic person suggest recently, "back to the catacombs" for the sake of protection is less supportive of that necessary social energy than one of "ahead to the twenty-first century." It is, in any event, the twenty-first century, and not the Middle Ages, that lies ahead.

We always start from where we are. We cannot, even though we might like to, start from any place else. The course of the journey and the nature of the future destination are always uncertain; but both the journey and the destination are affected by how we approach them—in despair or in guarded expectation. We need less euphoria than we once had, and less despondency than we now have, and more realism than we have heretofore displayed.

These are historic times particularly with the transition—the first in the world—into universal-access higher education; with the end of the much more rapid growth for higher education than for American society as a whole that has marked our past history; and with the possible birth of new mentalities, challenging the traditional "work ethic" both in youth and in the general population. Higher education does continue to require many constructive changes; but it does not really need to be "saved." In fact, we now have more time, with the "tidal wave" of students and the wave of political dissent currently behind us, to think more about purposes, to concentrate more on constructive change, to emphasize quality rather than quantity, to bring equality of opportunity closer to reality, to improve governance, to give more attention to the effective use of resources, and to do much else.

To those who see only gloom and doom, we can say that much that is good is also occurring. To those who say that everything fails, we can say that much is, in fact, succeeding. To those who see only problems, we can say there are possibilities available for their alleviation.

Higher education is too vital a force in any modern society for us to be in despair about it; it provides too much in the way of skills and of research, and responds too much to the human desire to understand. These are sound bases on which to move forward with a sense of cautious confidence.

Notes

* Address given at the annual meeting of the American Council on Education, Washington, DC, October 11, 1973. In *Education and the State*, ed. John F. Hughes (Washington, DC: American Council on Education, 1975), 267–75. Reprinted by permission.

† For citations, see addendum to this chapter.

1. Jacques Barzun, "Tomorrow's University—Back to the Middle Ages?", *Saturday Review*, 15 November 1969, 25.

2. James M. Buchanan and Nicos E. Devletoglou, *Academia in Anarchy: An Economic Diagnosis* (New York: Basic Books, 1970), xi, 168.

3. Judson Jerome, *Culture Out of Anarchy: The Reconstruction of American Higher Learning* (New York: Herder & Herder, 1970), xviii.

4. Lawrence E. Langdon, *Can Colleges Be Saved? A Critique of Higher Education* (New York: Vintage Press, 1969), vii.

5. L. G. Heller, *The Death of the American University* (New Rochelle, NY: Arlington House, 1973), 11.

6. Richard M. Nixon, speech reported in *New York Times*, 17 September 1970, 28.

7. Spiro Agnew, as reported in *New York Times*, 30 September 1970, 1.

8. Martha Mitchell, as reported in *New York Times*, 21 September 1970, 23.

9. Alan Pifer, "The Responsibility for Reform in Higher Education," *Educational Digest*, September 1972, 29.

10. Sheldon Rothblatt, *The Revolution of the Dons: Cambridge and Society in Victorian England* (London: Faber & Faber, 1968), 26.

11. *Priorities for Action: Final Report of the Carnegie Commission on Higher Education* (New York: McGraw-Hill, 1973), 83.

Addendum to "The Moods of Academia"

James M. Buchanan and Nicos E. Devletoglou, *Academia in Anarchy: An Economic Diagnosis* (New York: Basic Books, 1970).

Joseph Fashing and Steven E. Deutsch, *Academics in Retreat: The Politics of Educational Innovation* (Albuquerque, NM: University of New Mexico Press, 1971).

New York State, Temporary Commission to Study the Causes of Campus Unrest, First Report, *The Academy in Turmoil*, Albany, NY, February 1, 1970.

John R. Coyne, Jr., *The Kumquat Statement: Anarchy in the Groves of Academe* (New York: Cowles Book Co., 1970).

James Ridgeway, *The Closed Corporation: American Universities in Crisis* (New York: Ballantine, 1970).

Jacques Barzun, "Tomorrow's University—Back to the Middle Ages?" *Saturday Review,* 15 November 1969, 23–25, 60–61.

Peter Caws, S. Dillon Ripley, and Philip C. Ritterbush, *The Bankruptcy of Academic Policy* (Washington, DC: Acropolis Books, 1972).

Dikran Karaguezian, *Blow It Up! The Black Student Revolt at San Francisco State College and the Emergence of Dr. Hayakawa* (Boston: Gambit, 1971).

William Moore, Jr., *Blind Man on a Freeway: The Community College Administrator* (San Francisco: Jossey-Bass, 1971).

Morris Freedman, *Chaos in Our Colleges* (New York: David McKay, 1963).

Immanuel Wallerstein and Paul Starr, eds., *The University Crisis Reader,* volume 2, *Confrontation and Counterattack* (New York: Random House, 1971).

L. G. Heller, *The Death of the American University* (New Rochelle, NY: Arlington House, 1973).

Ken Metzler, *Confrontation: The Destruction of a College President* (Los Angeles: Nash Publishing, 1973).

Robert Nisbet, *The Degradation of the Academic Dogma: The University in America, 1945–1970* (New York: Basic Books, 1971).

Ben Morreale, *Down and Out in Academia* (New York: Pitman, 1972).

Stephen R. Graubard and Geno A. Ballotti, eds., *The Embattled University* (New York: The Daedalus Library, G. Braziller, 1970).

Christopher Driver, *The Exploding University* (London: Hodder and Stoughton, 1971).

Adam Ulam, *The Fall of the American University* (New York: Library Press, 1972).

CHAPTER 12

Vignette—
Students: The Exaggerated Generation*

The New York Times Magazine *called me to write about how I
viewed the student generation, then still a growing force (June 1967).
Actions by members of this generation and my responses had led to
events that caused the new governor of California to lead a movement
to replace me as president of the University of California. I said that
I thought the student activists had exaggerated notions about their impact on history, that conservatives (and I thought of Ronald Reagan)
had exaggerated fears, and that the media had exaggerated the whole
thing. The media people I talked to at the time agreed but said they
were "selling entertainment" and this was good entertainment; but I
am sure the others did not agree. While I did not say so, I thought
there was more to be looked at in the development of the University of
California than the revolts alone, and that the views of the activists,
the conservatives, and the media were all badly off-balance.*

The current generation of college and university students is the most-
berated, the most-praised—certainly the most talked-about—in America's
history. The names are varied, even contradictory. They tend to reveal more
of the biases of the observers than of the nature of the students.

To conservatives, this is a "discontented" generation—even though
youth never had it so good; or a "distrustful" generation—distrustful of its
elders, the schools, the Government, the Establishment, distrustful of all
the elements that have brought the good life to Americans, and to young
Americans in particular. University students of today are seen as "difficult" at best and "radical" at worst, disrupting society.

To liberals, students of today constitute a "generation of conscience"
in a nation that badly needs a conscience; or a "prophetic minority" point-
ing the way for an evil society to evolve. Or they are said to be "committed" to reform and good works; or to constitute a "New Left," presumably
carrying on the torch for the tired Old Left which sees in this new generation proof that it really was not defeated permanently and completely. Paul
Goodman has called the students of today the "New Aristocrats"—"America's emergent power elite."

From a more neutral point of observation, today's youth has been called "cool" or "activist" or "alienated" or "permissive." The current generation is many of these things to some extent some of the time. It is, for example, certainly occasionally difficult; often committed to some cause or another; to a degree alienated. There are many facets to this generation, perhaps more than to any earlier generation. It is going in more directions and at a faster pace. Thus, any simple designation may hold an element of truth but not the whole truth.

Exaggeration is one word that fits this new generation. It has exaggerated itself. It has been exaggerated by the news media. It has been exaggerated and also used, for their own purposes, by the left and the right. And, as a result, seldom in history have so many people feared so much for so little reason from so few.

The exaggeration is the work of many people. The students themselves are responsible in the first instance; some of them have wanted it that way. A few highly visible minorities, on a relatively small number of campuses, have become symbolic to the public at large of a whole generation. The dress has, at times, been outlandish. The speech, on a few occasions, has been without taste. The behavior of some, with sex and drugs, has been outside established norms. These characteristics have created an impression of widespread Bohemianism distasteful to large elements of the public. To distaste has been added actual fear and anger over actions of the political activists.

The student activists might be called the "McLuhan Generation." Their style is geared to the TV cameras and the flashbulbs, the bullhorn, the microphone and the walkie-talkie. Electricity powers this new student guerrilla warfare. It pulls in information, sends out instructions and carries the message of dissident views to a huge audience.

The media have also played their role in the exaggeration. Berkeley in the fall of 1964 and again in December, 1966, offered an example. The crowds were uniformly reported as being far larger than they were. Herbert Jacobs, a lecturer in journalism at Berkeley, has compared TV and press reports with analyses of photographs of the crowds. Thus, when reports said that 8,000 or 10,000 students voted to strike in Sproul Hall Plaza in December, 1966, the actual number of people there was 2,000—and this number included wives, curious onlookers and nonstudents. Another count, on another occasion, showed a count of 2,400 actually present, when 6,000 to 7,000 had been reported.

"Crowdsmanship," as Jacobs calls it, is a game played by the sponsor, the police and the media alike. They all have an interest in raising the score. Thus a demonstration becomes bigger and more violent than it really was. A sit-in becomes a riot, then a rebellion and finally the "revolution" at Berkeley.

I once said to some TV executives that, in the course of reporting history, they were changing it. They agreed, but said this was what their competition did—and what the public wanted.

Exaggerated accounts have, on occasion, produced exaggerated reactions. The Old Left has picked up each episode of campus protest around the nation and made it another omen of the second coming of the American Revolution. Its spokesmen saw these protests as involving more students, the students as more radical, the tactics as more effective and the "movement" as more permanent than the facts would seem to warrant. Some liberals went along, for they liked the goals, if not the methods; they wore their hearts on other people's picket signs.

The New Right, rising to the right of the Old Establishment, saw the long arm of Marx and trumpeted its discovery. The Old Establishment was the power structure and it did not like being pushed around; it liked law and order, and it did little to correct the exaggerations.

The middle class tended to be shocked. What it thought it saw of students disturbed it greatly—the biggest scare since the Korean war and Senator McCarthy. Politicians entered the game in more than one state to add their own misrepresentations. In California, "treason, drugs and sex" were said to be a part of the curriculum offered to the students on one campus, and student behavior was highlighted as involving an "orgy."

Amid these exaggerations, efforts to identify "cultures" and "typologies" of students are precarious at best. My own observation is that there are three main student types now vying to set the tone of campus life— Political Activists, Bohemians and the New Collegiates. These types, singly and together, constitute a minority of all students but contribute a majority of the off-campus impressions and impact of the modern generation.

The Political Activists: The protest element of issue-by-issue demonstrations first arose out of opposition to the House Un-American Activities Committee, atomic testing, capital punishment and other similar issues in the late 1950s and early 1960s, but particularly reflects in its style and content the civil-rights movement and then the opposition to the war in Vietnam. It rises and falls as issues rise and fall, and it attracts more or fewer or different people as the issues change. The radical element on campus finds its origins particularly in the Depression of the 1930s and the more recent developments in Cuba and China, and its fractionalization relates to the historical point of origin of each of its components. It has been undergoing a current revival particularly as a corollary to the rise in protest sentiment. The protest element and the radical element together constitute the political activists.

The activist students have wanted to influence the Establishment but have often ended up, partly because of exaggeration on all sides, by energizing the right, giving ammunition to their worst enemies. They have been, on some occasions, self-defeating prophets, better in the long run at building resistance than getting results, more adept at bringing the counter-revolution than at getting basic reforms, fated to achieve minor successes and major failures. A few of the activists, on the far left, wanted it this way, since they believed that destruction must precede reconstruction. But the great majority of activists wanted to do good things with and for the existing society.

The Bohemians: The Bohemian element in American universities is largely a product of the post-World War II period. It is basically incompatible, in its temperament and use of time, with hard academic work, and superficial evidence is a poor test of the real hold that this culture has on students. Yet this element is certainly growing and, given the conditions out of which it arises in modern society, it is almost bound to keep on growing. More fragmentation of life and less sense of purpose in the mass industrial society leads to more such behavior.

(Here we must note a subgroup, outside the campus itself but related to it. This comprises the nonstudents. It is a deviant group—deviant on politics, deviant on attitudes toward sex, morality, religion. Its members are children of affluence who often can make a life without having to make a living. They reflect the attraction of a large campus with its cultural programs, its political activism, its sense of freedom. They reflect the desire for the excitement without the hard work of intellectual pursuits. They reflect both Bohemianism and political activism—both of which reject the middle class. The period between emancipation from adult control and assumption of full adult responsibility can be prolonged almost indefinitely through nonstudent status. Left Banks are now found around a few of the great American universities. They will be found around more, and they will grow in size.)

The New Collegiates: Traditional collegiate culture took on its modern form before and after World War I with the development of intercollegiate athletics, formal student governments, debating clubs and the like. But, in terms of adherents, it has been losing ground rapidly since the G.I.'s came back to the campuses after World War II. What distinguishes the new collegiate culture is a sense of community service. It was hardly known in the 1930s and is particularly a product of the current decade, during which it has grown enormously.

In my student days at Swarthmore during the depths of the Depression, there were only two of us in my senior class who went to a Negro school in Philadelphia one morning a week to work on a Quaker project. Last fall, at the University of California, eight thousand students, or nearly 10 percent of the total student body, engaged in projects such as these: tutoring Negro children in West Oakland; volunteer teaching in Watts; running a camp in the San Bernardino Mountains for disadvantaged children; serving as

"Amigos Anonymous" in villages in Mexico; cleaning up freeways and parks as a beautification project around Berkeley; teaching in San Quentin prison; running summer schools for the children of migratory workers in the San Joaquin and Sacramento Valleys; helping to construct an orphanage in Baja California; working with delinquents in Riverside; providing free dental care to disadvantaged families in Northern California; "adopting" two orphanages in South Vietnam.

The report we issued on these and other projects was called "The Untold Story." The overtold story was about the "filthy nine" (only four of them students) who constituted the totality of the much-publicized Filthy Speech Movement on the Berkeley campus.

This generation, as a whole, has some characteristics that mark the influences that have shaped it. No one today would describe students, as Philip Jacobs did in 1957, as "gloriously contented" and "self-centered" and satisfied with the "American assembly line." They might better be described as "aggressive"—at home, on the campus, off the campus; "concerned"—about the meaning of life and the quality of society; "serious"—about their studies and their actions; "experimental"—in their way of life and their attack on problems; "impatient"—with an education that sometimes lacks relevance and a society that often practices hypocrisy.

This is a generation that was born under the sign of the bomb and suckled at the breast of TV. The bomb created a feeling that there was a time limit on getting a better world. Some students have another sense of urgency—to get something done before they disappear forever into the flatland of the suburb and the wasteland of the corporation.

TV brought to this generation at an early age, as the newspapers never did to children and young people in the past, a view of the whole world and all aspects of it. It became interested in all the world, including Mississippi and Vietnam, and saw vividly that participation was not something to be postponed until adult life. The means were there, through the electronic revolution, for students to be citizens, to be informed and to participate.

This generation was raised at home according to new manuals that stressed permissiveness, and at school under new views that stressed participation. Too often, its members arrived at colleges and universities which still reflected the old manuals and the old views, and both the students and the colleges were unprepared for the meeting.

The quality of education has been improved all along the line, particularly in the high schools, and particularly since Sputnik I. There is a new emphasis on grades and on going into graduate work. The meritocracy is taking hold and school is the way to move up and to avoid being moved down. The pressure is greater at all levels and students are better educated. Among other things, they are better educated in basic American principles like equality, freedom and the pursuit of happiness. And they see around them discrimination, restrictions on their freedoms, and poverty. They are troubled by the gap between aspiration and attainment. They were told all through high school about the sins of omission of the apathetic generation and the conformity of the "organization man" and exhorted to do otherwise. They are doing otherwise.

American society is now, by and large, affluent—students stay in school longer and fewer of them support themselves while going to school. One result is to reduce their dependence on the world of work and the sense of reality that goes with it. As Eric Hoffer said, "They haven't raised a blade of grass, they haven't laid a brick." They are also, frequently, less oriented toward getting a job after graduation, since that is taken for granted. Thus, materialistic considerations and pressures are less evident now that materialistic welfare is taken more or less for granted and also given a lower value.

The American society of the future troubles them. They have read "1984," "Brave New World," "Animal Farm," and they know about IBM cards and automation. The sense of a world in which the individual counts for less and less weighs heavily. Conformity to Big Brother and to science seems not so very far off. There is a countermove toward individuality as against the requirements of "the system." This move toward individuality is speeded as the new religion and the new anthropology remove some of the restraints on personal behavior.

The Rebel, to use the terminology of Camus, accepts society but wants to improve it. He accepts restraint but not the status quo. He rejects the absolutism of much of the left but not the need for reform. He rejects violence and seeks the possible. Part of his motivation is religious: part relates to a desire for a better future. The Rebel approach is at the heart of the community-service element as well as of the protest tendency among college students.

Confrontation politics, which has often been the special form of student protest, seems to be becoming a less significant weapon. Civil-rights victories are farther in the background. The radicals have taken over much of the guidance of confrontations, and conservative, religious and moderate support has dropped away. Vietnam, of course, remains an issue over which protest can easily be organized, but the great wave of student confrontations now seems to be passing. The sense of protest will continue, and may even rise in intensity, but it will find expression less through confrontation and more through other means.

New leaders are arising from what I have characterized as the New Collegiate group. The New Collegiate type has as one of its characteristics devotion to the campus and willingness to work with and through the campus power structure. The New Collegiate leaders, including those active in fraternities and sororities, are pushing academic reform instead of athletics, political discussion instead of activities, community projects instead of dances—and they appeal to the new interests of the students. They do not wish to bring a campus to a grinding halt, but to halt neglect of students and give voice to community and national concerns. The New Collegiate leaders reflect the student interest in service and protest and give organized expression to it. And then a number of them go overseas and become Peace Corps participants.

Nobody pays much attention to them, but in my opinion they are setting the tone of this generation. The campus revolutionaries are never going to win; this is not a revolutionary country. And the alienated Bohemians are parasites. What is most significant about this generation is the very high proportion of the Peace Corps type.

Society faces the campus just as the campus faces society. A reappraisal by society of the new generation is in order—a reappraisal which recognizes the diversity and the essential goodwill of the students of today. The communications media have a special responsibility to present the facts for this reappraisal. The public should read and hear and see the news about university students with sophistication and some tolerance. The excesses of youth are nothing new in history.

Aristotle once wrote: "They [young people] have exalted notions, because they have not yet been humbled by life or learned its necessary limitations; moreover, their hopeful disposition makes them think themselves equal to great things—and that means having exalted notions. They would always rather do noble deeds than useful ones: Their lives are regulated more by moral feeling than by reasoning—all their mistakes are in the direction of doing things excessively and vehemently. They overdo everything—they love too much, hate too much, and the same with everything else."

Notes

* *The New York Times Magazine*, 4 June 1967, 28–36. Copyright 1967 by The New York Times Company. Reprinted by permission.

CHAPTER 13

Vignette—

Society: Industrial Relations and University Relations*

*My field of study had been industrial relations, and the Industrial Re-
lations Research Association, which I had helped to found and of
which I was a past president and where I had many friends, asked me
(1968) to look at the student movement as I had once looked at the
labor movement; and at what it was like to be a president in the midst
of the student revolts. I also talked about how American society had
absorbed the labor movement with at least the implication that it
could also absorb the student movement. Some people then thought,
instead, that it was the end of all they held dear but not in this more
sophisticated group with more sense of history and more acceptance
of the role of conflict.*

Industrial relations has been concerned with the emergence over the
past two centuries of a new social force—the manual worker—under a different technology. The machine gave rise to the worker, the worker to
unions, unions to new political movements, and all of these to new social
arrangements of vast import. Industrial relations has been concerned with
the contrasting views of this process: of Marx on revolution and the "dictatorship of the proletariat"; of the Webbs on political evolution and the
rational socialist state; of Commons and Perlman on economic evolution
and "job control" unionism; of Slichter on changing market structures and
the "laboristic state." The field has been torn by the now fading controversies among the contending schools of thought.

Today there is a new social force growing out of a new technology and
it also may have vast import. There are now the students and the intellectual professionals—including the professoriate, the "scientific estate," the
"techno-structure." They constitute the new vanguard groups, increasingly
on a worldwide basis. In the United States today, over one-quarter of the
total population lives its daily life in a school as students and teachers and
administrators; and beyond the school are the "think tanks," and the
"R&D" enclaves in government and industry.

The workers are by now an older, more settled, more conservative
force. To the extent that industrial relations has been concerned with the

emergence and absorption of new social forces, it should now turn also to a consideration of the students and the intellectuals of many sorts. The student and intellectual class has some of the elements that Marx thought he saw in the working class: it is growing in size, and elements of it are becoming more radical. There are now over six million university students in the United States and soon there will be nine or ten million. The disaffected elements among them find allies in the intellectual professions and in the ghettos.

University relations deals with the people and the ideas that constitute this new social force, as industrial relations once did with the people and the ideas involved in the earlier and now largely assimilated force of the workers.

As the campus moves toward the center of the stage, some lessons may be learned from the history of industry. I should like to suggest a few for consideration:

1. A new social force need not necessarily emerge fully triumphant; Marcuse may turn out to be as wrong as Marx. In France in May of this year, a revolutionary transformation was temporarily a potential; but in California earlier, as more recently in France, it has been the reaction that is triumphant. The popular fears of 1964 and 1968 may turn out to have been as excessive in university relations as those of 1886 and 1919 were in industrial relations in the United States. An early stage of radicalism and violence may be followed, not by more radicalism and violence, but by containment and absorption and reform; and thus early violence may end not in revolution but in a more or less uneasy peace. The seemingly "logical" conclusion that flows from an anticipated unilinear trend may be the most illogical outcome of all.

2. The *in loco parentis* role of the college campus may prove no more viable than did the company town. It may be better to separate the functions of landlord and merchant and policeman from those of teacher.

3. The workers were turned into participating citizens with full political and legal rights, by the 1860s in England and even earlier in the United States. Were students to vote at eighteen and were political structures to become more responsive to their interests off campus, then a similar process will have taken place. The counterpart of this will be that the campus is no longer "off limits" to the police and the courts. Students will no longer be a class apart.

4. The workers secured more rights in the factory: their unions were recognized, contracts were signed providing shared authority over pertinent issues, the law came to protect them more. A similar

acceptance of students in aspects of the internal decision-making process on the campus, such as rule making, disciplinary matters, and curriculum formation, is now under way.

5. Peacekeeping machinery was set up in industry. Now it is emerging on campus—from grievance handling to settlement of organized disputes. It is no more possible to produce B.A.'s with billy clubs than "coal with bayonets."

6. Conditions were improved for the worker, with higher real wages and more considerate treatment on the job. On campus, the comparable possibilities are improvements in the quality of the curriculum and more personal treatment of students by faculty and staff.

7. The state came to assume a more impartial role as between capital and labor. Today, the state "owns" most of higher education. To become impartial, it will need to give up "ownership" by granting autonomy to the campus, by making all campuses essentially "private"; and thus, also, placing them more in competition with each other.

8. New attitudes of tolerance and "mutual survival" emerged out of conflict in industrial relations, and will need to evolve in university relations if the campus is to be a viable environment for scholarship.

9. The impact of the workers, viewed in its totality, brought new arrangements into industrial relations which made this new social force compatible with the productive functions of the firm. Once again the new social force of the students and associated faculty will have to achieve compatibility with the central functions of the campus.

All this makes what is now going on sound like a rerun of an earlier film—the perils of Pauline with a happy ending. But there are some very great differences:

1. The university students constitute a smaller mass than the manual workers did, their membership turns over much more quickly, and the chance of a "solidarity" point of view among students (and allied intellectuals) is much less likely than among workers; and thus they are less likely to be able to mount a cohesive political movement.

2. Students (and allied intellectuals) are less immediately essential to society. They can withdraw their efforts and not many may care. This places them outside the economic power structure.

3. The "new class" tends to be inherently more volatile, more given to fads, less stable in its views than the workers. The shifting

and divided views of intellectuals make it harder to create traditions, settled policies, and an effective permanent bureaucracy.

4. The comparative lack of political and economic power tends to turn this volatile "new class" toward periodic confrontations rather than toward long-term bargaining relationships. The tactics of confrontation lead to more permanent and violent opposition than do those of "responsible" bargaining by unions. Thus, while unions became more, not less, acceptable in the long-run, the agencies and actions of intellectuals may become less, not more, acceptable.

5. Students are comparatively "irresponsible" about the costs of disruption in order to get their demands, since disruption costs them nothing in their paychecks, does not mean that their families go without food, does not injure their permanent source of livelihood; and, additionally, they do not have the personal discipline of the daily job and of work. Consequently, they may be more destructive in their methods. The campus can stay closed longer from their point of view than the factory from the point of view of the worker.

6. Demands are more unlimited. They are not for higher wages and shorter hours; for "more, more, more, and now" in a materialistic sense. Demands are less for a good living and more for a good life, which means new styles of life and a higher quality to all of society. These are demands that cannot be bought off for another nickel or dime a year. Students may never be satisfied to the extent the workers have become. The workers are by now more conservative. Students may not follow this same pattern or at least to the same extent.

7. The movement of the workers led in the direction of the welfare state and even the socialist state, and this direction was compatible with the centralizing tendencies of industrialism. Schumpeter once thought the intellectuals would push society in this same direction with their attacks on the industrial innovators, with their predilections for rules and bureaucracy; so that capitalism would slide into socialism with hardly a whimper. The students (and their allies) lead more toward syndicalism or anarcho-syndicalism, with an emphasis not on the state but on individual and small group autonomy. We have tended to neglect the anarchism of Bakunin, the syndicalism of Sorel, the guild socialism of Cole, since capitalism, socialism, and communism alike rejected them. These views of society now need to be reexamined. The emphasis is now against both the consumptionist society of capitalism and the state control of socialism, in favor of producer (and student) sovereignty. Communism with its devotion to control and conformity may come to look like not radical reform but like total reaction, with pluralistic capitalism something in between.

But current ideology may not be the permanent ideology. We may be witnessing just the first Utopian stage, similar to the 1840s.

8. The campus is more complex than the factory. It is at once a market where people pick and choose, a guild where masters teach apprentices, a democracy where each person has a voice, a bureaucracy that administers rules, a corporation that holds property, a church that has its own religion of academic freedom and the rule of reason. Governance, as a result, is subject to few, if any, clear-cut solutions either theoretically or practically. Relationships are more fragile, more easily destroyed. The actions of quite small groups are potentially more likely to break the campus asunder. The campus is a hot-house plant that withers before the hot wind of disruption.

So this new social force may have other consequences than did the workers. Confrontation as a tactic is harder to absorb into society than is "responsible" bargaining; unrestricted demands more difficult to satisfy; syndicalism harder to adjust to, since it is essentially incompatible with highly organized, large scale, interdependent, advanced industrial society; the campus harder to preserve when subject to disruption. Consequently, this new social force may turn out to be more sporadic, more uneven, more unpredictable, more permanently—although intermittently—radical, more damaging to the existing social fabric than was the new social force of the workers one century and more ago; and thus the "happy ending" all around is less assured. But it may be as difficult in 1968 to divine the ultimate meaning of 1964, as it was in 1852 to see the full meaning of 1848.

Yet we need to try to be sensitive to the new realities. Advanced industrial society gives rise to affluence, encourages permissiveness in the home, church, and school, and creates a new volatility of opinion and conduct as communications and travel bring instantaneous contact with people and events around the world. University students reflect the new affluence, the new permissiveness, the new volatility, more than do the members of any other group. Their behavior gives some clues to the new culture being born. The workers by now represent the old culture of mass solidarity, the "standard rate," the supremacy of materialistic goals, statist solutions. The students are now the "forerunners." What happens first on the campus may happen later and to a lesser degree in the broader society. We should be alert to the new possibilities.

Thus there is this new social force to understand. Beyond understanding lies the development of reasonable responses; and what happens in the longrun depends very much on the wisdom of the responses in the shortrun. The most difficult set of adjustments may be those which involve making the new technology that integrates and dominates consistent with the new education (which it requires) that diversifies and liberates.

I should now like to turn to a discussion of "the role of the university president," which was the topic originally assigned to me. Quite obviously that role is now a more difficult one than it was in more "normal" times before the campus, along with the ghetto, took the place of the factory and the farm as a principal locale of social unrest.

I once wrote, in more "normal" times, that the president had three main roles: the role of the "mediator" who kept the peace and held together, rather loosely, the disparate elements of the modern "multiversity"; of the "initiator" who was responsible for such progress as there might be and who, since "progress is more important than peace," should be willing to "sacrifice" peace to get progress; and of the "gladiator" who fought for academic freedom and institutional autonomy. I noted that the "dividing lines" between being a mediator and a gladiator "may not be as clear as crystal, but they are at least as fragile."

I would now make three changes in this commentary as a result of the new situation and greater experience:

1. I would not say that "progress is more important than peace." This was said in the face of faculty conservatism, which was then the main barrier to change. I would now say that "progress in *most* important *to* peace." This is said in the face of the student revolt against the academic status quo. I would now emphasize the importance of quick solutions to reasonable requests; and I would point out the natural alliance between the president and moderate student leaders in getting some changes against faculty opposition.

2. I would not again use the word *mediator*. It seems to have been the one word remembered among the three words used. More importantly, it is a word that is frequently misunderstood. It seems to be commonly thought that the mediator plays only a passive role of passing messages back and forth. The larger role I had intended to imply of holding a community together through mutual understanding and persuasion is not the connotation the word *mediator* carries to many people, although I had insisted that the "mediator" should be concerned not with the "workable compromise" of the day but rather with the "effective solution that enhances the long-run distinction and character of the institution." What I had meant to suggest, and still believe, is that the president must work mainly with persuasion and not with dictation and force.

I would now use the phrase *campus leader*, which carries a more positive and less passive connotation, which emphasizes responsibility for the coherence, cohesion, integrity, and structure of the institution. I would add that it is important to have a sense of community on the campus and a sense of participation throughout it, and that this requires great attention to size, that it not be too excessive; to rate of growth, that it not be too rapid; to internal structure, that it not be too monolithic; to channels of communication, that they not be too clogged.

May I introduce a personal historical note that, as a university chancellor and president, I concentrated heavily on the roles of "innovator" and "gladiator" and by comparison less on the role of "mediator." In particular, I made almost no effort to "mediate" with Ronald Reagan or Max Rafferty or Hugh Burns (of the State Senate Committee on Un-American Activities), or with the leaders of the Far Left. History may tell whether this was the wise or unwise choice; whether it would have been better to be more of a "mediator" among *all* groups and less of an "innovator" and "gladiator."

3. I would add, with some regret, a fourth presidential role. This is the role of "image maker" creating a favorable image of the institution and of the president as the public symbol of the institution. In modern society, with the mass replacement of face-to-face relations by intermediate images, images become crucial. Reputation becomes perhaps more important than character; appearance than reality; public relations than actual results. This is particularly true of a large institution with many far-flung publics. Thus the president must be concerned with his or her own image and the image of the institution (and the two are so closely related) for the sake of the continuity and progress of the institution. The president must protect the position and its incumbent; let others be expendable; not always be in the front lines; associate himself or herself with the positive; and allow others to be associated with the negative, with trouble. The president may not be a giant, but should look like one; and may not be a saint, but should appear to be one.

I would append the note that the role of image maker can be overdone, and that "selective cowardice" can become simply cowardice. Under current circumstances, however, this last possibility can be a particularly attractive option as adversaries within and without the campus make the president their opponent, and these adversaries are more potent than ever before. A president always faces the major choice of "optimal" behavior to maximize the quality of the institution or of "survival" behavior to maximize his or her own longevity. In the conditions of modern university life, the tendency of many presidents is to place "survival" first; yet the need for "optimal" behavior has seldom been more urgent.

The role of president has once again become absolutely central. There is a new era that calls for "giants" as there were when Eliot and Gilman and Harper and Wheeler led the American university into its modern form; for presidents who will successfully perform all these major roles simultaneously; for people who will be initiators and gladiators and campus leaders and image makers. Herman Wells of Indiana once wrote that it was also important, above all, to "be lucky." There is this caveat, however—that it is less likely that one will "be lucky" now that university relations have taken on so many of the characteristics that once marked industrial relations in their bloodier days, now that the campus has replaced Haymarket Square and the Embarcadero.

To end on an optimistic note: industry in the United States in the 1960s is stronger than in the 1930s, and partly because of the successful adjustments to the problems of the 1930s; and the campus in the year 2000 may equally be more effective than in the 1960s if reasonable responses are made to the problems of the 1960s. I think these reasonable responses will be made.

Notes

* Paper presented at the 21st Annual Winter Meeting of the Industrial Relations Research Association, Chicago, Illinois, December 29, 1968. Industrial Relations Research Association, *Proceedings of the 21st Annual Meeting* (December 1968): 15–25. Reprinted by permission.

Vignette—A Possible Residue

The Intellectual versus Society: A Source of Conflict?*

The Committee on Lectures at the University of California, Irvine, a campus I had helped to create, asked me to come back (1973) to participate in an annual lecture series. I chose to talk on how some faculty members had reacted to the student revolts and what this might imply for some distant future time. But the student revolt, by then, had totally disappeared, and the sense I had from the audience, judging by the questions and the comments afterward, was that it was better to let sleeping dogs lie. And, it is quite true, they were asleep and still are asleep—but they also still exist.

I take as part of my text tonight an observation by Lionel Trilling. He says that an "adversary culture"—adversary to the dominant culture of the United States—is developing among intellectuals whose primary home is the campus. He notes, "Any historian of the literature of the modern age will take virtually for granted the adversary intention, the actually subversive intention, that characterizes modern writing."[1]

I take my text also from an article by David Riesman, who writes of the "collision course" being traveled by higher education and the surrounding society. It is a collision course for many reasons, including the political dissent between the campus and the community, as "higher education becomes more and more omnivorous of resources while it becomes less and less able to elicit community support."[2]

My text also comes from a comment by Alain Touraine, a leading French sociologist, who, in speaking not about the United States particularly but about all advanced industrial societies, claims that "the university, because it is a center of production and diffusion of scientific knowledge, is increasingly becoming the main locus of the social conflicts of our times."[3] He points to developments that have been more severe in Germany, France, and Japan than in the United States, but more severe in the United States than in Great Britain or the Scandinavian countries.

How true are these observations?

Who are these intellectuals that are the subject of such concern? They are not just educated persons. You can be an intellectual without being formally educated, and you clearly can be educated without being an intellectual. I would define an intellectual as one who takes a broad interest in the affairs of society, who is not solely concerned with these affairs for personal material reasons and who also is interested in philosophical and analytical approaches to their understanding. I do not suggest, by any means, that everybody who goes to college becomes an intellectual; but colleges constitute a major source from which intellectuals are drawn.

I would like to comment this evening on the rise of intellectuals as an important segment of modern American society; and on the positive roles they can and must play, and on the negative roles they can and may play (I realize that both positive and negative roles need definition). I would also like to give some data about current opinions among the American professoriate, in particular, and to suggest what we should be doing on campuses, now in a period of quiescence, to be sure that the role of higher education, and of intellectuals more generally, can be on the positive much more than on the negative side.

Any modern industrial society develops a substantial intellectual group. The wealth of these societies makes it possible to train intellectuals, and the complexity of society makes them necessary to the conduct of society—to what John Kenneth Galbraith calls the rise of the "technostructure."

The intellectual is no longer on the periphery of American society as was true throughout most of our history. The intellectual class or segment of society, is now central to the conduct of our cultural, economic, and political life. One might say today that the intellectuals are the vanguard group in any modern industrial society, including our own. Once economic growth depended upon new land, more labor, more capital. Increasingly it now depends upon more skill and new knowledge. Politically, more education is necessary as we have a more complex political system to manage. One of the consequences of education has been to create the second largest political party in the United States, the party of the independents. More people identify themselves as independents than as members of one of the two "major" parties.

The intellectuals have become a real force in society. In some ways they are taking the part once played by the peasants or the farmers, and later by the trade union movement in social change.

There are those who say that the intellectuals are now substantiating for labor as the vanguard group, and they assume that the intellectuals will have the same impact and will conduct themselves in the same way. I would like to suggest, instead, that the differences are absolutely enormous. It is not possible to take a theory of social development and just introduce "intellectuals" wherever the word "workers" was used before. In labor movements the tendency is toward unification; unity is the great cry. Among intellectuals, the tendency is toward factionalism. Among labor movements, the direction is toward practical goals—another nickel or another dime. Among intellectuals, the goals tend to be more idealistic. Labor movements build solid bureaucracies. Movements of intellectuals tend to be made up of very individualistic persons. The impacts of labor movements tend to be glacial, all the time in certain directions, having major impacts over a substantial period of time. The history of activity by intellectuals shows it to be very sporadic, rising and falling, shifting in tactics and interest. In looking at the role of intellectuals, one cannot draw on past theories of social change or social development. To do so would lead to totally false conclusions.

The particular role of the intellectual is to provide new ideas for an advancing society and the skills to make them work with some degree of efficiency. Intellectuals also provide much of the critical evaluation of society, the ideas for its effective self-renewal. Look back at the last decade. It was through the intellectuals, particularly on campuses, that the American people began to be alerted to the enormity of our conduct in Southeast Asia, and the enormity of the problem of preserving our natural resources for the generations of the future. The roles of critical evaluation for self-renewal and of the development of a higher level of cultural life in the nation are of great importance.

Some potential negative roles exist as well. Intellectuals are also capable of handicapping a democratic society in its process of constant self-renewal and improvement. (1) They have the capacity of conducting themselves so that they will invite a period of anti-intellectualism such as the United States saw in the past and as Richard Hofstadter so well documented; by conduct that engenders anti-intellectual responses, they can bring on periods of repression and even retrogression in a society. It is possible, in particular, to carry the tactics of confrontation beyond the limits of tolerance of society, thus leading to repression. (2) It is also possible to saturate a society with negative criticism without positive suggestions for improvement. (3) It is also possible to make so many excessive demands and build up so many excessive hopes in the people that it is harder for society to work effectively and make progress. (4) It is also possible through exploitation of methods of codetermination to make it harder for the society to operate. If you want to see a case of all this in practice, take a look at some of the German universities of today.

Let me now turn more specifically to the campus situation. Some thought that what was happening on the campuses of the United States in the 1960s was going to lead to revolution. That has proved to be wrong. It is now equally wrong to say that we are back to eternal apathy; that there never will be a period of activism again. That, too, is bound to be proved false. I do not know when and I do not know over what issues, but I am sure activism is going to occur again.

The campuses in the 1960s, and I think they will also in the future, took the place once held by the rural areas during the days of populism, once held by the factories during the days of trade union organization, as a central focal point for social conflict. This nation has had social conflict throughout its history; and it is bound to have it again. The focal point for the future is likely to be the campus and the intellectual circles of the nation. Let me say a word about the potential volatility of the situation. When one reads the history of higher education around the world, one finds periods of high political activity, almost incandescent periods, followed by periods of great apathy, not in a regular cyclical fashion, but in an erratic way. Periods of great activism drop into periods of great apathy, and then great activism rises again. We are currently in a period of apathy.

Now let me give you some data drawn from the Carnegie Commission survey of faculty and student opinion, and from a related survey, conducted over a period from 1969 to 1972. The Carnegie survey covered 70,000 undergraduate students, 30,000 graduate students and some 60,000 faculty members; the other survey was a much smaller sample. A central finding: compared with the older consensus among faculty members, there is now a significant lack of consensus on campus. This lack of consensus is likely to continue for quite a long time. About half of all the faculty members in the nation were recruited in the 1960s, when we doubled the size of higher education, and they will hold tenure to the year 2000; and it is largely faculty members recruited in the 1960s who have withdrawn from the old consensus.

The old consensus was that the university should stay out of politics; it should fight for its budget and its own independence, but stay out of external politics. This was largely taken for granted. Faculty members in these surveys were asked, "Do you think it is desirable for college and university faculty to put themselves on record by vote in major political controversies?" Once the answer would have been overwhelmingly "no." Now, the answer is one-third "yes." Another question was, "Do you agree or disagree with the statement that faculty members should be free on campus to advocate violent resistance to public authority?" The answer was in the range of one-fifth to one-fourth "agree." Another question was "Do you agree or disagree with the statement that meaningful social change cannot be achieved through traditional American politics?" One-third said "agree." The question was asked, "Do you agree or disagree with the statement that students who disrupt the functioning of a college should be expelled or suspended?" One-fourth said "disagree." A question was asked, "Do you agree or disagree with the statement that in the

U.S.A. today there can be no justification for using violence to achieve political goals?'' The range of one-fourth to one-third said "disagree." One-fifth to one-third of faculty members rejected the old consensus in each of these areas.

Now let me give you several caveats. (1) These questions were asked in the period of 1969 to 1972, which was a troubled period in the United States. It was the end of a decade when this country had seen a more divisive external conflict than ever before in history, and the second most divisive internal conflict. The questions were asked at the end of a very special period in American history. (2) People change their minds as circumstances change and as they get older. (3) Though I gravely doubt it, there may never again be an incandescent political period in American life which will call forth action from the campus community or from intellectuals. (4) People do not always act the way they answer questionnaires. (5) Beyond that, there may be some restraining forces greater than in the past. The labor market, particularly for faculty members, is going to be a difficult one for at least the next twenty years; and students may turn out to be more conservative than they were the last time around. If unionization does spread through the campuses across the country, it may turn out to be a conservative force in connection with political activity. This may surprise some people, but there are two reasons why this will be so. First, in industrial relations, initially the most activist workers are the union organizers. Gradually unions become institutionalized, develop their bureaucracies, develop their programs, and become increasingly conservative. If you were going to define the "establishment" of the United States today, you would have to define the American trade unions as part of it. This same historical pattern is likely to be reflected on campus. Second, if it is to be effective, a union wants to organize as large a group of people as it possibly can. It therefore wants to concentrate on those things which everybody agrees on—more money, for example. However, if politics start to come in and the union faces the question of whether or not it is going to be divided and lose some members on political grounds, it starts playing down political issues. Already in the United States, there are campuses where the union leaders have stepped in and said, in effect, "Please do not raise that divisive political issue; it will lose us members; it will make us less effective in bargaining with the board of trustees and the Governor; it will be a disservice to the faculty."

In any event, after considering these caveats, we have less consensus about the conduct of the campus in relation to political affairs than the United States has ever seen before.

More generally, in recent memory we have not been in a situation where American intellectuals were not generally in sympathy with the point of view of the nation as a whole and of its leaders. The intellectuals joined in with the New Deal; they welcomed it. The intellectuals then joined with the nation in opposing the threat of fascism sweeping around the world. The intellectuals subsequently generally joined in with the rest of the nation in opposing Stalinism and joined in support of "cold war" activities. We went through a period from the early 1930s until about the middle 1960s when the intellectuals in American society and American political leadership were generally in agreement with each other. Then we had the Vietnam War and the rise of the civil rights movement, and now we have Watergate; all of which separate the intellectuals of the nation from some of the leadership of society and from some or even many of their fellow citizens. We have a new situation.

I raise these issues this evening because I have a great belief in the positive role that needs to be played and can be played by the American campus specifically, by higher education more generally, and by the intellectuals more broadly. The roles played by intellectuals and by higher education in the future are going to be as important as those of any other group or any other set of institutions in America.

However, I am concerned that negative actions may again be taken, as they have been sometimes recently in the United States, and as they are now being taken in some other industrial nations of the world. In this period of quiescence, we have a chance to look at ourselves, not in the heat of controversy but in a more rational way. Higher education needs to decide how it will conduct itself in the future. It needs a "constitution" and a "bill of rights and responsibilities," as recently recommended by the Carnegie Commission on Higher Education. We need, on the American campus, a new consensus about how we shall conduct ourselves, particularly in the political arena.

Basic to the new consensus should be the absolute and total protection of the right to dissent. Dissent is not something which should be cherished for the sake of the faculty members or the student alone. Dissent on campus ought to be cherished also for the sake of society. I have often thought that the rules on academic freedom are really basically for the protection of society, so that it will be assured that there will be freely placed before it a variety of points of view from which it might choose—some viewpoints being quite critical. A greater effort to develop understanding on the part of the American people of the positive role played by dissent is necessary. Society can only renew itself adequately as there are people who will criticize it on the basis of scholarship.

A second aspect of the new consensus should be a rejection of the use of violence on campuses and by members of the campus community against society; and a third should be a rejection of the use of political tests for appointments and promotions. Rejection of violence and rejection of political tests for appointment are basic, with reliance instead on persuasion and on the preservation of academic standards.

In particular, I suggest that intellectuals are already an important part of society and are bound to become even more so, and that the campus is increasingly the focal point for intellectual activity. I also suggest that new attitudes on campus, and the new chasm between many intellectuals and much of the rest of society raise new possibilities for difficulties in the future. Thus, we have to continue to be concerned, as we have been for so long, about protecting ourselves and our right of dissent; but we also need to be more concerned with the greater and growing position of the intellectual in society with the resultant capacity to do more good but also more harm. Consequently, we have to be more concerned about our own self-restraint, about how we conduct ourselves so that we can maximize our capacity for the improvement of society and minimize the possibilities of aiding deterioration. A great challenge before higher education in this new world, in this post-modernized, post-industrial society, is to give considerable thought to how we can best contribute to the improvement of society through our intellects and how we can simultaneously restrain ourselves in legitimate ways in order to minimize the chances of any negative impacts of intellectuals on the surrounding society and on ourselves in turn.

I realize that this is raising an issue in a period when people are not concerned greatly about it. But I wish that some issues had been raised in advance of the middle 1960s about the nature of student life and about rising student concerns at a time when we were relying on the apathetic students not to take any action. We should have been thinking then about the changing nature of students and the changing impact of society upon them before it was brought so forcibly to our attention. We should have been better prepared to conduct ourselves in more effective ways.

Once again, we have a chance, which we missed last time around, to give serious thought to the way intellectuals on the campus ought to be conducting themselves for the sake of the welfare of higher education and the welfare of the nation. If we give thought now, we can potentially make a greater positive contribution later on than if we simply rely on the fact that, at the moment, there are no problems and if we wistfully hope that there never will be any again.

Notes

* Presented in the "Four Dimensions of the American Intellect" lecture series, the Student Affairs Committee on Lectures, University of California, Irvine, May 16, 1973.

1. Lionel Trilling, *Beyond Culture: Essays on Literature and Learning* (New York: Viking Press, 1965), xii.

2. David Riesman, "Universities on Collision Course," *Trans-Action* 6, no. 10 (September 1969): 4.

3. Alain Touraine, *The Academic System in American Society* (New York: McGraw-Hill, 1974), 279.

PART III

Governance and Leadership under Pressure

Introduction—Governance and Leadership under Pressure

The great transformation had substantial impacts on governance and leadership. This could have been anticipated just from the growth in size and in programmatic assignments, but mostly it was not. More decisions of greater potential consequences had to be made faster than ever before in American history. All this was then greatly complicated by the internal and external politicalization of the campus by student and faculty activists, and by politicians in the surrounding community. The "ivory tower" became a political platform; and then, subsequently, a victim of the "new depression"[1] in economic support for higher education at the time of the OPEC crisis. Overwhelming growth, then intense politicalization, and then depression, all taken together, created the greatest period of crisis ever experienced in American higher education by governance and leadership. These developments engulfed a system of governance and leadership that was loosely knit to begin with; and this loosely knit structure, it turned out, was one of its aspects that saved it.

Digression: Academic Governance as a Series of "Estates"

The literature on higher education is replete with discussions of whether the campus should be viewed as a vertical hierarchical structure, as Veblen saw it, topped off with boards composed of "Captains of Industry,"[2] with formal levels of reporting, formal rules, and institutional goals; or also with an informal life of alliances, shared values, and myths, and with individual and group as well as institutional goals, as others see it;[3] or as a horizontal collegial structure, as seen by the American Association of University Professors, of "shared governance"—mostly shared by the faculty; or as a political entity, as seen by Baldridge[4] and others, with constant struggles over who has the power over what; or as on atomistic market with individuals making choices; or just as chaos or anarchy.[5] In fact, it is all of these.

I have come to think that the campus is better viewed, rather than in any of the above ways, as a series of "estates," as in France before the Revolution with its nobility, clerics, and commoners. It is not best viewed as a highly unified organization with a single dominant form of governance. I see instead four major estates; and two minor.[6]

The first estate is "the administration" of president, trustees, and non-academic staff organized on vertical lines.

The second estate is "the faculty" organized on horizontal lines; with a variation, in times of political crisis, when it is disorganized like a mass political convention (à la Chicago 1968).

The third estate is "the students," which has, in turn, three governing formations: a market at all times;[7] the collegial student government of earlier times structured as a democracy; and the political movement of the dissident activists of more recent times relying on demonstrations and attention in the media—a movement sometimes united and sometimes fractionated.

The fourth estate is "external authority" with its decision makers and its professional staffs, ruling by decree and by budgetary authority. It might also be said that there is now often a three-and-one-half estate, partly external and partly internal, of systems of governance and coordinating mechanisms.

A fifth, and more minor, estate is constituted by "the alumni," strong in some places and weak in others.

The sixth, and again minor, estate, or actually estates, is composed of "associated enterprises"—the medical profession, industry, agriculture, the legal profession, and others, working with persuasion and pressure but with no direct authority to make decisions.

No major estate can succeed or even survive for long without the other estates.

Each estate controls or influences something, but no estate controls or even influences everything.

All estates are held together by a rich mixture of individual choice, conciliation, mediation, and arbitration.

The totality of governance contains similarities to other types of organizations but has no close counterparts in all of organized life.

Some of these estates are in close contact with each other most of the time—as faculty with administration; some in loose contact—as faculty with the student community outside the classroom; some in occasional contact—as alumni with faculty; some in almost no contact—as "associated enterprises" with students.

These estates share in varying degrees, however, the same physical, historical, and functional environments, and carry on related activities. Each affects the others, sometimes more and sometimes less. Some can make decisions in areas of their own autonomy; others share decisions; and still others can only take actions that influence those who make decisions. Some historically rise in strength, as did the third estate in France, and some fall, as did the French nobility. In the great transformation in higher education from 1960 to 1980, the first estate (the administration) fell, the fourth estate (external authority) rose permanently in power, and the third estate (the students) rose temporarily in power and shifted from the collegiate form to the form of a political movement or movements.

Governance within higher education is, by all odds, the most complicated I have known, and I have substantial experience with corporations, unions, government agencies, and foundations. More than any other, it is better understood as a strung-along series of independent or quasi-independent entities; and it is less well understood as a unified institution with one dominant form of governance. The intricate dynamics of the governance of academic institutions is founded on the fluctuations in the interactions of the several entities and on the changes in the inherent natures of each of the entities themselves. There is no such thing as *the* university or *the* college. To a much lesser extent, in my experience, this is also true, to one degree or another, of all organizations—none are fully unified, not even those made up of a single individual; but no others are so little held together by common formal structures.

And so, what happened to higher education in the recent great transformation might best be viewed as what happened within, between, and among the various estates within institutions rather than as what happened to institutions viewed in a more monolithic way. What happened to institutions was based on what was happening within and among the estates that composed them.

All this greatly complicates the life of the president. Within the first estate, the president takes (from trustees) and gives (to staff) directions; in relation with the second, consults and agrees; in relation with the third, tries to persuade and, very occasionally, orders; in relation with the fourth, negotiates and pressures; and in relation with the fifth and sixth, listens and sometimes concedes. Since the consensual mode of decision making in academic affairs is conservative, the president needs to be an initiator. Since many controversies arise among the estates, the president is required to be a mediator and arbitrator. Since external authority and "associated enterprises" seek sometimes to exert excessive or unwise control, the president is forced to be a gladiator. This requires a wide range of skills and temperaments seldom found in full array in a single individual.[8]

15. Changing Loci of Power. Loci of power have a long history of change in American higher education from ministers to lay boards, from agriculture to industry, from boards to presidents, from presidents to faculties, among others. But the most complex and important series of changes took place during the recent great transformation: among all estates—from internal estates to external estates; among internal estates, from the administration for a time to students and also, in some places, more permanently to faculties; and within estates, from the collegiate student leaders to the political activists, and from the collegial faculty, on some rare but important occasions, to political mass conventions; and also within estates from *economic* "associated enterprises" to *political*—to caucuses of women, Blacks, Hispanics, and Asians, among many others.

The issue of power was made more central, but power was, in and of itself, made more decentralized. More "power to the people" meant less to an accepted establishment and more to factions and fractions of factions. The politics of power also meant less consultation and more confrontation. New alliances were formed, as, for example, of politically active faculty and students. Old alliances were damaged as, for example, of Jewish and Black students; and of faculty and students in general, when the focus of the student activists moved from attacking the administrators to attacking faculty authority over the curriculum and over faculty appointments and promotions.

Some estates showed great persistence in their strength and goals, particularly the faculty and the external agencies; some showed only moments of intensity, as the politically active students; some developments reached early limits of expansion, as did the unionization of faculty members at a one-third level of the professoriate when the OPEC crisis, with its impacts of faculty salaries, was over—and when students stopped trying to take over faculty academic prerogatives, which had also aroused faculty members to organize to protect their turf.

The governance of academic life is better understood as it is more disaggregated.

16. Changing Administrative Styles. Administrative styles in higher education have shifted from the morality of the minister to the modernization drives of the "giants" among presidents after the Civil War, to the collegial presidents working with the faculty, to the aggressive planning of the builders at the time of the "tidal wave" of students, to the maneuvers of the political survivors of more recent times.

17. Holding the Center. Presidents were at the vortex of the great transformation. They were the persons under the most pressure and were placed in the most precarious positions. And they developed many grievances. Surprisingly, "student relations" did not head the list and were seen in a different light from how they were seen by the public at large. The center, by and large, however, did hold, and it was the presidents who held it, but it took some heroic efforts and led to some casualties along the way.

18. New Complications. One new complication was the rapid shift from the freestanding campus to systems of campuses in much of public higher education.

Digression: Centralization of Governance

The shift to governance strata above the campus level in the public sector took a great leap forward after 1960, as more students attended colleges and universities, as state expenditures greatly increased, and as higher education became more important to the states for the sake of equality of opportunity and advancement of economic capabilities.

As of 1960, ten states had formal coordinating mechanisms with at least advisory responsibilities over such issues as missions and budgets.[9] As of 1980, seventeen states had been added to the list of those with coordinating mechanisms.[10]

As of 1960, eleven states had consolidated governing boards, at least for their four-year institutions, with power to appoint campus presidents.[11] As of 1980, eleven states had been added to the list.[12]

States without either type of statewide system in 1960 numbered twenty-nine. States without any statewide system in 1980 numbered four.[13]

Thus the extent of statewide coordination had been both greatly extended among the states and intensified, moving from advisory coordination to centralized budgetary coordination to governing coordination via the appointment of campus executives by governing authorities above the campus level.[14] However, there was some offsetting reduction of control by state departments of finance, via line-item budgets, in some states in the course of establishing coordinating authorities.

Perhaps the best statistical indicator of centralization of governance is the proportion of students in the public sector who were on campuses in states with coordinated or consolidated systems: in 1960, it was 42 percent, and by 1980 it was 94 percent. Another indicator is that 54 percent of students on public campuses in 1980 were on campuses where presidents were appointed not at the campus level but at the system level.

The freestanding, self-governing public campus is becoming an endangered species.

19. Enter the Federal Government. The federal government entered into the affairs of higher education during the great transformation as never before. It came, in particular, to dominate the financial support of research and to lead in public support of students through financial aid.

20. Reenter the States. But the federal government began then to exit, particularly after the Higher Education Amendments of 1978, in terms of new initiatives, and the states again became dominant with the governors as the "new holders of power" in higher education.

21. An Eternal Issue. I have earlier noted that the fourth estate (external authority) gained power during the great transformation. Until 1960, it had generally been held at arm's length. By 1980, it had become the most important single estate in terms of overall policy. It went from being a minor estate to become *the* major estate, in just twenty years, within the public sector, which was by now also 80 percent of all of higher education. This raised grave questions of what belongs to Caesar and what to God— with "Caesar" being external authority and "God" being internal authority. But, in practice, as I see it, the Biblical contrast between what Caesar wants and what God deserves has not been all that great. It has been easier to "render" unto both of them than if there were the stark dichotomy that some have assumed. But the issue keeps arising, and always will, in small ways and in large. However, I have been surprised at how well it has all worked out—to date at least. That it has all worked out so well is mostly due to the restraint shown by the many Caesars; and, in part, because there were so many of them.

Notes

1. Earl F. Cheit, *The New Depression in Higher Education: A Study of Financial Conditions at 41 Colleges and Universities* (New York: McGraw-Hill, 1971).

2. Thorstein Veblen, *The Higher Learning in America* (Stanford, CA: Academic Reprints, 1954 [originally published 1918]).

3. Robert Birnbaum, *How Colleges Work: The Cybernetics of Academic Organization and Leadership* (San Francisco: Jossey-Bass, 1988); and Ellen Earle Chaffee and William G. Tierney, with Peter T. Ewell and Jack Y. Krakower, *Collegiate Culture and Leadership Strategies* (New York: American Council on Education/Macmillan, 1988).

4. J. Victor Baldridge, et al., *Policy Making and Effective Leadership* (San Francisco: Jossey-Bass, 1978).

5. Michael D. Cohen and James G. March, *Leadership and Ambiguity: The American College President* (New York: McGraw-Hill, 1974).

6. Also see Don K. Price, *The Scientific Estate* (Cambridge, MA: Belknap Press, 1965).

7. For a discussion of the rise of the student market as a determining factor in the development of higher education, see David Riesman, *On Higher Education: The Academic Enterprise in an Era of Rising Student Consumerism* (San Francisco: Jossey-Bass, 1980).

8. For some excellent advice on the governance of universities, see Henry Rosovsky, *The University: An Owner's Manual* (New York: Norton, 1990), particularly chapter 15. Rosovsky argues, in particular, that the university cannot be a

democracy since depth of academic knowledge and duration of participation vary so greatly among members of the constituent bodies.

9. Illinois, Kentucky, New Mexico, New York, North Carolina, Oklahoma, Texas, Utah, Virginia, Wisconsin.

10. Alabama, Arkansas, California, Colorado, Connecticut, Indiana, Louisiana, Maryland, Massachusetts, Minnesota, Missouri, New Jersey, Ohio, Pennsylvania, South Carolina, Tennessee, Washington.

11. Arizona, Florida, Georgia, Idaho, Iowa, Kansas, Mississippi, Montana, North Dakota, Oregon, South Dakota.

12. Alaska, Hawaii, Maine, Nevada, North Carolina, Rhode Island, Utah, West Virginia, New Hampshire, Wisconsin, Wyoming.

13. Delaware, Michigan, Nebraska, Vermont.

14. The above listing of states is based on Robert O. Berdahl, *Statewide Coordination of Higher Education* (Washington, DC: American Council on Higher Education, 1971), as updated by Aims C. McGuinness, Jr., in *State Postsecondary Education Structures Handbook, 1988* (Denver: Education Commission of the States, 1988), and in personal communication.

Changing Loci of Power—
Governance and Functions*

Daedalus *in 1970 had another in its series on higher education; this time under the title* The Embattled University. *Many battles were being fought. The one I wrote about was over governance. Overall, I worried that the old "consensus" was breaking down. Actually, a new consensus has by now (1990) emerged in a series of pragmatic adjustments, particularly in the direction of more external authority.*

The governance of the American college and university is a residue of traditions and arrangements that are more the gift of history than of conscious thought. This system of governance is now in crisis as never before, and history alone will not dictate the future. The way out of this crisis, if there is a way out, will be extraordinarily difficult because of the peculiarities and complexities of the academic institution. The campus is inherently difficult to govern—even in theory.

The Residue of History

Academic governance in the United States has at least four features that distinguish it from patterns elsewhere. The first is the heavy reliance on a board of trustees, regents, or managers composed of people drawn primarily from outside academic life and from outside governmental authority. There are boards or councils in Britain, Canada, and Australia, among other countries, as well as at some of the private universities of Japan, but they are nearly always much weaker than American boards in their exercised authority and are usually of a more mixed representation, including faculty and sometimes student representatives.

The second special feature is the comparatively strong role of the president, who is appointed without specific term of office as a full-time executive with a relatively large administrative staff. He or she has considerably more authority and opportunity for initiative, narrow as these limits may be, than the counterpart vice-chancellor or rector.

A third characteristic is the consolidated nature of the campus. To begin with, there is a campus as compared with the scattered endeavors, for example, in Paris or Buenos Aires. And on the campus, the central administrative organization is a single college of letters and sciences or arts and sciences. It includes most of the instruction and much of the research. Residence halls are simply residence halls, and not also academic units. Departments within the college are clearly subsidiary administrative units, as compared with the organization of a series of more or less autonomous faculties in many universities abroad—faculties of science and philosophy and law and medicine. Some of these consolidated colleges of letters and science in the United States are quite huge and have a single curricular policy and a single grading system.

The fourth identifying trait is the importance of external, but nongovernmental, forces in the conduct of the affairs of the campus. In the United States, the alumni have an influence found almost nowhere else. Industry, agriculture, and professional associations have their points of contact, their advisory committees, their influence over funds. Private foundations advise about and finance endeavors according to their own systems of priorities.

This system of governance contrasts with others around the world. In Britain, the organized faculty has predominant influence, with the power of the University Grants Committee growing steadily (as of 1970). Universities are generally smaller in size and more divided internally into colleges and institutes (as in London, the largest, which still has under 25,000 students). In France, authority resides with the separate faculties and their deans and with the Ministry of Education; in Germany, it rests with the individual full professor directing his area of scholarship and with the State government; in Russia, with the government formally and the Party informally and with the Academy that stands outside the universities with a degree of independence; in Japan, with the organized faculty; and in Latin America, officially with the faculties, under their deans, and unofficially and intermittently also with students and heads of states. In Latin America, as elsewhere, Catholic universities give more power to the rector and more influence to the church than do others. As a general rule, faculties and governments are the dominating forces outside the United States.

The American system bears the marks of its origins in the Protestant sects of the early colonies. These Protestant sects emphasized the supremacy of the parishioners over the ministers; it was natural that they should also provide control by leaders of the community over the new colleges. If there was a model outside the colonies, it was probably Edinburgh, which had a council largely composed of town councilmen and clergy. Similar arrangements existed at Leyden and Geneva. The earliest local councils were established in Italy when faculty members took refuge in the protection of the city fathers from the harsh rule of the students. Thus the rise of the city under control of its burghers was also a precedent for the board of the American college. It would have seemed natural, at a time when the church and the city were being placed under citizen control, to apply the same principle to the college. The populism of the nineteenth century in America added strength to this tradition—the college served the people and the board represented the people.

The president of the early college was like the minister of a Protestant church—in fact, most presidents were ministers drawn from the church. When the corporation became a more dominant institution, the president became more like the head of a corporation.

The single college of letters and science grew out of the unified classical college with its single curriculum and single faculty. Only at the University of Virginia, apparently following the French system, were the professors originally organized into eight separate schools. As the campus grew and departments were established, particularly after the Civil War and after the rise of science as against the classical curriculum, the college of letters and science became the administrative unit for the departments and the central unit for the budget, faculty appointments, approval of courses, and curricular requirements.

The involvement of private groups from outside the campus grew out of the dedication to service by the campus, particularly since the Civil War, the positions of power in society held by industrial and agricultural groups, and also the reliance on the private philanthropy of alumni and, later, of foundations as well.

Changes have taken place. Board members are no longer primarily from the ministry, but from business—as Veblen pointed out and did not like fifty years ago, but then he had not liked the ministers either. The president is no longer a minister, but an executive. The college of letters and science is no longer so dominant, with the growth of professional schools, research institutes, and graduate divisions. The outside private forces have shifted in importance from the churches to agriculture, to industry, to the professions, to the contiguous population. Faculty members have organized into senates and increasingly attained dominant power in academic areas, particularly since World War I. Students have gradually gained more freedom through the reduction of *in loco parentis,* the rise of the elective system for choosing courses, and the establishment of extracurricular activities under their own control, mostly in the period since the Civil War.

Changes have taken place, but the basic structural characteristics of a strong board, a relatively strong president, a largely composite internal structure, and a large role for private organizations from outside academic life remain about as they were in 1900 and in some respects in 1636.

The Pressures for Change

Substantive issues may or may not be settled easily and peacefully; but redistribution of power is always fought out with difficulty. The campus is currently passing from a concentration on individual issues growing out of interests to a confrontation over power growing, in part, out of principle.

There are more claimants for power than ever before, and there is no more power to be divided. Someone must lose if others gain—a zero-sum game. One gainer is the government, state and federal. The major shift in influence since World War II has been to public agencies. The reasons are clear. More of the institutions of higher education are under public control, and more of the money in both public and private institutions is public money. Public interest in higher education has also risen. More young people attend from more strata of society, and the actions of higher education, in research and service and dissent, increasingly affect more of the population. Higher education has become everybody's business. The campus is no longer on the hill with the aristocracy, but in the valley with the people.

State governments are exercising more fiscal control and more influence over direction of growth, usually through coordinating councils, than was the general situation historically. And, currently at least, there is a renewed state interest in the appropriateness of the relationships of students and faculties to political issues and to political action.

But the great new force since World War II has been the federal government. It now supplies one-fourth of all funds spent by institutions of higher education. It has contributed more than one fourth of the new initiatives: toward science, toward residence halls, toward more equality of opportunity to attend college, and in many other ways. And it, too, has an interest in the conduct of the campus within the political arena. Federal interest as yet is fractionized among many federal agencies and several congressional committees, contrary to the situation in most other nations and contrary also to that in the fifty states where control is more unified; but this interest is increasingly concentrated in the Department of Health, Education and Welfare.

Less power and less influence on the direction of change now reside on campus; on campus, the big losers, particularly in domination of the budget, have been the board and the president. Their best instrument of control is now shared with others, and the American pattern is approaching the world pattern.

The public campus in disarray internally is particularly open to further intrusions from the state and the federal government. Internal harmony is the price of autonomy, and this price is not now being paid.

Less power on campus is met by new claimants for that power. The great new force is the students. There are more of them; they are more activist; they have more grievances against the campus and against society; and they are already making gains, and they may make more. For the first time, they are challenging the inner sanctum of the campus where the faculty and the administration have ruled supreme, challenging control over the curriculum and the use of the budget. Earlier they had asked for more freedom for themselves; now they wish to reduce the established authority of others. This is a harder challenge. The initial loser before this new force is the dean of students and then the president; before long, it may be the faculty. The sharpest challenges may come to be between the faculty which once supported the students against the administration and the students who, having disposed of the administration as an intervening power, directly confront the faculty. On campus, the students are the new men of power.

The faculty is in a less clear position. It is gaining power from the administration in those segments of higher education where it has had little—the state colleges, the community colleges, and the lesser of the liberal arts colleges. About half of all faculty members are at such institutions. Gains take the form of stronger academic senates and faculty councils, but also, and potentially more significantly, of union organization. For the first time, unionization is penetrating higher education on an important scale, sometimes aided by state laws that favor unions and look upon academic senates as company-dominated organizations. When this happens, not only is some power shifted to the faculty, but it also comes to be expressed in the new form of employee–employer relations rather than the older collegial sharing of certain authority. There is a change in locus of power and in the philosophy of its expression.

In some places the faculty will gain power from the administration, often in major ways; but it may also lose to the students, sometimes in major ways. The net effect could possibly be a negative one for the faculty in terms of total power. It should be noted that not only are nearly all faculty members happy to take power from the administration, but also that some of them are happy to turn power over to the students. This is particularly true of younger faculty members who see the power of the older faculty members being taken away, and not their own—for they have little. Thus, while the faculty may lose power on a net basis, this does not mean that it will necessarily be unanimously unhappy about this shift.

The least clear trend in governance is what will happen to faculty power vis-á-vis the students. Students are historically changeable in their interests, and it is not certain how long the drive for influence in traditional faculty areas of dominance will continue. Also, faculties are historically conservative, and their capacity for resistance to change is quite substantial. Additionally, the public backlash against student activism can potentially strengthen the hands of the faculties as it did in Bologna centuries ago (and strengthen the hands of the public authorities at the same time). A crucial question will be the degree of unity within faculty ranks. Student seizure of faculty authority is likely only when it draws substantial support from within the faculty itself. Faculties recently have been on the run in the face of the sudden student attacks. If and when they consolidate their new positions, they may be virtually unmovable.

The two net losers are clearly the board and the president. The board is in an increasingly difficult position. Federal and state agencies make decisions it once made. The campus, particularly in the case of the universities and larger state colleges, is now too complex and too dynamic to be subject to detailed decision making; yet many boards historically have been managerial boards. It is difficult to become a performance review board since nobody knows exactly what kind of performance is being reviewed: There is no quarterly test of profit or loss. The campus concentrates on inputs, not outputs, and performance is concerned with outputs, with value added to inputs. As a consequence, many boards respond to the special interests of their members and the current headlines.

The president loses to everybody, partly because he or she has had the most to lose originally, but also because there is no firm base of support in the power struggle, no natural constituency. The president long ago ceased to have much of what Veblen called "erudition" and now ceases to be much of a "captain."

New outside groups also seek influence, chiefly the cities and the minorities, and they are not so discreet in their approaches as agriculture and the alumni have learned to become.

Several special situations exist. The Catholic colleges are moving from religious to secular control and from domination by the president to a sharing of authority with the faculty. Negro colleges are seeing the once masterful presence of the president—indispensable ambassador to the white power structure—reduced in stature as both faculty and students are less impressed than they once were. State colleges and community colleges, where the president historically has personally done all the hiring and firing, are witnessing faculty insurgence, and at some places even the commuter students have now become activist. Administrative authority is being reduced particularly in these three segments.

The forces that have the operative influence are those that can get the changes they want. Since World War II, these have been particularly the federal government and now the students. It is their changes which have prevailed and are prevailing. Nor is this surprising. The public interest in higher education has grown, and the methods of influence (money) have always existed. The influence of youth has arrived on the "tidal wave" of numbers and the new tactics of confrontation. So much of the recent history of higher education has been written by federally sponsored science and by rising numbers of students that governance could not well escape these forces.

The nature of the power struggle has changed. Formerly it was the faculty demanding freedom from the authority of the president and the board in the name of academic freedom with the American Association of University Professors determining the basic lines that divided freedom from unwarranted control. Now it is the campus asking for autonomy from the government, and as yet the lines have not been clearly drawn nor the protective agency devised that will differentiate autonomy from undue domination. The battle has moved to another part of the terrain, and there are new contestants.

Another change has been that part of the conflict has been internalized. The administration has always been looked upon as being partially foreign and thus subject to attack. The internal academic community has been viewed as composed of teachers and students. And now there is conflict within that community. Some of the students are against some of the faculty, and the faculty itself is divided. The academic community historically has faced its enemies outside and to the right. Now it finds attacks coming also from inside and mainly from the left. The "community of scholars" is now fighting within itself. The battle is not over a hated fascism without, but rather over a partially cherished syndicalism within.

A Confusion of Forms

The campus is a Tower of Babel in many ways, including governance. And hell hath few terrors like confusion sharply challenged—which is where higher education finds itself today.

A. J. Muste once wrote that a trade union had a divided soul. It was an "army," but also a "town meeting" and a "business enterprise." It could not be all of these things at once and yet it had to be. So also the university: It is many things to many people and many things to itself. It is a guild where masters train apprentices, where expertise is supreme, a guild run by the masters, by the faculty. It is also a marketplace where students choose one campus instead of another and move from one campus to another, where they choose one course of study and one professor rather than another. Campuses and professors offer their wares, and students individually express their preferences. The customers pick and choose. The rules of the marketplace apply, even though the curriculum does provide a good many "tie-in" sales.

The university is also, to some degree, a democracy. Decisions are made that require the consent of the governed; rules are issued; and discipline is exercised. In a democracy, one person has one vote and is entitled to a jury of his or her peers; and the students are in the majority.

It is a corporation with property, endowments, a reputation, a permanent life to preserve as against the difficulties of the moment. A board of directors should have the competence to manage the institution and look out for its long-run welfare. No group that comes and goes has the knowledge or the interest to do so. The directors represent the integrity of the institution.

It is a bureaucracy with rules to be applied impartially, accounts to be kept, and books to be stored as efficiently as possible. The executive runs the administration.

It is a series of semi-autonomous service bureaus. Each bureau provides information to interested persons in industry, government, and agriculture: It needs an executive secretary working under a committee of the people being served.

It is an agent of the state that spends state money and provides society with the research, skills, and consultation that are so essential to the progress of an industrial economy.

It is a church with a religion. It believes in the unfettered search for truth, in free expression of opinion without fear, in preservation of the past, including all books however offensive they may be currently, and in access on merit and the granting of grace on merit. Its principles are more important than service, or rules, or votes, or consumer preference. It is the keeper of the good, the true, and the beautiful; of culture. It perpetuates a spirit of inquiry and integrity. Its religion is not subject to compromise.

It is also a community, and the essence of community is that it is voluntarily held together by the common standards and interests of its members. Community follows the "will of the meeting," which requires more than a majority vote, and it is based upon a consensus about purpose and process. Traditionally, the academic community has been marked by tolerance among its members in their daily relations and by mutual persuasion as the basis of change; the application of power has been muted in the conduct of its internal affairs.

The university is all of these things, but it is also none of them in total. Perhaps most of all it has been a community with an implicit consensus that the guild of the faculty ran the curriculum and the research; the market choices of the students helped determine which campuses and which areas of study grew and declined; the democracy of the undergraduates governed extracurricular activities; the board watched out for the capital investment and the brand name; the president ran the day-to-day administrative affairs; the deans kept the students and the parents and the farmers and the doctors reasonably happy; the society was served in fact, but attacked on principle and expected to keep its distance; and everybody respected the academic faith and showed tolerance toward his fellow believer. Each element had its own domain. All elements had a common concern for the purposes of the community and the welfare of their fellow participants.

Much of this is now being challenged. The consensus is fading, and in some places, at some times, it no longer exists. The new crisis of governance is located in the dissolution of the old consensus. Without consensus, the campus can perish. . . .

A Pragmatic Pluralistic Strategy

The problems of governance in higher education are so complex that no single solution is possible—situations vary from campus to campus and within a campus from one major function to another. Nor are perfect solutions likely—perfection from one point of view is imperfection from another. Nor are permanent solutions likely—institutions change, and the interests and roles of their several constituencies change, and, also, experience accumulates.

Attempted solutions on the basis of ideology—all power to the faculty or all power to the students or all power to the regents who represent the people—are fraught with danger. There can be no clear preference for one solution versus another solution on principle, given the nature of the academic institution; and ideological solutions tend to be absolutist, authoritarian, and across-the-board in a situation that calls for tolerance, a large measure of individual freedom, and the precise fitting of governance to special situations. Attempted solutions on the basis of power alone—on who has the money or the votes or mob pressure—can tear a campus apart, and once torn apart it is hard to put together again.

A practical, pragmatic approach seems more sensible. An effort should be made to sort out the general issue of governance into its component parts, and then to approach each part in the light of the total problem. Area by area, the central questions should be who has an interest in the problem and who has competence to deal with it. The test should be performance. If performance is good, the argument for change is reduced. If performance is bad, the argument for change is enhanced. As an example, the undergraduate curriculum for nonmajors is a disaster area on many campuses. The faculty as a whole has little or no interest in it, and many students are dissatisfied with it. Here is an area where the faculty cannot be proud of its record, and where the students have a great interest and some competence. Where the faculty has done well, as in some liberal arts colleges, the case for student participation is less persuasive.

This practical, pragmatic approach can lead to a whole series of agreements, area by area, at any moment of time. In fact, this approach is being followed, hesitantly and too slowly, in the United States but particularly in Britain, Canada, and Australia. France and Germany, by contrast, are searching for across-the-board solutions of one-half power to the students or one-third power to the students in all areas. A more pragmatic series of solutions might lead to the conclusion that power should be total in some areas and zero in others.

Governance problems are best handled function by function. Also, academic governance is best conducted on a face-to-face basis within small communities. This suggests that separate institutions should be created to handle separate functions (particularly when the functions are not compatible—as, for example, specialized research versus general education for the nonmajors). Where several functions are combined in single institutions, there should be considerable decentralization of governance. It also suggests that institutions, both in total and in their component parts, should be of modest size. Structure and governance are interrelated.

Massive size is an enemy of effective governance in the academic world with its great variety of activities, interests, and personalities. A campus of large size might best be viewed as a series of communities within a common environment, rather than as a single monolithic community; this is how Harvard is organized.

Higher education in the United States is now reexamining the system of governance given to it by history. A new series of consensus is needed— not one overall "best" solution, not one single preferred form. Variety in solutions should match the variety of situations, and this is almost infinite. Many small agreements will come closer to providing effective governance in totality than will any global approach. An examination of functions is essential to the success of the endeavor. The task is to match the form of governance with the function—to use the guild where the guild works best, democracy where democracy works best, and so forth. We are fortunate in having a variety of forms available to match against the variety of functions. The test of the matching will be found in the performance—let the governance fit the functions. Clarity about functions is becoming essential to sanity in governance now that the consensus which embraced the confusions of the past has disintegrated into conflict.

Notes

* From *Daedalus* 99, no. 1 (Winter 1970): 108–21. Reprinted by permission.

Changing Administrative Styles—
Administration in an Era of Change and Conflict*

David D. Henry was the long-time and very successful president of the University of Illinois. When he retired, a series of lectures were established to honor him, and I was asked to give the first of them. I concentrated on the new assignment of trying to manage conflict on campus. David Henry would say this was not all that new. In 1975 he published a book in the Carnegie series (he had served on the Carnegie Commission) titled Challenges Past, Challenges Present: An Analysis of American Higher Education Since 1930.[†] *His theme was that there were "many stresses" in the period before 1960, including and not limited to the Great Depression, World War II and the return of the veterans afterward, the Senator McCarthy era during the Cold War, and Sputnik; and he reminds us of the "constancy of change" and of the fact that it was never all that easy to try to manage a college or university.*

Administration, defined as continuing arrangements for the conduct of affairs by organizations, is eternally the same in appearance. The daily preparations must always be made: the administrator sees people, handles paper, and makes decisions endlessly. But, although the tasks look much the same, the mood and tempo of the effort rise and fall.

The administration of higher education in the United States is a case in point. It passed through four major stages and is now entering a fifth—the most difficult passage of all.

The first stage of academic administration lasted from 1636, when Havard was founded, until just after the Civil War. This was the stage of the church-dominated board and minister as president; nineteen of the first twenty-one Harvard presidents were ministers. The institutions were quite small—Harvard had about four hundred students and twenty faculty members in 1860. They were also quite static, teaching the classics and the Bible in traditional ways, mostly by recitation. Administration was heavily involved with students, with enforcing *in loco parentis* rules, and with providing faculty members who were also good proctors. The president was essentially a dean of students.

The second stage of academic administration was dramatically different. This was the age of the presidential giants: White at Cornell, Eliot at Harvard, Angell at Michigan, Gilman at Hopkins, Harper at Chicago, Van Hise at Wisconsin, Jordan at Stanford, Wheeler at California. White fought any denominational bias in the selection of faculty, students, and subjects. He later wrote *The History of Warfare of Science with Theology in Christendom,* and he treated students as "men," not wards. Eliot brought in a system of electives and so completely transformed the classical curriculum that ultimately only two courses were required and those in the freshman year. He also initiated a three-year program (now being suggested again), modernized professional schools, and launched the ideas of tenure and sabbaticals. Angell took over a state university in the midwest, opening it to the "great world of scholars" and placing "generous culture within the reach of the humblest and poorest child of the soil." Gilman emphasized science and a graduate school for the academic disciplines. Harper innovated the community college idea, the quarter system, the regular summer school (year-round operations), the divisional organization of the academic disciplines, and university extension. Van Hise extended university service into the state, not only into the field of agriculture but also into the legislative halls, where faculty drafted bills as never before or since—"the borders of the campus" really were "the boundaries of the state." The university played a central role in the "progressive movement." Jordan and Wheeler created modern universities on the West Coast—Jordan from scratch and Wheeler by transforming an existing institution.

In this age of the president, Eliot, when asked by a faculty member why there had to be change after eighty years of stability, could answer, "There is a new president." A recent history of the early University of Chicago is called, quite appropriately, *Harper's Chicago.* Eliot and Angell served as presidents for forty years; the others served for what would now be considered long terms.

The third stage of academic administration came before and after World War I. Faculty gained greater authority; academic senates were created; academic freedom was enhanced; the American Association of University Professors was organized and began to set the basic policies for academic life. This was the age of the faculty. Administrators assumed a lower profile; they became more the servants of the faculty than masters, as they once had been. Among the outstanding presidents of the time were the counter-revolutionaries. Lowell at Harvard limited electives, introducing "breadth" and "depth" requirements, and initiated the Houses as more controlled environments for students; Hutchins at Chicago promoted Great Books rather than specialization and vocationalism: Aydelotte at Swarthmore introduced the British-type Honor's Program; and Meiklejohn at Amherst and Wisconsin sponsored a broad study of history. Each looked back to the forms and content of earlier times.

The fourth stage of academic administration, a period of great expansion, followed World War II. There were 1.2 million students enrolled in 1944; 2.3 million in 1950; 3.5 million in 1960; and 8.5 million in 1970. Science research exploded. Federal funds to universities for science research were about $100 million in 1950; $500 million in 1960; and $1.5 billion in 1970. Research universities, in particular, became big business. The University of Illinois now has 20,000 employees and an annual budget of over $300 million; by contrast the budget for the academic year 1955–56 was just over $60 million. And the University of Illinois alone now has as many students as all of higher education in 1870. Teachers colleges became comprehensive colleges, and hundreds of community colleges were founded in this postwar era. The college or university president during this period devoted his life to growth, plans for the future, and new projects. The great exception was in the segment composed of the private liberal arts colleges.

The president, in the first stage, was essentially a minister: in the second, often a revolutionary giant: in the third, a civil servant of the faculty and the status quo, and sometimes a proponent of the status quo ante; and, in the fourth, an executor of growth. The presidency and the administration generally were relatively unimportant in the first and third periods, and relatively important in the second and fourth. There were always exceptions, of course, but this was the general course and tenor of development.

Today higher education is entering a fifth period, one marked by change and conflict. What impact will this change and conflict have on higher education? How will these two elements affect administration in general, and presidents, deans, department chairs, and students in particular?

Higher education, and thus its administration, has always related to society. In its first stage, higher education related to a rural and commercial culture heavily influenced by religious views; in its second stage, to the "takeoff" of an industrializing nation under the influence of strong populist pressures; in its third stage, to a more slowly advancing—even contracting—society during the Great Depression; and, in its fourth stage, to a nation-state newly dominant in world affairs and increasingly subject to the rapidly rising expectations of most citizens for more opportunity. The future direction of higher education will also depend, in substantial measure, on how society develops—and that is an unknown.

Higher education, in its last period (1945–70), was marked by great growth. Growth is a type of change, but this particular period was characterized by changes in largely established directions, such as more students and more scientific research. Change in *new* directions *may* come to mark the current period—the two decades of 1970–90.

Response to the New Context

Change and conflict, if they are indeed to be major elements in the future of higher education, will greatly affect administration. Change will be both more necessary and less facilitated by growth than in the recent past. Conflicts over power and principle are much more difficult to handle than conflicts over interests (such as money for a department) within a consensus about power and principle. Administration, as a consequence, will become more important within the totality of higher education; both change and conflict require *more* administrative talent and effort. Administration, also, will be more difficult, because change comes so hard in the academic world and conflicts can be personal and intense. Academic administration will probably be less rewarding than in the periods after the Civil War and after World War II, when so much could be accomplished so quickly, but it will provide more opportunity for creativity than the periods before the Civil War and between the two World Wars.

Many administrators today are concentrating on a low profile and personal survival. The times, however, require a more activist approach to guide constructive change and to resolve conflicts in productive ways. The administrator, whether president, dean, department chairman, student personnel officer, or student leader, must be concerned with adaptation to change and to conflict. The role of the administrator today is different from that of the minister teaching and supervising morality, or from the great academic captain single-handedly setting new goals and devising new organizational forms, or from the civil servant efficiently carrying on the daily business, or from the executive driving forward a growing institution. The role is now more that of a political leader, such as a mayor or governor, using persuasion in working with others to move in progressive ways and to keep conflict within reasonable bounds—working with media, with coalitions, and more publicly with bigger constituencies. Leadership must be more political in its orientation both to internal problems and to external relations. "As the science of . . . who gets what, when, and why," as Sidney Hillman has said,[1] politics necessarily plays a greater role during a period when a campus undergoes change and conflict. Becoming more political in method does not mean, however, becoming more politicized in the sense of having an ideological basis for decisions. Perhaps to the contrary. New styles and new adaptations of old administrative styles are needed in the new context.

Administrative Requirements

The management of change requires an analysis of which problems need to be and can be solved, of the order in which they will be considered, of the number that can be handled at any moment of time, of alternative solutions, of ways to select among the alternatives to win acceptance of the chosen solutions. Administrators in a period of change must focus on the selection of goals, the procurement and assignment of means, the achievement of consent for new approaches, and the interpretation of the new order to interested publics. Each of these tasks is most difficult, but change will come. It is better, but not necessarily easier, that it be brought about by internal leadership than by external directive.

The management of conflict requires anticipation of points of conflict, dispersal of conflicts over time and place so they do not inflame each other, agreement in advance on the rules of the game, incorporation of all important groups into the political processes so each may have a stake in a peaceful solution, creation of mediatory and adjudicative agencies, and long-run constructive solutions. Conflicts, if allowed to accumulate, can become much more intense. Eternal vigilance is necessary to identify points of tension early; extra courage is necessary to confront them as they arise.

The management of change and conflict is a highly complex and important assignment for administrators of higher education. It is also a difficult assignment for students personnel officers, who have been largely driven out of *in loco parentis* responsibilities. They will also be driven out of roles as administrators of the company towns that so many campuses really are, because the company town is becoming less and less viable. They will be drawn more and more through student insistence into the difficult area of conditions for and assistance with emotional or developmental growth. They will be drawn more and more, through student insistence and despite faculty resistance, into academic affairs. Eventually, each university department must have a student affairs officer to assist students personally, administratively, and academically. This is a major area for development of the student personnel movement.

Administration is a means, not an end; but the ends of education cannot be well served unless the administrative means are effective. This is particularly so in a period of change and conflict. Lofty purposes and troubled times require the most effective of administrative approaches.

Notes

* Originally presented as the first David D. Henry Lecture, University of Illinois at Urbana-Champaign, October 10, 1972. In *Educational Record* 54, no.1 (Winter 1973): 38–46. Reprinted by permission.

† David D. Henry, *Challenges Past, Challenges Present: An Analysis of American Higher Education Since 1930* (San Francisco: Jossey-Bass, 1975).

1. *The Political Primer for All Americans* (Washington, DC: Department of Research and Education, Congress of Industrial Organizations, 1944), 1.

Holding the Center—
Presidential Discontent*

Everybody on campus was discontented in the early 1970s, but I thought that, among all others, the president had the greatest reason to be. This essay later gave rise to a series, under the auspices of the Association of Governing Boards of Universities & Colleges, looking at what was happening to the presidents and to trustees.[†] I was then impressed, as I still am, at how many able people keep coming along to be presidents when so many of the incumbents have so many discontents; and how many good trustees keep coming along as their roles also become more difficult.

Discontent on the campus and about the campus is one of the dominating themes of contemporary American society. Student discontent, faculty discontent, legislative discontent, public discontent are all well recognized and well documented. But the group almost certainly subject to the most nearly universal discontent—the presidents—has, by comparison, been the most neglected in our obsession with the malaise of others. The discontent of all the other groups piles up on the presidents, and the presidents add their own problems to the mounting totality. They endure all of this discontent largely alone and, with rare exceptions, in silence. Many presidents, for much of the time today, fall into the category of the walking wounded in the continuing wars in the groves of academe. The chief exceptions are the new recruits, and they constitute an increasing proportion.

The president remains the most important single figure in the life of the campus (although he[‡] is no longer the central personage he was during most of the history of American higher education). Consequently, his discontent should be of concern to the entire enterprise. Often, it is not. Attention is given to improving the lot of the student and the faculty member, and to bettering relations with legislators and the public. Yet the lot of the president and better relations with him are largely ignored. Partly this is a matter of numbers. There are seven million students and 650,000 faculty members, thousands of legislators, and millions of the general public, but only 2,500 presidents. They are comparatively few in number and surrounded by larger masses; the attention goes to the larger groups. The presidents also have no spokespersons, no merchants of their discontent, and, by the nature of their roles, must be largely mute about their own dissatisfactions.

The unhappiness of the president is not a new theme. It goes back to the early days of Harvard. The proof of it is in occasional statements by presidents, in biographies about them, and in the histories of campus controversies which almost always have clustered around the role, the policies, the personality of the president. Campus turmoil for over three centuries has concentrated on or near this one figure.

There are those who say the president deserves this fate: they say that he accepted the job voluntarily, sometimes even avidly; that he has the authority and the perquisites; that he represents the evils of the external world; that he perpetuates the evils of the campus. The theme of the president who must be overthrown—by students or faculty or alumni or trustees or legislators—runs through the literature about the campus, as does the theme of the president who feels himself betrayed by those he sought to serve.

"If a man wishes to be humbled and mortified, let him become President of Harvard College."[1] This was the lament of President Holyoke on his deathbed. He had served as president of Harvard from 1737 to 1769— longer than anyone else except Charles W. Eliot. He had reformed the curriculum to do away with the system under which one tutor carried a class through all subjects for four years. This development was historic for it began the trend toward greater and greater specialization by faculty members that has continued ever since. He had also been president when Old Harvard Hall, with all the records of the college, was burned, and he had seen many academic and student controversies. His lament has been echoed over the centuries by many others, including two of the college heads who served also as presidents of the United States. "Woodrow Wilson once remarked that he had never learned anything about politics after he left Princeton"[2]—and he did not like politics. Thomas Jefferson encountered severe problems of student and, subsequently, faculty discontent. He wrote that they gave him "a great degree of sufferance."[3] A survey of the history of the University of California leads to the conclusion that no president ever left office both happily and voluntarily. The discontented president of today has a long lineage.

The history of the college presidency, however, is not one of unrelieved gloom and doom. Many presidents have apparently been happy in their positions and greatly honored afterward, but this is not the dominant theme.

One test of the mutual contentment of the president and those with whom he works is survival. Presidents are usually appointed to serve until death or retirement. The position is looked upon as "permanent" rather than as for a fixed term. Given the average age at time of appointment, tenure might be expected to last fifteen to twenty years. Legend has it, however, that tenure actually averages four to seven years, or about one-third the normal expectation. If the legend is correct, most presidents leave voluntarily or involuntarily long before they might be logically expected to do so. Seldom is the departure made to take another presidential position, for there is no career line of movement from one presidency to another. Such movement is the exception and occurs in only 10 to 15 percent of cases. Thus it appears that most presidents leave their positions ahead of the expectation at the time of their appointment, whether by their own free will, under duress, or a combination of both. Turnover is a mark of the discontent of someone or some group or groups. The happy president surrounded by contented admirers does not cut his tenure to one-third the anticipated length of service; nor does he have it cut for him.

The presidents of the most prestigious universities have generally been thought to serve the longest terms. They are the most carefully selected, they are in the institutions that take greatest pride in their stability of leadership, and they are also the most visible symbols of higher education. An examination of tenure of the presidents of the universities included in the membership of the Association of American Universities gives some indication of maximum average length of term and of changes in it. This association is made up of the universities generally accepted as the academic leaders in the United States. Membership now totals forty-eight.

In 1899, the average years in office of this group of presidents was 10.9 years.[4] By 1969, this had dropped to 5.9. The decline has taken place throughout the seventy years, but the big drops came in the 1930s. from 9.5 in 1929 to 7.7 in 1939; and in the 1960s, from 7.4 to 5.9. It appears that the average may still be going down. In 1969, 27.1 percent of the presidents had been in office less than one year, and 52.1 percent less than five years—in each case, the highest percentage in history. The comparable figures in 1964 were 2.4 percent and 38.1 percent; and in 1899 they were 14.3 percent and 21.4 percent. This rapid change is an indication of growing discontent by somebody—often the president himself. It implies that the position of the presidency suddenly has become more difficult. There has been no similar increase in the dropout rates of students and faculty. The new dropouts are the presidents.

Averages are somewhat deceptive, for they include a small number of very long-service individuals. A person halfway up the AAU seniority list in 1929 had served seven years; in 1969, only two years. Thus the median years of experience has been cut by more than two-thirds. Half of the presidents of these leading universities in 1969 were, by comparison, "green hands." The "old hands" in 1969—defined as having ten years of service or more—numbered twelve, or one-quarter of the complement. It has been the "old hands" in particular who have lent wisdom and stability and guidance to all the presidents in the AAU.

The experience of the AAU institutions is that presidents once served one-half to two-thirds of "normal" expectancy, and now serve one-quarter to one-third instead. If comparable figures were available for other institutions of higher learning—and they are not—they would likely show a similar trend.

All of this leads to the observation that a permanent president is more temporary than permanent, and becomes more temporary as time goes on. I shall seek to examine why. First, I shall set forth the major problems now confronting presidents as they see them; second, the nature of the presidency itself and changes in it; and, third, possible solutions to some problems.

It is a sad commentary on American higher education that the central figure—the president—is apparently subject to the greatest discontent and has been so subject for the longest period of time. It could be said today, as it was said in 1940,[5] that "the position has become almost an impossibility"—but the important word is *almost*. It would be a still sadder commentary if that word were omitted; and it should not be.

Contemporary Problems

College presidents have recently set forth the "major problems"[6] that confront them, and the list holds some surprises. The problems they cited can be summarized under seven general headings in the order of frequency and intensity of mention:

Money
Faculty relations
Control of the institution
Student relations
New directions for programs
Aims and purposes
Personal considerations

Two surprises deserve special attention.

Money stands out as by far the dominant problem, surpassing all others and standing in a class by itself. This seems rather strange since higher education has just completed a decade when funds flowed more readily than ever before. Institutional expenditures rose four times over while student enrollments only doubled. Higher expenditures per student were partly the result of inflation but were caused by a rise in real costs as well. Also, by world standards, American expenditures are substantial. Higher education in the United States never was so rich or seemingly felt so poor.

A second surprise is the comparatively low rating given to student relations. The public conception is that they are the greatest, or even the only, problem. But presidents seem more concerned about the faculty and about external control. They also seem to be quite sympathetic to student complaints. Put another way: behind the public battles involving students lie more serious but also more hidden battles with faculties and with external authorities. The presidents, at the center of the conflicts, see these latter contests as being more currently intense and more fundamental. The more passing and more superficial crisis is the one with the students; the coming and more enduring crises are those with faculty members and with external authorities—according to this set of judgments.

Money

The standard presidential answer about "major problems" is "financial" or "money, money, money." Some mention money as the sole problem of importance and most mention it as a major problem. A frequently mentioned problem is how to get the funds for salaries and other benefits to attract and retain qualified faculty members. This difficulty is natural inasmuch as faculty costs are about half of total educational costs and the standing of an institution is largely determined by the quality of its faculty. The other stated major need for money is for capital improvements.

The institutions with the greatest emphasis on finances are the private liberal arts colleges; some of them speak of "threatened survival." For all colleges, the specific areas that give rise to the greatest complaints are: satisfying faculty demands for research time and facilities, particularly access to computers; and meeting the extra costs for disadvantaged students necessitated by scholarships and remedial work.

I should like to make several comments about the money problem. First, it is not new. A questionnaire at any time in history would probably have yielded the same results. A historical survey of presidential views noted that "Alma Mater" is always seen by presidents as "fast failing under the strain."[7] The president sees the financial problem more completely than anyone else, for this is primarily an area of his responsibility and, by comparison, he sees less of some other aspects of the institution. Also, the demands of the campus for more books, more buildings, more of everything are almost insatiable, and particularly so with the increasingly intense competition for status among campuses that has marked recent years. Additionally, the emphasis on money is partly a tactic. The president, like the minister, pleads poverty—poverty with parents, alumni, legislators, foundation executives. He does not have a standardized product to sell at the least price, but a specialized service to sell at the highest price he can get. His is an enterprise largely judged on its ability to maximize inputs, not outputs, Consequently, Alma Mater is always seen as being on the verge of bankruptcy as a method of raising money. The private goal is constant improvement; the public language is about constant deficits. Alma Mater is Pauline in peril—constantly threatened, always saved.

A case in point is the private colleges. They speak the most about impoverishment. Yet, by objective standards, they have been, by and large, better off during the past decade than public institutions. Their faculty salaries have risen faster, their expenditures per student are greater and have risen more rapidly, and their square footage of space per student is also larger and has increased more rapidly. They have been gaining, in fact, as against the public segment; but they have been fighting a losing battle according to their own rhetoric.

Second, the situation at the moment really may be worse than normal, unlikely as this may seem in light of the great financial gains of the last decade as the horn of plenty of an affluent society was poured onto the welcoming laps of the institutions of higher education. This period of prosperity has raised expectations—of faculty members for ever higher salaries, lower teaching loads, and better equipment; of graduate students for more fellowships for more years; of undergraduates for scholarships and loans more readily available. The curve of expectations is still rising. But the once-rising curve of income is now falling off in its rate of rise—income from the federal government, the states, the many private sources. A great gap is looming between the aspirations of the 1960s and the harsh realities of the 1970s.

The president is in the middle of this gap, trying unsuccessfully to close it and being pulled at from opposite directions. The institution may survive the process but he fears he may not. He has the hard task of replacing lush anticipations with the new facts of American life. He becomes, even more than normally, the proximate source of disappointed expectations. It is easier to parcel out plenty than scarcity, particularly when scarcity follows plenty. It may be better never to have been rich, than to have been rich and lost.

The institutions which seem, according to their financial accounts, to be in the greatest trouble fall into four categories.

The large research universities are caught with heavy research responsibilities as federal funds stabilize or even decline and as overhead allowances on continuing projects fail to meet overhead costs. They also are incurring the heaviest costs for libraries and computers, and are under the most intense pressures to add ever newer specialties on top of recently new specialties. The knowledge explosion is for them a financial calamity.

The small liberal arts colleges of no national distinction are also under great pressure. Their potential students are attracted to low-tuition community and state colleges. The institutions themselves are often too small for an effective scale of operations and too rural to be attractive to the new generation of students. The same is true of many of the private junior colleges. Catholic and Protestant institutions, of whatever size and wherever located, may also, by their very nature, limit their potential clientele in a less religious age.

The historic Negro colleges constitute a third group. Suddenly they are competing for faculty members in an overactive national market instead of in their formerly depressed and isolated market. They too must expand rapidly and diversify their curricula as they compete for students.

Another group comprises institutions that are engaged in special efforts on behalf of disadvantaged students. This group includes the large research universities, the historic Negro colleges, and, additionally, many of the more famous of the liberal arts colleges. It also includes the public comprehensive colleges—in New York City, New Jersey, and Washington, DC—which all of a sudden find themselves committed to "open access."

These institutions, together, number about half of all campuses in the United States. The financial strains within them vary greatly. Thus there is a financial problem, but it is not universal and, where it does exist, it is not uniform. The knowledge explosion, the urban explosion, and the opportunity explosion have varying effects on varying institutions. There are many financial crises on many campuses more than there is *a* financial crisis in all of higher education.

Third, the problem is likely to get worse in the 1970s and perhaps even worse in the 1980s. The nation is shifting its priorities from education after Sputnik to the environment, poverty, and much else. Much of higher education is now politically unpopular—some politicians make a career out of attacking it. Yet costs per student keeps rising. This trend is longterm, because higher productivity does not here, as in industry and agriculture, partially offset rising wages and salaries. There is also the shortrun factor that many of the new students come from less affluent homes and thus cost more in scholarships and remedial work—cost much more. Also, there are more students in prospect—a 50 percent increase in the next decade.

The 1980s may be even more difficult. Enrollments then will flatten out and, in some years, even decline. Rising costs per student will be recognized as such and will no longer be obscured by rising enrollments. The public may look with even less sympathy on greater demands year by year for more money, when the number of students is stationary or even going down.

The outlook for the next two decades is cloudy. And there is not a great deal that the president can do about it. One helpful factor will be that faculty salaries, under the new supply and demand situation for Ph.D.'s, will not rise so rapidly, but this development will have its debit side in the disgruntlement of faculty members after a long period of rising comparative incomes.

As a further comment, there is a money illusion—the illusion that money can cure all problems, satisfy all faculty and student demands. This illusion assumes that the demands for the things that money can buy are satiable, and they probably are not; it also assumes that all discontent can be bought off, and some of it cannot—some of it has a nonmaterialistic base. Also, while any one president might solve his own problems with more money if he got it and nobody else did, all presidents could not solve all their problems even if they all got more money, for then the competition for comparative advantage would only have been raised to higher levels. Presidents individually often hold to a money illusion—that money is at the root of all their solutions; but money, by itself, cannot solve all the problems of all of higher education.

Faculty

The presidents see faculty relations as the next great source of problems after money. The perversity of some of the faculty takes its place next in line after the scarcity of funds. Complaints take four major forms.

The first is that "faculty people are slow to change" in matters of institutional policies and structures, that the imperatives of academic change run up against implacable conservatism. This is an ancient complaint.

The second is that the faculty is too self-serving, too prone to place its interest in research above the students' interest in learning, its interest in external consulting above service on campus committees, its desire for higher salaries over other claims on funds. The more "cosmopolitan" a faculty becomes—and many have recently become much more cosmopolitan and less "home-guard"—the more "self-serving" it also becomes. Many presidents have seen this process at work to their dismay.

The third is that some faculty members are turning to unionization and thus confrontation against, rather than cooperation with, the administration, and turning to militancy on external political issues. As a consequence, a chasm is opening up between faculty and public thinking. This turn is largely new. Traditionally, faculty members have acted more like colleagues than employees, and more like objective observers of society than passionate partisans. The shift to unionization and to militancy, to the extent it occurs, places the president in a far more difficult situation.

A fourth complaint of the responding presidents is that the faculty has deserted the president or even betrayed him, that it does not give him the personal and institutional support he needs. Apparently many presidents entered office with a sense of being part of the faculty and having its friendship only to find, to their horror, that friends deserted them and they were bereft of the enthusiastic support they expected. This again is an ancient complaint; and fortunate are those who do not experience it. New administrative power and old academic friendships do not always go hand in hand; quite the contrary—"a friend in power is a friend lost."[8] The honeymoon is often over as soon as the marriage vows have been taken.

This concern of the presidents for faculty relations bodes ill for the future. Change will always confront academic conservatism, and the need for change continues, perhaps at an increasing level. Cosmopolitanism will grow with the supersonic jets. And the doctrines of the "dissenting academy" can split a faculty as well as create a chasm between the campus and the community. The last great faculty split came a century ago when the proponents of the classical curriculum were defeated by the new specialists and technologists. The ultimate outcome of that battle was inevitable.

The new battle between the supporters of "objectivity" and of "partisanship" has, as yet, no clear result. In this battle, society will stand with the old and not with the new, contrary to the situation a century ago. The presidential giants of a century ago stood with the new and with the public. The presidents of today will stand, of necessity, largely with the old and with the public, and yet many of the younger faculty will stand with the newer views of the dissenting academy. It is less certain that any giants will emerge from this historic conflict. Some of the bloodiest confrontations of the future may well occur within faculties, and the presidents will not be able to stand entirely aloof; nor will they be isolated from the public quarrels between organized faculty groups and external bodies. The giants who began rising a century ago rode a great new idea with the support of federal and state agencies and of a growing body of younger and more progressive faculty members. This combination is not repeated in the current situation. The efforts needed will again be herculean but more in guerrilla defense than in frontal advance toward a clear goal.

Gross and Grambsch[9] have noted recently the close similarity of goals between faculty and administrators, but this situation will certainly change as the dissenting academy becomes more influential on campus. It will split the goals of some faculty from those of most administrators in a most fundamental way. The unity of the recent past will dissolve into the partial disunity of the near future. For this reason, in particular, I agree with the presidential view that faculty relations are coming to be among the major problems. A sense of fear more than a conviction of unity marks the attitudes of many presidents today.

Control of the Institution

The presidents are concerned about who controls the institution, but in ways different from those that meet the public eye. The public sees demands for faculty power, or student power, or reassertion of trustee power or even alumni power. But these are not the main directions of presidential concern. Faculties already have a great deal of power in the better institutions and are more often holding onto what they have than they are demanding more. Students have little power and are getting more, and the presidents are generally sympathetic with this trend. Trustees, by and large, are more sophisticated and less interfering than they once were—with notable exceptions. And organized alumni may protest occasionally but they seem to have retired into a sullen silence. Their attachment is to the alma mater they once knew and that is fast disappearing. The attachment and the interest, however, continue to endure for the best and the oldest of the private universities and colleges even as they change.

The greater concerns lie elsewhere. They lie with the systemwide administration in the growing number of multicampus units, with the coordinating councils and superboards, with the state governors and their administrative assistants, with the legislative committees. They lie also with the closer, less friendly, and more sensational surveillance by the comunication media. Particular venom seems to be developing in the relations of campus administrators with the central administrators of systems and with governors and their assistants. The complaint is loss of autonomy, imposition of more and more stringent controls.

The really big power battles are not so much on as off the campus. The old power battles pitted faculties against presidents and trustees in matters of academic freedom. The rules of the American Association of University Professors grew out of these battles. The new power battles increasingly are between the campus led by the president, and external authorities led by the politicians and the bureaucrats, over independence and self-direction for the institution. That is where the hidden knives are really flashing.

In the midst of the remnants of the old and the intricacies of the new power battles, presidents cry for better communications, more of a sense of community, a greater consensus. One president comments about "the lack of a common moral base that permits faculty, administration, trustees, and students to function as a community. The modern university is held together by baling wire and chewing gum, economic advantage and lethargy. The university president presides over spreading chaos." Some of the chaos now comes from the outside as well as from the inside. More people and more agencies with more points of view try to control the campus than ever before. The chaos becomes more highly organized all the time. The old individualistic anarchy of academic life looks peaceful compared with the new administered confusion.

Student Relations

The presidents share the concern of most of the public about student political militancy, student moral standards, the "cultural revolution," black and "Third World" pressures, and student demands for power; but with several important variations.

Student moral standards—excessive use of drugs, anti-intellectualism, intolerance for the opinions of those with whom they disagree, a lowered level of civility—seem to be of greater concern than the more publicized political radicalism. Also, there is a good deal of sympathy with student demands for more power and with the demands of minority students for more consideration, provided solutions can be worked out within reason and through discussions. To the presidents, it is the new moral standards that seem the most troublesome, and some are alarmed at the conformity— "push-button radicalism"—of the growing student "counterculture." As a consequence of these views, presidents and faculties may be parting company about students. Faculty members are willing, even eager, to relinquish control over student conduct, while maintaining essential faculty control over academic matters.[10] Presidents, apparently, would prefer to keep more influence over student life, but give students more authority over academic affairs.

The presidents are almost as much troubled by the reactions to students as by the actions of students—the reactions of alumni and the public at large. A disturbance on a campus is a passing episode soon absorbed within the totality of campus life; but, to the general public, the headlines depict an unending series of episodes at many institutions that conveys a total impression of constant turbulence. Also, the public sees the big political event, and the president sees more of what he considers to be the daily deterioration of student standards of conduct.

New Directions for Programs

A number of presidents see problems in getting new programs under way. Generally they agree on the need for changes and the general directions of those changes: a better educational opportunity for undergraduates, a better break for minority students, a new emphasis on urban affairs, a general revitalization of the academic enterprise. Here again the faculty and administration may disagree. In a survey of "educational qualities," students ranked "teaching ability" as first and faculty rated it as next to last in a list of ten items; and faculty rated "office space," "sabbatical leave," and "parking" as the three top contenders (out of fourteen) for a claim on "college resources."[11] For the presidents to obtain their new directions, major shifts in faculty interests and institutional resources will be necessary. A special new direction for the state colleges, as perceived by their presidents, is to achieve "university status."

Aims and Purposes

A small number of presidents express doubts about the philosophical; goals of higher education. They see a loss of "traditional purpose" and a transition into the unknown and, perhaps, the unintended. They mourn the loss of consensus. They call for a "new understanding." They see the old emphasis on truth and individual academic freedom giving way to a new emphasis on societal service under peer group control. They wonder where it all leads. Some of the most thoughtful comments treat these matters. Until the American Civil War there was a consensus of faculty, administrators, and trustees broken by occasional rebellions by recalcitrant students against the classical college and its social and intellectual straitjacket. A new consensus was formed that ruled the next century—a consensus of faculty and administrators and public leaders about research and service—with the students relatively apathetic onlookers. Now the classicists are rising again on the right, the dissenting academy is being born on the left, and the students want in from all directions.

The schools of theology seem most concerned about aims and purposes. They sound like philosophical disaster areas. They have severe doubts about their place in a secularizing society.

Personal Considerations

A few presidents mention—almost all must experience—personal problems: "lack of sleep," "I have taken to drinking too much," "I am resigning," "My contract has not been renewed."

But the future is not entirely bleak; otherwise many presidents would not seek to continue with their jobs. When people are asked about their problems, they state their problems.

A study of future "events" gives a more optimistic outlook.[12] Institutional (presumably presidential) responses showed five of the most desired events as also among the ten most probable events:

> The great majority of high school graduates will take at least two years of instruction after high school.
>
> Faculty participation in major aspects of academic governance will become a widely accepted practice.
>
> Significantly more Federal and state funds will go directly to students, as scholarships or loans.
>
> Undergraduate curricula will undergo major revisions.
>
> In most undergraduate curricula, the number of required courses will decline to permit more electives and individualized programs.

The five other most probable events, but which were not also most "desirable," were considered to be these:

> *In loco parentis* will be much less important than responsibility for self-regulation as a basis for codes of nonacademic student affairs and conduct.

Statewide coordinating councils will have increasing influence over public colleges and universities.

The proportion of students enrolled in private institutions of higher education will decline at an even faster rate.

Formulas will increasingly be used to determine levels of state and Federal support for various academic programs.

Of all persons receiving earned doctorates in the 1970s, a steadily increasing proportion will be employed by bureaus, industry and government.

This listing of expectations, both good and not so good, is generally consistent with the presidential views summarized above. It is not the best of all possible worlds, but it is also not the worst.

Problems of the Past and the Future

It may be worth reflecting for a moment on the problems that do *not* now confront the presidents, but have confronted presidents in the past or may do so in the future. Two great issues dominated the period before the Civil War: the dominance of church leaders over the campus, and the enforcement of detailed in loco parentis rules over the unruly students. only the last vestiges of each of these once-consuming problems any longer remain.

From the Civil War to World War I, the great issues were the complete revision of the classical curriculum and the adding of research and service to the functions of the campus while fighting off the crude attempts of some agricultural and industrial leaders to turn the campus into a trade school dominated by the "interests." The elective system has now replaced the rigid classical curriculum, but new and less crude forms of influence, through money, have allowed the "interests"—by now mainly the federal agencies—to affect the academic enterprise.

From World War I to the end of the Korean War, the major battles were over academic freedom, which reached peaks during the early 1920s and again in the Joe McCarthy period, and over the rise of faculty power through academic senates. The courts and the new sophistication of trustees ended the first series of battles, and faculty dominance over academic affairs is by now well accepted in the leading institutions and is penetrating into all.

In the "apathetic" 1950s, the leading issues degenerated into "sex for the students, athletics for the alumni, and parking for the faculty," as I once commented to the Academic Senate at Berkeley.

The 1960s saw the great growth of scientific research and of student enrollments, and required an all-out effort at expansion in clear directions.

In retrospect, it was a golden age. It is notable that, at the end of a decade heavily influenced by the federal interest, almost no presidents complain of undue direct federal control as a major problem.

Certain potential problems have never yet come to plague the campus. Nonacademic employees have been largely quiescent, although there are now problems of minority representation in employment and on construction work. American higher education has never been faced with a lowering of standards across the board, as in India. Generally, standards have risen institution by institution. As new students, with lower academic accomplishments, have come into higher education, they have been absorbed mainly by institutions with lower admission standards within a system characterized by great diversity. There never has been a single "gold standard," as the British put it, to be debased. Were all institutions to be opened to all students, there would then be a crisis of standards. Nor has higher education, as yet, been faced by great technological changes, although TV was once thought by some to be bringing great change. The computer is a much more likely candidate in the future.

Higher education in America has met and surmounted many problems in its three and a third centuries. Many of the past battles were both difficult and important to win. The present age again offers difficult and important battles, but more of them simultaneously and with a shorter period for solutions than ever before. Presidents now, as then, will be in the midst of such solutions as may yet be found.

The Contemporary Presidency

Trouble rises to the level of the presidency and falls to the level of the presidency. The president is the institutional lighting rod. In a time of troubles, the president will be in trouble. Periods of change are periods of trouble, and we are in a period of change. Nothing can alter this fact. We have seen, above, through the eyes of the presidents, the troubles that now cluster around them. In meeting troubles, the president can work with money and power and policy and persuasion. There is now less money in prospect,[13] and the president has less power. His power was always restricted but has become much more so in recent times, with the rise of faculty and student power and the increased role of external authorities. A recent study concludes that the "most significant change" of the past decade has been the growth in faculty authority and the growth in student authority.[14]

The president must thus work mostly with policy and persuasion, a situation always difficult. The campus is loaded with negative power, with veto groups, William Rainey Harper wrote a memo in 1904 which was found in his files after his death:

when all has been said, the limitations of the college president, even when he has the greatest freedom of action, are very great. . . . in educational policy he must be in accord with (the faculty). It is absurd to suppose that any president, however strong or willful he may be, can force a faculty made up of great leaders of thought to do his will. The president, if he has the power of veto, may stand in the way of progress, but he cannot secure forward movement except with the cooperation of those with whom he is associated.[15]

The president can veto; the faculty can veto; so also can the trustees. It takes all three to enter upon a new policy. In more modern times and particularly in state institutions, there are still more veto points. Any really important measure in the University of California must pass at least twelve check points. This means lost time and, sometimes, lost chances. The head of a corporation, by comparison, has great positive power. As the person who most wants things done—to adjust to the market and for many other reasons—he has the most power to do them. No person or group on the campus has similar power to take positive action. The true sign of power on the campus is how much you can stop! Getting things done depends more on persuasion, less on power.

The campus has no clear theory of governance. It is partly collegial, with the president as one of the colleagues, and partly hierarchical, with the president as the chief executive. But it is other things as well. And there are many interest groups both inside and outside the structure of governance. Consequently, decision making can be both confused and cumbersome. This unwieldiness is particularly a handicap in times and situations that call for rapid action. If, for example, the president, acting in his role of chief executive, calls in the police during a disturbance, he will be called to task by his colleagues for lack of consultation and concurrence. If he takes time to consult colleagues, he may fail to fulfill his functions of trust as chief executive. It is a mixed-up form of governance. The collegial approach calls for time and unanimity; hierarchical governance calls for action and personal responsibility.

Also for the president, there are few clear tests of performance, as the profit-and-loss statement is for the business executive; and some of the imprecise proofs of performance that do exist become evident only over the long run, such as the eventual quality of a new faculty member or of a new endeavor. The president cannot point to one or a few clearly defined, universally accepted, and quickly available demonstrations of his stewardship. He does not have available the evidence of a profit earned or an election won to substantiate and authenticate his leadership. Nor has he civil service status or seniority rights. He is more like a minister who cannot prove how many souls he has saved, but nevertheless must satisfy both his parishioners and the hierarchy above him, or like an actor who must please the audience once a night and twice on Saturday—and there are many types of audiences.

The difficulties have been compounded over the past decade. The average campus enrollment has doubled, and in many institutions has increased several times over. Some colleges that once were small communities have become more impersonal environments. The president at such institutions can walk through the campus and meet few people he knows personally, but the academic world prefers personal contact. More people feel he never sees them and does not understand their problems: they may be quite correct. The campus has also become more complex—with a bigger budget, more relations with outside groups and agencies, more varied activities. New service activities, such as those with the local community, add to the burdens on the president's time and to the heterogeneity of his constituencies. The president's attention is both fractionalized internally and drawn externally.

Size and complexity run against the collegial tradition. The collegial president should know all his colleagues and understand their problems. The hierarchical president need not, even should not, know all his employees and understand all their problems. The big and complex campus becomes more hierarchical and less collegial, but collegial expectations still continue

Further compounding the difficulties is the loss of consensus over powers and goals, already noted, and without consensus on both there is less basis for making decisions and less assurance of their acceptance. Additionally, the students have often become activists. When they were passive, the president, on campus, could be concerned almost exclusively with the faculty. But with students more active and with student and faculty interests diverging, he cannot equally satisfy both. A new and complicating element has entered the situation.

Beyond all these factors lie some personal considerations. Once the president received far more in salary and perquisites than any member of his faculty. Now many faculty members, from all sources available to them, may earn more than the president. He alone on the campus once had a chance to travel widely and participate in public affairs. Now these opportunities are equally open to many faculty members. The comparative rewards to the chief executive have been greatly reduced. Medical deans may have suffered even more in relation to the advantages available to some of their colleagues; and they also have infinitely more complex jobs than they once did.[16] Many presidents and many medical deans reduce their incomes, as well as complicate their lives, when they accept their positions.

And there are other changes. This is not an age of unquestioned loyalty to leaders nor an age of intense school spirit, a change that shows up in faculty and student attitudes toward presidents. On campus, the attitude is generally anti-Establishment. The president no longer has a natural constituency from which he can expect support. Only in such areas as schools of agriculture and football teams is there still some sense of unquestioned institutional and personal loyalty. The president is more alone in the academic world. It is not simply a new age, for the mega-campus and the multiversity are not the types of institutions that in any age could be expected to elicit a spirit of intense loyalty.

We have noted in passing the problems of medical deans. Deans of students and other personnel officers are even less to be envied. The faculty once turned over personal guidance of students to the dean, who with goodwill did his best; but the students no longer want the guidance, even with goodwill. The dean once handled individual discipline, but the students are now turning discipline into a collective problem and placing it directly before the president. The dean once helped the students with their organized activities, but some of their new activities are not so properly subject to the support of the dean. The dean was once helpless in the face of cigarettes and alcohol; he is now also helpless in the face of sex and drugs. I know of no academic administrators today more uncertain about their roles than those in student personnel.

The pressures of the new situation are not uniformly felt in higher education, any more than the financial difficulties are uniformly experienced. It is my impression that state colleges, community colleges, and regional universities go along much more as they once did than is true of the national research universities, the historic Negro colleges, the liberal arts colleges, and the schools of theology. The greater troubles now seem to center on the presidents in this second set of institutions. This may not be true indefinitely. In the next decade the state colleges and the community colleges will experience the greatest growth among institutions. Thus they will recruit more of the new generation of college teachers, many of whom are already disenchanted with the world and will be particularly disenchanted about teaching at a community college or state college instead of at a great university like the one where they got their Ph.D. Supporters of the New University Conference, with its dissenting academy approach, may end up having their greatest employment in and greatest impact on the nonuniversities. But at the moment, the problems are concentrated elsewhere and, particularly, on the great university campuses. The "large university" has undergone "the most far-reaching changes,"[17] and the greatest problems are centered on its presidents. Solutions, such as there may be, are particularly needed where the problems are the greatest.

Directions for Solution

There are no panaceas for presidential discontent. The position is inherently a difficult one. In seeking remedies, it is the beginning but not the end of wisdom to know what is given, what cannot be changed. The president will never have enough money to solve all his problems and particularly not over the next two decades; nor is his power likely to be much increased. Society will continue to be in trouble and the campus in need of reform. The ordeal of change through which the United States and higher education are going will continue to disrupt the campus. The faculty will become even more cosmopolitan; the students will continue their experiments with new styles of life; a new age of loyalty is not on the immediate horizon; and the public will be disturbed by what it sees and hears. These are among the largely fixed attributes defining the situation within which solutions must be sought.

The task is to find out what both can and should be changed. Since the president is at the center of the administrative processes, his lot can be improved only in smaller part by direct attention to the office he holds. The larger part of any improvements lie in the general environment, the system of governance, and the general atmosphere of understanding. Additionally, the characteristics of the president himself need to be reexamined.

The General Environment

Size of campus should be subject to direct policy consideration and not allowed to increase indefinitely. The tests of appropriate size are effective use of resources and quality of program. The burden of proof should be on those who want to increase the size of an institution beyond the requirements of these two tests. I should like to suggest that resources can be used and a quality program developed certainly at the level of 15,000–20,000 students per campus for the national research universities, 7,500–10,000 for the regional universities and comprehensive colleges, 2,000–5,000 for the community colleges, and 1,000–2,000 for the liberal arts colleges.

Rate of growth should be modest and as regular as possible. Unduly rapid growth brings problems of building faculty attachment, administrative competence, and new policies; and sudden starts and stops are upsetting.

The academic enterprise works best if the decision-making units are kept as small as possible and if decisions are made as close to the point of origin of the problems as successfully can be done. Thus, in multicampus systems, the move would be toward maximum effective decentralization to individual campuses and the breaking up of monolithic and huge colleges of letters and science into smaller multidisciplinary schools or into cluster colleges. Decisions, again as many as possible, should be made before the level of the president, and the responsibility for decisions should be spread widely over deans and provosts. But the solution of Paul Goodman of tiny self-governing communities of students and resource leaders is not generally feasible.

Partial and selective disaggregation of the more complex institutions is desirable, and in two directions. First, many campuses are still "company towns," and company towns are notoriously filled with tension as the employer seeks to serve also as landlord, grocer, police chief, and judge. The campus should, unless there is an academic component involved, seek to turn over residence halls, eating facilities, and bookstores to private contractors or consumer cooperatives; and violations of general laws or interference with persons, property, and programs, to external police and external courts.[18] Second, many campuses have taken on activities that are not central to their academic functions, including some external service and developmental research. Many of these could either be made completely independent or at least semiautonomous, with their own governing boards and budgets. Some of these nonacademic activities have accumulated like barnacles.

There are those who favor more complete disaggregation than outlined above. Flexner would have stopped all service and all semiprofessional activities; Hutchins and Barzun would also stop most of the research as well; and many radicals join in the opposition to traditional service and research functions. Others, who have no philosophical antagonism to any of the current functions, still feel that the multifunction campus is no longer viable, is too subject to disintegration; and they would split off research in one direction, graduate training in another, undergraduate instruction in another, and so forth, for the sake of survival. I reject the philosophical arguments on the grounds that the complex environment is a highly stimulating and productive one and should be preserved, and the realistic arguments on the grounds that reality is not all that desperate and that we need not turn to tactics of last resort.

In general, the fewer the rules and the more the options for free choice offered to individuals, the less the burden on both central and local administration.

The campus can be made a more manageable community if size and rate of growth are controlled, if reasonable decentralization is undertaken, if there is selective disaggregation of unwise or unnecessary functions, and if rules are minimized and options maximized. A central strategy should be to disperse discontent over as many separate units and as much time as possible, rather than allow it to be concentrated at one place and at one time. More of the community more of the time should be given the responsibility for the reconciliation of differing points of view and for decisions made. Not just the president.

The System of Governance

Faculty and students must be associated appropriately with the process of governance to make policies more effective and the process more legitimate. One way is to give each a standard percentage of membership in each governing body, as is now being done in France and Germany. A more satisfactory way, in the American context, is to award authority on a pragmatic basis in accordance with the specific functions performed: faculty and students would be assigned—depending on the function—anywhere from no authority to all authority in accordance with their interest, their competence, and their responsibility. This division of labor approach is not as elegant as an overall percentage formula, but it is better adapted to getting good decisions area by area. The sorting-out process to make the governance fit the functions involves much detail and, in the end, there will be overlapping responsibilities. One task is to sort out collegial and hierarchical situations, and to apply collegial decision-making to collegial situations, and hierarchical decision-making to hierarchical situations, and not unduly mix the two. There are other types of situations—for example, inherently democratic or inherently master-apprentice—requiring still other types of relationships.

The whole community, however, must be held together. Historically, this has been the function of the president, who has gone from committee to committee and group to group and person to person. This process has caused much loss of time in going from one checkpoint to another, and has led to the dictatorship of veto groups. I can be greatly simplified by the creation of a central advisory council where representatives of all groups can be met by the president, and where responsibility for getting a consensus is borne by the council as a whole. In such a council, forces that now meet only through their mutual contact with the president can meet directly and, if necessary, confront each other face to face. Within such a council, the more progressive forces in relation to change (trustees, administrators, students) can bring their efforts to bear more directly on the more conservative forces (mainly the faculty). Such a council should concern itself only with broad policies that affect the entire community. It would not replace more specialized consultative instrumentalities.

There are dangers in this approach. Direct confrontation may agitate antagonisms that are now muted through the president as intermediary, and the whole process can be highly politicized according to external political orientations. Consequently the selection of members, the appropriate items for the agenda, and the parliamentary arrangements are of utmost importance.

Such a council, through an executive committee, can provide the president with a quick avenue for consultation and action.

At its best, such a council can provide the president with a better mechanism for his persuasive efforts, and the community a better opportunity to develop a consensus on matters of fundamental importance.

The president lives most intimately with the trustees. They select him, they continue him in office, they make some of the most essential decisions. The composition of the board, consequently, is of great importance. Membership by public officials, in an ex officio capacity, brings in the possibility of an unfortunate element of external politics and of conflict of interest (of governmental policies as against campus welfare). Faculty and students should be associated in the process of selecting at least some of the members to assure understanding of their points of view and their acceptance of the ultimate decisions.[19]

New layers of authority are being added outside the campus and complicating academic life. External planning, coordination, and surveillance should be kept to a minimum. We need a set of principles (as has been worked out to protect academic freedom), an evaluative body (the equivalent in this area to the American Association of University Professors), and appropriate mechanisms for giving money (general formulas, applications judged on individual merit by impartial panels, land disbursement through the many hands of the students).

Additionally, we need agreed-upon rules controlling the forms of expression of dissent to avoid violence and the suppression of points of view by peer groups. Historically, the American Association of University Professors and the American Civil Liberties Union have worked out rules to protect individual faculty members and students from undue control by administrators, trustees, and public authorities. The attacks on free expression of opinion then came from the right and the outside. Attacks now come from the left and from within as well. A new set of rules is equally necessary here to protect free expression of opinion and the uncoerced search for truth. The American Association of University Professors and the American Civil Liberties Union have both special competence and a special obligation. The dissenting academy should not be allowed to suppress the dissent of others on the basis of its own intolerance.

The purposes of governance are to obtain effective actions and to achieve essential consent; these are also the basic responsibilities of the president. These purposes can be furthered as governance is related to functions, as the will of the whole community finds better means of expression, as trustees are better selected, as external authority is minimized, and as rules of conduct inhibit attacks on academic freedom from right and left and outside and inside alike. Under these circumstances,the role of the president as chief persuader or constructive mediator or community leader can best be enhanced.

The Presidency

Within the modest limits possible, the power of the president should be preserved and even enhanced in a period when it takes leadership to move in new directions. I any event, he should take and keep the initiative in making proposals. His chief influence is as initiator. Most academic reforms, most new programs come about through his efforts.

It has been suggested that the presidency be divided into two parts: an external-affairs president and an internal-affairs president. Except under unusual circumstances this would, I believe, prove unworkable. External and internal affairs are too intertwined. One person must coordinate them. Otherwise there could develop a two-headed monster. Rather, the president should have adequate assistance at the vice-presidential level, particularly in external affairs, now that much more of his time is taken up with internal affairs.[20] Instead of an academic provost, he now needs more a provost for external affairs. Also, where this is not already the case, the president should have all administrative and staff officers, including the legal staff, reporting to him and not directly to the board. Additionally, he needs the highest quality of technical staff. In the new situation he does not have the time for detailed supervision and review of staff work, and yet he is absolutely dependent upon the competence of the staff endeavor.

Most important, I believe, among changes is to place the president on a term appointment of reasonable length. This will give him, except under exceptional circumstances, a fixed period on which he can plan. At the end of the term, he will have an easy opportunity to review his own desires and for others to review his conduct. If he is reappointed, he will have received a reaffirmation of his authority as he meets new crises. In any event, opponents will not feel that they must wait forever for a change unless they mount massive opposition. A term of office could relax their opposition. This is not to suggest, however, that under exceptional circumstances a president may not be terminated at any time.

The term of office should, I think, be made not less than five and not more than ten years. My preference is for six, partly on the grounds that this is now the actual average term of office at the leading universities.[21]

Exits should be made easier; reaffirmations should be more clear cut. However long the term, the president should have available and should take substantial vacations and periodic leaves, much as do faculty members.

The General Atmosphere

An understanding of the limited and complex role of the president by faculty, students, trustees, and the public is of great importance: an understanding that his powers are not unlimited and that his responsibility for both good and evil is not total. He should not be held fully responsible for the conduct of people and the nature of developments over which he has little or no influence, let alone control. Too often his role is that of Mr. Lazarus in the firm of Undershaft and Lazarus as depicted by George Bernard Shaw in *Major Barbara*: to serve as the convenient personage who is consistently "blamed" for the faults of others. But it is too extreme to say that all the president does is preside over a "tangle" that "is full of queer animals, old, young, and middle-aged'' with the sole ability "to stand on a height above it and squirt perfume on the ensemble."[22] It is more accurate to say that the latter is the essence of some of his more ceremonial speeches and statements.

Beyond this understanding of the presidency should lie an appreciation of and tolerance for the manifold problems that beset the modern campus, a realization that it cannot and should not be entirely quiescent, a perception that it cannot and even should not meet the ideals of all groups. Political leaders and the mass media have a central position in the spread of both understanding and misunderstanding in the public mind, and thus a very special responsibility. The American public has come to accept strikes of workers without fearing revolution. It must also come to accept campus unrest without fearing the end of all it holds dear. Violence, however, is quite another matter—it neither should be nor will be accepted.

The Style of the President

Most of the presidents before the Civil War were clergymen. They now appear, in retrospect, as stern figures standing for morality and character. After the Civil War, the great leaders and models were the academic entre-preneurs who were building research programs and new professional schools and recruiting scholarly faculties. They were great public figures, highly visible and even flamboyant. They ruled in a very personal way, often as academic autocrats, usually but not always benevolent. The style changed after the initial period of university building. There were more checks and balances, bigger budgets, more diversified interests. By the end of World War II, the preferred style was that of the competent academic executive handling resources, personnel, policies, and public relations in a quietly effective manner. The method was the small and private discussion with representatives of all the interest groups concerned and the working out of satisfactory solutions to be promulgated without fanfare. The executive sought to maximize, from a long-term point of view, the facilities available and their effective utilization. He was custodian of a permanent trust making long-range plans. Reforms were undertaken and new endeavors started when appropriate and when possible without unduly disturbing consequences. He dealt with interest groups and appealed to a rationality, to goodwill, to concern for the general welfare, to tolerance.

Now new styles are being born. Some presidents, in a more polarized situation, are appealing to one pole as demagogues crying for law and or-der; others, to the opposite pole as the new sycophants seeking to flatter every whim of radical students and professors, and to embrace every idea provided it appears sufficiently new.[23] Many are seeking a low profile by serving, so to speak, as staff officers without opinions of their own, as reticent civil service officials. Still others turn to an emphasis on current tactics like politicians facing a hotly contested and proximate election, cautiously balancing actions and words, tiptoeing on the high wire—surviving but not advancing.

The dominant new style will come to be, I think, that of academic statesman. The academic statesman will seek the same goals as the academic executive—of resources well used, effective policies, reform, quality, consent—but with new methods. Generally his conduct will be less in the committee room and more in the open. He will appeal more to mass groups and less to representatives. Thus he will be more attentive to sentiments and attitudes, even when irrational. He will speak more in terms of principles and less in terms of interests; but he will not ignore interests. Public relations, on campus and off, will be a greater concern. He will be more visible, more accessible, more of a public personality. Thus he will be more like the mayor of a big city walking in the streets, meeting the people, wrestling in public with the great issues of the day and less the executive with his experts working in comparative silence with other elites.

The academic statesman will be more the political leader dealing with large publics, with his own image, with the image of his institution, with the image of his programs, with the organization of mass political support. His obvious concerns will be more short-term; his expenditures of funds more for their immediate and noticeable effects. He will continue to be the chief persuader, the mediator, the community leader, the ''unifying force''[24] holding the campus together, the initiator, the policy maker seeking to move it ahead to meet its problems; and the defender, the gladiator seeking to protect it from internal and external attack; but he will also be the image maker and the political leader and the public relations expert trying to turn mass sentiment on campus and off in the directions he wishes to go. He will be in the plaza and on TV, as well as in the office and in the faculty club. The new leaders will be seen more directly and less indirectly, will marshal mass support more than just leadership support, will appeal more publicly to principle than privately to interests, will win and lose battles more openly. Popularity in the short run will be more of a test; quite effectiveness in the long run, less.

Good men keep coming along to be presidents, although more reluctantly and in lesser numbers than a decade ago. Some respond to duty; others to the honor and recognition; others to the challenge and the chance to test their leadership abilities; others to the call to an exciting life including social and public affairs; but most to the opportunity for public service, for helping to solve some of the pressing issues of the age. The availability of good men to be presidents is the ultimate test of the viability of the college and university system. The faith of these men and their willingness to try is now the key resource of higher education.

Solutions to grave problems of higher education have been found in the past and the presidents were central to their implementation. Graver problems exist today. Their solutions will depend more on the quality of the presidents than on any one other factor—on the quality of the new academic statesmen. They will need the best of environments, the most effective of governing arrangements, the greatest of understanding, and the most appropriate of styles. They will be in the midst of the trouble and the midst of the changes and the midst of the new advances for higher education and for society.

Notes

*From *Perspectives on Campus Tensions: Papers Prepared for the Special Committee on Campus Tensions,* ed. David C. Nichols, (Washington, DC: American Council on Education, 1970: 137–62. Reprinted by permission.

†Commission on Strengthening Presidential Leadership, *Presidents Make a Difference* (Washington, DC: Association of Governing Boards of Universities & Colleges, 1984); Clark Kerr and Marian L. Gade, *The Many Lives Of Academic Presidents: Time, Place & Character* (Washington DC: Association of Governing Boards of Universities & Colleges, 1986); Clark Kerr and Marian L. Gade, *The Guardians: Boards of Trustees of American Colleges and Universities—What They Do and How Well They Do It* (Washington, DC: Association of Governing Boards of Universities & Colleges, 1989).

‡[In accordance with the style of the time this piece was written, the president is referred to as "he" throughout. To remove this language would require so many changes that it has, in this case, been left as originally published.—C.K.]

1. Samuel Eliot Morison, *Three Centuries of Harvard* (Cambridge, MA: Harvard University Press 1936), 99.

2. Harold W. Stoke, *The American College President* (New York: Harper & Row, 1959). 149.

3. *The Writings of Thomas Jefferson,* vol. 18, ed. A. E. Bergh (Washington: 1907), 346.

4. I am indebted to Charles P. McCurdy, Jr., executive secretary, for the basic data from which the averages given here have been calculated.

5. Edgar W. Knight, *What College Presidents Say* (Chapel Hill: University of North Carolina Press, 1940), 346.

6. I am indebted to Harold L. Hodgkinson of the Center for Research and Development in Higher Education, University of California, Berkeley, for access to the answers to a questionnaire filled out by 1,200 college presidents in 1968. This

questionnaire was developed in connection with a study of "Institutions in Transition" supported by the Carnegie Commission on Higher Education. The material which follows is drawn largely from answers to a question which read: "What major problems that you are currently facing are of most concern to you?" I shall draw on my own many conversations with many presidents.

7. Knight, *What College Presidents Say,* 349.

8. Henry Adams, *The Education of Henry Adams* (New York: Random House, 1931), 108.

9. Edward Gross and Paul Grambsch, *University Goals and Academic Power* (Washington, DC: American Council on Education, 1968).

10. Robert C. Wilson and Jerry G. Gaff, "Student Voice—Faculty Response," *Research Reporter* (Center for Research and Development in Higher Education, University of California, Berkeley), no. 2, 1969. Two-thirds of faculty members would give students "equal vote" or "entire responsibility" in "social matters," but less than one-tenth would make the same concessions in "academic matters."

11. Harold L. Hodgkinson, "Governance and Functions—Who Decides, Who Decides," *Research Reporter,* no. 3, 1968.

12. John Caffrey, "Predictions for Higher Education in the 1970s," In *The Future Academic Community* ed. John Caffrey (Washington, DC: American Council on Education, 1969), 261–92.

13. New money is essential to influence. Old money is nearly sacrosanct. And, among new money, much of it—perhaps 50 to 90 percent—is essentially beyond presidential control. Of 100 percent of old money and 10 percent of new money, a president may himself be able to control only 1 to 5 percent; with no new money, he can control almost no funds at all.

14. Harold L. Hodgkinson, *Institutions in Transition* (New York: McGraw-Hill, 1970).

15. *The William Rainey Harper Memorial Conferences*, ed. Robert N. Montgomery (Chicago: University of Chicago Press, 1938), 28-29.

16. Their average length of tenure has also been reduced, from seven to four years in the short periods from 1962 to 1969. (Robert J. Glaser, *Journal of Medical Education* [December 1969]: 1124.)

17. Hodgkinson, *Institutions in Transition*.

18. Thomas Jefferson reached this latter conclusion in 1826: "But the most effectual instrument we have found to be the civil authority" *(The Writings of Thomas Jefferson, 356)*. He had started out as a strong supporter of "self–government" on campus.

19. [Further study of the operations of boards of trustees has convinced me that it is a conflict of interest for students and faculty to be involved in trustee selection or in service as trustees in their own institutions.—C.K.]

20. The president of Columbia was out raising a huge endowment when trouble broke out at Columbia in 1968. His successor stayed home and helped reduce the trouble, but did less toward raising the endowment. This illustrates the dilemma.

21. [On the basis of further evidence and consideration, I now believe that evaluations should take place at stated intervals and I no longer believe that any set term is wise.—C.K.]

22. Somnia Vana, "College Education: An Inquest," *The Freeman*, 1 March 1922. (I am indebted to Professor Seymour Martin Lipset, of Harvard University, for calling this article to my attention.)

23. None yet have fully accepted, however, the view of some radicals that the campus should become a "center of disloyalty" and the president should serve as "chairman" of the center.

24. Stoke, *The American College President*, 171.

Vignette—

New Complications: The Multicampus System*

Our Carnegie Commission had the first study made of the rise of systems of campuses, and this was my foreword to the ensuing report, which has become a classic in the field.

The multicampus system has become a significant feature of higher education in the United States since World War II. Forty percent (1987: 55 percent) of all students now attend schools which are parts of multicampus institutions, and more than one-fifth (1987: one-third; two-thirds of all public campuses) of all campuses are constituent elements of these new higher education conglomerates (see table 1). Particularly a phenomenon that marks public higher higher education, it is, however, not unknown in the private sector as well. Whether the multicampus system will become the dominant method of organization in the future remains to be seen, but past trends, if continued, would make this seem likely. Already three-fourths of the students in public universities are enrolled within such systems.

Three organizational changes of great importance have affected higher education over the past quarter of a century: (1) the introduction of students into governing mechanisms, (2) the creation of statewide coordinating councils, and (3) the rise for the multicampus system. The first of these developments has been the subject of nationwide attention; the second, of a number of studies; and the third, of almost complete neglect—yet it is at least as important in actual governance as either of the other two.

Two of these developments (coordinating councils and multicampus systems) have been part of the fundamental process of shifting power in recent times from the campus to instrumentalities outside the campus to a greater extent than ever before in American history. While most eyes have been directed to the struggle over power within the campus (students versus faculty versus administration), the really important phenomenon has been that there is constantly less power on campus; the more meaningful but largely hidden battle has been over how much less campus authority there should be.

The freestanding campus with its own board, its one and only president, its identifiable alumni, its faculty and student body, all in a single

TABLE 1

Number and Enrollment of Multicampus Colleges and Universities, 1968

Type of institution	Number of Institutions		Number of Campuses			Enrollment		
	All Institutions	Multicampus Institutions*	All Institutions	Multicampus Institutions	Percentage of Campuses in Multicampus Institutions	All Institutions (in Thousands)	Multicampus Institutions (in Thousands)	Percentage of Enrollment in Multicampus Institutions
Public								
Universities	90	54	389	344	88.4	2,342	1,808	77.2
Other four-year colleges	235	20	332	117	35.2	1,636	680	41.6
Two-year colleges	530	29	590	89	15.1	1,492	374	25.1
TOTAL	855	103	1,311	550	42.0	5,470	2,862	52.3

Private							
Universities	65	9	86	28	32.6	704	127	18.0
Other four-year colleges	1,132	16	1,176	45	3.8	1,249	71	5.7
Two-year colleges	271	4	277	10	3.6	149	7	4.6
TOTAL	1,468	29	1,539	83	5.4	2,102	205	9.7
Total colleges and universities**	2,323	132	2,850	633	22.2	7,572	3,067	40.5

*A multicampus institution is defined as one that reported in the U.S. Office of Education *Opening Fall Enrollment, 1968* questionnaire that it had two or more campuses (except that institutions that reported a main campus and one theological seminary branch campus, or one medical school branch campus, or one extension branch at a military installation are excluded); or the institution did not report enrollment data for branch campuses but further study revealed it did have at least two campuses (e.g., the Junior College District of St. Louis); or campuses were listed as separate institutions in *Opening Fall Enrollment, 1968* reports but further study revealed they were part of a unitary system (e.g., University of Nevada). The level of a multicampus system is determined by the level of its most senior institution.
**Does not include "specialized" institutions such as law or medical schools.

Source: Estimates developed by Carnegie Commission staff from U.S. Office of Education data.

location and with no coordinating council above it, is now the exception whereas in 1945 it was the rule. A whole series of new complexities, as a consequence, enter into what was already a highly complex system of governance even at its simplest. Two more layers of government have been added into many situations, and these new layers are also highly competitive with each other for authority—sometimes they are locked in mortal combat.

The superstructure of higher education has been gaining great weight in recent years just at the same time that the infrastructure on the campus has been undergoing substantial turmoil; and it has been the quiet revolution from above that has had the greater impact rather than the noisy revolt from below. Between the two developments, the governance of the campus has become a great issue.

Systems are the order of the day. National systems dominate in France, England, Russia, Sweden, and many other countries. The American counterpart has been the coordinating council and the multicampus institution, separately or in conjunction. So that here, as in much of the rest of the world, more is now done centrally and less is done by the campus itself. Several forces are working almost universally in this direction:

- The heightened interest in enrollment opportunities for more youth, skilled manpower for society, and the burden of mounting costs places more of higher education policy within the public domain and centralized control.
- The new dynamics of the growth of enrollments and of the enlargement of functions require more advance planning for new campuses, new admission policies, and new endeavors than did the older status quo of slow growth and change.
- The vastly improved techniques of centralized direction in industry and government are also applicable to higher education, and the new technology aids and abets these techniques.

So systems, in one form or another, proliferate.

The multicampus form is not entirely unique to the United States. The mammoth universities of India, such as Calcutta, are really systems of many largely independent colleges and institutes, running sometimes to more than one hundred, but, contrary to the United States, the central function of the "university" itself is examining—on the model of the older University of London with its external degrees. In Japan, groups of campuses comprise informal systems with all or nearly all the faculty drawn from the same "flagship" campus—thus a number of colleges recruit only from Tokyo, others only from Kyoto, and so forth; an American equivalent would be the "farm system" for baseball teams. The multicampus system in the United States, however, goes far beyond the examining of students and the farming out of faculty members.

The American multicampus system, as I have seen it and lived within it has some great advantages:

- It concentrates certain external relations, particularly with state and federal authorities, in a single office where they can usually be better performed.
- It facilitates long-range and overall planning of the creation of new places for students, of the provision of new services to new areas of the state, of the assignment of new endeavors among campuses, and of the continuing differentiation of functions between and among campuses.
- It makes possible (although by no means certain) the determination of diversity among campuses, as compared with the standardization that results from their competitive imitation of each other in the absence of central policy. Diversity is more likely to flow from central authority than from local autonomy.
- It facilitates greatly the creation of new campuses, and some of the most innovative have come from within multicampus systems, as in California, New York, Illinois, and Wisconsin.
- It encourages better management with the aid of specialists in the central administration and the exchange of experiences among campuses.

But the multicampus system inherently has some major liabilities as well:

- With its extra layer of management, it is almost inevitably more bureaucratic, more slow to move; it is less collegial in management and less personal in approach.
- Faculty senates and student governments have less influence. Both operate best on immediate, local, individual problems. It is the central expert who sees better and often analyzes better the more general and long-run problems. As a consequence, faculty unionization and student confrontation against the distant experts may be encouraged in lieu of more informal participation in decision making.
- The very process of centralized planning results in denying many expectations to many people at the same moment through the plan, as compared with case by case action where ''gifts'' are made to many over a period of time and denials take the form of individual postponements for later consideration. The case by case approach may be less rigorously thoughtful, but it is more adaptably politic.
- The lay board of the system is farther removed from the local atmosphere of the campus and the current practicalities of relationships. It is, as a

consequence, more likely to react ideologically to problems, to respond to the personal whims of influential members and to current headlines, and to be concerned with external considerations. It is harder for even the best of boards to perform as well as it could if it were concerned only with a single campus with which its members are closely identified and intimately knowledgeable.

• There are more points of possible friction over who does what and how, and more places for personality clashes—especially between the campus executive and the system executive.

• The political impact of an untoward event on a single campus can affect the whole system rather than being isolated to the one campus; but, conversely, the whole system may protect the single campus from political retaliation—it is harder to get at and punish the particular campus.

• The multicampus system is more open to control by external authority, particularly by governors, than would be a series of separate campuses. Among other reasons, a governor can be effective on one board in a way he could not be on ten or twenty or fifty campus boards.

• The roles of both the campus executive and the system executive are made more difficult. They must share authority and symbols of authority. The influence of each is diluted. Both must relate to the more potential veto groups in trying to get anything done—the president of the University of California has had to take any matter of basic importance before at least a dozen separate instrumentalities each with the assigned or, at least, the assumed power to confirm or deny the action.

Thus, a multicampus system is strong on the possible positive results—diversity, specialization, cooperation, effective use of resources, advance planning, and so forth—and weak on the negative aspects of process—bureaucratization, disenfranchisement of faculty and student informal influence, complexities in administrative relationships, political interference, and so forth. The possible positive results are more likely to be seen in advance but the negative aspects of process only as history unfolds. The central question about any multicampus system is whether it improves results—particularly the adequacy of advance planning, the enhancement of diversity and quality, the effective use of resources, and the successful representation to external authorities—more than it impedes the processes of governance. Is the value worth the cost? Any answer to this question must be given system by system and not for all systems at once.

It is not necessary to have multicampus systems. They may be highly likely, nevertheless, with block grants from public authorities. If reliance, however, were to be placed on financing higher education through the students, then the market might supplant the central planning. Since that has not happened and may not happen, it is important to see to it that multicampus systems work as well as possible. Based on personal experience, I suggest the following:

- Decentralize to the maximum extent possible. The burden of proof should be on the centralizers. In particular, it is important to decentralize personal relations among people, while it is easier to centralize the handling of things—like purchasing, accounting, etc.
- Work with broad formulas for financing and broad policies to guide actions, rather than with line-item control and specific rules.
- Rely more on postaudit than preaudit.
- Create local boards with final authority in the maximum number of areas like grounds and buildings, faculty appointments and promotions, student disciplinary actions, and so forth. The central board, of necessity, will handle total operating and construction budgets; admissions requirements; policies on size, rate of growth, and functions of each campus; creation of new campuses; and major personnel appointments. I favor the selection of the members of such local boards from persons outside the campus itself but personally interested in it, with some chosen by the faculty, some by students, some by alumni of the campus, some by the local community, and some by the central board—perhaps two or three by each group. The nature of the assignments to the local board calls for identification with the campus and specific knowledge of it.
- Provide adequate administrative assistance of high quality so that delays will be minimized and the civil service of the system can be fully effective. There will be more formal documents to handle and they will be more important in the life of the institution; they should be carefully prepared and thoughtfully reviewed.
- Select chief executives, in part, on their ability and willingness to be cooperative members of the system.

The multicampus system may be viewed, overall, as one facet of bureaucratic centralism in American society—in its government, its industry, its trade unions, its education at all levels. Particularly in higher education, the tidal wave of students, mounting financial costs, the increased interest of all elements of the public, the new methods of management, land the new technology have encouraged bureaucratic centralism.

The multicampus system, combined with the related rise of coordinating councils, has turned higher education increasingly into a quasi-public utility with its prices (tuition and budget) controlled outside the campus, its services (functions) specified, and its customers (through admissions policies) determined; and with outside agencies also prepared to hear complaints about prices, services, and the acceptance and rejection of customers. The campus is less part of free enterprise and more part of the controlled public domain.

But the future is not likely to be simply a mirror of the past. Bureaucratic centralism is under attack in many places from many sources. The new theme is local control, voluntarism, and spontaneity. From right and from left comes the challenge to simplify and to personalize. It is unlikely that the multicampus systems of higher education in the United States will escape entirely from the impact of these new demands. This is a great unknown.

Notes

* Foreword to Eugene C. Lee and Frank M Bowen, *The Multicampus University: A Study of Academic Governance* (New York: McGraw–Hill, 1971), Copyright 1971 by The Carnegie Foundation for the Advancement of Teaching. Reprinted by permission of The Carnegie Foundation for the Advancement of Teaching.

CHAPTER 19

Vignette—
Enter the Federal Government: The Evolution of the
Federal Role*

The Brookings Institution published a volume called Agenda for the
Nation *(1968) looking at about twenty major items on this agenda at
home and abroad. My agenda for higher education was for the federal
government to keep on doing more as it had, gradually, historically,
and particularly adding more money.*

The federal government, now facing policy decisions for the next decade, has entered upon its role in American higher education by gradual
steps.

The Dartmouth College Case

The first step was unintentional. Most early colleges, including Harvard had been founded with a special relation to the government of their
colony or state. The Jeffersonians argued that the public interest was dominant, that the state had a natural right to control. The Supreme Court decided to the contrary in 1819. The state of New Hampshire was prevented
from infringing upon the charter of Dartmouth College and changing the
nature of the private college into a state university. Dartmouth was assured
its independence and the trustees were confirmed in their control.

As a result, the movement for private colleges was accelerated and
scores of them were founded in the period before the Civil War. The distinctive American pattern of many private institutions evolved, each able to
go its own way, each started by private initiative, each financed wholly or
largely with private funds. Public institutions, as a consequence, had a
harder struggle for public funds and prestige. This pattern of private and
public higher education, in which the private segment at its best has always
stood for independence and quality, is unusual among university systems of
the world, most of which were started by public initiative and are publicly
financed and controlled.

The Land-Grant Universities and Service to Society

The second step by the federal government came at the time of the Civil War. The Morrill Act of 1862 authorized grants of land to the states to provide colleges giving instruction in agriculture and the mechanic arts. Thus the Congress took the initiative in establishing land-grant institutions, but it worked through the states and did not create federal universities. The land-grant college movement built chiefly on the few state institutions which existed at the time. It borrowed from German universities the combination of teaching with advanced research, added direct service to agriculture, industry, and government, and thus evolved a distinctively American pattern, not only for the state institutions but also for the greatest of the private universities, which adopted a similar course. Nearly two hundred universities, public and private, now follow this pattern, and at least twenty of them have international distinction.

The land-grant model created great possibilities for cooperation with the federal government. Distinguished universities accustomed to giving service to the surrounding society were available to work with the government—willingly and competently. Thus, during and after the Second World War, the federal government turned to them for scientific research at the highest level of capability, while other countries relied more on government agencies, academies, or scientific societies largely separate from the universities.

War and Science

The third step came with the Second World War and the subsequent cold war. Military might was based increasingly on scientific capability. The United States, under emergency conditions, turned to the universities for the atomic bomb, radar, and much else. The results were phenomenal; and they were obtained from a handful of universities. Six universities at one time shared one-half of all federal funds spent for scientific research through universities. Special federal agencies were established to work with the institutions. By 1960, 75 percent of all university research was funded by the federal government, most of it in scientific fields. Thus was established one of the most productive relations in history—the nation became stronger, the leading universities more distinguished.

Sputnik and the "Tidal Wave"

The fourth evolutionary stage began in 1958, following Sputnik and facing the decade of the "tidal wave" of students. Federal aid took multiple forms in response to multiple problems. The National Defense Education Act of 1958 supported science training, but added language instruction and teacher training. Support for construction beyond research facilities began on a large scale in 1963. Assistance to needy students was greatly expanded in 1965. Support was increased to institutions as such, to selected budding "centers of strength" in the sciences, land to "developing institutions," which meant, in fact, largely Negro colleges.

The first stage of federal involvement with higher education assured the integrity of the private colleges; the second initiated service to society; the third expanded scientific research; the fourth provided broadened support in the decade of assistance to growth.

Notes

* Originally titled "New Challenges to the College and University." in *Agenda for the Nation*, ed. Kermit Gordon, (Washington, DC: The Brookings Institution, 1968), 238–43. Reprinted by permission.

CHAPTER 20

Vignette—Reenter the States

The States and Higher Education: Changes Ahead*

The National Governors' Association gave a note of support to a conference at Wingspread in 1985 on "The Governors and Higher Education." I said that by now, about twenty years after the Brookings volume (selection 19), the federal period was over and a renewed state period was now in place. One observer said that I "shocked many listeners" but he agreed that "we have entered a new era."†

My first point is that the great period of federal initiatives in higher education is clearly, totally ended. I define that period as roughly from 1955 to 1985; from Sputnik, which was technically in 1957, to appointment of a new Secretary of Education in 1985.

Recently, I was at a meeting listening to an extremely passionate address with the message that the "golden age" had ended and we are now entering a new dark age for higher education. This college president said that a new Henry VIII has been let loose on our land. He is out to destroy the monasteries, to disperse the priests over the landscape, to leave only the walls of the abbeys standing there holding their arms up to the skies as though pleading for salvation from heaven which will never come. He went on to say that this Henry VIII, as compared with the original Henry VIII, is a very ignorant man. He does not realize that the only two basic necessities of daily life for the modern college and university student are a hi-fi set and an automobile. Then he went on to talk about the academic world. He said, "I fear that the academic world is playing Hamlet, pacing around the castle in Elsinore, saying 'to be or not to be,' while this new Henry VIII is still at large." I sat there, thinking to myself and wondering whether it is really a good idea for a college president to read too much Shakespeare too late at night.

However, I do agree that an age has ended although I do not think in quite such a dramatic way or with such drastic results. The end of the federal age has taken place, in part, because of the direct policies of the federal government, of the U.S. Secretary of Education, of the president of the United States, and with their new policies they are capping off the federal period. This would have happened anyway, I think, without these new policy decisions, because it would have to be capped off as a result of other policies.

Given the budget deficits which we are running, it is highly unlikely that higher education, regardless of policy desires, would receive any new money. Beyond the current deficit and looking into the future, we are building up a huge federal debt which is going to take a very substantial portion of all of our federal revenues for a very long period of time to pay the interest, and possibly someday to pay it off. We are also building new weapon systems at tremendous costs and, regardless of what happens in Geneva and elsewhere, weapon systems in the United States are carried on to their ultimate conclusion in obsolescence regardless of their need. So more money for higher education would not be there even if new initiatives were.

The Federal Period

Contrary to my presidential friend, however, all is not being lost. The gains of the past thirty years will be (and should be) preserved, by and large, and they have been great. We have built up research activity in universities and colleges all over the nation such as the world has never seen, and this will continue. The student aid program, while almost certain to be revised to some extent, is also going to continue. It has a great deal of popular support. The affirmative action program, in one way or another, will also continue, and, in my judgment, the developments of this federal period in affirmative action are in the process of largely being won for women. Unfortunately, we have not made such a breakthrough wit some of our minority groups; progress, but not a breakthrough. So, all will not be lost, but there are not going to be many more gains from federal initiatives for a long time ahead.

The New State Period

My second point is that we are once again entering a state period in higher education. This has been the standard situation for higher education since the founding of our republic, except for the land-grant period from 1860 to 1890 and the recent period from 1955 to 1985. The states, by and large, have taken good care of higher education; otherwise we would not have the best system of higher education in the world. Perhaps I should say that we are entering a state–private period of higher education when, once again, the major initiatives will come from state and private sources.

The states, in fact, may do better than they have ever done before in supporting higher education as higher education becomes more important to interstate competition. With all the concern about jobs in economic development, the states are becoming even more competitive and advancing their higher education systems, since one of the greatest assets a state can have in the competition with other states and with foreign nations is its system of higher education.

Also, the states may be even more interested in and do better by higher education than they have historically for another reason. There is more pressure from parents to get a good education for their children because of what it means to their lives, what it means to their incomes. This pressure rises, in part, because more and more of the potential students come out of households where their parents and even grandparents have had a college education and know what it has meant to their lives.

So I rather welcome, under the conditions of these times, the return to state initiatives and to the states as the principal source of new money.

Governors and the New State Period

My third comment is that, within most states, the governor has now become the most important single person in higher education. This is different than it was in 1955 when the recent federal period began. Then the governor in hardly any state would have been said to be the most important person in higher education. Now we go into a new state period with the governor in a more crucial position than ever before.

Before 1955, while some governors and legislators may have been very much involved in patronage, they were less interested in policy and they were generally more reticent about getting into policy whether interested or not than they are today. Now it would be almost inconceivable that, over this thirty-year period, governors would not have become more concerned with policy. Higher education enrollments tripled in the 1960s. Over the 1960s and 1970s, they quadrupled, and the sums of money in state budgets going into higher education have gone up enormously. That has to bring the governors into policy, even if they are totally out of patronage as California has been for a very long period of time.

Further, there is a lot more public interest in what happens within higher education. Parents want more places and better places for their children. Higher education, additionally, is more important to the economy of the states. And higher education, over that period of thirty years, has taken over much of the cultural life of the nation. The great mass of the American people now get their cultural opportunities through our three thousand campuses. That makes it more important for the governors too. And more of the entertainment life of the nation, for good or ill, comes through some of our large universities that are heavily active in sports.

Governors also have mechanisms they did not have in 1955. They have bigger staffs and they have better staffs. There has also been the development of state coordinating mechanisms that permit governors to become involved, not campus by campus, which would frequently be impossible, but through coordination where it is possible to have an impact.

I think the student revolts of the 1960s were terribly important. They brought the governors into campus life as almost never before, under public pressure or by their own desire or by both. There began to be a kind of intervention we had never seen before. I think that the autonomy, the independence of the university, has been something like the autonomy of the church. To a large extent, higher education comes out of the churches and was long protected by the idea of the separation of church and state. We lost our church status in the late 1960s. We are now in the marketplace of politics, and we are no longer looked upon as an institution apart. I think that was a very important development.

So the governors, as we go into this new state period, are the most important people in higher education across almost all of the nation. There are some dangers in this, I think, as the governors can become too important. In the recent AGB study I directed, members of our group talked with eight hundred people in all fifty states. I was impressed in talking with heads of consolidated systems, coordinating councils, and big land-grant universities how important, almost overwhelmingly important, the governor has become to these people.

Several told me that not just the most important person in their professional lives but the *only* important person in their professional lives was the governor. If they got along with the governor, the board was going to support them and the faculty was going to support them. If they did everything else right, and did not get along with the governor, they were going to lose the support of their board and of their faculty. And so I believe that governors can become too important. The heads of systems, the heads of coordinating mechanisms, the heads of big campuses can become too tied to one single individual. It runs against my own feeling for pluralism and, I think, the standard American feeling of the importance of pluralism—separation of power.

The danger is not when there is a supportive and understanding governor, but governors vary in the intensity of their interests and also in the direction of their interests. Some are for and some against higher education. I wonder whether, as we go into this new state period, we may not have too few checks and balances and too few filters against the power of an unfriendly governor.

Issues in the New State Period

My fourth point is that, if the governors are the most important education officers in their states now, and for higher education too, there are some very grave issues ahead for them to decide. There is a great deal at stake:

1. There is a contest in so many states between the public and the private institutions, almost open warfare in some places around this country. What are the governors going to do about it?

2. It seems to me that there is a coming conflict in the states between what they will want to do for the more elite and the less elite institutions. To draw in industry, states will want to put more emphasis upon the more elite institutions with their research facilities and their ability to train people with the highest skills. In the 1960s, the emphasis was on the community colleges. Now what are the governors going to do as between the elite and the less elite academic institutions?

3. What funding formulas are they going to establish? Enrollment-driven formulas worked very well in a period of expansion, but when enrollment declines, what were once variable costs under expansion suddenly become fixed costs.

4. Unionization is another major issue. The number of faculty in unions has been steady for a long period of time, but as faculties get threatened and tenured people start being let go, unionization could increase again. What position are governor going to take on negotiations, because increasingly the negotiations are going to take place at the level of the state government. The tendency, always in the trade union movement, is to go where the money is, and the governor has it. How are they going to handle unionization.

5. How are they going to react to shifts in the labor market? To what extent are they going to put more pressure on colleges and universities to strengthen technology as compared with the humanities and the social sciences?

6. Teacher education is in trouble everywhere too. What are the governors going to do?

7. Affirmative action, I think, is going to move more and more from the federal level to the state level. And what about the situation of minorities? There are no riots in the streets right now, but there have been in the past, and there could be again. There are unsettled problems in this nation, real tensions.

So the governor as chief academic offer has some very, very difficult problems to solve.

Notes

* From *State Government, 58, no.2* (Summer 1985): 45–49. Reprinted by permission.

† Stanley O. Ikenberry, Opinion: "Higher Education and the States: A New Era Begins," *Higher Education & National Affairs*, 29 July 1985, 7.

CHAPTER 21

An Eternal Issue—
Caesar and God*

The University of North Carolina held a national convocation of Kenan professors in 1982, under the leadership of William C. Friday. The central theme was university autonomy. The central tone of the discussion was how much was being lost. I took a contrary view that it was not all that much, but not with any support that I could detect from anyone else—external authority was still and always an enemy.

This conference centers on certain areas of current difficulty with respect to university autonomy. These selected areas are seldom better set forth than by Professor Edward Shils in a report, in the Spring 1979 issue of *Minerva*, entitled "Government and Universities in the United States" with a subhead of "Render unto Caesar . . . ;"[1] and by Senator Daniel Patrick Moynihan in his December 1980 article in *Harper's* on "State vs. Academe."[2] I have been asked to comment, in particular, on these two presentations of the issues.

Professor Shils identified government as "Caesar" and higher education, by implication, as "God." He is particularly concerned with the federal government and with the research universities. His catalogue of current sins by Caesar includes exploitation of the universities by not paying adequate overhead on research contracts, by infringing on the confidentiality of records, and by interfering with academic appointments based on merit alone, particularly the latter. Senator Moynihan's list includes the federal government, through one of its instrumentalities, demanding to know and demanding access, through another instrumentality, to confidential university records on academic appointments and promotions; forcing "time and effort" reporting by faculty on federal contracts; and creating a Department of Education "that will make regulation more extensive." I agree that the federal government has sinned in each of these areas, and I have fought on the battle lines for higher overhead allowances, for concentration on merit in appointments and promotions, and against the creation of the Department of Education; and I oppose breaches of confidentiality in voting on tenure cases and in managing records. There are, in my judgment, even more categories of sins by government that those noted by Shils and Moynihan, and I shall refer to some of them.

Yet I disagree, in differing degrees, with the analyses of Shils and Moynihan. To begin with, there is no Caesar and there is no God. There are many Caesars and there are many Gods; and evil and good are not, respectively, concentrated so nearly on the one side or on the other. Both evil and good are well distributed on both sides. The world of reality is not so divided into the forces of darkness and the forces of light, into the black and the white, into the sinners and the sinned upon. The State is many agencies and many people; and Academe the same. And I am more optimistic than Senator Moynihan. I do not agree that "nothing" can be "done" about the "conquest of the private sector by the public sector" except "to be aware of it" (Moynihan). Thus I associate myself with specific complaints made and see even more to complain about than Shils and Moynihan, but not with the general assignment of fault; and I think that more can be done than the "nothing" of Moynihan and even more than the generally excellent suggestions of Shils. I wish to disassociate myself both from the theme of an overall confrontation between Caesar and God or between The State and Academe, however qualified, and from a sense of despair or of the inadequacy of possible remedies.

My theses are: (1) that there should be more specificity and balance in the analysis of the sources of the threats to the integrity and autonomy of higher education and, thus, a different emphasis in the remedies to be undertaken; and (2) that, in particular, we should be more concerned with the evil we do unto ourselves and less with the evil that others do unto us than are either Shils or Moynihan. I shall conclude with suggesting a six-part program of action.

Many "Caesars" and Many "Gods"

There are many Caesars—the national government, the fifty states, the local jurisdictions that deal with community colleges. The federal government itself includes the executive, the legislative, and the judicial branches, each, in turn, subject to many, many subdivisions at the operating level. The same is true at the state and local levels. I take great comfort in the fact that there are many Caesars mostly acting alone; that there is no conspiracy among them.

I doubt the advantage of going too quickly from the specific to the general, of speaking of *the* state, or *the* the federal government; of reaching broad conclusions from a few individual events however serious they may be, such as, for example, the conclusion that "universities are now wards of the state" (Moynihan), or that "Caesar . . . had no tradition to restrain him in relations with the universities" (Shils). Which state? Which Caesar? It was federal judge in Georgia (Judge Owens) who sentenced a professor at the University of Georgia to jail because he would not say how he voted on an academic promotion. It was the Secretary of Labor who ordered the University of California at Berkeley to surrender its confidential records. And neither case has yet been finally settled. Federal accounting rules to "keep track of time and effort" by professors are still in dispute. The status of the Department of Education is still not settled, and its creation has not been so damaging, as yet at least, as some of us who opposed it once thought it would be. Overhead allowances involve many federal agencies and the OMB, and arrangements keep changing; and the nicest thing about money is that it is not a principle, that it is subject to endless compromises. The national Supreme Court decided the Bakke case on a precarious split vote. It was HEW that tried to require the University of North Carolina to get advance approval of academic plans; a policy later reversed by the new Department of Education. "Dependence is the key issue" as Moynihan states; but it has not yet been so conclusively settled adversely to the universities.

So my first plea is to be specific—which agency did what to whom and when? And not to raise what have thus far been specific issues into broad confrontations between "Caesar" and "God," and the "State" and "Academe." That might come later, as Moynihan notes that Schumpeter indirectly implies, but we should not encourage movement in that direction by saying that it has already happened.

There are also many Gods—three thousand quite various institutions of higher education. And each of these institutions, in turn, is its own combination of trustees, faculty, staff, students, administrators, alumni; and each of these groups breaks down into subgroups and individuals. I know what is meant by the "groves of academe" as a place, but I am less sure of what is meant by Academe itself. Whatever Academe does mean, it clearly is one of the most divided of all institutions by subject matter, by opinions about proper institutional and social policy, by types of internal governance. Who acted wrongly? Who took the wrong path?

Parenthetically, may I say that I would prefer, instead of the images of Caesar and God or The State and Academe or the possible contrast of "The Power and the Glory," images of Patron and Artist—the Patron occasionally too heavy-handed and the Artist often too mercenary, or of Foundation and Scholar.

Evil and Good

All the different Caesars have done much evil but they have done much good as well. Humboldt helped to inaugurate the modern university movement from his position as Minister of Culture in Prussia. Napoleon helped to renovate the moribund French university system and expand the Grandes Écoles. It was Royal Commissions that served to stir Oxford and Cambridge out of their lethargy in the middle of the nineteenth century. The land-grant university movement in the United States originated in the national Congress. It was the national administration that decided to make universities the "home of science" during and after World War II. The community college movement was initiated by states and localities. All this must be set against the activities of the un-American activities committees at the national and state levels; against the governors that intervened too much; against the agencies that became too zealous. Academic freedom has been increasingly more, not less, respected by nearly all branches of government over the past century. Restraint by the states in recent times in intruding into the affairs of colleges and universities has been quite phenomenal. Looking broadly at state funds appropriated per student across the United States in real terms or at direct legislative action taken, one would never know that the public at large was irate about student political activities in the late 1960s and into the 1970s. State legislators were very protective of public higher education in the face of the public outcry and despite their own critical rhetoric.

All the different Gods have done much good but they have done some evil as well. Too many institutions for too long ignored the talent available among women and minorities. It was boards of trustees that fired Professor E. A. Ross at Stanford and required a special oath of allegiance at the University of California—later declared unconstitutional by the California State Supreme Court. It was students and faculty that went beyond careful analyses and peaceful persuasion in the period of unrest in the late 1960s; that sought to "reconstitute" the university into a political agent of social change. More damage, by far, has been done to academic freedom by individuals and groups within higher education over the past two decades than by all those outside Caesars. And many other individuals and groups defended or stayed silent about these internal attacks; more than ever did when similar attacks came from external sources. Higher education has been so quick to support academic freedom when threatened from outside and so hesitant when the enemy was inside.

Moynihan and Shils do castigate the universities but their general view seems to be that it is Caesar that is more inclined to be evil—with exceptions; and that God is more inclined to be good—with exceptions. For Moynihan, "the universities politicized themselves in the 1960s," have been guilty of a "profound failure of leadership" in not fighting for their autonomy, have been able to agree only on "greed-by-consensus." For Shils, the universities "have all too often nestled" in the arms of Caesar, have too readily become "service stations," even "multiversities," have taken "lying down" the intrusions of the federal government into the selection of academic staff, land have been too lenient toward or even supportive of "disorders" in the 1960s. Yet it still is the federal government that is mainly at fault for having an "inordinately inflated," according to Shils, "conception of its rights and powers." I agree instead with Derek Bok that the federal government has generally exercised "proper restraint."[3]

This mixed situation also greatly comforts me—that evil and good are widely distributed; that the many Caesars are capable of good as well as of evil; and that the many Gods can appreciate that even Gods can err. So my second plea is to be careful to balance as accurately as possible the praise and the blame, to emphasize the good as well as the evil in the opposing group; to recognize the evil as well as the good on our own side; and never to confuse the two on either side.

What Can Be Done?

The issue is the preservation of a necessary and reasonable degree of autonomy for institutions of higher education.

To begin with there are more things to be done about and more transgressions than the items noted above. Let me note particularly the following two:

The introduction into the states of "1202 commissions" by Congress in 1972 seeking to determine essential aspects of state coordination of higher education. Fortunately, the federal government has not pushed this approach in subsequent years.

The long-term imposition of line-item budgeting on institutions of higher education in many states.

The remedies to be considered for these and other intrusions on autonomy are several.

1. Higher Education Should Know Better What It Will and Will Not Do. Here Shils is very helpful in defining so eloquently the central obligation of higher education as the "discovery and transmissions of truths." I like also the formulation of Trow[4] of "transmission of high culture" and the conduct of "pure scholarship"; and I would add the definition and preservation of academic morality. What higher education will not do is more difficult. It should not, of course, violate its central obligations. It should also not allow exploitation of institutional resources for political or economic gain by specific individuals or groups inside or outside higher education.

2. *Higher Education Should Favor the Continuation of Many Caesars.* Moynihan notes the importance of decentralization within the federal government of relations with higher education. This is one reason to oppose a too-inclusive Department of Education or any department at all. This reason also means keeping the fifty states involved in sport of higher education as well as the federal government; preserving in health the many private foundations; encouraging private giving; and charging tuition to those students who can afford to pay.

3. *The Private Sector of Higher Education Should Be Preserved.* There are many reasons for this. One important one is that the autonomy of the private institutions serves as a protection for the public institutions. The private institutions set the standards, serve as the models.

4. *Higher Education Should Favor a Limited Role for the Federal Government.* Aside from supporting access to higher education, the Carnegie Council supported federal responsibility for funding basic and applied research, and federal help to construction particularly in times of depression to stimulate the economy or in a period of great enrollment expansion when state funds would be inadequate.[5]

5. *Higher Education Should Be Better Prepared to Defend Its Own Autonomy.* This requires some clear understanding of rights. Shils has a good list in relation to the federal government. It includes: no interference with the "power of appointment," no access to "confidential records," payment of full costs for services rendered without unduly burdensome accounting requirements. I hesitate only about the first. I think the federal government has the right to insist that merit be fairly defined, that it not be clouded in its application by clear acts of prejudice, and that the search for talent be energetically pursued in all places where it might be found.

The Carnegie Commission once set forth a list of rights versus state governments (*Governance of Higher Education*[6]), which was quite explicit, including: the right to assign all funds for specific purposes, to select and promote faculty members, to approve course and course content, to determine grades and issue degrees, to make policies on and to administer research, to set conditions for academic freedom, and to select leadership, among a number of others.

Rights, however, are not enough. To be effective there must be strong institutional leadership and, as Shils points out, this is impeded too often by the "unthinking prejudice" of faculty members. It may also require the equivalent of the AAUP in the area of academic freedom. The Carnegie Commission once suggested that the American Council on Education establish a "Commission on Institutional Independence." For reasons I have never understood, while considered, this suggestion was never accepted. Perhaps the Association of Governing Boards might now be willing to consider the same possibility.

Higher education should, in reciprocation, recognize the legitimate expectations of government, which, as Shils sets forth, include the training of enough persons to meet the occupational needs of the nation, the conduct of research that is responsive to the "proper purposes of government," and the carrying on of disagreements over policy by members of the academic community in a "temperate way." Here again, the Carnegie Commission[7] set forth a list of proper claims by the states including respect for the law, the political neutrality of institutions of higher education, the proper accountability for funds, and the assurance of equality of access for all qualified applicants, among others.

6. *Higher Education Should Earn its Independence.* It can earn its independence by:doing the following:

> Performing, at a high level of quality, functions that are important to the people in the larger society
> Demonstrating capacity for effective self-governance
> Making effective use of resources provided by society
> Abiding by the law on campus
> Assuring institutional neutrality in partisan politics and in public controversies external to the institution
> Preserving its own intellectual integrity from attacks from within as well as from without
> Giving full and honest explanations to the public in general and to legislators and elected administrators in particular about all matters of broad public concern

Shils properly notes that independence has not always been fully earned; that universities have not always adhered to "the intellectually most stringent standards in their appointive action"; that they bear much of the responsibility "for the disorders" on campus that have occurred; that some academics have indulged "in demagogy" and given "patronage to subversion"; that universities have permitted their resources and prestige to be exploited to advance "some transient political cause."

Higher education needs more explicit moral codes and better statements of institutional "rights and responsibilities" and "fair practices" of faculty members and students, as the Carnegie Commission and subsequent Council have suggested and outlined.[8] We once called for the development of an "academic constitution" and gave an outline of its essential points.[9]

The firmest basis for independence is integrity. I have been surprised and even shocked with how reluctant organizations of higher education, accrediting associations, and individual institutions are to face directly the creation of codes of good conduct and the means for their enforcement. These matters, it is true, are controversial. They involve very careful thought. Any limitations on action run counter to the wishes of some members of the academic community who want to be guided only by their own judgments and desires. And no priesthood likes to reform itself. The academic priesthood can and often does claim that it is a moral community and thus needs no rules of conduct. But integrity is the most precious possession of higher education and is necessary for its continued autonomy; and it deserves careful definition.

I conclude, sadly, by saying that I am more impressed with the restraint shown by most of the many Caesars most of the time than with the integrity of academic conduct demonstrated by some within the temples of higher education some of the time. We need to look at ourselves as well as at the conduct of others.

Notes

* Originally titled "Higher Education and the Federal System," presented at the Second Convocation of Kenan Professors, University of North Carolina, Chapel Hill, June 4, 1982.

1. Edward Shils, "Government and Universities in the United States: The Eighth Jefferson Lecture in the Humanities," *Minerva*, 17, no. 1 (Spring 1979): 129–77.

2. Daniel Patrick Moynihan, "State vs. Academe," *Harper's*, 261, no. 1567 (December 1980): 31–40.

3. Derek Bok, *Beyond the Ivory Tower* (Cambridge, MA: Harvard University Press, 1982), 59.

4. Martin Trow, "Elite and Popular Functions in American Higher Education," ed. W. R. Niblett, in *Higher Education: Demand and Response*, (London: Tavistock, 1969), 182.

5. Carnegie Council on Policy in Higher Education, *The Federal Role in Postsecondary Education*, (San Francisco: Jossey-Bass, 1975).

6. Carnegie Commission on Higher Education, *Governance of Higher Education: Six Priority Problems*, (New York: McGraw–Hill, 1973), 25–27.

7. Carnegie Commission; *Governance of Higher Education*, 25–27.

8. Carnegie Council on Policy Studies in Higher Education, *Fair Practices in Higher Education: Rights and Responsibilities of Students and Their Colleges in a Period of Intensified Competition for Enrollments*, (San Francisco: Jossey–Bass, 1979).

9. Carnegie Commission on Higher Education, *Reform on Campus: Changing Students, Changing Academic Programs*, (New York: McGraw–Hill, 1972), ch. 6.

PART IV

Academic Innovation and Reform:
Much Innovation, Little Reform

Introduction—Academic Innovation and Reform: Much Innovation, Little Reform

Never in the history of the United States, or for that matter any other nation, has there been such a wave of academic innovation—large, medium, and small—with such miniscule results as during the great transformation. There were "cluster" colleges and "optive" colleges and "afloat" colleges and "mini" colleges and "free" colleges and "federated" colleges and "storefront" colleges and "newspaper" colleges and "without walls" colleges; also "work-study," "field study," and "study abroad"; and every other innovation that the mind could possibly devise.[1] It was almost obscene not to have some kind of an experiment in progress on your campus. Few of the innovations survived, and those few had little general impact on higher education—everything was tried; nearly everything failed. The same largely disappointing results were experienced also in Europe.

The flurry of new endeavors in the United States is easy to explain:

It was the time of the "new frontier," and of endless hopes.

Growth created opportunities for new directions in both old and new institutions.

Students had many grievances as a result of growth—larger classes, more teaching by graduate assistants, more bureaucratic impersonalization of the administration, and much else.

Students wanted a "philosophy of life" and got only bits and pieces of specializations.

Students wanted more choices and more freedom of choice in all of their lives.

Many young faculty members were less tied to traditional approaches; some carried over complaints from their student years.

A few older faculty members had waited for years to have a chance to try out their pet projects.

A reaction was taking place among some faculty members and some administrative leaders against what they considered to be excessive specialization of subject fields.

Academic reform was one response to student activism, sometimes genuinely intended to remedy problems and sometimes undertaken as a diversion from political extremism.

Some institutions were trying to find a distinctive market niche.

Some administrative leaders were seeking distinguishing records of their own.

The actual results of all these explorations were mostly these:

Fewer required courses.

More student-demanded courses, as in women's studies and Black studies.

A continuation of the long-term decimation of "liberal education" in the name of free choice. The increase in electives came from reduced general education requirements as the faculties held on to the requirements for the major.

The wave of reform was very revealing in that it demonstrated that reform was not the wave of the future—the status quo ante was. Seldom in the history of education have so many said so much and ended up doing so little.

22. Rebuilding Communities of Scholars. My own particular concern, shared by many others, as we built three new campuses of the University of California, was to create smaller human communities within the ever-larger total university, and to create better opportunities for more-rounded intellectual communities less fractionated by specialization. At Irvine, the effort was to organize around broad "divisions" of knowledge instead of narrow departments. At San Diego and at Santa Cruz, it was to establish "cluster" colleges relatively small in size but large in intellectual coverage. The results in each case were marked, as they were elsewhere, by erosions from the original plans.

The concern for environments more conducive to a more liberal education, now more than twenty years later, has been expressed in two recent national best-sellers that have also captured national media attention.[2] In my opinion, these essays simplify both the sources of the decline of liberal education and the possible solutions.

23. Who Should Lead? The solution, if there is any, lies not with the "Great Books" or any other single definition of best content, but lies instead, I believe, in leadership. The faculty will protect the majors, the students will protect the electives, but only the president and/or the provost or dean will protect liberal learning. Yet most presidents have, in fact, been pushed or pulled out of or have wriggled out of responsibility for the academic curriculum. They preside, instead, over the nonacademic aspects of academic institutions. We are a long way from the advice of Harold Dodds that presidents should spend "half their time on academic concerns."[3]

Digression: New Approaches to Liberal Education.

I think it is realistic to aim for one-quarter of an undergraduate education to be devoted to liberal education.[4] The major has a solid grip on one-half of the undergraduate time (more in some areas, such as engineering). This would leave a final one-fourth for electives, for any minor, and for any remedial or additional skill training. The main argument to me for a liberal education is that a person lives a life as well as earns a living, and that a life involves citizenship duties and the effective use of leisure as well as work. And I note that alumni particularly wish they had spent more time on liberal education.[5]

But what? Distribution requirements have usually been a political compromise among departments, and many of the courses are taught for those students majoring in the field and not for the general student; and, in any event, high school gives contact (and should give more) with distribution. Great Books are great for the very few. "Western Civilization" has run up against a contest with "non-Western" and nonmale and nonwhite aspects of "civilization"; the issue has become politicized; and, "Western Civilization," as the sole approach, is, I believe, out of date.

I have been involved with the development of two other suggestions.

One is "global perspective in education"[6] that involves specifically these guidelines:

A one-year course in world history with special attention to U.S. history within the context of world history.

A one-year course on the world as a series of interrelated systems—a physical system, a biological system, a political and economic system, and a system of information and evaluation.

A one-term course on understanding comparative cultures; followed by another term studying a non-American (or at least nonmajority American) culture of the student's choice.

A one-term course on how to analyze public policy issues in general; followed by a one-term course of choice that includes discussion of one or more specific national or international policy issues.

This proposal was first made for high school students but fits the college level even better.

The other is an "integrative learning experience."[7] The central idea is that the major is organized along vertical lines but that people need experience in thinking along horizontal, or cross-disciplinary lines, also. A series of such integrative learning groupings would be made available—for example, Far Eastern Civilization (history, art, philosophy, current politics); or The City (history and the great cities of history, the city as an engineering project, the sociology of the city, the redesign of the city); The Environment (biology, the environment, the impact of humans, saving the environment, the ethics of the environment). Each professor would teach within his or her own specialty (they generally dislike "core" courses that lead them outside their specialty). Each student would be offered a series of choices, rather than a single set requirement, and might be allowed to piece together his or her own integrative learning experience.

But there is no one solution. The important thing is to have one or more alternative solutions.

As I see it, there are four major approaches:

"Distribution," or "ways of knowing." One that impresses me is that of Brooklyn College.[8]

"Civilization," as at Stanford and Columbia, and earlier the "Ancient Greats" at Oxford, and, historically, French Culture in France. The "Great Books" is another example.

"Global," as noted above.

"Mentalities," also as noted above. The long series of courses at Harvard, which each cover broad subjects broadly taught, is an example.

And there are, of course, mixtures, as outlined in the recent report issued by the National Endowment for the Humanities, which combines the first and second above.[9]

24. How Hard It Is. European experience, as well as American, shows how hard it is to get reform, whether in liberal education or in any other direction. Partial successes and failures are more likely than full successes.

25. An Urban Versus a Rural Society. A major concern of mine, as we attempted to project the future of the University of California (specifically in San Francisco and downtown Los Angeles), was to add an urban-grant dimension to the existing land-grant dimension, with problems of youth and of community health among the central focal points, as food and fiber had once been for the land-grant universities. It is by now, however, politically impossible, as the debate over my urban-grant proposal showed, to pick by name sixty-seven urban-grant institutions to stand beside the sixty-seven land-grant. Yet there is still a possibility for some institutions to emerge along the lines of this model. This did not happen as I once hoped it might in San Francisco or Los Angeles.

26. A Residual Role for Higher Education. If higher education is to move increasingly toward urban problems in an increasingly industrialized society, then I believe that it, and particularly the community colleges, will have two additional essential assignments: (1) to ease the difficult transition from education to work; and (2) to be a support of last resort, by way of advice, care, and coping instruction, for all young adults.[10]

27. The Longer Term. Higher education should look at the longer term. Historically it has added functions as society needed more knowledge, more skills, and more solutions to its problems. What might the new contributions be?

28. The Eternal Verities. The most important academic reform always is to continue the centuries-long effort to protect and intensify the roles of truth and merit in the academic world. The role of merit is of particular importance in mixed-race societies, such as the United States and South Africa.

Notes

1. For a partial inventory, see Ann Heiss, *An Inventory of Academic Innovation and Reform* (Berkeley, CA: The Carnegie Commission on Higher Education, 1973).

2. Allan Bloom, *The Closing of the American Mind* (New York: Simon and Schuster, 1987); and E. D. Hirsch, Jr., *Cultural Literacy* (Boston: Houghton Mifflin, 1987).

3. Harold W. Dodds, *The Academic President—Educator or Caretaker?* (New York: McGraw-Hill, 1962), 60.

4. Lynne V. Cheney, chairman of the National Endowment for the Humanities, suggests that 40 percent of an undergraduate's time be spent on a core curriculum in general education. (*50 Hours: A Core Curriculum for College Students* [Washington, DC: National Endowment for the Humanities, 1989].)

5. Joe L. Spaeth and Andrew M. Greeley, *Recent Alumni and Higher Education* (New York: McGraw-Hill, 1970).

6. Study Commission on Global Perspectives (Clark Kerr, Chair), *The United States Prepares for Its Future: Global Perspectives in Education* (New York: Global Perspectives in Education, Inc., 1987).

7. The Carnegie Foundation for the Advancement of Teaching, *Missions of the College Curriculum.* (San Francisco: Jossey-Bass, 1977), 173–79.

8. Brooklyn College of The City University of New York, *The Core Curriculum,* September 1975.

9. Cheney, *50 Hours.*

10. For an elaboration of this view, see Carnegie Council on Policy Studies in Higher Education, *Giving Youth a Better Chance: Options for Education, Work, and Service* (San Francisco: Jossey-Bass, 1979).

CHAPTER 22

Rebuilding Communities of Scholars—
Toward the More Perfect University*

Robert Hutchins asked me to participate in a conference (1967) on The University in America. He gave me the title of "Toward the More Perfect University" although he knew perfectly well that I did not think there was such a thing, since I was always concerned with what was better and it was he, in our many discussions, who sought what was best. Hutchins said in his introduction that the American university had "combustible tendencies"—always trying to offer every possible service to anyone that might possibly want it. That was not his idea of the "best." Actually I talked not as the "cannibal" he rather thought I was but about efforts to reconstitute university life into more human and intellectual communities.

"Toward the More Perfect University" is the title most thoughtfully and kindly provided me by President Hutchins. I have no reasonably clear idea of what he thought this title would call forth in my mind. He may have thought it would evoke no clear idea—in the sense of a vision of the "perfect university" unrelated to time and place, of an institution without spatial or temporal constraints. If so, he was right. There is not now, never has been, and never will be the "perfect university." There is, or should be, however, always the search. My remarks will relate to one current aspect of this search by the modern American university.

The search is intrinsically a difficult one. Most defintions of perfection involve inherent contradictions, inconsistent elements. "We the People of the United States" once sought to "form a more perfect Union, establish Justice, insure domestic tranquility, provide for the common defense, promote the general welfare, and secure the blessings of liberty to ourselves and our Posterity. . . ." We have spent a century and nine decades disturbing domestic tranquility in efforts to promote the general welfare, curbing liberty in order to establish justice, and so forth. So, also, it is with the university. There are inevitable contradictions inherent in the nature of the institution itself. This gives it many of its problems but also much of its dynamism. The search for the Holy Grail is the important thing; and it might be too bad if we ever really thought we had found it. As Robert

Louis Stevenson said of El Dorado, "To travel hopefully is a better thing than to arrive," It might almost be said that the perfect university is an imperfect one urgently seeking perfection.

We should, consequently, set a reasonable goal for the contemporary university which will help to draw it closer toward such perfection as it may attain. James Perkins has recently suggested the goal of "internal coherence" so that each activity could "strengthen the others." If this were to be the firm goal relentlessly sought for Cornell, then much of Cornell as we now know it would quickly disappear. Do fraternities strengthen Southeast Asian studies? Does rowing on the lake strengthen the agricultural experiment station? Does the medical center in New York City strengthen industrial relations at Ithaca? If they are held to do so, then this criterion is so broadly applied as to provide little definition. Now there are those who really do think that much of the modern American university should disappear. But I do not agree that this is necessary or even desirable.

It seems to me that a more reasonable goal would be to require that activities carried on within a university should be able to coexist effectively with each other, each drawing strength from, and hopefully also adding strength to, their common university environment; and that each activity should be worthwhile and suitable in and of itself and be of university level quality. In this connection, I realize full well that the phrase "university-level quality" is subject to a variety of definitions. This more modest goal will be difficult enough to achieve, for it will require major changes in content, in form, in attitude.

It is often said that the modern American university is in crisis. I do not believe this to be true in any general sense. A segment of the university is in crisis, and an important segment; but most of it is not. Most of it is moving along with unparalleled vitality and productivity, and in harmony. This is part of the trouble. It is partly in crisis, but mostly contented, and because it is mostly contented it is only halfhearted about doing something about the part in crisis.

The modern American university draws primarily on three strains of history. First, on the British tradition of high-quality training for a select group of undergraduates; second, on the German tradition of research for society and specialized training for graduate students; and, third, on the American genius for service to many, if not most, elements of the surrounding community. Out of these three strains of history have come the three major functions of our contemporary universities. The second and third functions—research and graduate training, and service—have proved quite compatible. The first, undergraduate instruction, is finding it harder to co-exist in its entirety with the other two.

The reasons for the growing conflict between some aspects of undergraduate education and the other major current functions are clear.

Research, graduate training, and service are carried forward through specialization, and they increasingly relate also to the outside community, to government, to industry, to the professions, to agriculture. The specialist draws funds and problems from the outside and supplies ideas and skilled personnel to the outside. Undergraduate instruction, on the contrary, is inherently more internally oriented—toward the student—and some of these students are interested more in generalization than in specialization.

There is also a problem of scale. Research, graduate training, and service are best carried out in a very large institution, large enough to accommodate an increasing number of specialties and to provide large libraries and laboratories. But, though they take place in a large institution, the relationships they foster are personal. The professor works closely with relatively few graduate students and research assistants, or as consultant or adviser to a few clients. Undergraduate instruction, on the other hand, can be, and in the large institution often is, carried out on a mass basis—the large impersonal lecture. The small-scale relationship with the graduate student within the large-scale institution works better than the large-scale relationship with the undergraduate in the same large-scale institution.

The demands of those functions which can be carried on in a specialized and still personalized way within the large institution have so overwhelmed undergraduate instruction that it has ended, too often, by being handled in a specialized but depersonalized fashion. Universities have grown larger and larger. More and more faculty time and more and more facilities have been devoted to research, graduate training, and service. Specialization has been the key both to publication and to opportunities for consultation by the individual faculty member, and consequently to distinction for the institution.

The organizational structure has responded by creating the department with its own curriculum and the research institute with its own usually narrow segment of knowledge. The undergraduates have been offered specialized courses often imposed in a sequence developed for those majoring in the subject. And universities have come to be measured more by the distinction of their faculties and the quality of their graduate instruction, and less by the distinction of their undergraduate work, which has been much harder to rate on a comparative basis.

There has always been an inherent conflict between undergraduate instruction and the other functions of the university—a conflict caused by the differing degrees of specialization needed by each function, by the scale of the total institution within which each function is best performed, and by the comparative emphasis of the functions on external and internal orientation. But this latent conflict has become fully apparent only since World War II. Over the past twenty years, faculty members have increasingly been drawn into more and more specialized research with the new opportunities available to them, and into service, as external demand for their specialized knowledge has greatly increased. Concurrently, the undergraduates have entered the university better prepared than ever before, more of them have been oriented toward serious academic study, and more of them also have had broad social concerns. The gap has widened between what was offered from behind the lectern and what was demanded by those who sat in front of it.

This gap—between the new missions of many professors and the new desires of some students—might have gone largely unnoticed except for another development. Student styles changed. Apathy turned to activism. More students wanted more control over their institutional environment. Vocationalism also was replaced, in the case of a substantial number, by an even more intense interest in the world as a whole and their role within it. More students wanted to gain from their education a personal and social philosophy as well as, or even instead of, a vocational skill. Faculty members and undergraduate students, who should be in close contact, too often were moving rapidly in divergent directions. And a system of undergraduate education which had been, in part, undesirable became in some situations also less viable. Thus the crisis.

The crisis in the American university is much narrower than undergraduate instruction in general. There is no crisis in the professional schools. There, students have clear vocational aims, the curriculum is designed to further these aims, and the school is usually small enough so that the student is known as an individual. Nor is there a crisis, by and large, in the sciences. There, also, the student usually knows what he or she wants to do and what he or she wants to do leads down the path of specialization. Also, the laboratory is a more personal environment than the classroom.

The crisis is largely in the humanities and the social sciences. They have adapted themselves to teaching on a large scale. On a campus I know, one professor has sixty-three teaching assistants under his direct supervision. Large departments in particular tend not to view themselves as having any identifiable group of undergraduate students under their auspices. The students in the humanities and the social sciences are also more likely to have broad concerns about values or public policy which are not satisfied by specialized, segmented courses. Then, too, the political activists are mostly found in these areas of study.

This crisis in the humanities and social sciences at the undergraduate level carries over to a degree into the graduate level and thus into the ranks of the teaching assistants—for somewhat the same reasons, but for an added one as well. Selection and financing of graduate students are generally not as adequate in the humanities and social sciences as in the scientific and professional areas and standards for performance are not so clear-cut; thus, too many graduate students stay around for too many years and in the end achieve only disappointment. Moreover, some faculty members, particularly in the humanities, have felt neglected as the largesse of recent years passed them by, and as honors and acclaim went to the work of others.

Thus the crisis of the university is a limited crisis—limited to areas comprising perhaps one-quarter or one-third of a typical university viewed in terms of numbers of students, but considerably less than that in terms of total faculty time and far less than that in terms of money spent. And within this one-quarter or one-third of a university, there are great variations from student to student, from faculty member to faculty member, and from department to department. Among students, for example, the vocationally oriented major in economics is little different from his or her counterpart in business administration; and generally the student pursuing his or her major with vocational aims is much like the student in the sciences. But the crisis, though a limited one, is real. It is the dominant, although by no means the only, internal crisis in the modern university. It needs to be resolved.

Three potential approaches might lead to a resolution of the crisis in undergraduate education. Which solution best meets the problem and is most compatible with the other functions of the university?

The first is to withdraw from the crisis area; do away with the lower division or even with all undergraduate instruction. This solution overreaches the problem. The problem does not involve all of lower division or all of undergraduate instruction. Much undergraduate instruction, even at the lower division level, is highly effective. University efforts at this level help set standards for the high schools, the junior colleges, and other institutions. They force the university to be concerned with the long span, rather than only the upper limits, of the educational process—and this works to the advantage of the university and the process. Undergraduates bring a spirit of freshness and enthusiasm to a campus. They provide an opportunity for graduate students to gain experience as apprentice teachers. Many undergraduates also benefit from spending a reasonably extended time in the same institution.

The second approach is to make improvements and adjustments within the existing university structure. Much can be done. Much has been done. Much is being done—perhaps more than ever before. The specific remedies are almost endless—freshman seminars, honors programs, credit for field study and other extra-university activities, more selective admission policies, spreading of liberal or general education throughout four years instead of the usual two and perhaps even into the graduate level, better advising procedures, devotion of more faculty time to undergraduate students in general and to lower division students in particular, more careful evaluation of teaching performance, introduction of pass–fail grading to encourage broadening of the student's study program, courses specifically designed for the nonmajor, more opportunities for independent study, introduction of "problem-oriented" as well as survey courses, consultation with students in the formulation of educational policy, better selection and supervision of teaching assistants, easing of methods for students to drop and resume their studies, improved and earlier orientation programs, and more effective machinery for the encouragement and approval of new and experimental programs.

All these devices have value. Some of them have great value. Their general impact will be to give the student a greater variety of choice and more individual attention. Their introduction marks an important change in attitude—from rigidity to experimentation, from uniformity to variety in the treatment of students, and particularly from a view of the undergraduate students as a grudgingly acknowledged responsibility to a view that these students are a potentially exciting asset to an institution of higher education.

As more and more universities make more and more use of these improvements within the existing structure, undergraduate instruction will become increasingly rewarding to teacher and student alike. The university itself will become a better balanced institution, less preoccupied with its noninstructional responsibilities which so frequently are externally oriented; more concerned with its internal cohesion and coherence. It will be more nearly what it once was—a community of scholars. All reasonable support should be given to these endeavors.

But some questions remain. Will these endeavors solve the crisis completely? Is the existing structure of the university an adequate one within which to administer these endeavors effectively? It seems doubtful to me that we can give a clear affirmative to either of these questions.

Will these endeavors solve the crisis completely? There is now a sizable group of students, particularly in the social sciences and the humanities, who want a really broad and coordinated program for their general education; and who often also want to work within an environment which provides some sense of community, where they can be known as individuals, where they can have an impact on their surroundings. These devices for reform can give them more choices but not a coordinated program; more individual attention but not a sense of community. Thus, for this group, there will still be a crisis, although one of lesser proportions. It should be understood, of course, that a university need not and cannot respond to the interests of every group.

Is the existing structure adequate for administering these endeavors effectively? For some of them it is, but for others it clearly is not. The department is the main administrative agency of the university. It generally handles its undergraduate majors quite well and its graduate students even better. But it is not well equipped by interest or by knowledge to advise or to supervise or to design a curriculum for the non-major; or to provide broadly oriented freshman seminars, or problem-oriented courses, or some new and experimental programs. And the traditional university structure usually contains no other administrative mechanism for handling these endeavors.

The third approach, then, leads to structural changes in the university as a further means for solving the crisis. Structures often seem immune to change, for they are not only the homes of the vested interests but also the judgments drawn from long experience by many people. Nevertheless, structures can and do change as new needs become evident.

We have in the past century created the department, the institute, the service bureau, to handle graduate instruction and undergraduate majors, research, and service. It should be equally possible to create structures that fit the needs of undergraduates not fully served by programs for departmental majors. If so, the department could concentrate on its majors and give them a more personal home. I should like to urge that we now give increasing attention to structures designed to fit the needs and interests of the nonspecialized or broadly-interested undergraduates. This group includes some of our ablest students. Society needs the talents of generalists as well as specialists, and attention to their needs can bring a broader intellectual focus to the university as well.

The new Irvine campus of the University of California represents a significant attempt to revise the internal structure, while retaining the traditional framework, of the modern American university to serve better the particular needs of undergraduates. At Irvine, subject matter is organized less by the standard departments and more by broad divisions and interdisciplinary groupings. This structure, the culmination of eight years of planning and development of this new campus, is designed to counter the current tendency to overfractionalization of knowledge, discourage premature specialization by undergraduates, and promote the broad-ranging approaches that are proving to be so beneficial to the solution of many current questions. Students at Irvine are allowed great leeway in organizing their own academic programs within this structure, with careful attention given to individualized advising. There are, in fact, few general university requirements for students. Requirements instead are set forth in the approved program for each individual student. Pass-fail options have been permitted from the beginning to encourage exploration of unfamiliar subject fields. Independent study is encouraged, with course credit available by examination in many instances. The historical separation between teaching and research is minimized. Thus, there are fewer structural barriers to student choice across the entire undergraduate curriculum.

This approach, however, is not the most promising structural change to solve the undergraduate crisis on older campuses. There, the traditional departmental structure is long and firmly established, and the conversion to divisional structure or to new types of departments could only be accomplished by extensive and often costly reorganization of the entire institution.

A more feasible and thus a more promising structure for present undergraduate needs is the cluster college, the relatively small and broadly oriented undergraduate college within a university. Organizationally, these units can be added to established campuses with a minimum of disruption of ongoing programs. Or they can be developed in sequence on new or rapidly growing campuses in conjunction with central libraries and other core facilities. The cluster college concept is being used in slightly different forms, for example, on the University of California's new campuses at San Diego and Santa Cruz.

President Hutchins was a proponent of a somewhat similar idea at Chicago before World War II. When I was chancellor of the University of California at Berkeley some years ago, I had a study made of the performance of students who had transferred there from other colleges and universities throughout the United States. I was impressed then, and I still am, that the students with the best records after transfer to Berkeley had come from the undergraduate college at the University of Chicago. Mr. Hutchins was said to be five hundred years behind the times, harking back to Oxford and Cambridge of old, or two thousand years or more behind the times, looking back to the Academy and the Lyceum. If he had been fifty years behind the times, he would have been judged "sound," or if five hundred or two thousand years ahead of the times, he would have been out of harm's way. I prefer to think that he was fifty years ahead of the times— not in the sense of a general solution to a general problem, but rather of a partial solution to a partial problem. The modern university must and will pursue specialization, but it can and should preserve some elements descended from earlier models. The Great Books cannot teach biochemistry. They can help teach broad understanding of broad problems.

The cluster college to be effective should be reasonably small in size, have a broadly oriented curriculum, and possess its own separate administrative identity. Reasonable size permits a sense of community. The broad curriculum will serve the student with general interests. The separate administrative identity will make possible a specialized style; more important, it will provide a more intimate group that can treat each student and faculty member as a unique individual. Within such a structure, personalized programs of independent study, field study for credit, dropping in and dropping out can effectively be developed. Students and faculty can consult on educational policy. Teaching assistants can be made a more integral part of the teaching staff. Many of today's piecemeal remedies can become more meaningful within such a structure. The cluster college can bring into the undergraduate level some of the personalized features that already mark graduate study, research, and service even in a large institution, and that help provide these functions with more effective relationships despite the scale of the total endeavors. Size need not mean depersonalization at the undergraduate level any more than at the graduate level.

The great success of the many excellent liberal arts colleges throughout the United States in attracting and training superbly the best of the undergraduates encourages imitation, and possibly even some efforts at improvement on their outstanding performance. The cluster college can operate under fewer restraints than the isolated liberal arts college. It need not cover the same range of subject material, for it can rely on its associated colleges and specialized departments in the central university for some of the total coverage. Thus, it can experiment more with diversity—in style, in emphasis, in method. Each of the colleges in a cluster can be more different from its associated cluster colleges than the single liberal arts college can be from other lone colleges. In 1958 when we at the University of California began planning colleges within our new campuses at San Diego and Santa Cruz, we considered it not only possible but desirable that each cluster college have its own quite distinctive personality and pattern. And each of these two campuses will relate the colleges to each other and to their general campus in quite different ways.

One or more cluster colleges within a university campus can offer to students and faculty members central library, laboratory, and cultural facilities inaccessible to the isolated institution, albeit with some loss of identity for the college in the cluster as against the single institution.

The nature of the faculty of a cluster college within a university will not be the same as in an isolated college or university. The faculty will contain more specialists than will the separate college and more generalists than will the traditional university department; and particularly may enlist more specialists with a deep concern for generalization than either the liberal arts college or the university department can command. To serve the research interests of this faculty, there can, of course, be the usual specialized institutes. But there are also unusual opportunities for institutes with broad orientation toward public policy and toward philosophical and esthetic issues. Then the university might really help shape the minds that influence the age, quite beyond the bits and pieces of new knowledge it now chiefly supplies. It is disquieting to note how many of the broadranging commentaries on the world at large that are read by students and faculty alike are written outside of the university. One remembers how science in England first developed largely outside the universities, which only very gradually accepted it as one of their intellectual concerns. The new age we now face might well benefit from efforts to comprehend it more broadly than through the separate fields of knowledge alone. The cluster college with this broad orientation might not only help undergraduate instruction to coexist with the other functions of the modern university but might also actually strengthen the university and its other functions. The cluster colleges within universities might also find a role to play in extension work by carrying their broader orientation to qualified adults, as the more specialized departments and professional schools now do in their areas of competence.

The cluster college within the university may well have some beneficial side effects in addition to service to undergraduates. It can give faculty members who wish contact across the two or three or four cultures a better opportunity for dialogue. It can also help decentralize administration, particularly of student affairs, within the large campus. Too often now, undergraduate students belong to the Dean of Students rather than to any identifiable academic unit; or they just get lost (some of them, of course, like it that way). A modern university cannot be small but it can seem small to its individual participants. One of its challenges is to seem smaller even, indeed, as it gets bigger.

The cluster college may even possibly add to public understanding of and public benefit from the involvement of those persons identified with the university who participate in public affairs and political action. Too often, now, this involvement takes the form of simplistic slogans and even occasionally that of violent or potentially violent actions. Neither the slogans nor the actions are at a very high intellectual level. Yet the university, of all institutions, should encourage the application of reason and facts and persuasion to the solution of problems. The cluster college can provide a forum for the careful and informed discussion of broad issues of public policy far superior to that offered by the streets, the sidewalk, or the plaza. As a result, the impact exerted on policy by persons identified with the university can also be potentially more effective in the long run. Mind should influence mind, rather than passion pit itself against passion. The university should have ways of serving as a model for high-level public debate, as has the Oxford Union, and the program of the cluster college may provide one such way.

Oxford and Cambridge in England, and the Claremont Colleges and the University of the Pacific in California, have shown the possibilities of clusters of colleges within a larger system.

Not all universities, of course, need to have or perhaps should have cluster colleges, for although this solution may be desirable, it is by no means imperative. The established campus, in particular, may find it difficult to add colleges to itself—even physically, although residence halls can be remodeled or special facilities added to them. The present era, however, presents unusual opportunities. New campuses are being built. Old ones are being expanded. Michigan State and Michigan, for example, are undertaking some of their expansion in the form of undergraduate colleges, and the Santa Barbara campus of the University of California is doing likewise.

Growth holds within itself special capacities for new and, hopefully, better solutions. But new solutions, such as cluster colleges, hold within themselves some inherent problems too; and the new approaches will need to be viewed critically. Firm decisions about their precise form must be held open until we have more experience with them, and judgment of their full value must be kept subject to constand reexamination.

The university is becoming subject to a new set of judgments. For many decades now, since the impacts of the German university and the land-grant movement were felt throughout large American universities, they have been judged mostly by their research output, the quality of their graduate work, and the effectiveness of their service. Only in the older, private universities has the quality of undergraduate instruction been an important continuing criterion—this partly through the strong influence of the alumni. Now there is a greater interest among the the public generally and within legislatures in particular in the quality of undergraduate teaching. The public universities will respond to the stimulus of this interest as the private universities have to their alumni. Beyond these external tests of performance lie the new intensity of undergraduate concern for the most effective educational environment and the reviving conscience about and interest in undergraduate teaching on the part of the faculty member. Moreover, there are now better means of rating undergraduate instruction—national test scores for entry into graduate schools, lists of scholarship winners, and the like. And nobody will wish to be last.

This limited crisis is not the first nor will it be the last to confront the American university, whose history occasionally seems to match the plot of the Perils of Pauline. Like Pauline, the university always escapes the immediate peril. I am certain that it will escape this one also. But there is always the next installment. We can face the future with full confidence, and even absolute assurance, that some new peril will come along to make life in the university more exciting. It may also make the university, in the process, more nearly perfect.

Notes

* From *The University in America* (Santa Barbara, CA: Center for the Study of Democratic Institutions, 1967), 9–16. Reprinted by permission.

CHAPTER 23

Who Should Lead?
Liberal Learning: A Record of Presidential Neglect*

The Association of American Colleges put me on the program of its annual meeting. This is an association of presidents, provosts, and deans. I chose to tell them that they should lead rather than follow in the effort to restore liberal education but that most of them did not, although I did note that the in liberal arts colleges were less devoid of such leadership than most others.

Higher education in the United States, overall, is in excellent condition. Compared with other industrialized nations, the United States has the best system of higher education now existing. More accessible to young people than higher education in any other country, the U.S. system offers more choices among both types of institutions and programs. The best research in the world is done in American universities. And, within the United States, higher education is one of the systems which works extremely well, compared with other parts of the American infrastructure such as the criminal justice system, or secondary education. Though many reasons could be given as proof of this statement concerning secondary education, it can be noted in particular that, while high school standardized test scores have gone down so tragically for two decades, higher education standardized scores have by and large remained stable. This implies that higher education not only has maintained the quality of its contributions, but actually has made up for some of the deficiencies at earlier levels.

Various opinion research studies of Americans have shown that confidence in institutions of higher education and their leadership is topped only by confidence in the medical profession, which is, of course, a product of our institutions of higher education. Higher education rates considerably above such institutions as government, the courts, industry, and unions, in the opinion of most Americans.

While our system of higher education is excellent overall, one of the reports of the Carnegie Council, *Missions of the College Curriculum* (1977), said, with respect to general education, that it is a "disaster area." The Carnegie Council, and the Carnegie Commission before it, made the most intensive survey of higher education ever undertaken in this or any other nation. General education is the only area of higher education in this country which was considered critically deficient. There was particular concern, especially in the early days of the commission, with the problem of equality of opportunity for all young persons, but that is an area where, while there are still grave deficits, there has been progress. In the area of general education, the commission found only deterioration. General education, defined to include training in the basic skills and the provision of liberal learning opportunities, has clearly been losing ground for a long time.

Liberal learning, once almost the totality of the curriculum in American higher education, has been giving way for over a century to the increasing concentration on majors in many academic and professional fields. Thus, it has been playing less and less of a central role compared to majors and, beginning in the 1960s, to electives in undergraduate instruction.

One Carnegie study found that in the 1970s, not only was more attention being given to majors but that increasingly the majors were in professional fields, and not in more traditional academic fields. In a six-year period, the number of undergraduates majoring in professional fields outside the arts and sciences had gone up from 38 percent of all students to 58 percent, which is an enormous change in the course of such a short time. It was also found that electives, which were greatly increased in the 1960s to enable students to take more socially "relevant" courses, were increasingly used to strengthen the major or develop some kind of minor field as a second opportunity.

With less of a student's time going toward general education, there has been a decreasing sense of the value of liberal learning. To the extent it still exists, too often what goes for liberal learning on the nation's campuses is just the historical result of a series of political compromises concerning which departments acquired distribution requirements and thus which got the extra faculty positions to teach these required courses. Much of what is labeled "liberal learning" has come to be just an artifact of past political battles.

There are, of course, programs that were and are more than vestiges of past compromises; programs that have a real sense of purpose, such as the western civilization program at Stanford, or the "Great Books" program at Chicago in the days of Hutchins, and its continuation to some extent at other places. In the Carnegie reports, it was particularly recommended that consideration be given to what was called "an integrative learning experience" for the individual student, where every student has a chance to study some subject in a very broad way, rather than in the piecemeal fashion of most courses of study.

An example would be a series of courses put together to give a student a chance to see Far Eastern civilization quite broadly—courses on the history of the Far East, the philosophies of the Far East, the politics of the

Far East, and so forth. Another illustration given was man and his environment, a conception drawing on sociology, economics, and even engineering. This was an attempt to take into account the fact that it is very difficult to get faculty members to teach outside their specialties, but at the same time that students ought to be able to get a more rounded educational experience. By putting together groups of courses, faculty members could teach in their specialties and yet students would have a chance to see something in a more integrated manner.

American higher education has been excellent in most respects; however, in the area of liberal learning there are great deficits, as there are in the teaching of basic skills. General education, and within it liberal learning, has no effective constituency on campuses around the country—at least no effective constituency of any size. The faculty is not a constituency for liberal learning: faculty members are concerned primarily, as they should be, with what goes on within their departments and within their majors. This must be their first concern. But, too many faculty members know only their own department, or perhaps a few adjacent departments. Most do not know the range of offerings across the campus, and do not have a broad grasp, even on smaller campuses, of the totality of what is available.

Students are the natural constituency for electives, not for liberal learning. They want to take what they want to take and generally do not favor requirements of any sort, as in the late '60s and early '70s when they organized against them in the name of free choice.

There is one potential constituency of some size supporting liberal learning, but it cannot bring to bear any real influence; this is the alumni. One of the studies made for the Carnegie Commission, undertaken at the National Opinion Research Council at the University of Chicago, was *Recent Alumni and Higher Education* (1970) by Joe L. Spaeth and Andrew M. Greeley. The authors made a very extensive survey of what recent alumni thought about their education and what they would like to change. Things they would do differently if they were now in school included spending a lot more time getting a liberal education, for both personal and professional benefits, and much less time on specialization. Unfortunately, the alumni are not an influence on the curriculum.

As is well known, there are many reasons for emphasizing liberal learning. People have to live a life and not just earn a living, and they are citizens in a society as well as individual human beings. Where jobs are nonroutine, liberal learning can contribute a certain sensitivity about the feelings of others, and also a sense of values in making decisions, both of which are worthy goals.

Every college should have a conviction about the knowledge most worth knowing, and this ought to be the result of careful intellectual consideration. The curriculum should be more than just the sum of the consequences of internal and external pressures. However, the curricula of today reflect more the internal pressures of student choice and departmental rivalries, and external labor market pressures to add this or that subject, than they do any careful intellectual consideration.

Only the academic administration can provide the leadership assuring a proper curricular role for general education and liberal learning, even though the faculty is said to have primary responsibility for the curriculum. The academic administration is here taken to mean the president, the academic provost, and the deans, particularly the dean of letters and sciences. Primary responsibility and the central role, however, rest primarily with the president. The president sets the goals for the institution, is most involved in selecting the other members of the academic administration, and is the person who encourages and guides others as a leader, in ways impossible for other members of an administration.

There are many in academe who feel it is the professors who have fomented a "subversion of liberal learning" and at whom the finger of responsibility should be pointed, and that if anything is going to be done it is going to be done by the professors or not at all. Professors, however, are not now positioned to think creatively and responsibly about what a comprehensive and coherent college education ought to be; nevertheless they have the power and they must be encouraged to use it responsibly.

The only persons who might, if they wished, encourage the professors are the presidents, the provosts, and the deans. The professors must give their "advice and consent" but they will not, with few exceptions, take the initiative. Professors do have the power; but if anything is going to be done about the deterioration of general education, the academic administrators must take the initiative with respect to a proper role for liberal learning and basic skill training, and then appeal to the professors.

Perhaps I have been unduly influenced by my own early experience in academic life. I went to Swarthmore as a student and participated in the honors program during the presidency of Frank Aydelotte. I saw the impact he had upon that college, not only through the new academic program he implemented, but in how it changed the image and aspirations of the school. I did not know then the price he paid for his leadership, not just for the academic changes which caused consternation in some quarters, but also because of his de-emphasizing of athletics. The year before I entered as a freshman, his presidency had hung on the slender thread of a single vote to maintain majority support in the board of managers.

Later, my first teaching job on the way to a Ph.D. was at Antioch College, just after Arthur Morgan had left to go to the Tennessee Valley Authority. It was his impact as president that gave Antioch a distinctive personality, raised its sights, and created a program which quite impressed me.

It is only the president, and the academic officers around him, who can see beyond the department, be responsible for looking at the future, and control the overall quality of the education provided. Either they provide voice and influence for the cause of liberal learning and general education, or there is no leadership. Faculties, through their departments and schools, are the natural champions of the majors; students naturally champion electives. If general education and liberal learning are to have champions, they must be found among the academic administrators; and, in fact, the major defenders in the twentieth century have been presidents, provosts, and deans. For example, at Harvard, in the twentieth century, the champions have been Lowell, Conant, Buck, Rosovsky, and Bok.

Presidents, provosts, and deans regretfully did not, by and large, fight for the preservation of liberal learning during the battle against requirements in the late 1960s (faculties did fight successfully to preserve the majors), or against the demand for vocationalism beginning in the early 1970s. What efforts have taken place have been mostly to regain a small portion of the ground that has been lost.

It is very difficult to give such leadership, generally because of the changing nature of the presidency. Harold W. Stoke in *The American College President* (1959) called attention to the big change from what he called the "academic leader" to the "manager." All of those associated with the 1984 Association of Governing Boards study of college presidents have had that change brought to their attention vividly, as Stoke's observation has been confirmed and reconfirmed by presidents, and generally endorsed across the country.

Many presidents say they have been pulled out of a concern for academic life: by the demands on their time caused by fundraising—often, in fact, they have been hired for that purpose primarily; by the demands on them to help recruit students; by the additional time spent in state capitals if the institution is a public one; by the time they have to spend on federal government problems, whether public or private; and, by the additional time taken by boards of trustees as they change, becoming representatives of constituencies—particularly public boards—rather than guardians of the long-term welfare of the institution as a whole.

Constituency boards insist on becoming more involved in administration and less in policy, because they serve their constituencies better through administrative involvement than through policy making alone. Presidents are also diverted from academic affairs by the demands which have been created as more and more colleges become parts of systems (more than half of all college students in the United States are on campuses which are parts of systems) and coordinating councils.

Many presidents also feel that they have been pushed out of academic affairs—pushed out by a student market which now determines academic policy. What do the students want? What new specialties do they want? What new courses do they want? They feel that increased faculty influence has often served to push them out of academic policy, as departments and schools have become stronger. Where there is collective bargaining, contracts in some cases largely remove presidents from having an influence on academic policy. Others feel that the relatively short terms many presidents now serve do not give them the opportunity to exercise leadership, in the academic field in particular. Getting heavily involved in academic policy takes years—much more time than it takes to influence the budget, which can be done in months.

Rhetoric in support of liberal learning is rising, at commencements, inaugurations, and other ceremonial academic occasions. But as the rhetoric goes up, the reality is going the other way. All the inspirational speeches should not obscure the facts: liberal learning has been neglected and one of the reasons it has been neglected is that presidential or other administrative leadership once available is no longer present.

One usual solution for the presidents of today is to move the responsibility for curricular policy to the provost, deans, or department chairs. The further down the responsibility moves, the more closely related to some special interest it becomes and the less related to the total intellectual endeavor of the institution. Another, and even more common, solution is to just let the student market dictate policy.

There are, however, other possible solutions, those found by the approximately 20 percent of presidents who still have a substantial personal concern for the academic development of their institutions, and who insist upon such a commitment from other academic officers as well. How do they go about it? First of all, they are very careful about saving time for academic affairs. This means getting strong assistance in other areas of administration such as business, finance, and public relations, and delegating greatly in these areas. Presidents who have thought about their time carefully and who want to reserve substantial time for academic affairs cut out a lot of the things that occupy the other 80 percent of presidents. Some have said they participate in very few purely social engagements or, in one case, none at all. Others say they give up all the opportunities they have for service on corporate boards and nonprofit boards, or strictly limit their acceptances; they concentrate their service on their campus to maintain some time for academic affairs. Some have foresworn all external speeches, such as commencement addresses on other campuses or speeches to Rotary clubs.

Based on information given for the AGB study, under 20 percent of the three thousand presidents of American colleges and universities are now, even by their own descriptions of themselves, substantially involved in the academic side of their enterprises. This percentage does vary greatly depending on the type of institution. Involved presidents constitute a much higher percentage in the liberal arts colleges than in any other segment of American higher education. In some segments, the percentage approaches zero.

The other part of time-expenditure policy is to set the highest priority on time devoted to academic affairs. The following are the major areas of concentration with which the presidents say they take a personal concern:

- The selection of the provost and the deans; they do not turn these obligations over to one committee or another.
- Each tenure appointment and/or promotion.
- Development of an academic plan including a statement of mission; they insist on having the academic plan guide the physical plan and the financial plan, not vice versa.
- The world of knowledge; they develop some sense, through reading and talking with people, about where the intellectual world is going, about new developments that have the greatest opportunities for research and instruction, and about which areas are moribund.
- The distribution of resources, reflecting the directions in which the world of knowledge, as well as the world of work, is moving.
- The undergraduate curriculum, particularly for general education.
- Teaching; expressed, among other ways, by actually teaching a course or seminar or participating, from time to time, in the courses or seminars of others.
- The academic needs of the campus; presenting them effectively off campus, and developing support for learning skills and liberal learning on campus and off.

Only about 20 percent of the presidents surveyed are, at least, significantly involved in all of these aspects of the academic lives of their institutions—what may be defined as "substantial academic involvement." Not more than 2 percent of the total, defining interest in academic affairs as above, could be said to play a central role, in all eight of the academic activities just listed. The 20 percent of all presidents, and 21 percent within the 20 percent, are the ones who may be said to qualify as chief academic officers. The other 80 percent are mostly executive officers. Within this 80 percent, it should be noted, however, that most presidents are significantly involved in one or more of these academic activities, and only a few in none at all.

As a president, it is not possible to be effective by guiding the undergraduate curriculum as an isolated academic item only. To do the most good for the curriculum, the president must be involved in the fuller range of academic affairs—must be an academic as well as an executive officer.

Among the many tests of college and university leadership over the long term, the ultimate test is whether the institution has been strengthened, weakened, or unaffected by that president's involvement in its academic affairs. Early criteria that alumni and boards of trustees apply are how well the president functions at cocktail parties, his or her effectiveness as a public speaker, whether the budget is balanced, or whether administrative appointments are strong enough. But in the long run—over ten or twenty or thirty years—the ultimate test is whether the institution has moved forward academically as a result of that president's involvement.

It is the president, the provost, and the dean or deans (above all the president) who must lead the battle of liberal learning against excessive specialization and insist on careful consideration of the knowledge most worth knowing. There is no substitute for such leadership. This is not a task for the faculty alone or a task for the students at all. It is of great importance that the faculty provide advice and consent to make any administrative initiative effective. Future students must also give "consent," and this, of course, is essential. But the basic responsibility must be assumed by the academic administration: as the presidency and the academic administration go, so goes general education and liberal learning in American colleges and universities. To paraphrase President Harry Truman, the buck stops there; but it also starts there.

Notes

* From *Change*, September 1984: 33–36. Reprinted by permission.

CHAPTER 24

Vignette—

How Hard It Is: Foreword to *Great Expectations and Mixed Performance**

This was the foreword to the leading study of the efforts at reform of higher education in Europe.

The 1960s and early 1970s were the greatest period of attempted reform of institutions of higher education in the Western world in eight hundred years. There were, of course, earlier attempts but none so widespread among nations: in the France of Napoleon, in Germany after the Napoleonic wars, in England around the middle of the 19th Century with the renovation of Oxford and Cambridge and the establishment of the Red-Bricks, in the United States after the Civil War, in Japan after the Meiji restoration, in the U.S.S.R. after the Revolution, in the socialist countries conquered by the U.S.S.R. at the end of World War II, and in China during the Cultural Revolution.

This study, thus, reviews a phenomenon of great importance and, in the course of this review, illuminates not only the reform process but the inherent nature of higher education and the influence of the societies that surround and often engulf it. Fortunately, this study is equal to the size and importance of the task. It is a product of what has become the outstanding center for the study of higher education—the European Institute of Education and Social Policy; and its senior author is the most knowledgeable scholar of European higher education. The study covers nine reforms in seven countries with in-depth examination. Additionally, Burton Clark contrasts, with great perception, as always, the European with the American reforms of the same period.

I shall confine myself to several observations. I make these observations as an American who participated in several attempted reform efforts: in the Master Plan for higher education in California, in the establishment of three new and to various degrees experimental campuses within the University of California, and in the many studies (some highly oriented toward reform) of the Carnegie Commission (later Council) on Higher Education.

1. The 1980s may not be the most sympathetic time to look back at and to understand the 1960s, not so much because so little time has passed but because the atmosphere has so greatly changed. The ambience of the

1980s and the 1960s are so different. The 1980s in higher education emphasize the traditional, as the 1960s enthroned the experimental. A common theme of the 1980s is that everything fails; of the 1960s, that many efforts can succeed. The 1980s concentrate on survival, as the 1960s did on expansion. A renaissance almost certainly lies ahead for higher education perhaps only a decade away. From that future perspective, the 1960s may seem more relevant, more of a guide to what can be done and how, and less of a record of high hopes matched only by low results. The experiment may then seem more attractive; new endeavors may then again appear more possible; renewal may draw attention away from survival alone. When that time of resumed progress comes, this study, with its balanced analysis, may seem not just an interesting record of times past but a useful guide to times future.

2. The major reforms chosen show three partial successes (widening access, contributing to regional development, and advancing vocational and short-cycle higher education) and one partial failure (searching for comprehensive reform). If this list had been expanded, achievements might weigh less in the balance, and the failures more. For example, curricular reform, particularly in interdisciplinary directions, has nearly everywhere been a near total failure. And, reform of governance has, at best, had only mixed success and, at worst, has been a disaster.

3. "Achievement" and "failure" are so hard to define, as this study notes. Does the reform lead to imitation and to expansion of its territory? Or does it survive intact in its original territory? If the answer is "yes" to either question, then success may be declared and these seem to be the central tests applied in this study, particularly the second. If the question is, does the reform meet the "great expectations" of its original proponents, the "success" is never likely—original expectations are almost always excessive. I should like to propose two more modest tests: did the reform serve a good purpose at the time? (for example, at least giving constructive change a chance); and, however modified the reform in longer term practice, is the continuing situation better than it otherwise would have been? (for example, giving junior faculty members a voice when they previously had none).

However, I have come to doubt the use of the word *reform*. Reform means "new and improved." At the time undertaken, it can be known whether the effort is "new" in that context but not whether it will turn out to be an improvement. This evaluation must wait until later and the criteria must be specific. Thus I have come to prefer the word *change*, leaving to later the question of whether or not the change turned out to be an improvement as its proponents, of course, except.

May I also note the importance of distinguishing between "reform" and "response," at least in the American context. Reform is something someone wants to do in relation to a set of values; response is something someone must do in reaction to the situation. Both involve change. But the first is active and by choice, and the second reactive and of necessity. The prophet chasing visions and the entrepreneur chasing markets may each bring about changes, however different they may be. In the United States, the early 1960s belonged more to the former and the early 1980s more to the latter. Some changes, of course, such as the Open University in Britain, have elements of both reform and response, and these may often be the most effective of all.

4. This leads me finally to the importance of two additional observations often made by observers both yesterday and today:

The importance of the contemporary context, politically and economically.

The influence that society has on higher education—enduring change is more likely to originate in what the society outside wants than in what some reformers inside may dream about.

Notes

* Foreword in Ladislav Cerych and Paul Sabatier, *Great Expectations and Mixed Performance: The Implementation of Higher Education Reforms in Europe* (Stoke-on-Trent: Trentham Books Ltd., 1986), xv–xvii. Reprinted by permission.

CHAPTER 25

An Urban versus a Rural Society—
The Urban-Grant University: A Model for the Future*

The City College of New York was holding a celebration of the centennial of its receipt of a chapter of Phi Beta Kappa. I talked about City College as a model for an urban-grant university movement. My suggestion got good editorial support, some interest among several university presidents, and some indication of interest in Congress. But the idea floundered when it became clear that there would be a terrible battle over which institutions would be chosen if there were a federal program with money behind it and that most faculty members looked on local problems as below them, although they might, and some even did, discover great interest in local problems in urban areas at a great distance—Cairo and Karachi and Rio.

For a good many years I have watched City College from afar. I've known many of your graduates as graduate students at the University of California, and many also as faculty members. I sometimes thought that if the City College alumni were to leave the University of California, certain departments would disappear entirely. I am, of course, quite conscious of the fact that one out of every twenty-five Ph.D.'s in the United States is a graduate of City College or one of her sister institutions in the City University. I know that City College shares with the Berkeley campus of the University of California and the University of Illinois the distinction of being the leading source of undergraduates who go on to receive doctoral degrees.

A Centennial meeting is a time to look back and also to look ahead, and I should like to make a few comments in both directions. A hundred years ago, in 1867, City College was emerging from the Civil War years. It had just changed its name from the Free Academy. It was a fairly traditional liberal arts college, with clubs and fraternities and sports being extremely important in college life. But there were two events taking place which helped set some of the distinctive characteristics of City College for the ensuing century. A hundred years ago, there was established here a Phi Beta Kappa chapter, the second in New York and the sixteenth in the nation. And there was also established the first freely elected student government in the United States. These two events cast their shadow across the future, as City College raised the intellectual stature of students and faculty, and also became a center for student participation in all sorts of activities. Over this hundred years, City College has grown with the city and changed with the city. It will continue to grow, and I am sure it will continue to change.

Now I should like to turn to the future, and I have chosen to talk this evening about the "urban-grant university"—a new university model, its new assignments and the intensified controversies which may surround it.

The land-grant university movement, as you know, is a little more than a hundred years old. A key purpose of the land-grant movement was to help agriculture throughout the United States. Today these land-grant institutions have risen to great heights of service to much of society. They presently number sixty-seven out of some 2,300 colleges and universities in the nation, but they turn out one-third of all the Ph.D. degrees. In some fields the rate is much higher: 100 percent in agriculture, for example, and 50 percent in the biological sciences, 50 percent in engineering, and 50 percent in the health professions. Showing their heritage to this very day, they turn out a far smaller proportion of advanced degrees in areas like philosophy and law, foreign languages, and the other humanities.

The land-grant idea was one of the great ideas in the history of the United States and of higher education throughout the world. These institutions have contributed enormously to American agriculture and technology, making both the most productive in the world. And they have made great contributions to their particular regions as well as to the nation. How did they accomplish this? They did it, to a large extent, by turning their backs on the then-established model of a college. To the traditional classical curriculum, they added research on the problems of agriculture, and then extension directly to the farm to help the individual farmer. But beyond the research and beyond the extension work, there was in many of these land-grant institutions a spirit—a spirit of concern, of responsibility, and of service—which was really quite remarkable.

Tonight I should like to suggest that we need a new model to add to our existing models for universities in the United States. I have called this new model the "urban-grant university." I have specifically not spoken of the "urban university." The term *urban university* is used in some very strange ways. It is used for universities that receive some financial support from the city. It is also used for any university located in an urban setting, however uncomfortable that institution may be in its setting, however much it may wish it were located someplace else, and however much its concern with the urban community may be limited to combatting the urban blight in its immediate neighborhood. Many institutions around the country called urban universities have turned their backs on their own cities.

I use the term "urban-grant", instead, to indicate a type of university which would have an aggressive approach to the problems of the city, where the city itself and its problems would become the animating focus, as agriculture once was and to some extent still is of the land-grant university. Specifically, I should like to propose that we create, to stand beside the sixty-seven land-grant universities, some sixty-seven urban-grant universities, at least one for each city of over a quarter of a million and several for the very large cities. Not all of these would have to be new institutions, although I hope some would be new. Some institutions could be reoriented; some institutions could have their involvement with urban affairs intensified. A great many new colleges and universities are going to be created in the United States by the end of this century. My proposal is that some of these new institutions each year be of the urban-grant type, to be fully useful to the modern society.

I use the term *urban-grant* to imply something beyond location and orientation, namely, that the federal government should aid the urban-grant university as it has the land-grant university. The federal government might help make the land available as part of urban renewal. Perhaps as new urban transportation systems are developed with federal support, some urban-grant universities could be located at the great central stations of such systems, rising above them and thus easily accessible to all the people in the surrounding community. Or the urban-grant university might be part of the new educational park concept. We talk these days of educational parks, serving large areas of a city, to meet problems of *de facto* segregation and to allow other improvements in our grammar schools and high schools. Perhaps at the center of such an educational park should be a university.

Obviously, there are problems of finding the necessary land for central urban locations. But there are usually areas where land can be made available and where the construction of a new campus will serve to raise the level of activity of the whole surrounding neighborhood. In California, for example, I had proposals before our Board of Regents suggesting new University campuses in central San Francisco and in downtown Los Angeles. Our studies indicated that efficiently designed high-rise buildings can accommodate a large enrollment on perhaps as few as thirty-five acres.

The suggestion that the federal government should help with the land and with the money to build these new campuses or to change existing campuses is altogether reasonable. When the land-grant movement began, over 50 percent of the people in the United States lived on the land; today, only 10 percent do. The reasons for an urban-grant university now are at least as compelling as were those for the land-grand university in 1862. If you look at the history of federal aid to education in the United States, you see that it has been responsive to the great problems of the nation. The land-grant movement, initiated by the federal government, was responsive to agrarian demands and to problems of national economic expansion. Then, during the depression, the federal government through the NYA aided some students who otherwise could not have afforded to attend college. During World War II, in response to the nation's needs for science, the federal government stepped in with support for scientific research—support which has continued to the present time. The government also provided aid to the returning GIs, and thus launched the tremendous recent expansion of the American college and university system. After Sputnik came the National Defense Education Act, and then, as people became more concerned with community health problems, tremendous sums of federal money for the medical schools and for health research.

Today, great national problems have to do with the cities, with equality of opportunity, with the ending of poverty, with the quality of life, and I think that the federal government might logically respond to these problems by again aiding the proper activities of higher education. The urban-grant university might parallel the land-grant institution not only via city-oriented curricula and on-campus research studies but also by setting up experiment stations to work on the problems of the city as they once worked on the problems of the land, and by setting up intensified urban extension services like agricultural extension. As a counterpart to the county agent, I can visualize a school agent, for example—one who through the research at his university is informed about the best new techniques for language teaching and who can take this knowledge directly into the public schools in his particular city area. It is true that many urban problems are more complex than those of the land, but this very complexity makes the prospect of confronting them more important and more challenging.

There is one point were I would suggest that the urban-grant university specifically depart from the land-grant model. Rather than a system of selection of institutions by the state governments, I would much prefer to see a system of direct institutional applications to and grants from the federal government. These applications could be submitted by public or private institutions, by existing rural or suburban colleges willing to launch new urban campuses or new activities relating to urban problems, by existing urban colleges for expansion and reorientation of their programs, or by public agencies or private groups proposing to establish entirely new institutions. In this way the private "prestige" institutions of the country could participate along with leading state universities and other types of colleges. The grants would be awarded on the basis of merit and initiative, rather than merely by automatic geographical distribution among the states. The participation of some prestige institutions, both public and private, I believe to be highly important to the initial success of the urban-grant movement.

American colleges and universities now face some urgent new assignments. One is to draw in those people who aren't with us today—to their loss and to ours as well. Townsend Harris, the father of City College, of the Free Academy, set forth this destiny for City College:

> To open the doors to all. Let the children of the rich and the poor
> take their seats together and know of no distinction save that of in-
> dustry, good conduct and intellect.

And this destiny has been fulfilled—up to a point—by City College. From
the very beginning, it has extended equality of opportunity through education to new groups of people, particularly the children of immigrants, just
as the land-grant institutions extended educational opportunities to the children of farmers and workers.

But access to college is not sufficiently broad today. We have what
Gunnar Myrdal calls an "underclass," and we are not drawing out from
this underclass the ability that is there. A start has been made, but we must
do far more. Without intending to neglect the problems of other groups, let
me note that only half as many Negroes go to a college or university today
as is true of the rest of the population, and half of that one-half go to
completely segregated Negro colleges and universities. We have an enormous task of opening the doors to all and of bringing in those groups that
have not yet been made full members of American society. And I think this
is a key responsibility of the urban-grant university.

Whenever a new college or university campus is established—at least
we found this to be the case in California—the number of people going on
to a college or university from that area is increased, even though not all
may attend the new local institution. The mere existence of a campus close
by seems to raise the aspirations of the people surrounding it. Moving directly into the areas of deprivation, as the University of Illinois has done
with the Chicago Circle campus, hopefully will bring new people into the
colleges and universities.

Every effort should be made, of course, to draw in students from outside the immediate community as well, so that the urban-grant university
does not become as segregated as its suburban or rural counterparts. The
drawing power will depend in part on the general excellence of the institution. Beyond that, however, I believe there are many students today from all
walks of life who are eager to participate in new approaches to our social
problems and who would find the urban-grant university an attractive and
stimulating setting for their college work.

Beyond drawing in new groups and making their talents available more
fully to the nation, the urban-grant university will find many city problems
that need to be attacked more directly. In recent years there has been much
talk but little effective action. In fact, I think I could make a case that some
universities and colleges of the nation are less involved in municipal problems today than they were a third of a century ago. The University of Chicago is less involved than it was in the thirties when Paul Douglas and
Charles Merriam were active. And this is true of many other places as

well. Rather than moving toward the problems of our cities, we've been moving away from them. There is, for example, an Association of Urban Universities which dates back to 1914 and has one hundred members, including Harvard. It is only recently, however, that Harvard has paid attention to the blight of sections of Cambridge or to urban problems more generally. Many of these universities have been *in* the urban setting, but they have not been *of* it.

May I say that I went back and looked over the City College Centennial addresses of 1947. What were they on? Looking to a new century of service, they spoke of the new science, the new international order, liberalizing the liberal arts college, the problems of organized labor and of the business college. There was no mention of the ghetto. There was no mention of equality of opportunity. There was no mention of urban blight. There was no mention of the inadequacies of the school system at the primary and secondary levels. But these are precisely what the concerns of the urban-grant university, I think, should be. It should come in with its shirt sleeves rolled up.

I think it should take some responsibility for the overall school systems of its city. I recently attended a conference in Williamsburg on "The World Crisis in Education"—it is really the world *crises* in education. There was a very persuasive point made, in a section called "The Democratization of Education," that those systems which were the most democratized, in the sense that access was based most on merit, were in those nations whose universities had a major responsibility for the entire educational system, including the high schools and the elementary schools. Not only the urban-grant universities but universities generally ought to be looking back more to the high schools. There has been improvement in science and mathematics teaching, for example, because of the interest of the universities. But, by and large, the universities have taken what has come to them and have not really tried to give full assistance to the high schools and their very difficult problems. The universities could assist in a number of ways, helping to improve the quality of the curriculum and the text books, helping to identify people of great potential who, because of their home life or their cultural background, have not seriously considered the prospect of higher education. My experience in California was that the high schools were eager for more contact and assistance than the universities generally were willing to give to them. Of course, this has to be a two-way street. The high schools and the grammar schools can say something about the university and what it does, too, because university curricula and requirements have an impact all along the line on the operation of the earlier schools. The urban-grant university could help provide the framework for this interaction with the city's public school system.

I think, also, the urban-grant university should take some responsibility for the health services of the area. I think that the medical school of the future, if it does its job properly, will be more involved with the health of the surrounding community than the land-grant university was ever involved with the farmers of its state. It will be concerned not just with its university hospital, but with the quality of other hospitals and the development of health centers.

The urban-grant university should be concerned with the urban environment in its totality, its architecture, its space use, its cultural programs and recreational facilities.

Let me add emphatically, however, that the city should not be the sole concern of the urban-grant university. Certainly that should be a central emphasis, but the urban-grant university should from the first plan to follow the land-grant model in its concerns for all the main-streams of intellectual thought and discovery.

There are a few existing colleges and universities in the United States today that approach in some respects the urban-grant institution I have sketched, but I know of none which could be held up as a full model. The land-grant university turned away from the model of the classical university and eventually had a profound impact on that type of university, so that the Harvard of today is more a land-grant institution—without the land—than the classical university it once was. And so, I believe, the urban-grant university can enter the American scene as a new model, eventually affecting all the others. And some universities will rise to heights of distinction on the urban-grant model, as have many on the land-grant approach.

This new type of university will inevitably find itself embroiled in controversy. There will be a controversy within it over the question of quality. A former president of the University of Minnesota once said that the state universities hold that there is no intellectual service too undignified for them to perform. I disagree with that. But I also disagree with the idea that because something is a city problem, it is not worthy of high-quality attention. I have seen faculty members who would work on an international problem, or on a national problem, or on the problems of local government in some other country, but not on the problems of their own city, because they regarded such work as somehow beneath them. Granted, it can be done at a low-quality level, as can work on national and international problems. But that is not necessary. We should recognize that local city problems today need and justify work of the very highest quality.

Nor should the student body be expected to be of lower quality, even though it might be desirable to adjust admission standards somewhat to help make the urban-grant university more accessible to minority group students whose earlier educational experience may not have been completely adequate. I have a sense that faculty members across the country increasingly want to make a contribution to the problems of these students, and they feel that they can. They certainly do not intend to lower the quality of the final product that comes out of the college. Rather, by greater attention and greater concern, they intend to help make up for the deficiencies of the earlier years.

These new endeavors will also see some battles among those who want to remain secluded and aloof from immediate problems, as against those who want to work toward the solution of those problems, and as against those who believe the problems can be solved only by changing the entire system. The land-grant institutions did not face so great an internal dispute about their role. Given the nature and intensity of the problems of the cities and the nation today, however, I can easily see disagreements involving students and faculty members over whether it is better to ignore the problems or to work with them or to work against the entire system. To handle the controversy on the campus among these points of view, there will have to be some rules on how opposition is mounted, and I think this is basically the responsibility of the faculty. Surely, we want free speech. Surely, we want criticism. But it must be within the law and it must be in a form that does not interfere with the proper functions of the campus.

Beyond the internal conflicts, this kind of university will be bound to face a great deal of external conflict about what it is doing. There will be those, for example, who will view with apprehension the potential political alliance of the students and the ghetto dwellers. Others will fear the potential involvement of the university in partisan urban politics. The already existing urban institutions, which are for the most part not doing the job of the urban-grant university as I visualize it, will nevertheless view any new institution or new activity as a competitor.

The land-grant institution encountered some external opposition, but not really very much. There were occasional disputes over findings about the relative merits of oleomargarine and butter. I recall a case I had in California, where one of our professors made a study which got headlines, concluding that whiskey not only tasted better than milk but was better for you, and that the older you got, the better it was, until at a certain age milk was an absolute evil and whiskey an immense benefit. I heard a good deal about these findings from the dairy interests and the allied agricultural interests. And there are always some problems from the external community when a faculty member says, for example, that farm wages ought to be higher. But the early land-grant institution faced essentially in one direction, toward the farmers, and served them, and naturally found little criticism there—except that there be more service and that it be more practical.

The urban-grant university, dealing with the problems of the city, will have to face in many directions, not one. When you deal with urban problems, you deal with urban controversies and with urban politics. And so, for this university to work effectively, there will have to be a considerable amount of public understanding—especially understanding of the distinction between service based on applications of knowledge and positions taken because of partisan politics. Beyond that, the institution will need an excellent system of buffers, and this is particularly a challenge to the trustees. I think that they should be selected on a nonpolitical basis and carefully screened, and that they should appreciate that their job is to protect the institution rather than to intensify the pressures from the external community.

There are strong indications today of a widening gulf between our universities, whatever their setting and orientation, and the general public. Some view the universities as elitist institutions apart from the everyday problems of the community. Many resent the criticisms of society that originate on university campuses. Others see the universities as sources of new ideas that are changing people's lives in ways they fear or don't understand or approve. What we need is more contact, not less, between the people and the universities. We must bridge the gulf between the intellectual community and the surrounding society because, if that gulf is permitted to widen, the intellectual community cannot get the resources and support to make it effective and the people cannot be served by intellect. The urban-grant university can provide such a bridge and, if the greater participation will result in greater controversy, we must be prepared to accept it and deal with it.

And so I would like to urge that we consider the urban-grant university as a positive approach to some of the greatest of our national problems. During World War II we turned to our universities for a vital contribution to national survival. Cannot the intellectual resources that created the new age of science now tackle the equally explosive problem of our cities? The threat is as real and the obligation surely as great.

The university can come increasingly to aid the renovation of our cities, and in return the university can be inspired by the opportunities and strengthened by the participation. If we make this new step forward, if we aggressively accept the challenge of the problems of the great city, if we desire to participate intimately in their solution and to make knowledge serve to the full extent it can, then and only then will higher education in the United States have risen to the challenge of the times.

Notes

* First presented as the Phi Beta Kappa–Gamma Chapter Centennial Lecture, The City College of New York, October 18, 1967.

Vignette—A Residual Role for Higher Education

Education and the World of Work: An Analytical Sketch*

This "sketch," also done for a conference of the International Council for Educational Development, was an effort to outline the sources of the "youth problem" in modern societies, and to serve as a basis for a discussion of how education might ease the difficult transition of youth into society.

My comments focus on three general questions: What is the fundamental source of our current problems? Is there such a thing as *the* youth problem? If there is, what might be its possible solutions?

1. The Industrial System. On the first question, I believe that our current problems stem from the basic change in the economic structure of industrial society with the heavy dependence of economic structure on the new technology. With the new technology has come a system of management which makes most people into employees, subject to the rules of others.

Going beyond the economic structure but associated with it are two crucial factors: the increasing longevity of the population and the enlarging role of the media. Longevity is a result of the new economic system, and has fundamental implications in sociological and psychological terms quite beyond the economic. But from an economic point of view, longevity has at least these impacts. First, it pays people to invest a lot more in their human capital. They have a much longer payoff period than when the average person's life expectancy was thirty-five years. When one's working life can be forty-five or fifty years, the payoff period is very long, and it pays to invest a great deal more in our human productive capital. It also pays to invest much more in what the economics call a durable consumer good. That usually means such things as refrigerators, but the individual has within him durable consumer goods in such ways as appreciation of music, art, and literature. These two considerations have, of course, big impacts on education. If you are going to be living a long time, the choice of your lifestyle and occupation is a much more important choice than if you have only a short period to look forward to. Hence the importance of longevity.

Turning to the media, Daniel Lerner's *The Passing of Traditional Society,* which essentially discusses six Middle East countries, categorizes people as traditional, transitional, or modern on the basis of their reliance upon the mass media to gain their knowledge and expectations of life. Bringing in radio communication even before there are newspapers makes an impact upon people's lives that is fundamental. However, the role of the media and the impact of longevity are still subsidiary to economic structure in determining what happens in the world of work.

In analyzing the world of work, I see five mainstreams of life. The new industrial system changes the proportions of people in these different streams, changes the content of them, and creates new ones. People can cross over from one stream to another, but there are some people who live in one stream all their lives. Four streams are preindustrial but today take somewhat new forms.

The first preindustrial stream of life includes established occupations entered through one's family: farming, the crafts, and the ancient professions of medicine, law, and theology. People typically entered these occupations as apprentices to their father or another relative. As late as 1870 about 80 percent of Americans were in that stream of life, and today the number is still about 20 percent. In most of these occupations formal education, however, is now more important than formerly.

The second preindustrial stream is the stream of the aristocracy, a stream based not upon occupation but upon wealth. That stream continues and probably with more people in it, although the chain gets broken more rapidly with inheritance taxes and the like. In the aristocratic stream, one's life pattern is determined by inherited wealth rather than by inherited occupation.

The third stream is that of structureless employment. In it people are not committed to one employer or to one job. The crafts worker is committed to one job and the industrial worker to one employer, although he or she may do many different tasks for that employer. For those in structureless employment—and there are many—life is not organized around a single occupation or single employer. Whereas some time ago these were the many people who did odd jobs in rural communities, now this structureless employment is largely urban. It involves the people who work in restaurants, in car washes, and in gas stations. They go from one type of work to another, from one employer to another. They tend to be low-skilled, high-mobility people, and there are substantial numbers of them.

The fourth stream, the culture of poverty, used to involve mainly the subsistence farmer, of whom we still have some in the United States. Now subsistence living tends to take place either on public or private welfare—the public welfare through all kinds of relief, the private welfare through the family supporting the young person in the culture of poverty. Some people now choose the culture of poverty voluntarily because they want it, but many more are propelled into it by industrial society. Today in the United States we have a third generation of young people in a culture of poverty. Their families have been in this culture of poverty, and they too are in it. Partly it is because the jobs that many such people used to have have been abolished in the industrial system. Instead of newspaper boys, a machine dispenses papers. People selling flowers on street corners or people running elevators have disappeared or are disappearing. We have abolished many occupations which used to absorb people of low ability, either physical or mental. We not only abolished their jobs with machinery, but also in part by the high standard of minimum wages. We can no longer afford to pay people to do these kinds of work.

On top of these four preindustrial streams, each of them now changed somewhat, there is a fifth, the industrial stream with its established new occupations, whether private or public. One enters it not out of inherited occupation or inherited wealth or from the lack of such inheritance (the structureless segment) or from the culture of poverty. One enters it through school and competition. For the first time in the history of our planet a very large number of people get into their stream of life predominantly through education and competition within it. This has created three basic problems.

The first of these is that in developing the industrial system we have built in excessive rigidities. The Webbs wrote, with great approval and fervor, about the establishment of the "common rule." Put into effect by employers, trade unions, and government, it was considered a great thing because it eliminated prejudice and the traditional personal way of running society on the basis of preferment and discrimination.

Developing the "common rule" was a great theme of reform in the last century, but now may bring *rigidities which handicap society.* We have lost the flexibility characteristic of more primitive societies, and to some extent of agricultural society today, where each day you decide what to do that day, depending on the weather, the season of the year, your inclinations, and so forth. In industrial society this is not possible because we have put everything under rigid rules, and this has had a very big impact upon youth.

The phasing of education, of work and leisure is subject to or the product of these rigidities. With respect to formal education, we start with none at all for the young child. Then all of a sudden we put him into full-time formal schooling for a certain period of his life, and then drop it altogether again. Formal education as the focus of a person's life goes from zero to essentially 100 percent to zero again. Then comes work. All of a sudden, we tell people "you are now going into work," and they then are immersed in work until at a certain age they are out of it 100 percent. It is a traumatic experience, both going in and getting out. In more primitive societies and in agricultural society today, you keep on working as long as you can, less per day, but you still keep working.

Leisure is another element in the pattern. The preschool child can be said to have a great deal of leisure. Then you put him in school and reduce the leisure to a lower level, and then into work and reduce it still more. When all of a sudden you retire, it is, as with the preschooler, full-time leisure again. These changes happen to people in a single day, in twenty-four hours. In terms of earnings (not income) we start people out with nothing at all. We then all of a sudden give them earnings, generally increasing these through seniority or skill, and then all of a sudden we drop their earnings again to zero.

To summarize, I would therefore say that the first basic problem for the people who are in the industrial stream in society is that a variety of forces, including government, employers, and trade unions, create various kinds of rigid rules and patterns and that these rigidities then come to govern people's lives.

The second basic problem, which is closely related to the first, is the fact that as compared with preindustrial society, we have two extremely difficult *transitions built into industrial life*. One is the transition from school to work, and the second, which can be just as difficult, is the transition out of work and into full-time leisure again at the end of life. These are two very traumatic experiences of youth and age.

The third basic problem in this fifth industrial stream is that to do well you have to have an institution watching out and caring for you. The people inside the *"care system"* are very well taken care of, compared with anybody in past history. If you get inside General Motors or inside the University of California, for example, somebody is looking out—taking care of your health, providing you your income, and so on. Those left outside are in a really difficult situation, especially the youth.

Institutional coverage in the industrial stream is inadequate for youth as nobody has a residual responsibility for it. The family and the school watch out for children and adolescents, but then there is a largely uncovered period. Then one goes into the corporation or trade union or government agency. When one comes out again, he or she may be covered by some form of income, usually depending, in the U.S. system, upon the employer, not the government; but nobody is watching out for one as a total human being. So I would say that our industrial stream has these three basic problems to it: the rigidity of the rules, the difficult transition points, and the inadequate institutional coverage at some points in life.

2. *Problems of Youth.* In discussing the problems of youth and employment, I have a question about terminology. The word *youth* does not seem exactly appropriate, nor do the traditional terms *childhood, adolescence,*

and *adulthood*. I think we are seeing the development of an in-between stage, for which I suggest as a possible name the one used by John R. Gillis in his study, *Youth and History,* namely *young adulthood.* It suggests an in-between period which is different from adolescence and adulthood and for which the term *youth* does not fit because it carries the impression of being young and not in charge of oneself. When we are talking about young adults, in the sense that they have responsibility for themselves, I wonder if we do not need a term which is different from the concept of youth and more in the direction of "young adulthood."

On my general second point: *the* problem of youth. First, I do not think one can talk about "the youth problem" because it makes a major difference which of my five streams a young person is in. To talk about youth *in toto* ignores basic factors such as which stream is the person in and to what stream does he want to go.

Second, and related to the first, the nature of youth problems depends on the characteristics by which one defines young persons and the different cells into which one puts them. One way of looking at people is by age. If you take 16- to 24-year-olds, in 1970 the chance of a 16-year-old being unemployed was 14.5 percent and of a 24-year-old, 5.2 percent. So each year makes an enormous difference. To talk about the 16-to-24 age group can obscure major differences within it.

If one looks at youth and employment from the point of view of education, in 1973 those with less than twelve years of education had a 15 percent unemployment rate, those with sixteen years or more under 5 percent. Race is another important factor in the United States: in 1970 white unemployment for ages 16 to 24 was 8.6 percent, compared to 10.6 percent for Spanish-speaking and 13.6 percent for Blacks. These rates differ little by sex but do by location. It is better for young males to be in a rural situation, and for young females to be in an urban situation, from the employment point of view. To look at several characteristics together, white males with sixteen years or more of education had an unemployment rate of 3.1 percent in 1973 when the overall rate was 8 or 9 percent, or one-third the average rate. At the other extreme, in the fall of 1975, for Black youth who had dropped out of school in 1974–75, the unemployment rate was 61.4 percent. Because the youth problem from the point of view of unemployment goes from 3 percent to 60 percent, I question if we can talk about *the* problem of youth. It breaks down into a whole lot of different situations which need somewhat different solutions.

Martin Trow, a sociologist at the University of California, Berkeley, is preparing a paper on the subject of youth which also goes into the plurality of problems. He has a schematic presentation according to which he categorizes youth in four compartments, as shown in chart 1 below, on the basis of their financial resources and their preparation for industrial life, which involves their family situation, personal qualities, schooling, and career motivation.

First are "The Advantaged," those that have both the resources and the preparation for life to fit into the meritocracy, and for them one could say there is no problem.

In the second group are "The Alienated," the young people who are not being prepared for life, either because of family circumstances, personal circumstances, or schooling, but who have financial resources.

The third group comprises "The Disadvantaged," those who lack the resources, but are being prepared, for example, out of what we call "ethnic" families, to take their place in the meritocracy. The problem for them, which the Carnegie Council and the Commission before it largely had addressed, is how to get them the funds needed to do what they want to do.

Finally, there are "The Deprived," those who have neither the wealth nor the resources, the ghetto youth.

For the United States, I would say about 80 percent of American youth is now in category one. The second category, where there are the resources but not the preparation for life, i.e., some of the children of the well-to-do and the wealthy, I would estimate at less than 5 percent.

Another 5 percent have adequate preparation for life, but not yet enough resources from either private or public sources; this category is a residual and disappearing one. The fourth category—the ghetto youth with no resources and no preparation—I estimate at maybe 10 percent or more.

When one considers solutions to the so-called youth problem, they clearly are much more complex than the term *youth* implies, whether you take the five streams or the numerous statistical cells or Martin Trow's four categories.

Having said that there is no such thing as the youth problem, I shall be quite inconsistent and discuss solutions to it. For this I return to the concept

CHART 1

Preparation for Life

		Early Education and Socialization	
		Adequate	*Inadequate*
Family Financial Resources	*Adequate*	I The Advantaged	II The Alienated
	Inadequate	III The Disadvantaged	IV The Deprived

Source: Martin Trow, "Reflections on Policies for Youth," paper prepared for the Conference on Young People in Contemporary Industrial Society, Ditchley Park, England, October 1976.

of transition points, and these are depicted in chart 2 below. The bottom triangle depicts childhood, in which the individual is initially almost totally dependent for environment on the parental family and the school, at first mainly the family. As one goes further through childhood, the peer group becomes more important, as do the media, and then in young adulthood the experience of work increasingly takes over along with the creation of a new family structure.

3. Solutions? When you look for solutions—and some of the problems may have no solutions—I would say that you ought to look first of all at the family, because it is the family that gets people into the streams of life and gives them the motivation to move on. The Coleman study and many others confirm that the way people get started in life makes an enormous difference in what happens later. Second, the combination of work and education through part-time courses and work, and through apprenticeship jobs, is the second crucial area to explore. And third is how to get some kind of an institutional structure that will be a residual base for youth and

CHART 2

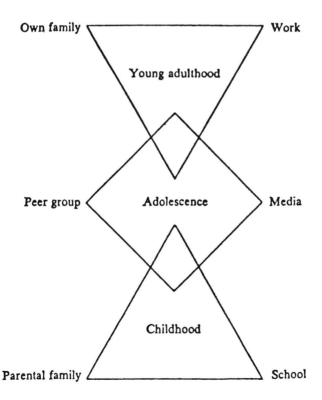

enable it to be covered by institutional care. In the U.S. context, that means looking particularly at two places: first, higher education in its totality and the community colleges in particular, and second, some kind of a service corps, or a combination of the two. I am convinced that we have to start building in some institutional base for young people, some institution in between the parental family and compulsory schooling and the work institutions, and the best I can see are community colleges and a kind of service corps.

So far we have been talking about capitalism, western capitalism, particularly the American version. I would suggest that the problem of the tendency toward rigid rules is universal in industrial societies and inherent in their logic, whatever kind of industrialism it may be, whether capitalism or eastern communism or western communism. The colonial industrial societies put in their rigid rules, too. Technology is the basis of rigidities for all kinds of industrial societies.

In terms of the institutional coverage of youth, both eastern and western communism have it, although we might not approve of the particular institutional coverage. A lack of institutional coverage is not inherent in industrialism, but tends to be the case in capitalism with its emphasis upon individualism. A society based more upon state than private initiative is more likely to have institutional coverage of youth and age. In comparing systems, if one divides the more developed industrial world into capitalism, of which there are many, many varieties, and eastern and western communism, and there are also many varieties of them, I would say that China probably handles the transition problems, both of youth and age, better than other industrial societies. It is impressive how the Chinese have put work and education together. At the age of three, the young people start working in the garden and also in the factory, and they do more work with more responsibility as time goes on. So there never is the dichotomy of schooling versus work. The two go together the whole way along. Also, in terms of the aged, the Chinese make good use of them. Block committees see to it that the older people are given something that they can keep on doing. There are, of course, however, heavy human costs in terms of loss of personal liberty within the Chinese system.

So I would say that while the problem of rigidity is inherent in all industrial systems, the problem of lack of institutional coverage is more inherent in capitalism than in socialism or communism. But the problem of the transition depends not so much upon whether it is capitalism or communism, but upon the particular policies of the system.

One final word, and this is just a suggestion. There is a tendency in all industrial societies to create a class of outsiders. The insiders are the people in the well-cared-for system, the productive people inside the big agencies of production and government. Unless it is deliberately combatted, there is a tendency to turn the youth and aged people into outsiders because both are outside the economic process. It is being inside the economic process that makes one an insider, whether a worker, a manager, owner, or something else.

Unless one does something about it, the many people in the undesirable jobs in the structureless market and in the culture of poverty are outsiders. And I would estimate for the United States today, assuming one-third of youth as being put outside by choice or necessity, most of the aged, and all the people in the structureless market and the culture of poverty, that about one-third of our people would have to be put in the outsider category. One-third of the nation. One of the great tasks is how to reduce that one-third of outsiders and not just the youth component within it. It takes an attitude toward people and toward society, not just to solve the youth problem, but to solve what it is a larger part of and that is the outsider problem: people outside or not fully integrated into the organized productive process.

Notes

* From *Access, Systems, Youth and Employment*, ed. Barbara B. Burn, (New York: International Council for Educational Development, 1977), 133–42. Reprinted by permission.

Vignette—

The Longer Term: Review Article, "An Agenda for
Higher Education"*

*Howard Bowen was a good friend of mine over many years, and we
often told each other that we were the last two optimists about the
future of higher education in the United States. This is a review of his
optimistic* The State of the Nation and the Agenda for Higher Education, *which I considered a little too optimistic.*

The agenda for higher education in the United States today is over-
flowing with current problems: with cutbacks in student aid, with reduc-
tions in funds for research except as related to national defense, with the
consequences of financial stringency in many states, with the adjustments to
the great demographic depression that is just beginning. Seldom, if ever,
have so many urgent problems with such potentially negative impacts confronted our colleges and universities. But there is a longer term agenda,
much less certain in its content and almost certainly less disastrous in its
implications, that also lies ahead. It is asking a great deal that higher education should raise the level of its sights as it stumbles along today's rocky
path. However, the spirit with which the problems of today are approached
and the solutions sought for them can and should be affected by a more
long term view.

This longer-term view is the subject of Howard Bowen's new book:
The State of the Nation and the Agenda for Higher Education.[1] This book
should be a high priority for all persons concerned with the future of American higher education. Today, yesterday, and tomorrow, the actual agenda of
higher education has been, is now, and will be mostly concentrated on the
problems of survival in a time of troubles. But this time of troubles will not
last forever, and the current troubles of future periods will be of a different
nature. It is helpful, even and perhaps particularly at a time such as this, to
look beyond present troubles at the possible worlds of the future for American higher education as they may be and as we wish they might be. This is
what Howard Bowen invites us to do. With this book he continues his important series on the benefits of higher education,[2] on the costs of higher
education,[3] and now (with benefits and costs both in mind) on the prospec-
tive futures of higher education. This book is the best current discussion of

the longer-run future of American higher education. While I shall disagree, in part, with what Howard Bowen sets forth, this in no way detracts from the great admiration I have for the thrust and the general content of his study. I comment upon his views at some length because they are eminently worth commenting upon. He asks the right questions and gives most thoughtful answers. He encourages a debate that can be quite productive about the longer-run future of higher education and on the role of higher education in affecting its own future and that of the nation.

Let me say, at the start of this commentary, that I agree with Bowen's optimism about the medium-run future of American higher education, although I am less sanguine than he is about short-term prospects for the next decade or decade and one-half, specifically in the area of enrollment prospects.[4] I am a firm believer in the contemporary validity of Plato's law that "when the wheel [of education] has once been set in motion the speed is always increasing." This law has not been true at many times in history and in many places around the world, but it is certainly true, in general, in the modern world. The modern world has needed, and as far as one can see ahead, will need the higher skills and better ideas that higher education generates.

Higher education, as Boyer and Hechinger have recently noted, has, nevertheless, suffered a "loss of confidence" because it is "no longer at the vital center of the nation's work." "For the first time in nearly half a century, America's colleges and universities are not collectively caught up in some urgent national endeavor"—to win a war, to educate veterans, to advance American interests in the cold war, to implement programs of social justice. "Higher education appears to be adrift".[5] It no longer has the same sense it once did of "positive dedication to the service of an evolving dynamic, democratic community," of serving so actively "the basic needs of American life".[6] This leads, quite naturally, not only to much malaise but also to a search for new goals, a new sense of purpose, new inspirations.

Bowen takes as his premise that higher education will continue with what it does now—with the education of students, with the conduct of research, with the preservation and interpretation of the cultural heritage, with the patronage of the arts, with policy analysis, with its many forms of public service; doing each of these better. With this I totally agree. I would particularly emphasize that we can still make great gains in our contributions to the achievement of greater social justice.

The first major item suggested by Bowen for the new agenda is to help create a "nation of educated people." The potential advances to be made here are enormous. I am particularly persuaded that higher education can make a great contribution to the ability of people to cope with an ever more complex society and to advance the quality of their participation in political and community life. I am less persuaded than Bowen, however, about the potential additional contributions it can make to economic gains in productivity. They may still be substantial but not so central as in the past. I do not agree, as some now suggest, that higher education has become economically counterproductive because overeducated people are dissatisfied with the jobs they hold and sabotage, or, at least, withhold output. I think that the declines in the growth in productivity can be explained by other causes. However, higher education may have already made its peak contributions to enhanced productivity; but not to individual and to community life.

To accomplish this goal of a nearly entire nation of educated people, Bowen counts on increased participation rates in college attendance and suggests that the national rate may come to match the current level in California. This would raise attendance by one-third. I think this is quite possible, although attendance rates have not risen as fast as I, and many others, once thought likely. The Carnegie Commission once suggested an even higher potential attendance rate comprised of the high school graduation rate of Minnesota (90 percent) and the college entrance rate of high school graduates in California (75 percent).[7]

Bowen also counts on a renaissance for general education in colleges and universities. I share his conviction of the desirability of this but not his high hopes. General education has been in decline for most of the past three centuries. It was almost devastated in the late 1960s and early 1970s. A Carnegie Foundation report called it a "disaster area."[8] The near demise of general education was the greatest of the "popular"[9] academic "reforms" of the 1960s. This was the one overwhelming change that took place. It was not planned. It just happened in response to the pressures of the times. It was given up for external not internal academic reasons; but internally there was neither the conviction nor the strength to defend it effectively. The faculty community gave up control of the general curriculum, although still holding on to control of the curriculum within each disciplinary major. The general curriculum was surrendered, by and large, to the student market reflecting, among other things, the presumed wishes of potential employers. Students came to prefer, and often insist upon, electives and vocational courses. a major academic responsibility was abandoned. The pendulum may, and I think will, swing back a bit in the future but, I fear, not much. There is much guilt about the decline of general education in the United States but little action. There are exceptions to this generalization, mostly in the more selective liberal arts colleges.

Bowen also counts on substantial assistance from institutions of higher education to the high schools with all their problems. Once again, I share his conviction about the desirability of this but doubt the practical accomplishments that may lie ahead. The gap between the two types of institutions is enormous, marked by lack of interest on the one side and by resentment on the other. The mentalities on the two sides are at great odds with each other. It can, I think, be well argued that higher education has done the high schools more harm than good in recent times by lowering the comparative attention given to teacher education, by lowering admission standards into higher education, by being the source of little useful and some very counterproductive research. I do not see this record being substantially improved. The performance of the high schools can and will be raised but mostly from other sources of inspiration than from the colleges and universities.

This leaves me with great expectations for a nation of more educated people but mostly because a higher proportion of people will attend our colleges and universities, and not because our colleges and universities will behave much differently than they have in the recent past in the development of their own curricula and in aid to the high schools.

The second major item of Bowen is an increased "emphasis on values" for the sake of the nation. He believes that we need "to alter the values of our people"; that "higher education may be a strategic point of leverage in modifying the values that actuate the system"; and that "in education lies the main hope for a good society."[10] This, he believes, is "perhaps the most important function of higher education as related to the agenda of the nation."[11] Here I have some doubts and for several reasons, and, consequently, I do not think that higher education should seek to put on the agenda it offers the nation an increased "emphasis on values." I think that this is a dangerous suggestion. I am not sure that we can produce on such a promise. Many, perhaps even most, faculty members do not like to confront the issue of values in any broad way. The commitment to the doctrine of ethical relativism may be fading, but a doctrine of ethical commitment has not yet taken its place. Any effort to move toward an explicit ethical commitment by the campus for the sake of the nation can be very divisive among faculty members and among students. Also, such a commitment would invite efforts at external interference in the affairs of colleges and universities, particularly under current national circumstances. Additionally it can be "arrogant," as Bowen notes.[12] There is no proof that morality is higher on campus than off. The level of cheating, the theft and destruction of library materials, the heavy default rate on loans even offer evidence in some areas to the contrary. The selection and advancement of moral issues and the attachment to moral principles are much more subject to fads on campus than in the community at large. The methods used to advance moral issues by elements on campus have, at times, gone beyond the persuasion that is central to academic principles and democratic practice.

I should like to suggest another approach: that an "emphasis on values" be made part of the internal agenda of higher education for the sake of the integrity of the academic community, as part of its aspirations about its own highest conduct, for the sake of its own soul. This leads me to strong support for the following:

> Making clearer and emphasizing more strongly the ethical principles of the academic community, as Martin Trow has proposed—the commitment to truth, tolerance for alternative views, defense of free expression of opinions, respect for the facts, attention to careful analysis, interest in the experience of the past, search for a cosmopolitan outlook, advancement of ideas and persons on merit, opposition to plagiarism, and emphasis on civility in debate.[13]
>
> Raising ethical issues in training for the professions, in discussing problems in the social sciences, in understanding situations presented in the humanities, and in advancing the scientific method; ethical issues are central to the full examination of each of these areas. Too often faculty members have avoided as too uncertain, or too controversial, or too unimportant, the ethical component in human affairs.
>
> Adding more courses in ethics and in comparative religions.
>
> Conducting the life of the campus community along ethical lines. This involves carefully developed codes of rights and responsibilities for faculty members and students. It involves standards of fair practice in all aspects of campus endeavors. The ethical standards of campus life today should be subject to periodic scrutiny—particularly in such areas as cheating, theft and destruction of library materials, and default on student loans.[14]
>
> Conducting relations with the surrounding community in ethical ways. This involves reliance on thought and persuasion, and not on the passion and violence that has marred relations in recent times. Ethical relations with the surrounding community have become much more difficult with the advent of a concern for affirmative action, with the rise of fears about the consequences of certain types of scientific research, with the introduction of greater temptations in the use of new knowledge for profit, with the addition of moral concern to the placement of investments.[15] In earlier times, the essence of relations with the surrounding community was a stance of political neutrality by the campus in return for acceptance by the community of institutional autonomy and academic freedom. The issues are now much more complicated.

All this should be done because it serves the welfare of the academic community and is in keeping with its own best values. One result might be that the level of "morality" in the nation might rise. But we should be careful not to suggest that we are by nature more moral than the rest of the nation—I think that would be very hard to prove in some areas; and not to promise that we can raise the moral standards of the nation—I think that would be a commitment very hard to fulfill. I agree with most of the specific actions that Howard Bowen suggests be taken; but I would like to see these actions pursued as part of the academic community's sense of purpose about itself and not as part of its service to the nation, not as part of the agenda for the nation. I would not like to see us approach the morality of the nation head on. To Bowen's critical question of whether higher education is, or has the capacity to become, an independent and effective moral force, I reply "possibly" but only if it seeks to become such a force in the course of its own conduct in accord with its own highest principles and not through direct, frontal assault on the morality of the nation.

Bowen's third major item is for higher education to make greater contributions to solutions to the many "problems of youth." Some of these problems are quite horrendous. I fully agree with the emphasis on this problem. The Carnegie Council in one of its last reports also made a number of proposals for improvement to which Bowen refers.[16] This report was one major basis for a bill that was making its way through Congress with bipartisan support in both houses prior to the national elections in November 1980. This, or a similar range of proposals, will some time again be considered, both because of the severity of the problems and because youth is an increasingly scarce resource in demand by the military and by the economy as seldom before. I do think that, at some time and perhaps gradually, higher education will be given a "residual responsibility" for youth where all other sources of support have proved inadequate; a responsibility to give advice, guidance, and educational help to all youth. This responsibility will fall most heavily on the public community colleges. The main assistance that higher education gives to a solution to youth problems now is to provide many young persons a more constructive alternative than they otherwise would have. This makes financial aid to students from low-income families of such great importance. The main solutions to the youth problems of the nation, however, lie outside higher education—in the family, in the community, in the primary and secondary schools, in the job market, in public service opportunities.

I should now like to add some items to the potential agenda and to highlight others that are already on Howard Bowen's list but not so specifically emphasized as those listed above:

> That higher education take more of a lead in developing materials for use with the new electronic technology. Control Data Corporation alone has done more than any American university. This new avenue to "a nation of educated people" at last seems to be opening up for substantial use. Eric Ashby called this the "fourth revolution" in educational methods.[17] It will be unfortunate if higher education does not make good use of the new opportunities.

That higher education extend more of its attention to service to other often neglected groups, in addition to disadvantaged youth, particularly to the aged and the handicapped, whose lives could be greatly enriched by more educational and cultural content. Use of the facilities made available by the fourth revolution is one means.

That higher education pay more attention to counseling on academic programs and on occupational careers. The number and complexity of choices to be made by students is staggering. A basic course on how to make good use of the college years could be central to this effort.

That higher education seek to introduce more of a global perspective into its curriculum and many of its individual courses. I am doubtful of the value of more courses in international relations, as some now insist upon, and even of more attention to foreign languages except for those students who will become really expert in one or more; but I believe that global perspectives should stand with "moral values" as one of the great internal concerns of higher education. Higher education began as an international enterprise in the late middle ages and it has as one of its internal concerns knowledge of the whole world, even the whole universe; knowledge should not be so confined to developments within national boundaries.

That higher education find ways to encourage more integrative approaches to knowledge to go along with the still increasing specialization. We pay too much attention to the fractionalization of knowledge into more and more bits and pieces; too little to its recombination into more explanatory wholes. We have a nation of specialists needing better generalizations. We need more attention to wisdom; and to organized thought about the future of society.

That higher education be alert to, help analyze, and refine the new mentalities that are now being born. It played a rather dubious role in the spread of the counterculture of the 1960s and 1970s, never providing much analysis of it. There are now other new mentalities: the "hard hats" emphasizing production, the egalitarians emphasizing distribution, the conservationists emphasizing the environment and quality of life, the preservationists emphasizing older outlooks and ways of doing things. People are choosing among these several mentalities and these mentalities will help shape the world of the future. The mentalities of the capitalist, the worker and the peasant are fading into history.

That higher education give more encouragement and rewards to the members of its community who participate constructively in public debate. I have been impressed, in reading public opinion studies, with the similarity in knowledge of and views about policy alternatives between experts and opinion makers, but also with the gap between both of them and the public at large. Alexander Meiklejohn once wrote of the teachers in our colleges and universities "as the creators of the national intelligence."[18] This puts it, I think, much too strongly but our colleges and universities should be, more than they are now, intellectual experiment stations and extension services; should "help make public opinion more self-critical and more circumspect, to check the more hasty and unconsidered impulses of popular feeling, to train democracy to the habit of looking before and after."[19] The new schools of public policy can greatly help with this.

There are, I am sure, many other items that could and should be added to the list for consideration as part of the future agenda.

My estimate of the prospects for positive future contributions, in the several areas noted above, is "good" for those items that have grown out of historic experience and that may be classified as continuing and expanding functions; and only "moderate" to "poor," but mostly "moderate," in the newer agenda items that add functions or methods. I see no enormously successful new contributions such as those made after the Civil War and, to a much lesser extent, after World War II. We are entering for the medium-term, I think, a period with less dramatic new potentials than either of those periods, but there are still opportunities which, if effectively developed, can substantially improve both higher education and the nation.

It can be helpful to look ahead of the moment, to try to see where we might like to go. I hope, through the initiative, the careful thought and the imagination of Howard Bowen, that higher education may be encouraged to look beyond the next steps that so occupy our attention today to the horizons we some time might like to reach. I think that substantial progress can be made in the directions that Bowen points out to us; that there are other areas for advancement as well; and that, in addition to mourning the Golden Age recently past, we should anticipate some, at least silver, opportunities that may lie ahead. We are all indebted to Howard Bowen for suggesting that we stop looking only down at the rocks on which we seem to be walking today. There is more to the future than that: the nation changes, and higher education will continue its perpetual goal to serve the changing nation within the boundaries of its great talents and the constraints set by its own essential character.

Notes

* Reprinted from *Higher Education*, 11 (1982): 593–600. Reprinted by permission of Kluwer Academic Publishers.

1. Howard R. Bowen, *The State of the Nation and the Agenda for Higher Education* (San Francisco: Jossey-Bass, 1982).

2. Howard R. Bowen, *Investment in Learning: The Individual and Social Value of American Higher Education* (San Francisco: Jossey-Bass, 1977).

3. Howard R. Bowen, *The Costs of Higher Education* (San Francisco: Jossey-Bass, 1980).

4. Bowen seems to define the long term as lying in the period up to about fifty years ahead. I should like to suggest these definitions for the purposes of viewing the future of higher education: "short term"—the period to about 2000, when the demographic depression will have ended and students not yet born will enter higher education; "medium term"—the period to about 2020, when the current faculty will have retired; and the "long term" as the period after that. I think it is very difficult to look beyond the medium term so defined.

5. Ernest L. Boyer and Fred M. Hechinger, *Higher Learning in the Nation's Service* (Washington, DC: The Carnegie Foundation for the Advancement of Teaching, 1981), 3. Boyer and Hechinger explore, more briefly than Bowen, a similar range of problems; and they come to somewhat the same conclusions. They emphasize three of the same agenda items as Bowen: "advancing civic learning" (Bowen: "a nation of educated people"); "using knowledge wisely" (Bowen: "education for values"); and "educating a new generation" (Bowen: helping "American youth"). They also add: "generating new knowledge."

6. John S. Brubacher and Willis Rudy, *Higher Education in Transition* (New York: Harper & Row, 1968), 394.

7. Carnegie Commission on Higher Education, *New Students and New Places* (New York: McGraw-Hill, 1971), 2; Carnegie Commission on Higher Education, *The Capitol and the Campus* (New York: McGraw-Hill, 1971), table 2 and Appendix 7.

8. The Carnegie Foundation for the Advancement of Teaching, *Missions of the College Curriculum* (San Francisco: Jossey-Bass, 1977), 11.

9. Gerald Grant and David Riesman, *The Perpetual Dream: Reform and Experiment in the American College* (Chicago: University of Chicago Press, 1978), ch. 6.

10. Howard R. Bowen, *The State of the Nation and the Agenda for Higher Education* (San Francisco: Jossey-Bass, 1982), 78, 79, 81.

11. Bowen, *State of the Nation*, 132.

12. Bowen, *State of the Nation*, 93.

13. Martin Trow, "Moral Problems in the Context of American Higher Education," an *Occasional Paper* of the Center for Studies in Higher Education, University of California, Berkeley, 1980.

14. Carnegie Council on Policy Studies in Higher Education, *Fair Practices in Higher Education* (San Francisco: Jossey-Bass, 1979).

15. For an excellent discussion of this range of issues, see Derek Bok, *Beyond the Ivory Tower* (Cambridge, MA: Harvard University Press, 1982).

16. Carnegie Council on Policy Studies in Higher Education, *Giving Youth a Better Chance* (San Francisco: Jossey-Bass, 1979).

17. Eric Ashby, "Machines, Understanding and Learning: Reflections on Technology in Education," *The Graduate Journal* 7, no. 2 (1967).

18. Alexander Meiklejohn, *The Experimental College,* ed. John Walker Powell (Cabin John, MD/Washington, DC: Seven Locks Press, 1981 [orig. pub. 1932]), 120.

19. American Association of University Professors, "General Report of the Committee on Academic Freedom and Academic Tenure," *Bulletin of the AAUP* (December 1915): 26, 32.

CHAPTER 28

The Eternal Verities—
Universities: Open to Truth and Merit

Every four years the "open universities" of South Africa hold a lecture, sometimes on one campus and sometimes on another, to commemorate their battles against apartheid within the universities. My lecture was in 1976 and I was greatly pleased to receive an honorary degree along with Helen Suzman. The British newspapers reported the event but the Afrikaaner did not. My central line was that denial of merit is a recipe for revolution.

Twenty years ago this coming December, the Council of the University of Cape Town and the Council of the University of the Witwatersrand separately resolved that each was opposed to "academic segregation on racial grounds." This lecture, which I am privileged to present here today, commemorates the subsequent occasion in April 1959 when the general assembly of this university similarly dedicated itself "to uphold the principle that a university is a place where men and women without regard to race and colour are welcome to join in the acquisition and advancement of knowledge." This was a principle upon which each of these two great universities had been founded and upon which each had conducted itself until no longer permitted to do so by external authority.

Later, in 1968, the right of appointing teachers at the sole discretion of the university—a second basic principle on which these two universities were historically conducted—was restricted. By 1975, also, according to a report by the Academic Freedom Committees of the two universities,[1] 26,000 written works had been banned as "undesirable" and placed on a limited-access basis only. There have been other infringements as well on the right to teach and to conduct research, as their report so carefully documents.

Consequently, I have chosen to speak, on this commemorative occasion, on the subject of "Universities: Open to Truth and to Merit." Truth and merit are the two most basic principles of modern academic life in the Western World; and the principles of a university are its most cherished possession.

I speak, I well know, as a guest in your country, hesitant to talk about your laws, about which I am ill-informed. I also speak, however, as an academic colleague in the worldwide community of scholarship, where I am not a guest and not ill-informed. I also speak from the vantage point of a citizen of a nation which has had experience, and continues to have experience, similar in kind to yours, although clearly not currently similar in intensity of degree, in facing the educational (and other) problems of a multiracial society. I also speak as a citizen of a nation which, because of its position in the world, cannot be unconcerned with how you solve your problems. Nor would you wish us to be unconcerned when others are, in part, because both the United States and South Africa have basic, although quite imperfectly executed, commitments to democratic and to Christian beliefs. These beliefs act as restraints in bad times and as beacons in better times in both our nations. They create one basis for mutual understanding.

I speak from one addition perspective and a quite personal one. I have been through the wars of academic freedom and institutional autonomy. I know how difficult these wars can be, how they can strain internal amity, how they can exacerbate relations with the surrounding community, how they can compel unwilling concessions, how they can force fine and even agonizing distinctions—inside the easy-sounding global principles—between what one will and will not fight for and against. Out of my own experience, may I express my admiration for the resolute, dignified, and thoughtful way in which you have generally carried on your many battles. Even though you have been overcome on occasion, even on very important occasions, you have never been defeated in the only places where defeat would be total—in your own minds and spirits. We would not be meeting here tonight if you had been.

I also know out of my experience how universities, fragile as they sometimes seem, can survive times of stress and how their high principles can ultimately be triumphant. As a young professor, I was a member and later chairman of the Committee on Privilege and Tenure of the Academic Senate of the Berkeley Campus of the University of California during the great "oath controversy." Those were the days when, as Lord Ashby put it in the first of these Chancellors' lectures,[2] "the fanaticism of Senator McCarthy passed like an ominous eclipse over some of the universities of America"—including particularly my own. Later, as Chancellor (Vice-Chancellor in your terminology) at Berkeley, however, I welcomed back the returning "nonsigners" of the oath who had earlier been dismissed against the recommendations of our committee. Still later, by then as president of the nine-campus University, I saw Mario Savio, in what Lionel Trilling has called "the age of hysteria" in America, try to bring the "wheels of the university to a grinding halt" through massive confrontations, try to stop orderly processes of decision making, try to interfere with the assigned duties on campus of others. Savio, nevertheless, a few years later, chose to return to the university to try to benefit in his education from the fact that the wheels had never been stopped. By the irony of fate I was in the same year, 1964, both given the highest award made to an administrator in American academic life—the Alexander Meiklejohn award of the American Association of University Professors for outstanding contributions to the cause of academic freedom, and condemned by student radicals for my opposition to what they called "the free speech movement." Subsequently, basically because I had twice opposed the use of massive police force on campus, I was dismissed as president of the University under the urging of a new and reactionary governor of the state; but public opinion in the United States has by now progressed to the point where such use of force or attempted use of force on a campus would be less likely under similar circumstances.

The principles of freedom from an oppressive oath, of maintenance of orderly processes, and of basic reliance on peaceful persuasion ultimately were in each case in fact accepted. But, on each occasion, there were many that saw only the end of all they held dear, that saw almost nothing but gloom and doom, that yielded to despair. They were wrong. There was hope instead. Similarly I believe that the two plaques in the Jagger Library at the University of Cape Town leaving open the dates when your basic academic rights are restored will not be left forever uncompleted. These dates will some day be filled in both because of the worth of the principles at stake and because of the logic of necessity in the current world.

I should like to comment tonight upon both the worth of your principles and the necessity of their realization, but I should first like to make three observations from my experience:

1. Academic freedom and institutional autonomy can be threatened from within a well as from without, from the left as well as the right. Support of freedom and of autonomy should never take such forms that opposition to one enemy may strengthen another and perhaps greater enemy.

2. Force on campus is counterproductive in both external and internal relations for whomever first uses it. Peaceful persuasion is not only the right but also the superior means. It is better to appeal to the good in others than to respond to the evil in one's self.

3. It is essential to maintain your faith, your confidence and your efforts, as you have done.

Vice-Chancellor T. B. Davie of Cape Town in 1953 set forth his understanding of the basic academic freedoms. His statement later became the basis for the 1957 declaration of the representatives of the Universities of Cape Town and the Witwatersrand, under the title of *The Open Universities in South Africa.*[3] There it is set forth that "the four essential freedoms" of a university are "to determine for itself on academic grounds[4] who may teach, what may be taught, how it all be taught and who may be admitted to study." This has become your basic declaration of faith. Lord Ashby in 1962, Lord Birley in 1965,[5] Lord Butler in 1969,[6] and Professor Leo Marquard in 1973,[7] my predecessors in giving this lecture, have each endorsed and reaffirmed these principles, as I also gladly do.

These four freedoms, and certain other associated ones, stem from concern for the truth of ideas and for the advancement of individuals on the basis of academic merit.[8] The pursuit of truth requires free access to information and freedom of expression, which in turn means freedom of speech, freedom to choose, conduct, and publish research, freedom to determine the contents of courses and the methods of teaching, and freedom of peaceful assembly and petition. Advancement on merit requires that faculty appointments and promotions be based solely on academic qualifications and accomplishments and related academic contributions, that admission of students be based upon prior academic achievement and innate academic ability, and that grades and degrees be given on the basis of academic performance.[9]

The evolution of basic academic rights. The pursuit of truth and advancement on merit in academic life are acquired rights—acquired by the actions of teachers and students, and granted by or even insisted upon, or at least acquiesced to, by society. They have evolved as principles over an extended period of time. They are not part of the birthright of academic endeavours. You are part of that process of evolution. In one regard, at least, you have actually given unusual leadership, as I shall note later.

I wish that I could say that persons in academic life had always and everywhere subscribed to these principles. They have not. There have been many internal as well as external battles in the course of establishing these principles. In ancient Athens, there was a commitment, by Socrates and by others, to what we would now call academic freedom for citizens and for intellectuals, but not for the slaves. When universities began in the twelfth century, they were oriented more toward past authority and its interpretation and refinement than toward intellectual freedom and the discovery of new ideas—to the authority of the Bible and the classics at Paris and at those universities moulded on Paris, and to the authority of Roman law at Bologna and the universities modelled after it. The Bologna model, of the two, was the more open to science (witness Galileo) and to research in the humanities. In both models, students were welcomed from many "nations" but there was no outside search for merit and, in fact, the students came from the upper classes—often the younger sons. Even in England, as late as a century and a half ago, orthodoxy by the dons still handicapped full intellectual freedom; and only members of the Anglican Church were admitted to Oxford and Cambridge; and women were only admitted to "full membership" in the university by Oxford in 1921 and Cambridge in 1948.

There was no Golden Age in the distant past to which we can refer and from whence we can say we derive our rights. The distant past was one of a frequently dismal performance,[10] a few bright episodes only to the contrary. The ambiguity of past academic conduct is obscured by the lack of any good general history of academic freedom,[11] by our natural desire to seek historical precedent for our now most cherished principles, and by our concentration on the pathology of recent times as though we had retrogressed from some Golden Age. We have tended to concentrate on problem cases, not on the general course of history—even Eric Ashby entitled his lecture "Universities Under Siege." He talked about Hitler's Germany, McCarthy's America, and the then-current South Africa.

The Golden Age, to the extent it is golden, is now—when one looks at the history of universities of the Western World. The situation, generally, has been getting better and better, not worse and worse. The history is one of great progress overall, not of great retrogression; although the progress has often been slow and halting, and there have been periods and episodes of retrogression along the way.

The active practice of academic freedom on any large scale has been around for only two centuries.[12] The "lehrfreiheit" of the German universities, established in the first half of the 19th century, was the first general assertion of academic freedom. The development of this movement had begun earlier but progressed more gradually in England. It only became a force of importance in the United States after the Civil War. The rise of academic freedom has been associated with the rise of science, and with the rise of democracy and of individual rights following the American War of Independence and the French Revolution (with the Renaissance and the Reformation standing in the background). The scientific method, to be successful, required freedom of inquiry, and democratic societies were more willing to grant individual rights than most earlier forms of society. Faculty members and students who fought for their rights did so with their own colleagues as well as with external authority. Similarly with advancement on merit, it also has relied for its accelerated development on the rise of a more professional faculty with the advent of science, and on the rise of democracy and the right to equality of opportunity.

Universities have been around for eight centuries but only in the past two centuries have they been increasingly devoted to academic freedom and to advancement on merit. At least 99 percent of the actual experience of faculty members and students, however, has taken place during these two centuries.[13] This experience has been that successful universities have been those that have given the most attention to academic freedom and to advancement on merit—it has been there that the new knowledge has mostly been created and the highest skills trained. This experience of the past two centuries has been so universally favorable that, in the Western World, the pursuit of truth and advancement on merit in academic life are by now looked upon as "inalienable rights"—to borrow a phase from American history; "inalienable" in the sense that they have been won in the course of and tested by vast human experience; "inalienable" in the sense that they are now never given up voluntarily, that even when taken away by others the claims for their restoration are not relinquished, and that they are restored—as in Germany after Hitler—at the first opportunity.

These rights, also, are usually recognized by now as legitimate by citizens at large in the Western World when they are free to do so. The two human institutions most devoted to the search for truth—the church more by revelation and the university more by research—have customarily in recent human history, even in dictatorships, been accorded more self-determination than other institutions, possibly because there appears to many to be something sacred in or at least inviolate about the search for truth. It has become part of general social beliefs that "know the truth, and the truth shall make you free" (Gospel according to St. John), and that—with the rise of science and the nation state—"knowledge is power" (Bacon). And merit too has come to have a popular appeal to the sense of "fair play". Whether in sports, or in entertainment, or in services performed or in products sold or in politics, it is generally accepted that the better should be preferred over the poorer. The phrase of Shakespeare is "The force of his own merit makes his way (*The Tempest*).

Thus it seems that, as a general rule of modern social life in the Western World, scholars insist upon and the people accept the principles of truth and merit. They have come to be normal, fundamental aspirations of independent scholars and they appeal to the common sense of the people. They have re-enforcing advantages—making academic life more vigorous and service to society more effective. Truth and merit are, in any event, after eight centuries of university life, the principles asserted and reasserted; and applied and reapplied in the evaluation of the quality of academic life. They have come to be the guiding principles in all free universities in all free nations.[14]

There are, however, some difficulties with these principles and these difficulties can give rise, as they do now in the United States, to bitter controversy. Few principles are clear-cut—they require careful definition and consideration of borderline cases. I should like to illustrate here with just one difficulty although I shall raise others later on. The pursuit of truth requires free choice by competent scholars of subject matter and of method. But some research threatens the physical safety of others. Thus controls and safeguards can legitimately be placed upon it, as, for example, in the use of radioactive substances and in some genetic experimentation. Such qualifications, I realize, will trouble the purists and even realists must fear that exceptions can destroy the rule. But good judgment must be used about even the most basic principle and what is good judgment is, of course, controversial. This university once judged, as did the University of Cape Town, that it was more important to insist on merit in academic matters than on desegregation of residential living, social occasions, and athletic contacts—a judgment which I would find repugnant in the American context, but, perhaps quite necessary for you at the time. I shall return later to some difficult judgments we face in the United States and which, I hope, you will later have the opportunity to face in South Africa.

To talk about qualifications and judgments is not in any way to take away from the importance of the basic principles. I should like now to return to them and to present the view that the pursuit of truth and advancement on merit in academic life are not only universally desirable within the academic world, but are necessary to the proper progress of society, are of particular value to a multiracial society, and are of special importance to South Africa today within the world of nations.

By referring to the role of society, I do not want to seem to subscribe to the conclusion of Karl Jaspers, as noted by Lord Butler, that "The university exists through the good graces of the body politic. Its existence is dependent on political considerations. It can live only as and where the state desires."[15] Jaspers was a famous philosopher suspended from his chair by the Nazis but after their defeat was made president of the University of Heidelberg. His observation was certainly correct looking back on the Germany of Hitler; but it is not generally true of the Western World—universities can to a significant degree determine their own fate. Society, however, everywhere must either grant, or at least acquiesce to, the acquired rights of universities; and so a society's view of academic life is important.

Truth. Socrates, as Lord Birley noted in his lecture, argued that Athens needed him as a "gadfly." He told his fellow Athenians that he was "not going to argue for my own sake, as you may think, but for yours." He said, "If you execute me, you will not easily find a successor to me . . . and the State is a great and noble horse which is rather sluggish owing to its very size, and requires to be stirred into life." Society, for its own sake, needs the pursuit of truth—to know that the world is round, to know what may be the real causes and thus cures of economic depressions, to know what effects on the environment an insecticide may have, to know what the side effects of a new drug are, to know how to develop new sources of energy—the needs to know are endless.

Truth changes. It is always being pursued. There are new facts, new problems, new methodologies, new systems of analyses, new insights, new discoveries to be made. Truth emerges in conflict. Some earlier solution proves inadequate. It is challenged and defended. New truth evolves in a never ending process, and this is the process of the advance of knowledge.

The university is the main instrument of society for the most wide-ranging and most constant pursuit of knowledge. It is the place where there is the greatest and firmest belief in what Cardinal Newman called "the sovereignty of truth."[16] "A university is a place," he wrote, "of concourse whither students come from every quarter for every kind of knowledge . . . it is a place to which a thousand schools make contributions; in which the intellect may safely range and speculate, sure to find its equal in some antagonistic activity, and its judge in the tribunal of truth. It is a place where inquiry is pushed forward, and discoveries verified and proved, and rashness rendered innocuous, and error exposed, by the collision of mind with mind and knowledge with knowledge."[17]

Society needs error to be exposed and truth to be found for the sake of its own progress and proper conduct. That is why it needs universities with assured academic freedom for its own protection and advancement. Society, in its own interest, should insist upon academic freedom, should demand that contrary views be open to presentation and debate in its universities. For its own protection, society needs academic freedom both as against external efforts to stifle it, and as against internal efforts to subvert it—it needs freedom for the younger as well as the older professor, for new as well as old points of view, for heretical as well as dominant schools of opinion; and freedom from capture of centers of teaching and research by proponents of a single ideology. The greatest civilizations in world history, those that have made the most significant contributions to intellectual thought and artistic expression, have also been those most open to new and contrary ideas. It is a sign of confidence by a society in itself that it be open to the free exploration of truth. It is a sign of weakness that it be closed. The degree of freedom given to its universities is a sign of the assurance that a nation has in its capacity to cope with its future.

Merit. Society also needs advancement on the basis of merit.[18] Modern societies are so complex that it takes many persons of substantial ability to make them work effectively. Any nation that cuts itself off from access to its total pool of talent only handicaps itself. One can only stand aghast at the loss to the world throughout history of all the great works of art and literature, of all the better ideas, of all the great leaders that have not emerged because of the suppression of so many human elements—of talent among women and within underclasses and segregated racial and ethnic groups. In how many places in the world, and not just an English village, may it be said that "some mute inglorious Milton here may rest"? In the current world, in particular, when the requirements for high talent are so great, all sources should be fully explored.[19]

There is another, and ominous, side to this coin. Persons of merit who are denied opportunities to exercise their merit in the support of a society are the ones who are most likely to give leadership to destruction of that society. Denial of merit is a recipe for revolution. If merit is not used one way, it is likely to be used another.

Societies neglect this reality at their peril. Education, particularly higher education, is one of the best instruments that a society has to discover merit, to develop it and to advance it. It is, or can be, a great sorting mechanism. One of its greatest contributions can be to find and to advance talent wherever or whatever its origins—however obscure, however humble. To quote Cardinal Newman again: "This, Gentlemen, is why I say that to erect a university is at once so arduous and beneficial an undertaking, namely, because it is pledged to admit, without fear, without prejudice, without compromise, all comers, if they come in the name of Truth."[20]

Truth and merit in multiracial societies. A multiracial society has very special problems. It is hard enough for people of similar backgrounds to get along in peace. When religion or race or class, or all of them together, intervene, it becomes all the more difficult. I do not believe, contrary to Karl Marx and others, that industrial society is inevitably condemned to revolutions until that day when the "dictatorship of the proletariat" (which, in fact, usually means domination by what Djilas called "the new class") has been spread worldwide. I believe, rather, that industrialization inherently tends to reduce social conflict, after its initial period of introduction which may be quite turbulent, for a number of reasons. It blurs class lines with the almost infinite gradation of jobs. It mixes the races (when there is more than one race) more than tends to be the situation in a settled rural society—there is more mobility. It even tends indirectly to reduce the hard edges of religious conflict. But still there are severe social conflicts in advanced industrialized societies. They come, I believe, not because they are ordained by the "social laws of history" but essentially because of poor management of human affairs. Human affairs, however, can be well managed. Class barriers in higher education, for example, can be reduced as they are now being reduced in Western Germany; and racial barriers, as currently in the United States; and religious barriers, as earlier in England.

To work well, multiracial societies, and there are a number of them around the world, require understanding among people, friendly personal contact, mutual respect, common standards of conduct and a sense of fairness of treatment beyond the ordinary to offset the potentially divisive tendencies. Education, and particularly higher education, has a central role to play.

Personal contact in the classroom can lead to greater understanding and respect among individuals, and to friendships that can make it easier for the future leaders of society, who inevitably must treat with each other, to conduct the affairs of that society in greater harmony. The academic world has its standards of morality. They include respect for the facts, concern for careful analysis, tolerance for opposing points of view, civility in argument, acceptance of functional authority, appreciation of merit, rejection of brutal simplifications. These elements of academic morality can be helpful in the conduct of the affairs of state when the graduates of today become the leaders of tomorrow if they share similar standards of conduct and, to some extent, share similar ideals.

Let me illustrate from the United States. It is a great strength to our nation that there can appear on the same national platform in mutual support, as happened this past July, persons from as diverse backgrounds as Representative Barbara Jordan and Governor Jimmy Carter. Barbara Jordan comes from the black ghetto of Houston, Texas; Jimmy Carter from a once poor farm in the "redneck" country of southern Georgia. Both went to segregated schools but Barbara Jordan received her law degree from the integrated Boston University and Jimmy Carter his B.Sc. degree from the integrated U.S. Naval Academy. Both were, of course, influenced by many other experiences aside from the environments of their universities but presumably also by these environments. Barbara Jordan, as a member of the Rodino Committee in the House of Representatives investigating the Watergate scandals said, "My faith in the Constitution is whole, it is complete, it is total, and I am not going to sit here and be an idle spectator to the diminution, the subversion, the destruction of the Constitution." It was in accordance with this Constitution that the Supreme Court had declared that "separate educational facilities are inherently unequal."[21] Jimmy Carter, as candidate for the President of the United States, has called the Civil Rights Act of 1964 "the best thing that ever happened in the South in my lifetime." The American system of higher education helped, in however small a way, to make it possible for Barbara Jordan and Jimmy Carter to come from opposite sides of a segregated society to support the development of an integrated nation.

May I note that the great enduring societies of past history survived, in part, by drawing talent from all parts of their societies. Those that developed a "universal" aspect, to use a phrase of Toynbee, generally fared better than did those that confined their leadership to a single ruling class or caste or nationality. This was true, as one illustration, of Rome—Trajan and Hadrian were both Spaniards and Diocletian was an Illyrian and Justinian a Macedonian. The incorporation of able persons from diverse sources, in part through the educational system, is a recurrent theme in the history of successful civilizations;[22] an effective "circulation of the elites" as Pareto put it.[23]

Also in managing any society, it is I think important to avoid the phenomenon of an "isolated mass" of any sort, including a racial one. I once made a study, with Abraham Siegel, of the interindustry propensity to strike.[24] We found enormous variations in the propensity to strike from industry to industry. Some industries were always strike-prone in every nation studied; some always comparatively strike-free. The strike-prone industries were those with an "isolated mass" of workers whether in a lumber camp, or a coal "patch," or a one-industry textile town, or on a waterfront. The strike-free industries were ones where the workers were more integrated into the larger community. Members of the "isolated mass" tend to have the same grievances at the same time against the same common enemy. These grievances fester into major outbreaks of passion; into an attitude of "us" versus "them." The same thing can, and does, happen within higher education, as you may recently have noted in the closing of certain of your universities.

The open university in a multiracial nation thus provides for society an opportunity for personal contact among future leaders, for the development of a common framework of conduct, and for the integration of able individuals into the support of, rather than opposition to, the society.

Some universities, of their own accord, have not admitted students on the basis of academic merit. Then society has, I believe, the right and the duty to insist upon merit. The British government, through a Royal Commission, broke the religious barrier at Oxford and Cambridge in the 1850s; and later Parliament provided for the awarding of fellowships on the basis of merit. In the United States, federal officials in 1963 ordered Governor Wallace to stand aside from the entrance to the University of Alabama and they then escorted Black students inside for the first time in the history of that university. The government of Sweden currently has changed the admission requirements of its universities to reduce the earlier class bias. All these acts infringed upon the autonomy of the universities but in the name of a basic academic principle and for the sake of the welfare of the society—a welfare that is impeded by religious, racial, and class barriers and is aided by reliance on individual merit.

It is a sad commentary on academicians that more efforts to find and train what Jefferson called the "aristocracy of talent" have come historically from outside than from inside institutions of higher education. In the case of the United States, it has been government that sponsored the land-grant universities, the teachers' colleges that became comprehensive colleges, the community colleges, the financing of low-income students on a large scale, and much else that greatly expanded the pool of talent. The scholars were more likely to decry the possible decline of standards than to praise the wider search for talent. Actually the mental ability of college and university students rose from 1920 to 1960 as the pool of talent was greatly enlarged.[25]

There are good reasons why government should press for the discovery of talents—it wants to make good use of its educational investment, it wants the ablest doctors and engineers and skilled personnel generally, it represents all of the people in the democracy, it is looked upon as the protector of individual rights including the right to equality of opportunity, it wants the social peace that rests, in part, on the recognition of merit. Thus it is somewhat unusual that, in South Africa, it is the academics—not the government—who demand advancement into higher education on merit as found within the total population; that you should have been in the forefront, not the rear guard, of this effort.[26]

Defining merit. Merit is essential in principle, but it is a confusing concept in practice. I should like now to turn, for a few moments, to some practical questions.

1. How shall merit in the admission of students be defined when some students have met earlier deprivation for reasons beyond their control? Past achievement and current knowledge is the standard test of merit. However, where prior circumstances have been grossly unequal, for example, where there are major differences in the funding of schools on a per student basis, then equality of opportunity has not been provided by society—the "deck is stacked." Many suggestions have been made. The Carnegie Commission on Higher Education, of which I was Chairman, came to this conclusion and it is, perhaps, the most commonly accepted one in the United States today: that, above a certain necessary level of attainment, reliance should be placed on tests of aptitude and of innate ability or on class standing in the students' own school or on other indications of academic potential or on all of them, as well as on current knowledge as shown by achievement tests, with provision for subsequent remedial work where necessary but with no reduction of standards for graduation. The goal is to find and to develop innate capacity without loss in the quality of degrees.

2. How shall merit be determined in the selection and promotion of teachers? The standard tests are quality of teaching, research, and community and public service. But some other minor considerations are also customarily taken into account, such as the age distribution of the faculty, the coverage of fields to be taught, the degree of interest in student affairs and so forth. Should any consideration be given to race and to sex? Our Commission concluded that, where everything else was roughly equal among candidates, consideration should be given to the extent that the members of a "minority group" (in our terminology) or women would serve as "models" and sources of inspiration to minority or to women students, respectively, or would serve as "mentors" and sympathetic advisers; that such consideration would add to the quality of the total academic environment and to the performance of all the students taken together; that these contributions are an appropriate aspect of "university service."

3. Is consideration on the basis of merit enough? It is argued, by some, that proportional quotas based on race and sex are the only fair so-

lution, because the tests of merit are so imprecise and so subject to possible manipulation, because the need to overcome the consequences of past discrimination is so urgent, and because restitution is due for past denials of opportunity. Generally, quotas have been rejected in theory, although they are sometimes applied in fact. Our Carnegie Commission opposed them. Quotas discriminate on the basis of race (or sex) and not on the basis of merit. They treat individuals as members of a group, not as individuals in their own right. They easily could lead to a reduction in standards. They could easily reduce incentives to perform. They say to members of minority groups and to women, in effect, you did not make it on your own, you are here by sufferance of the law; and this could be a degrading experience. Instead we supported the national policy (1965) of "affirmative action" in employment, which says that full effort must be made to seek out and to advance persons with the necessary qualifications regardless of race or sex, and to seek to correct any "underutilization" in comparison with the pools of qualified talent available. Overall, we supported equality of opportunity, not equality of results.[27]

4. Have academic standards, in fact, deteriorated because of integration in the schools? The only fair answer is that it cannot yet be proven either that they have or that they have not. There has been some deterioration in test scores both for entry into college and into graduate schools. In both cases, this may merely be explained by the greater numbers and different compositions of persons taking the tests as higher education has greatly expanded since 1950. At the level of graduation from high school, one explanation is the reduction in requirements in the high school of work in subjects like mathematics and English composition—the scores have gone down almost exactly in proportion with the decline in hours of class work. Other explanations are the decline of homework with the hours spent on TV and with more mothers away from home in the labor force; the alleged general decline in the work ethic; and greater permissiveness in the home and school in American society. At the undergraduate level in college, grading standards did deteriorate during the Vietnam war because faculty members were reluctant to give low grades to men subject to the draft, because of student unrest, and because a loss of faith by some faculty members in the worth of their own educational efforts; and the standards have not as yet been raised again. The reluctance to give low grades to members of minority groups may have been another factor. On the other hand, there has been more competition to get high grades because of the downturn in the labor market and the more intense competition to get into graduate school. Since test scores have declined rather similarly in all parts of the nation and in both integrated and segregated schools, it would appear that integration, to the extent that it has had an effect, has not been a major cause of this deterioration. In any event, integration must be

evaluated on other grounds as well as on any impacts it may have on academic performance.

I note these several questions to make the point that the transition from a principle to an effective practice is not easy, but also to make the point that it is possible to work out reasonable solutions. The principle is of primary importance but the timing of its application and the specific practices that interpret and apply it are crucial. Morality in action requires not only the commitment to high principles but also consistency and effectiveness through time in seeking their application; and concern for the concrete difficulties in turning them into reality, including advance thought about these difficulties. May I also note, having seen long-term developments in both industrial relations and university relations in the United States, that reforms seldom turn out to be so good as their supporters expect in advance or as bad as their opponents fear.

Conclusion. Next, as I approach my conclusion, I should like to treat briefly with a delicate point. As a nation, South Africa will do what it thinks best for itself. But it most obviously lives within an international community. It is in one of the three areas of the world (Southern Africa) which are the greatest potential flash points for international tension, potentially involving the great powers. (The other potential flash points are the Middle East and Korea.) Opinion abroad, including within the United States, is consequently of importance to you. You already know that the policies of South Africa are of concern among people in the United States. You already know that the people of the United States have a hope that you will make a steady, a rapid and a peaceful transition in the direction of more provision for the human rights of all persons resident within South Africa. You also know that, after Vietnam, anticommunism alone is not sufficient to attract support within American public opinion. What you may not know, to quite the same extent, is how developments within your universities are taken as a particularly visible measure of progress or retrogression, partly because your universities more than most other of your institutions are part of an international community, and partly because American intellectuals are more informed about and more vocal about your situation than other elements of the population. You obviously need time to work out your problems and freedom from improper foreign intervention in doing so. Others may be helpful, in a small way, perhaps, in helping you gain time and freedom—given the proper circumstances. This position of hope and help is the official position of the United States, but it stands in direct opposition, among others, to those who favor instead a policy of academic boycott. Concern over such a boycott is poignantly raised under the heading of "the academic boycott" in the 1974 report on the *Open Universities in South Africa and Academic Freedom* to which I earlier referred.

The key phrase used in this report about the academic boycott is "deeply regret." I share this sentiment.[28]

In summary, the world changes even as we meet here tonight. You face these changes with some substantial assets—your principles, your scholarly reputation around the world, your very considerable academic freedom despite regrettable infringements, your attendance of students drawn from other elements of the South African population than the white community alone—which is an entering argument for expansion of their numbers, your receipt of budgets from the government apparently not reduced in retaliation for your disagreements with it, your support in the scholarly communities of the Western World. You also have on your side the fact that the pursuit of truth, aided by academic freedom, is an essential element of long-term effectiveness in a scientific age amidst intense international competition. You also have on your side the fact that advancement on merit is essential alike to economic efficiency and to social peace in an industrial democratic society.

You have dedicated yourselves to the "principle that a university is a place where men and women, without regard to race and colour, are welcome to join in the acquisition and advancement of knowledge." You are committed to autonomy in determining "on academic grounds who may teach, what may be taught, how it shall be taught." You are supported by many others around the world in your efforts to restore in full these earlier rights for the sake of the integrity of your university and all the other universities of South Africa, for the sake of the most effective service to your nation, even for the sake of peaceful developments in this part of the world community.

Notes

*Originally presented as The Chancellor's Lecture, University of the Witwatersrand, Johannesburg, South Africa, September 14, 1976.

1. The Academic Freedom Committees of the University of Cape Town and the University of the Witwatersrand, *The Open Universities in South Africa and Academic Freedom,* 1957–74 (Cape Town: Juta & Co., 1974).

2. Eric Ashby, *Universities under Siege* (Witwatersrand: Witwatersrand University Press, 1962).

3. Published on behalf of the conference of representatives of the University of Cape Town and the University of the Witwatersrand, held in Cape Town on 9, 10, and 11 January 1957, by Witwatersrand University Press, 1957.

4. I should like to stress the phrase "on academic grounds". I do not believe, as I shall note later, that universities should have the right to choose or to exclude teachers or students on such nonacademic grounds as race.

5. Robert Birley, *Universities and Utopia* (Witwatersrand: Witwatersrand University Press, 1965).

6. Lord Butler, *Academic Liberty* (Witwatersrand: Witwatersrand University Press, 1969).

7. Leo Marquard, *Academic Freedom and Responsibility* (Witwatersrand: Witwatersrand University Press, 1973).

8. I take as my definition of truth—"the agreement of the mind with reality"; and of merit—that which is earned on the basis of accomplishments and/or is deserved on the basis of ability, that which has been achieved or can be achieved on the basis of ability rather than that which is ascribed on the basis of status or special preference.

9. The two principles are tied together in these ways. The pursuit of truth is best carried on by the ablest teachers and students, by those with the greatest merit. Merit, in turn, is defined as competence in the pursuit of truth. Were advancement based on other grounds, it would, clearly, hamper the pursuit of truth.

10. And not just the distant past. In the twentieth century, even before Hitler, the German professoriate was informally largely excluding members of the Jewish faith and of the Social Democratic Party. (See, for example Max Weber, "The Alleged 'Academic Freedom' of the German Universities," *Minerva,* October 1973; originally published in 1908.)

11. There is, however, an excellent history for the United States—Richard Hofstadter and Walter P. Metzger, *Academic Freedom in the United States* (New York: Columbia University Press, 1955).

12. The concept, of course, goes back in our intellectual traditions to ancient Greece. In more modern times, Bacon and Descartes and Spinoza were among its earlier proponents. They supported the new intellectual freedom as against the old reliance on authority. All three of them, and most of their like-minded contemporaries, however, acted as individual scholars outside of the universities. The universities continued, largely unaffected, for two centuries as fortresses protecting scholasticism and orthodoxy—a few exceptions, such as Cambridge at the time of Newton and Padua at the time of Galileo, aside. (See, for example, Lewis Feuer, *The Scientific Intellectual* [New York: Basic Books, 1963].)

13. Oxford and Cambridge had about 1,000 students together in 1800; but the United Kingdom has 650,000 students in higher education today. (Michael Sanderson, *The Universities in the Nineteenth Century* [London: Routledge & Kegan Paul, 1975], 243.) The colleges of the United States (about twenty-five of them at the time) had less than 2,000 students in 1800, but higher education now enrolls over 11 million students. (Edwin Grant Dexter, *A History of Education in the United States* [New York: Macmillan, 1904], 269.)

14. The irony, however, is that both of these principles were largely introduced into academic life from the outside—by independent scholars and by leaders of modernizing societies. The early heroes mostly emerged outside the groves of academe.

15. *The Idea of the University* (Boston: Beacon Press, 1959), 121. Jaspers also says (p. 1), however, in a possible contradiction, that "the university is a community of scholars and students engaged in the task of seeking truth. It is a body which administers its own affairs." Jaspers may be talking at one point about the reality and at the other point about the ideal.

16. John Henry Cardinal Newman, *Idea of a University* (San Francisco: Rinehart Press, 1960 [originally published 1852]), 360.

17. John Henry Newman, "What Is a University", Lecture, Dublin, 1852 (in *A Newman Treasury,* ed. Charles Frederick Harrold [London, Longmans Green, 1943], 41).

18. The basic argument for equality of opportunity to advance on the basis of merit, however, is not that it makes for a more effective academic community or for a more successful society but it is an absolutely fundamental human right. The basic consideration is justice to the individual.

19. The United Kingdom has been falling badly behind other countries in the growth of its per capita income. For views that the educational system, and particularly the system of higher education, may be partly at fault by drawing talent from too small a pool and by directing it away from technology and business management, see The Hudson Institute, Europe, *The United Kingdom in 1980* (New York: John Wiley, 1974); and G. C. Allen, *The British Disease* (London: Institute of Economic Affairs, 1976).

20. Newman, *Idea of a University,* 344.

21. *Brown v. Board of Education of Topeka,* May 17, 1954.

22. See Edward D. Myers, *Education in the Perspective of History* (New York: Harper & Brothers, 1960).

23. See Vilfredo Pareto, *The Mind and Society* (New York: Harcourt-Brace, 1935).

24. Clark Kerr and Abraham J. Siegel, "The Interindustry Propensity to Strike—an International Comparison''; included in Clark Kerr, *Labor and Management in Industrial Society* (New York: Doubleday, 1964).

25. Paul Taubman and Terence Wales, *Mental Ability and Higher Educational Attainment in the Twentieth Century* (Berkeley, CA: Carnegie Commission on Higher Education, 1972).

26. Generally academics have been more concerned with giving grades and degrees (to students), and appointments and promotions (to faculty members) on the basis of merit, than in supporting the expansion of the pool of talent among students and for potential faculty members. They have, however, also generally favored choice on merit of those who have actually applied to them for admission or employment, within the categories that they have recognized as eligible (which has sometimes eliminated women, or non-Whites, for example).

27. For excellent discussions of these matters from opposing points of view, see Nathan Glazer, *Affirmative Discrimination* (New York: Basic Books, 1975); and Robert M. O'Neil, *Discriminating Against Discrimination* (Bloomington, IN: Indiana University Press, 1975).

28. There have been mutually profitable academic and scientific contacts between our two countries. One example that impressed me on an earlier visit to South Africa was the close relations between your scientists working on citrus crops and ours at the Citrus Experiment Station of the University of California at Riverside.

Epilogue—Reflections

Edward Shils, out of his great knowledge, in his review of the nearly fifty-year period from 1930 to 1975, particularly including 1960 to 1975, saw mostly deterioration in higher education—even permanent deterioration. He saw "The Academic Ethos Under Strain"[1]—even severe strain. He was looking at developments in Western Europe, Britain, and the United States. After World War II, there had been a time of "Great Expectations." These great expectations were based, particularly, on "the idea of a society based on science," on "equality through higher education," and on "the perfection of society and the individual through the universities." But the great expectations quickly began to be disappointed. They gave way, first, to "ambivalent expectations," next to the "loss of the sense of buoyancy," and then even to "the disparagement of the academic ethos" itself. What were once "endless horizons of opportunity" became more nearly endless horizons of despair.

The causes for these disappointments were, among others, as Shils saw them, (1) the massification and bureaucratization of higher education, with many of the new students not having "strong intellectual interests in the traditional sense" and with a tendency for the academic staff to become alienated from "the administration"; (2) the dispersion of academic effort from more noble to more trivial pursuits—so that "the exercise of the intellect was made secondary to the expansion of personality"; and (3) the politicization of aspects of academic life as "universities became centers of criticism," as "many of their students behaved atrociously and have not been censured or punished for doing so," and as some radical faculty members came to "hate society"—and came to "hate the universities that serve society" and to "regard the academic ethos as having nothing to do with them."

Shils concludes: "All those strains and distractions and 'busyness,' of the desire to please one's patrons by flattering subservience and large promises, of self-advancement and radical partisanship, and of all the burdens of large numbers and insufficient resources, are significant because they weaken the academic ethos. The same is true of student radicalism and public dissatisfaction with scientific technology. They becloud the minds of academics and weaken their adherence to the ethos of academic life. This weakening spreads its injurious efforts in many directions."

This review of developments by Shils is the single most thoughtful and comprehensive effort that has come to my attention. All that he says is true and yet I disagree—at least with respect to the United States. I disagree not because what he says is not true, but, to my mind, because it is true only in part; because there is also another side to the story. What I consider a more balanced overall view requires severe disaggregation of the total situation and more equal attention to the good as against the bad.

Massification and bureaucratization—yes, in many but not all institutions, and some consequent alienation; but some of it was inevitable in the process of accommodating the "tidal wave" of students that could not realistically be turned away. Reduction in the "intellectual interests" of some students—again yes; but levels of test performances out of college have at best held even and at worst deteriorated less than test scores out of high school, and many of the new professions and occupations to be served did not, in any event, require all that much intellectual interest. Many new and more trivial assignments accepted by higher education—again yes; but this was in response to what the people wanted in a democracy and no other institution could have responded so well, and these new assignments fell within the historical functions of teaching and service. "Politicization" of aspects of academic life—once again yes; but this took place mostly in elite institutions and mostly there in the social sciences and humanities; and politicization has become, at least temporarily as of the late 1980s, less extreme in expression and less manifest in totality.

We should all worry about the concerns of Shils. We should also give consideration to offsetting considerations. My more favorable view than that of Shils reflects at least these three considerations: (1) He was looking at Europe as well as the United States, and I only at the United States; (2) he was writing in 1975 and I, in part, later on, and some of the fears of 1975 have retreated, at least momentarily, into the memory banks; and (3) his attachment is more to the elite aspects of higher education and mine to the land-grant ideal—Chicago versus California.

Digression: Value Added by Higher Education

The record of higher education in terms of value added over the period 1960 to 1980, net, is a positive one. Over that time, Scholastic Aptitude Test (SAT) scores out of high school declined as follows:

	1960	1980	Percent Decline
Verbal	474	424	10.5
Mathematical	495	466	5.8

According to the best evidence—which is not all that good—test scores out of college, on the average, also deteriorated but not to the same degree. Thus, value added actually increased. The colleges made up for some of the deficiencies at the high school level. Yet the colleges operated in much the same environment as did the high schools. Among other things, the colleges added a substantial amount of remedial training to offset the inadequacies of entering students.

The record shows the following for higher education:[2]

Eleven areas where tests are used for admission to graduate and professional schools showed increases in scores or no change or only slight declines, in this order:
  Mathematics
  Law
  Physics
  Biology (medical)
  Chemistry (medical)
  Graduate Record Examination (Quantitative)
  Biology
  Economics
  Medical (Reading)
  Chemistry
  Graduate Management Admission Test

Twelve areas showed medium to large to extreme declines, in this order:
  Medical (Quantitative)
  Engineering
  Music
  Psychology
  Education
  Geology
  Graduate Record Examination (Verbal)
  French
  History
  English Literature
  Sociology
  Political Science

Overall the declines added up to more than the increases and the little or no changes. However, this statement must be qualified. The fields most connected with the professions and the economy (with the exception of engineering—with a moderate decline) generally showed better results than those less involved. Thus mathematics, the sciences, economics, and management had more advantageous developments in their scores than did such fields as literature, history, and sociology—the "hard" fields did better than the "soft"; the mathematical better than the verbal.

I conclude, overall, that colleges increased value added over high school performances to the benefit of the nation.

What Was Happening Overall?

1. Surviving. Higher education did survive into the 1980s in good condition. It had grown almost four times in size without loss of, and most likely with improvement in, the quality of its most academically elite functions—research and graduate training in the most rigorous fields of knowledge. Henry Rosovsky of Harvard, and former Dean of the Faculty of Arts and Sciences, has noted:

> In these days when foreign economic rivals seem to be surpassing us in one field after another, it may be reassuring to know that there is one vital industry where America unquestionably dominates the world: higher education. Between two-thirds and three-quarters of the world's best universities are located in the United States. This fact has been ignored by the many recent critics of higher education in America. (We also are home to a large share of the world's worst colleges and universities, but that is beside the point.)
>
> What other sector of our economy can make a similar statement? There are baseball, football, and basketball teams—but that pretty much exhausts the list. No one has suggested that today America is home to two-thirds of the best steel mills, automobile factories, chip manufacturers, banks, or government agencies. Our position at the upper end of the quality scale in higher education is unusual, may be a special national asset, and needs to be explained.
>
> In higher education, 'made in America' still is the finest label. My only advice is to add 'handle with care,' lest we too descend to the level of most other American industrial performance.[3]

Some of the reasons why higher education survived the time of troubles better in the United States than in some European nations are that it is a very diverse and flexible system able to absorb shocks one institution at a time; that decisions were mostly made by institutions themselves and not by a Ministry of Education or Prime Minister or Parliament; that the United States did not have any socialist governments with a tendency toward an overall plan; that the American states, by and large, acted in a restrained and generally supportive fashion during the student troubles and the OPEC crisis; that the public at large was remarkably tolerant over the longer run of the excesses and fundamentally favorably inclined to higher education; that higher education had many friends among alumni, within industry and agriculture, and among related professions; that it had effective leadership in its boards of trustees and its presidents; and that society needed it particularly strongly at that time in history after Sputnik, with the requirements for greater social justice, and with the need for new skills in massive numbers. If Shils had singled out the United States for separate treatment from Europe and Britain, he would, I am sure, have noted a comparatively better performance and prospect.

Higher education not only survived:

It added to quantity across the board and to quality in its most elite segments, particularly in research and graduate training.

It satisfied the demands of the labor market, with only temporary exceptions, for more persons with more and higher skills.

It added to its service activities generally and to its provision of centers of cultural activities across the nation, in particular, in so many smaller towns and cities as colleges spread across the states and as they put more emphasis on their cultural programs.

Digression: state support per student enrolled. It would not be clearly evident from the statistics on state support for current operating expenses per student enrolled in public institutions that there ever had been the most significant student revolt in national history in the middle and late 1960s.

The rate of increase in per-student support actually rose from 1965 to 1970, which was the period of the greatest student unrest. It did go down from 1970 to 1973, when there still may have been some political repercussions (as there were in California). However, the big drop was in 1973 to 1980, by which time the OPEC oil crisis was the dominant economic event. The third column also shows changes in national income per person employed, which is an indication of state ability to pay as affected by the tax base. The positive gap between column two and three was relatively favorable from 1965 to 1970.

Two additional notations:

There were exceptions to the general trend. State support per student at the University of California during the governorship of Ronald Reagan (1967–75) fell by 10 percent in real terms.

The federal government in 1972 passed the most supportive program for student aid in all national history in the Higher Education Amendments of that year.

2. Confirming Plato. As I have noted, Plato observed that the "wheel of education" keeps moving at an ever-faster pace. This certainly has been

Year	State Support per Student for Current Operations (1967 Dollars)	Percentage Change per Year from Prior Date	Percentage Change per Year from Prior Date in National Income per Capita
1960	$800	—	—
1965	$814	+0.4	3.6
1970	$933	+2.9	1.8
1973	$980	+1.7	4.0
1980	$897	−1.2	1.5

Sources: Enrollment: U.S. National Center for Education Statistics, *Digest of Education Statistics, 1982* (Washington, DC: U.S. Government Printing Office, 1982). State support: M. M. Chambers, *Higher Education in the Fifty States* (Danville, IL: Interstate, 1970), Appendix 2; M. M. Chambers, *Higher Education and State Governments, 1970–1975* (Danville, IL: Interstate, 1974); "Fact-File: Analysis of State Funds for Higher Education," *Chronicle of Higher Education* 11, no. 8 (October 14, 1980): 10.

National income per capita: Edward F. Denison, *Trends in American Economic Growth, 1929–1982* (Washington, DC: Brookings Institution, 1985), 78.

true around the world in the twentieth century. For the United States, enrollments as a percentage of the college-going age cohort (18–24 years) have been steadily increased:

1790	0.5
1870	2
1940	9
1960	22
1980	40

Participation has moved from elite to mass to universal access. It will, of course, however, never move on to universal attendance. In the process, many citizens have become more productive, more active in community life, more advanced in the quality of their individual lives.[4]

The 1980s have been a case in point. Enrollments in prospect, for the period of 1980 to 1997, were estimated to decline from the low Carnegie figure of 5 percent (in a range of 5 to 15 percent)[5] to an average prediction of about 25 percent—the approximate rate of decline in the size of the age cohort, to a high figure of 40 percent after making additional allowance for the decline in the private returns on an investment in higher education that began after 1968[6] (but did not continue indefinitely thereafter). This decline in enrollments has not yet happened. Enrollments were 12.1 million in 1980 and will be almost 12.6 million in 1990. There are more women, more minorities (except Black males), and more adults, and institutions have worked hard to raise retention rates.

The tendency for secular expansion has, at least thus far, offset more temporary factors. The "wheel of education," 1980 to 1990, has ridden right over the many bumps along the way.[7]

Digression: What Happened to Enrollments in the 1980s?

Illustrative of standard advance predictions for enrollments were those of WICHE,[8] which foresaw a decline from 1979 to 1994 of 26 percent. The lower Carnegie range of minus 5 to minus 15 percent (by 1997) was considered, in some quarters at the time, to be "totally irresponsible." The Carnegie Council reached these lower figures, in particular, by giving greater than usual emphasis to

the long-run trend of rising percentages of the age cohort attending college,

rising attendance rates by part-time and adult students, and by women and minorities, and

greater efforts by colleges and universities to retain students to graduation.

The figure of minus 15 percent is certain to be excessive for 1997 (the year we used), but minus 5 percent is still possible since the size of the age cohort will still fall by an additional 10 percent. In retrospect, where we made our greatest error was in underestimating the rise in the private rate of return on a college education. We noted the possibility of an increase but did not expect that the rise would be as great as it turned out to be, in part because we were highly conscious of the decline after 1968, although we did know that rates were rising again but very slowly. The essential figures for "trends in college wage premiums with one to five years of experience" ("differences in weekly wages of high school and college graduates") are as follows:

1968 +45 percent for college graduates
         (the highest point for the 1960s)
1976 +31 percent for college graduates
         (the lowest point for the 1970s)
1979 +32 percent for college graduates
         (the time of the writing of the Carnegie report[9])
1986 +69 percent for college graduates
         (the most recent figure available[10])

However, we clearly overestimated the attendance by Black males.

The closest prediction I know of (other than the low Carnegie figure) to what now seems likely to be the eventuality of was that made by Dennis Ahlberg, Eileen M. Crimmins, and Richard A. Easterlin[11]—of a decline by 1995 of 3 percent (their most likely—as it is turning out—of several projections they made). They particularly took into account the impact of the total size of the age cohort (in this case small) on rates of enrollment.

The great gap between the rate of decline of the age cohort and of actual enrollments at colleges and universities is a phenomenon of great significance in the history of American higher education.[12]

3. Setting the dominant pattern for the future. After all the testing of 1960 to 1980 and the new developments that have emerged, higher education in the United States may now be said to have reached its mature pattern:

> All segments have now been filled out with the conversion of teachers' college into comprehensive colleges and universities, and with the extension of community colleges nationwide.
>
> Differentiation of functions into institutions with two-year programs, with four- and five-year programs, and with Ph.D. and advanced professional programs is now accepted in all of the states. There is not just one degree level as in Italy; or the absence of community colleges as in Britain; or the incorporation of all programs into single institutions as in Sweden and in the consolidated universities in Germany, and as is now taking place in Australia.
>
> The private sector has stabilized at about 20 to 25 percent of all students—25 percent in 1970 and 22 percent in 1980.
>
> The federal government has found its settled role in supporting research and in financing individual students; and the states their special role in providing institutional support.
>
> The curriculum has come to be dominated by occupational and professional studies, and liberal education requirements have fallen from the original 100 percent in the classical colleges to a range of 0 to 10 percent. The house of intellect has become a school for skills.
>
> Efforts at interdisciplinary or transdisciplinary teaching and research have largely failed. Instead, new specialities within disciplines have arisen. The department, more than ever before, is now the basic unit of academic life—that is where most faculty members live most of the time. The faculty member teaches within his or her discipline, reads within it, publishes within it, has friends within it. This is all very natural. There is a limit to time and to what one mind can comprehend. There is a desire to feel secure within boundaries. Consequently there is more of what Bertrand Russell once called "fiercer specializations."

Shared governance with faculty is now almost universal, having been extended by unionization into areas where it was not well developed.

Seniority has risen and merit has fallen in affecting faculty promotions. The orbit of seniority practices has risen comparatively as community colleges and comprehensive colleges and universities have become the dominant sectors in higher education in terms of numbers of faculty positions, as unionization has spread, as some women and some minorities feel they can rely better on seniority in avoiding adverse discrimination than on merit in the hands of nonwomen and nonminorities. Seniority considerations now dominate in well over half of the total professoriate.

The many attempted academic reforms have mostly failed; and there is no current likelihood that a similar such wave will occur soon again or in the foreseeable future. This is proof that existing academic patterns generally work well or at least satisfactorily from the point of view of most academics. It is also proof that most academics agree with Shils in having "no doubt that great mischief is done in the name of innovation."[13] Plato, in *The Laws,* wrote, with reference to education, that "change, we shall find, except in something evil, is extremely dangerous." At a minimum, faculties seem to have agreed with the principle set forth by Edmund Burke "not to tamper with existing institutions without good cause."[14] The only changes that are readily accepted come from new intellectual developments in each discipline, changing student interests in relation to the labor market, new public claims for service, new directions in federal and foundation research subsidies, and new technologies. These are, of course, the most essential areas for change to take place. Outside these areas, the going is difficult and the survival rate of innovations is low, and the imitation rate nearly zero.

All in all, the American pattern of higher education is now more set than ever before, more entrenched, more solidified. It seems that the dominant professional opinion is that "what is, is right" in the academic realm.

As these essays indicate, I do not agree in several areas with what seems to be the now generally accepted judgment that the existing pattern is satisfactory and may even be the best possible.

Digression: Influencing the Pattern—The Master Plan in California

Higher education in California was in chaos. Everybody wanted to do everything—two-year colleges wanted to become four-year, four-year colleges wanted to give the Ph.D., university campuses all wanted to have medical schools, and the private institutions were feeling very threatened. The state legislature was moving in and adding to the chaos. Every crossroads wanted a college. One crossroads in the Central Valley got one because its state senator was chair of the Committee on Education.

As the new president of the University of California in 1958, it seemed to me that the state needed a Master Plan, or better a treaty or a general framework for higher education, so that each segment could then make its own detailed plans; and I set about immediately to initiate the development of such a plan. I had in mind the following:

Higher education should make its own plans on academic grounds; not the state legislature on other grounds.

Universal access should be provided to all high school graduates via an expansion of the community college movement, in response to developing egalitarian expectations.

The new occupational skills needed by the economy should be provided particularly by extending the state colleges from four-year to include also five-year programs, and by opening them to all programs at these levels, going far beyond teacher education.

The University of California should be protected in its elite functions of research, and training for the Ph.D. and for the highest level professions.

These levels of functions should not be mixed—they involved different types of students, differently oriented faculty members, and different sets of rules on admission and advancement of students, on appointment and promotion of faculty members, and on levels of financial support. These differences could not all be handled well within a single set of institutions. This was clear in Italy and became clear later in Germany and Sweden, where the "consolidated" approach caused many fundamental problems. Also, putting all levels together in California would result in an enormous system, as it did in New York with sixty-four institutions under a single board.

There should be a mechanism for advisory state-level coordination with strong participation by leaders of the academic institutions themselves.

The vision overall was that we should have an "aristocracy of talent," as seen by Thomas Jefferson, and a democracy of the educated at one and the same time; and this vision became a substantial reality. This was all accomplished and has now functioned with growing acceptance for thirty years. And it turned out that this established not only a pattern for California but a model followed, with many variations, widely across the nation. This model was one of differentiation of functions among institutions and of advisory coordination above them. This is now the dominant American pattern; and one that has been studied by other nations, and most recently by the OECD [Organisation for Economic Co-operation and Development]: "This plan for the combination of equality with excellence meant that in effect in 1960 logic was superimposed on history."[15]

4. Elevating the significance of the unforeseeable and the unforeseen. The period 1960 to 1980, as no other before it, held major surprises within it. One was the intensity of the student revolt; a second was the series of OPEC economic crises; and a third was the sudden drop around 1965 in the net reproduction rate of women of childbearing age from 3.6 to 1.8—a drop never before experienced in such proportions and so suddenly.

Actually, the first of these might have been anticipated but not its intensity. Student revolts in ascending volume have marked American history—the last prior one had occurred during the Great Depression. Some students and young faculty members of the 1960s were "red diaper" babies of participants in that earlier wave of revolts in the 1930s. Also, growth did often lead to more anonymity for the individual student, to more bureaucratic rules, larger classes, longer waiting lines, crowded facilities, and the "IBM card syndrome." Radical students were more likely to attain a critical mass on campuses that doubled, tripled, and quadrupled in size. On top of all this, greater social justice was a leading theme on the agenda of the "New Frontier" of President Kennedy, with a sympathetic reception on many campuses. The Vietnam war, however, could not, of course, have been foreseen.

I did warn the chancellors of the University of California in late July of 1964 of the likelihood of student unrest the coming academic year, but on other more proximate grounds. A hot presidential campaign was under way between Barry Goldwater and Lyndon Johnson, and there had been disturbances at the Cow Palace in San Francisco during the Republican Convention; there was an explosive racial issue of "fair housing" on a referendum before the electorate in California that fall; there had been some troubles at Stanford and Chicago over the two prior years and in San Francisco and in Oakland since 1960; and my contacts with left-wing union leaders, whom I had come to know in my earlier industrial-relations experiences, led me to think that there was a radical effort to heat up grievances and contract negotiations and that this might indicate a new widespread campaign of disturbances. The "long, hot summer" in the South, however, was not yet in full evidence; and the current perception of college students was still of the "apathetic generation."

Had higher education not been so overwhelmed by preparing for growth in numbers and in assignments, its leaders might have thought more about some of the potential side effects of growth and other contemporary developments that could have been foreseen. It was likely that growth in numbers of students and in budgets would lead to more state-led coordination and the building of systems out of individual campuses; that the very fact of growth and of the foundation of new institutions would encourage a wave of attempted academic reform; that growth by itself would put pressure on governance with all the decisions that had to be made too fast; that the "New Frontier" would lead to "affirmative action" demands on higher education as access to the "American Dream" was becoming the right of all Americans; that a booming economy (twenty years of sustained growth, with productivity increases at a rate of two to three percent per year) would give rise to many new demands from the labor market.

Why were the leaders of higher education generally so blind? Presidents are on short-term assignments, and they think about one institution at a time. To them the past was the best guide to the future, and historically change had been gradual. Additionally, they were overwhelmed by the preparations for the anticipated large numbers of students that lay ahead, and that was their big agenda item. Decision makers, also, often neglect the problems of execution in making their plans—Burke once wrote that the plan should never be "separated from the execution;"[16] and many side effects come in the course of execution. Academic decision makers additionally often neglect, as radicals always seem to do, to consider reactions to actions—the backlashes. And contingency possibilities are by nature so uncertain that speculation seems to be a waste of time.

Would it have made a difference if the leaders of higher education had been more farsighted? In my judgment, I think it would. Higher education might have been more in charge of its history and less a plaything of external events.

In the future, there are likely to be even more unforeseeable events as higher education becomes more tied into all of the life of society and as American society becomes more tied into the life of the world. Consequently, leaders of higher education may find it advantageous to try harder to see what has been in the past the unforeseeable, and to be more alert and to respond quickly as the unforeseen becomes reality; to be more conscious of the costs as well as the benefits of the programs they advance; and to see more than one possible scenario unfolding.

5. *Recognizing the importance of underlying historical forces.* Much of the history of 1960 to 1980 was written not so much by what the actors did or did not do but by the plots that lay behind the play:

> The military challenges of Sputnik and Breshnev that so propelled the advance of the research universities
>
> The demand for greater equality of opportunity that so exploded the community college development
>
> The discovery that "human capital" was as important as physical capital, which so helped to transform the former teachers' colleges into the great sources of middle-level expertise that they are today

The changing demographics that so affected all segments
The rise of the youth culture that so challenged all traditional
virtues and placed all authority under attack

As Abraham Lincoln said: "We cannot escape history." Higher education
did not escape the impacts of these five great forces. Earlier in our history
we had not escaped the force of religion in affecting our historic colleges in
their early years or of the great faculty drive for "shared governance" in
the twentieth century. In the future we may not escape the impacts of the
fractionalization of our society, the rise of ethical concerns on campus and
off, and the need for renewal as older faculty members retire and as older
buildings and facilities deteriorate.

Disappointments

The Carnegie Commission (and Council) on Higher Education from
1967 to 1980 (years that covered much of the period under discussion here)
studied developments and made recommendations for improvement. Based
on our many discussions of what we thought needed to be done and also
could be done, I conclude that the major disappointments in meeting the
existing challenges were that higher education did not help adequately to
achieve

• greater equality of opportunity to secure a college education,
• more and better attention to liberal education for undergraduates,
• more and better contributions to solving the problems of youth in general,
• more and better assistance to the deteriorating high schools,
• more and better service to an urbanized society in general, and
• better codes of conduct for the academic community.

The greatest disappointment was in the first area—greater equality of opportunity through education. We underestimated how difficult the problem
were and overestimated what higher education could do in solving them.

Another reflection is how dependent higher education was, for such
advances as were made, on the fact that this was a period of federal initiative. The greatest successes generally came in the form of federal legisla-
tion, and not in initiatives by higher education itself.

Puzzles

There were some puzzles along the way—for me, two in particular
where fully satisfactory explanations still elude me.

Puzzle I. Why the student movement disappeared so suddenly and so completely. In May of 1970, it reached its peak. In September, it was sunk almost without trace. It is easy to understand why the movement started. It had to happen. There were the predisposing conditions of the early and middle 1960s noted above. On top of that, there was the most divisive internal issue since the Civil War—the Civil Rights Movement, and the most divisive external issue ever in American history—the Vietnam war. It is inconceivable that there would not have been trouble on the campuses under these circumstances. And television added to the drama.

During the summer and early fall of 1970, I visited many campuses across the nation and talked with many students about what was happening. The most common responses I got to "why the disappearance of the student movement?" were these:

> Students were disappointed that the effort to influence national policy—in particular, efforts to stop the Cambodian "incursion" had been a failure; the American public had failed them.
>
> They were disappointed with themselves that they spent the summer not organizing to continue and to increase their endeavors in the fall but went to the mountains and the beaches and Europe instead.
>
> They were turned off by the violence at Kent State and Jackson State, in Greenwich Village and in Madison. They wanted no part of it.
>
> The movement had been taken over by the Weathermen, the Maoists, and the Black Panthers.

Additionally, I would add my own observations, that, while the main causes were just, the methods were not always just or wise:

> From the beginning, with the seizure of the president's office at Chicago in 1962, the disruptions of ROTC ceremonies and commencement exercises at Stanford also in 1962, and the capture of the police car at Berkeley in 1964, the movement embraced illegal acts. This was counterproductive.
>
> The movement, starting with the Port Huron Conference in 1962, did not protect itself from subversion by its radical left, as the democratic socialists at that time clearly warned it should. Instead it chose to include all dissidents regardless of their chosen means.
>
> The movement was more interested in actions than in reactions. Andrew Greeley, then of the University of Chicago and the National Opinion Research Center, observed in 1970:
>
> > It has been a bad summer for the academy. In a recent Gallup Poll, the campuses found themselves described as the most

serious problem the country faces, bar none. They rank ahead of Vietnam, inflation and the Black Panthers as a cause of national concern. The academy has been appalled to discover that the majority of Americans thought that the Kent State murders were the fault of the students, and it has been amazed to learn that its support for a political candidate could easily become the kiss of death. Convinced as it was in the spring, as indeed it has been these several springs past, that it was the avant garde of a great popular revolution, the academy now finds itself wondering about its very survival, about the survival of its institutions, about the survival of education itself. Characteristically, it blames the situation on 'the hard hats' or 'the silent majority' or 'the fascist mass' and does not pause to ask whether it is remotely possible that its own course has gone awry somewhere in between. . . . Surely the . . . movement, because of its tactics rather than its sentiments, has consistently hardened the stand of hawks in American society.[17]

Reagan was elected Governor of California in 1966 and Nixon as President of the United States in 1968.

The movement, instead of building coalitions of support, antagonized many potential supporters of its efforts at racial justice and at ending the war in Vietnam: people over thirty were not to be "trusted"; liberals were actually "fascists"—as Norman Thomas had earlier been called a "social fascist"; middle-class values and prejudices in cultural areas (including regarding sex, drugs, and patriotism) were denigrated; union members were called "hard hats"; university administrators were to be put up against the wall; faculty members were attacked in sensitive areas of their control over academic policy and promotions.

The movement misjudged the situation by believing that a minority of college students (not more than 5 percent of all college students were radical activists) could carry out a revolution all by themselves in a highly stable democracy.

The movement had unsolved internal contradictions. Where did it want to go—to Castro's communism or to the anarchy of Haight-Ashbury? How did it want to go—the way of the storming of the Bastille or the way of Mahatma Gandhi? Was it rebellion for rebellion's sake, or rebellion with a goal in mind and a strategy, as the Old Left had once had?

And yet I remain puzzled that from May to September 1970, the movement vanished without a whimper; and that college students of that gener-

ation became the most conservative political age element in the American
public and the strongest supporters of the most conservative president in
American history—the real "movement" was to make money economically
and to go right politically.

*Puzzle II. Why were the efforts at greater equality of opportunity not
more successful?* All those billions of dollars were spent on student grants
and loans, and all those efforts were made at affirmative action. With what
results? Great progress has been made with the enrollment of women generally and with middle- and higher-income women in particular; some with
Blacks, generally more with women than men; some also with Hispanics;
and great progress with Asians; but little progress with students from low-
income families generally and particularly Blacks and Hispanics (see table
1 and figure 1).

Expectations were once so high. The Carnegie Commission in one of
its early reports (*A Chance to Learn,* 1970) said that by 1976 "all economic
barriers to educational opportunity" should be eliminated; and that by 2000
all of the "last vestiges of limitations" for the less advantaged should be
totally eradicated—no more "compensatory educational programs" and no
more "flexible criteria for admission and grading" should be necessary. It
was thought that, with enough money[18] and with a few encouraging rules,

TABLE 1

Percentage of 18- to 24-Year-Olds Enrolled in School or College

	1960	1986
Males	28.8	33.3 (28.2)*
Females	14.4	30.6 (27.6)*
Blacks	15.8 ("nonwhite")	28.6 (21.9)*
Males	18.0	29.8 (20.0)*
Females	13.9	27.5 (23.4)*
Hispanics	n.a.	23.2 (17.6)*
Males		21.7 (16.7)*
Females		24.9 (18.7)*

*Percentage enrolled in college

Source: Enrollment rates, 1960: U.S. Bureau of the Census, *Current Population Reports,* series P-20, no. 110, "School Enrollment, and Education of Young Adults
and Their Fathers: October 1960" (Washington, DC: U.S. Government Printing Office, 1960), table 3. Enrollment rates, 1986: U.S. Bureau of the Census, *Current
Population Reports,* series P-20, no. 429, "School Enrollment—Social and Economic Characteristics of Students: October 1986" (Washington, DC: U.S. Government Printing Office, 1988), table 1.

FIGURE 1

Percentage of Families with One or More Members Eighteen to Twenty-four Years Old Attending College Full Time, by Income Level—1986

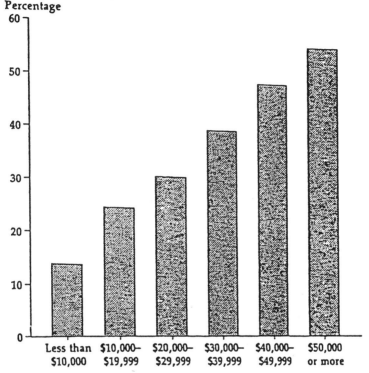

Source: Cecelia A. Ottinger, ed., *Higher Education Today: Facts in Brief* (Washington, DC: American Council on Education, 1989), 11. Based on U.S. Bureau of the Census, *Current Population Reports,* series P-20, "School Enrollment—Social and Economic Characteristics of Students: October 1986" (Washington, DC: U.S. Government Printing Office, 1988).

this could all be accomplished. It has not and it will not be. More money and new rules at the higher education level have not by themselves been enough; and they will not be.

Alice Rivlin, in her "Reflections on Twenty Years of Higher Education Policy" for the College Board,[19] says that "with hindsight, the faith of the sixties was quite touching . . . that simply increasing resources would make many difficulties and disparities disappear." As she points out, we now realize that higher education should not be treated as a "distinct activity" all by itself but rather as part of a "continuing lifetime process. It starts at home; it goes through school; it does not end with college or graduate school. It is not a good idea to try to carve out a few years in the middle and call it higher education." Higher education is part of a great continuum that starts at birth.

The problems start with poverty and with the family—with the degree of family concern and of the capacity to help with the education of the children. Early motivation and early preparation are the key elements—those who start behind mostly stay behind. The high schools, additionally, have deteriorated, and youth is too much left to the not so tender mercies of peer groups and the mass media.

I was surprised at how quickly and how greedily middle- and higher-income families insisted on sharing, at the higher educational level, the federal largesse for student aid, particularly in the Higher Education Amendments of 1978. This reduced the funds potentially available for support for students from lower-income families. Middle-class hedonism and middle-class political power triumphed. The "American Dream" was interpreted less as equality of opportunity and more as "me too" than I had expected it would. At the college and university level, as another factor, there was some resistance to affirmative action,[20] and I believe this is now increasing among many majority students who feel they have been discriminated against in admissions, in their financing by loans instead of by grants, and by what they perceive as the comparative neglect of their interests.

As Alice Rivlin notes, however, "we are still trying." But we need to try more at the fundamental levels of reducing poverty and of renovating the effectiveness of the family as the most important of all educational institutions. Beyond that we need to move from a policy of equality of opportunity to more emphasis on compensatory equality of opportunity in the early years to offset deficits.

The contributions of higher education to greater equality of opportunity are necessary but far from sufficient. The greater problems lie elsewhere.

Yet I am still puzzled. Universal access was provided. National and state policy became that no young person should be denied attendance at college for financial reasons alone. And yet, so many fewer came along among those it was most intended to help.

Legacies of the Great Transformation

The greatest legacy was a system that entered the 1980s having been severely tested on the firing line of social tensions in a stabilized mode of operation and with revived public confidence. The 1980s were again a period of normality, of business as usual, of few special problems, of comparative tranquility, of little that was new and with little evidence that most participants wanted anything different—a world apart from 1960 to 1980. It was a period both less exciting than the Golden Age and less disturbing than the Age of Survival.

But there are other important legacies:

A private sector that is now only about 20 percent of higher education and that, if it should become a still lesser part, will be less beneficial to the totality of higher education.

Weakened governance at the top, with less influence by and more restraints on boards of trustees and presidents, and this could be costly in a new period of dynamic change.

Second-stage repercussions of the great growth of the 1960s and 1970s that will conduce to a new period of more dynamic change. More than half the faculty will need to be replaced over ten to twenty years (1995 to 2015). Many facilities of the growth years will need to be renovated or replaced. The third stage of repercussions to the demographic explosion of the 1960s will come about another thirty years later but in a once-again diminished amplitude; and, then again, about thirty years still later.

A professoriate, particularly in the more academically elite institutions, that reflects the activism of the 1960s. Faculty members in the Carnegie-Trow survey of the mid-1970s[21] identified themselves politically as about 5 percent "Left." That figure by now may have risen by half or even doubled, as alumni of the movement have taken their places in the professoriate. This has implications for politicization of the campus, if and when a new wave of activism arrives; and for harmony within the campus. Shils[22] noted how departments had been split along political lines: "Cleavages within whole faculties and particular departments still persist and find new issues on which to be sustained. Those who sympathize with the radical students are still bitter against their colleagues who opposed them." Two supporters of the movement have written: "The spirit of the sixties did not die as its bearers got older, nor did they betray that spirit. Perhaps the spirit waits for a new opportunity that will permit the tides of collective action once more to rise."[23]

Campuses fractured along lines of sex and ethnic and racial groupings as never before. We have gone from the historic doctrine of separate but equal to the new doctrine of equal but separate. The earlier doctrine rested on law; the newer doctrine rests instead on choice. May the resultant tensions ratchet up?

A decimated program of liberal education. Yet citizens need a liberal education and many professionals can benefit from it in their employment. And new ideas often develop on the borderline of disciplines, and nearly all policy issues cross disciplinary lines.

And an as-yet-unmet national promise of equality of opportunity through education with smoldering embers lying scattered throughout American society.

Future history will be written by some, and perhaps all, of these legacies, as well as by the new developments that will come along—foreseen, unforeseen, and unforeseeable. My estimate is that the steady times of the 1980s will not long continue and that a new, less settled period may well lie ahead. In any event, in the future as in the past, as Heraclitus noted so long ago, "all things are in flux," and it is change and strife that write history. To the extent that change and strife write history, the 1960s and 1970s lasted a very long time but the 1980s were over in a flash.

In the prologue, I noted that Pindar in 500 B.C. wrote that the test of a person "lies in action"; and action is also the testing ground for institutions. Higher education met the test of action from 1960 to 1980 overall quite well, and emerged from this period clearly larger and mostly better. In particular, it was providing more services to more poeple in the American society than ever before. It had, in many ways, been transformed, and, in the process, it had become a more central aspect of the life of the nation and was, consequently in turn, a greater potential source of transformation for the nation.

Notes

1. Edward Shils, "The Academic Ethos Under Strain," *Minerva* 13, no. 1 (Spring 1975).

2. Based on Clifford Adelman, *Standardized Test Scores of College Graduates, 1964–1982* (Washington, DC: National Institute of Education, 1985).

3. Henry Rosovsky, "Highest Education," *The New Republic*, 13 & 20 July 1987, 13–14.

4. See, for example, Howard R. Bowen, *Investment in Learning: The Individual and Social Value of American Higher Education* (San Francisco: Jossey-Bass, 1977); F. Thomas Juster, ed., *Education, Income and Human Behavior* (New York: McGraw-Hill, 1975; Joe L. Spaeth and Andrew M. Greeley, *Recent Alumni and Higher Education: A Survey of College Graduates* (New York: McGraw-Hill, 1970); and Stephen B. Withey, et al., *A Degree and What Else? Correlates and Consequences of a College Education* (New York: McGraw-Hill, 1971).

5. Carnegie Council on Policy Studies in Higher Education, *Three Thousand Futures: The Next Twenty Years for Higher Education* (San Francisco: Jossey-Bass, 1980).

6. Stephen P. Dresch, "Educational Saturation: A Demographic-Economic Model," *AAUP Bulletin* 61, no. 3 (Autumn 1975): 239–47; and "Demography, Technology and Higher Education: Toward a Formal Model of Educational Adaptation," *Journal of Political Economy* 83, no. 3 (June 1975): 535–69.

7. The immediate future, however, remains uncertain. The number of students graduating from high school between 1989 and 1994 is expected to decline about 10 percent. (American Council on Education, *Higher Education Today* [Washington, DC: American Council on Education, 1989], 7.)

8. Western Interstate Commission for Higher Education, *High School Graduates: Projections for the Fifty States* (Boulder, CO: Western Interstate Commission for Higher Education, 1979).

9. Carnegie Council on Policy Studies in Higher Education, *Three Thousand Futures* (San Francisco: Jossey-Bass, 1980).

10. For the source of the above figures, see Kevin Murray and Finis Welch, "Wage Premiums for College Graduates," *Educational Researcher* 18, no. 4 (May 1989): 17–26.

11. Richard A. Easterlin, "The Outlook for Higher Education: Cohort Size Model of Enrollment of College Age Population, 1948–2000," *Review of Public Data Use* 9 (1981): 211–27. See the comment by Easterlin that "blind faith in naive demographics is unwarranted" ("Demographics is Not Destiny in Higher Education," in *Shaping Higher Education's Future,* ed. Arthur Levine and Associates [San Francisco: Jossey-Bass, 1989], 135.)

12. For another discussion of this development, see Paul E. Harmington and Andrew M. Sum, "Whatever Happened to the College Enrollment Crisis," *Academe* 74, no. 5 (September–October 1988): 17–22.

13. Shils, "Academic Ethos."

14. See introduction by B. W. Hill in *Edmund Burke on Government, Politics, and Society* (New York: International Publications Service, 1975), 12.

15. Organisation for Economic Co-operation and Development, *Review of Higher Education in California,* Examiners' Report and Questions (Paris: Organisation for Economic Co-operation and Development, February 1989).

16. Hill, *Edmund Burke,* 8.

17. Andrew M. Greeley, "Malice in Wonderland: Misconceptions of the Academic Elite," *Change* 2, no. 5, (September–October 1970): 32.

18. For a discussion of how there may not have been much impact on attendance from greater student financial aid, see W. Lee Hansen, "Economic Growth and Equal Opportunity," in *Education and Economic Productivity,* ed. Edwin Dean (Cambridge, MA: Ballinger, 1984), 2.

19. Alice M. Rivlin, "Reflections on Twenty Years of Higher Education Policy," in *Educational Access and Achievement in America* (New York: College Entrance Examination Board, 1987), 3–10.

20. See the discussion in Carl A. Auerbach, "The Silent Opposition of Professors and Graduate Students to Preferential Affirmative Action Programs: 1969 and 1975," *Minnesota Law Review* 72, no. 6 (June 1988).

21. Carnegie Council on Policy Studies in Higher Education, *Carnegie Council National Surveys, 1975–76: Faculty Marginals* (Berkeley, CA: 1978), 268.

22. Shils, "Academic Ethos."

23. Jack Whalen and Richard Flacks, *Beyond the Barricades* (Philadelphia: Temple University Press, 1989), 283. See also the comment by Philip G. Altbach and Robert Cohen that "activism is not dead" ("American Student Activism: The Post-Sixties Transformation," in *Student Political Activism,* ed. Philip G. Altbach, [Westport, CT: Greenwood Press, 1989], 457.)

Index